Dynamics of Effective Secondary Teaching

FIFTH EDITION

William Wilen
Kent State University

Janice Hutchison
**Kent City School District
and Kent State University**

Margaret Ishler Bosse
University of Northern Iowa, Emeritus

Richard Kindsvatter
Kent State University, Emeritus

PEARSON

Boston ■ New York ■ San Francisco
Mexico City ■ Montreal ■ Toronto ■ London ■ Madrid ■ Munich ■ Paris
Hong Kong ■ Singapore ■ Tokyo ■ Cape Town ■ Sydney

Series Editor: Traci Mueller
Editorial Assistant: Krista E. Price
Marketing Manager: Elizabeth Fogarty
Editorial-Production Service: Omegatype Typography, Inc.
Manufacturing Buyer: Andrew Turso
Composition and Prepress Buyer: Linda Cox
Cover Administrator: Joel Gendron
Electronic Composition: Omegatype Typography, Inc.

For related titles and support materials, visit our online catalog at www.ablongman.com.

Between the time Website information is gathered and published, some sites may have closed. Also, the transcription of URLs can result in typographical errors. The publisher would appreciate notification where these errors occur so that they may be corrected in subsequent editions.

Library of Congress Cataloging-in-Publication Data

Dynamics of effective secondary teaching / William Wilen . . . [et al.].—5th ed.
    p. cm.
    Rev. ed. of: Dynamics of effective teaching. 4th ed. c2000.
    Includes bibliographical references and index.
    ISBN 0-205-39536-8 (alk. paper)
    1. High school teaching—United States.   2. Classroom management—United States.   3. Motivation in education—United States.   I. Title: Dynamics of effective teaching.   II. Wilen, William W.   III. Dynamics of effective teaching.

LB1737.U6K56   2004
373.1102—dc21

                     2003041867

Printed in the United States of America

10   9   8   7   6   5   4   08   07   06   05

Photo Credits: p. 7: Will Hart; p. 26: Steve Skjold/Photo Edit; p. 65: Mary Kate Denny/Photo Edit; p. 98: Brian Smith; p. 136: Will Hart/Photo Edit; p. 170: Dennis MacDonald/Photo Edit; p. 217: Will Hart; p. 273: Will Hart/Photo Edit; p. 314: Will Hart/Photo Edit; p. 334: Paul Conklin/Photo Edit; p. 370: Cleve Bryant/Photo Edit

Contents

7 PRIMARY INSTRUCTIONAL METHODS 214

Preface

The basic premise underlying all five editions of *Dynamics of Effective Secondary Teaching* has been that teaching is a science implemented by artists. The science of teaching is evident when competent teachers are well informed by current theory and research and, together with their own personalities and perceptions, the potential for a dynamic pedagogical presence in the classroom is increased. While much of this text naturally supports the artistry of teaching, its primary purpose is to establish a base of rational sources on which preservice and in-service teachers can rely to make informed decisions about what and how to teach.

Research on instruction has changed dramatically over the past 40 years. From an emphasis on investigating teacher characteristics and then teacher behaviors during the 1960s and 1970s, the field has become more inclusive by focusing on student and curricular variables. Teacher behavior is still extremely important with new researchers focusing on quality as determined by changes in student behaviors. During the 1980s, researchers were able to identify those instructional behaviors in which teachers engage that positively influence students' learning. The first edition of *Dynamics* was written to translate the findings of this massive body of what has come to be called the effective-teaching research into classroom practice. Why is this important? So that preservice and in-service teachers can be even more influential in their impact on students in the classroom.

Ten years later in the 1990s, teachers were still expected to be effective in the traditional sense of influencing students' achievement. This is clearly evident today with the major emphasis on state- and district-level educational standards and periodic testing to determine the extent students have come to know content. But emerging modern perspectives on how students learn are changing educators' views of best practice. Cognitive and developmental psychologists have found that students learn best by first making connections between what they know and have experienced with new content. Learning is further enhanced when they are encouraged to apply knowledge in authentic situations, or those that come as close as possible to reflecting life outside the classroom. The active construction of knowledge, rather than the sole passive absorption of knowledge, increases the probability that students will go beyond simply knowing to developing true understanding. This is where we are as we progress into the new millennium.

The fifth edition of *Dynamics* continues to reflect the best ideas and practices from both the effective-teaching and constructivist worlds of ideas and research. We believe a realistic perspective is that teachers need to competently address the demands of both educational worlds—effectively preparing students to demonstrate proficiency in knowing and applying content and encouraging students to develop higher-level understandings by making connections between new and prior learnings through applications to real-world tasks and problems. In accordance with this reality, with this edition we have added other perspectives on the standards movement and testing and expanded constructivist connections between instructional techniques, methods and strategies, and teachers' applications of these approaches in their classrooms. In this way, we believe we are better serving teachers' needs.

As with the previous editions, we have designed the fifth edition of *Dynamics* for middle school and high school teacher-preparation students in general-methods courses, student or interim teachers who need a solid reference book and a comprehensive set of analysis instruments, and beginning teachers who intend to achieve at their level of optimum effectiveness. In a broader sense, though, we believe that any teacher who engages in instruction or supervision will find something of value in *Dynamics*. It will appeal to readers who share our views on the following:

Effective teaching is basically sound decision making.

Teaching is an art informed by science.

A sound knowledge base is the bedrock of every bona fide profession.

Translating this knowledge base into thoughtful classroom practice is the challenge and task of every professional teacher.

Effective teachers accommodate the diverse abilities, needs, and interests of learners.

Effective teachers have a repertoire of instructional techniques, methods, and strategies on which to draw to stimulate active learning.

Empowering teachers is the key to heightening their esteem and improving the image of the profession.

We have tried to embody these positions in *Dynamics* by introducing decision making in Chapter 1 as a process fundamental to educators and by revisiting the application of that process in every succeeding chapter. Our view of decision making considers it from a constructivist view of teaching and learning based on reflection and "meaning making." In addition, these positions are built into the structure and organization of the text. Because a strong knowledge base is so important to our vision of decision making, most chapters contain at least one section entitled Research and Theoretical Base that grounds the discussion in the most current thinking and facilitates the readers' acquisition of knowledge that is personally meaningful and useful. We have updated and given a stronger focus to material throughout these sections. Because they are relatively discrete segments of each chapter, instructors may easily choose how and to what degree to integrate the theory and research into their classrooms. Related sections entitled Application to Practice focus the research findings and theoretical approaches and help readers begin to consider practical classroom implications.

A realistic scenario contained in each chapter serves to add faces, names, and a narrative structure to the issues we present. These scenarios are predicated on our assumption that we often learn most effectively when we feel some sense of connection and personal relevance to the content, and our feedback from instructors using earlier editions has wholeheartedly supported this contention. We have also included many highlighted Hints for the Beginning Teacher and Application for Diverse Classrooms boxes throughout the book to help teachers. New to this edition are Website Resource boxes to assist teachers in identifying key websites related to chapter themes.

In addition, graphic organizers introduce each chapter to assist the reader in visualizing key ideas. Questions for reflection close each chapter, serving to encourage personal exploration and insight. Periodic summary points focus reader attention and reiterate important topics. Finally, observation/analysis forms are included at the end of many chapters. We and other instructors have found these forms useful for facilitating comprehension by developing personal understanding, promoting a common language for the community of educators, and providing tools for the teacher-as-researcher approach we hope to stimulate. Altogether, we hope that these various parts of the text will continue to serve to organize instructional methods into a sound and eminently teachable structure that promotes reflection, insight, and discussion.

Of course, our revision has not simply extended to rethinking and revising the pedagogy and skeletal structure of *Dynamics.* In keeping with our mission, new topics have been sought out that have become important since the publication of the fourth edition; for instance, we have added a chapter on differentiated instruction primarily to assist teachers in meeting special needs of students. Also, there is expanded coverage of cooperative learning, multiple intelligences, and performance assessment in light of their growing application in the classroom and testimony to their effectiveness.

The text breaks into four large areas. The first, made up of Chapters 1 and 2, considers the meaning of teaching and being a teacher, and the climate of the classroom. The second—Chapters 3 and 4—examines discipline and curriculum, two topics that undergird all other parts of professional instruction. Chapters 5 through 10 present teaching as an integrated instructional process and build on the first four chapters. Chapter 11 both closes the book and shows the openings in the professional world beyond.

As mentioned, Chapter 1 presents our view of decision making and its importance in the minds of professional educators. We also advance our view of education as a professional discipline here. Because all classroom teaching occurs within a social setting, Chapter 2 addresses the teacher's role in providing a productive climate and attending to students' motivation. Motivation, in our view, is the most basic task of the teacher, and much of this book is directly or indirectly concerned with the topic. Because discipline emerges naturally from our discussion of classroom climate and motivation, and because it is a pervasive aspect of teaching, we have placed Chapter 3 ahead of the chapters on instruction. We have selected pertinent aspects of democratic discipline rather than attempt a broad coverage of this complex topic.

Chapter 4 addresses curriculum. Very simply, to teach, one must teach about something. What one chooses to teach and how one teaches it determine teaching effectiveness. Constructivist approaches that focus on encouraging students to discover personal meaning beyond the accumulation of factual knowledge make the selection of content especially critical.

We see teaching as a three-step process: planning, instruction, and evaluation. Chapter 5's discussion of planning continues the logical transition from Chapter 4's discussion of curriculum. We conceive of planning as a human process of decision making rather than only the routine development of written plans. Planning should be the beginning of an adventure in learning for students, so it deserves to be done with a sense of excitement and commitment.

Chapters 6, 7, and 8 deal specifically with instruction—a central focus and the heart of this book—as the second component of teaching. We begin this component in Chapters 6 and 7 by describing behaviors and techniques that are the basis for instruction, showing how they evolve into methods and strategies through manipulation by the purposeful teacher. In Chapter 8, we stress the elements of effective teaching that have the greatest impact on student achievement and those strategies such as direct teaching and cooperative learning that have the potential to help students find relevance in their learning.

Chapter 9 focuses on differentiated instruction. We have listened to our students and others who have used previous editions of *Dynamics* and realized the need to address more directly the changing character of our classrooms. Students are more diverse than ever, and we need to construct a framework in order to make decisions about meeting the needs of all the students. This framework consists of the research, theory, and practical teaching ideas of differentiated instruction. The "one-size-fits-all" mentality is a thing of the past. Teachers need ideas about effectively accommodating a full range of students from the student with specific academic weaknesses to the gifted student. Many ideas that are presented are primarily related to adjusting curriculum and instruction to accommodate students with special needs to collaborative teaching with special education teachers.

Evaluation, the third component of teaching, is addressed in Chapter 10. Like discipline, it is presented concisely. The areas of assessment and evaluation are changing rapidly and much controversy exists here. We have tried to synthesize important traditional and new topics in evaluation to establish a reasonable foundation for further and more specialized exploration in the professional literature. Commentary was expanded on alternative and authentic assessment, and the use of rubrics is accompanied by a variety of examples and illustrations to enhance understanding and application.

In the final chapter, we describe the use of this book beyond the general-methods classroom. As students become involved with instruction through student teaching, internships, and finally in their first in-service year, the book will continue to be an applicable and useful resource; for instance, the analytical instruments at the end of most of the chapters, especially if they are used in the context of the action research we encourage, will aid in the analysis of the various teaching components in clinical or field settings and will promote improved performance.

■ WHAT IS SPECIAL ABOUT THIS BOOK?

As with previous editions, the major feature of this book is our emphasis on decision making as the thread that links all the topics together. We have tried to balance two major perspectives influencing teacher decision making about instruction today: findings from research on effective teaching and the ideas of constructivism. Unique to this book is the inclusion in each chapter of a scenario in which a middle or secondary school teacher, representing a wide range of subject areas and grade levels, applies key ideas to the classroom. These scenarios, which appear near the beginning of each chapter, are referred to and analyzed throughout the chapter to provide a running commentary on the theoretical content being presented.

Various pedagogical elements are designed to help you understand and use this book:

Graphic organizers begin each chapter, emphasizing key ideas.

Summaries of key points appear both throughout the text and at the end of each chapter.

Questions for reflection, at the end of each chapter, guide you to begin making your own decisions about classroom practice.

Observation instruments appear in appropriate chapters to enable you to engage in self-analysis or in shared analysis with colleagues.

Each chapter includes strategies for using the chapter content effectively with students for diverse or special needs.

A complete, updated reference list points you to other resources in the field.

■ WHAT IS NEW ABOUT THIS EDITION?

Dynamics has been revised extensively, ensuring that the content reflects the most current research and best practice. In addition to the features already listed, the fifth edition includes several new features designed to help you use this book more effectively:

The current research and theoretical literature section of each chapter has been updated.

Annotated website resource boxes have been added to each chapter to help teachers identify and use internet-based information.

A new chapter, Differentiated Instruction: Meeting Special Needs of Students, emphasizes why and how teachers can meet the needs of individual students in our diverse classrooms.

Many additional classroom applications have been added to give teachers ideas as to how major trends might be realistically applied in the classroom setting.

More emphasis has been placed on establishing democratic discipline, encouraging reflective teaching, developing students' critical-thinking skills, understanding standards-based curricula, applying cooperative-learning and grouping practices, using multiple intelligences, and creating rubrics and portfolios.

■ ACKNOWLEDGMENTS

As is always the case with projects of this kind, many people have contributed to the final result. We are especially indebted to the colleagues who reviewed the manuscript in its various stages and provided their insight and expertise: Susan R. Smith, Westminster College, and Martin J. Ward, Texas A & M, Corpus Christi.

Teacher Decision Making

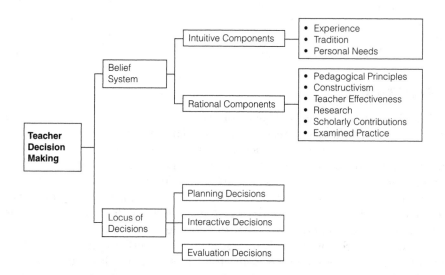

Why a chapter on decision making? Westerman (1991) points out that until the mid-1970s, most research in education focused on teachers' observable behaviors and students' learning outcomes. With Jackson's (1968) close look into the complexity of classroom life, research on how teachers think about students, lesson objectives, content, evaluation, and so on has increased dramatically. What nearly three decades of research points out, according to Westerman, is that "decision making is involved in every aspect of a teacher's professional life" and that "a teacher's thinking and decision making organize and direct a teacher's behavior and form the context for both teaching and learning" (p. 292).

Furthermore, as Hunter (1984) explained, professional decision making and effective teaching are interrelated concepts.

> *Education professionals need to move from the extremes of either intuitive or "recipe-based" behavior to deliberate professional decision making based on research plus experiential wisdom. There still remains plenty of room for intuition. Clearly, we desire educators who are inspired, empathetic, and sensitive to the needs of students and dedicated to the value of education. Those traits are more likely to emerge and be maintained, however, if educators see that students learn successfully as a result of effective teaching. (pp. 189–190)*

Finally, decision making is a thread that links all the topics in this book. Decision making is pervasive, so any improvement that is made in a teacher's decision-making skills will be reflected in every aspect of that teacher's practice. In this respect, any change in decision making has the possibility for a broad-based impact.

■ OVERVIEW

Decision making is personal behavior. It does not lend itself to tightly designed prescriptions. Nevertheless, there are certain common aspects of the process that you as a teacher or prospective teacher should consider. This chapter's most important point is that a well-informed belief system is the most credible basis for rational teacher decisions. The first concern is that you are purposefully aware of the assumptions and beliefs that comprise your belief system. Then, as you develop particular attitudes and habits of practice (i.e., patterns of decision making) based on those assumptions and beliefs that define your personal teaching style, you should examine each one carefully to ensure its conformity to accepted educational principles. As you later plan your instruction, interact in the classroom, and evaluate instructional outcomes, the parameters of thinking you have established will be a safeguard against specious and anti-intellectual reasoning.

■ ASSUMPTIONS AND BELIEFS

Assumptions and beliefs are the basis for much of our everyday behavior. Assumptions tend to be informal, whereas beliefs are more structured. However, one blends into the other so that, in many cases, it is impossible to distinguish between them.

Teachers make assumptions and depend on beliefs in their everyday teaching lives; for example, a teacher who lectures to a class about a particular topic assumes that the class will assimilate a sufficient understanding of that topic from the remarks, or the teacher who assigns a detention to a misbehaving adolescent believes that punishment is a deterrent to future misbehavior. Some may not share the assumptions or the beliefs of these teachers and would, therefore, use a different approach in these situations.

Decision making, with its attendant assumptions and beliefs, serves as a thread throughout this book. As authors, we realized that we needed to make explicit the beliefs that reflect the particular preferences, perceptions, interpretations, and priorities to which we subscribe. You, as the reader, deserve to be informed about them to understand the decisions we made about the content, tone, and style we used in writing this book.

Belief 1   Quality of teaching is directly contingent on the quality of the decision making that precedes the teaching. Decision making is a process, as will be described in this chapter, but more pervasively it is a concept that integrates the various elements of teaching. Decision making is integral to establishing classroom climate, planning for teaching, interacting with others, and evaluating performance and achievement.

Belief 2   Teaching is complex behavior. To interpret it in too-simple terms leads to misunderstanding. This, in fact, is what is done by many noneducators and results in distorted notions about the role of the teacher and the needs of schools. More tragically, some teachers are also guilty of this kind of simplistic, if well-intentioned, thinking as reflected in classroom approaches that disregard professionally endorsed pedagogy and rely on unexamined traditional practice and personal intuition. Their concept of teaching is more likely to be a bag of tricks than a synthesis of sound principles.

Belief 3   Teaching is learned behavior. One often hears about the "born teacher" and that nobody had to teach Socrates or Christ how to teach. A charismatic personality, personal sensitivity, or the gift of verbal dexterity contributes to some people's effectiveness in informing and influencing others. Certainly these characteristics are desirable traits in a teacher. However, pedagogy, as the study of education, is based on systematically derived principles that have been established and recorded by thousands of scholars and practitioners. To assume that a teacher can be optimally effective without a reasonably sound grounding in this science is naive. One can draw the analogy of a kindly family doctor, a general practitioner, being called upon to perform quadruple-bypass heart surgery, the task of a highly trained specialist. It is unthinkable. How then can one rationally assume that it does not take extensive preparation to teach with optimal effectiveness?

Pedagogy, which is available to educators in the professional literature of education, deserves a prominent place in your academic thinking and decision making. It brings respectability and dignity to the teaching profession. In fact, without pedagogy, teaching could not claim to be a profession. Throughout this book we will emphasize that pedagogy takes precedence over personal experience as a referent for teaching decision making.

Belief 4   Instruction should be based on the most effective strategies, methods, techniques, and behaviors as determined by current research and learning theory. Actually, this belief is an extension of statements made in beliefs 2 and 3. A science of teaching, or pedagogy, is derived from research and learning theory and—please take special note of this—is validated by practice. As a professional practitioner, you must have faith in the science of your profession, for without faith you approach it essentially as a craft. A totally personal approach hardly serves in guiding the development of the most complex entity known in the universe—the human mind. In this book we have attempted to translate the most up-to-date, credible ideas from educational literature into practices you can integrate into your own teaching style.

Belief 5   Students must be motivated. This is hardly a controversial statement; in fact, it is so obvious and pervasive that it is regularly taken for granted. As this book was written, the concept of motivation could not be ignored, any more than any current or prospective teacher can afford to ignore it. Students must be motivated in the areas of emotional and academic needs, interests, and abilities for learning to occur. This is the cornerstone of instruction. Your initial and most essential responsibility as a teacher is to arouse these students' intention to learn. To assume that students should want to learn or will make the effort—especially if they already lack a personal sense of purpose—is naive. The truest measure of teaching effectiveness is the extent to which a teacher re-creates conditions that promote student motivation.

Belief 6   The social setting in which learning occurs is a major factor affecting instruction. Admittedly, the possibility of tutorial teaching and independent learning exists, but when one thinks of schooling, one envisions teachers instructing a group of students in a classroom or in a laboratory or on the athletic field. The nature of such interaction is termed *group process*. A body of knowledge has been developed on the subject of group process, and principles related to its application have been established. Clearly, the classroom cannot be fully understood solely in terms of intellectual considerations. The quality of life in the classroom is also contingent on social factors. Therefore, the classroom environment as it is affected by group process is the backdrop of productive learning.

Belief 7   Teaching is, in the final analysis, a personal invention. Although pedagogy is the foundation of optimally effective teaching, it tends to be more suggestive than prescriptive. Individual teachers, meanwhile, are as different from one another as everyone else in the population is. For example, a teacher who has a highly developed sense of humor may banter with students and use quips, the overall effect of which can be quite positive. A more serious-minded teacher may conduct a more structured class and yet also be effective in helping students achieve intended learning outcomes. Teachers will be most effective if they maintain their own personal identity and integrity while being guided by the tenets of pedagogy. Please note, however, that not all persons, no matter how true to themselves they remain, have personalities that are well suited to the demands of teaching. This is especially true of persons who have limited social sensitivity or an inordinate need of security, recognition, or authority.

The observation has been made that effective teachers tend to be more diverse among themselves, whereas mediocre teachers tend to be more alike. We believe that teaching is a personal invention of each practitioner, and this book is intended to contribute to the personal inventing process by helping teachers develop their own unique teaching styles within a framework of established principles.

Belief 8 Students learn both individually and as a group. An important decision the classroom teacher makes during the planning phase of instruction is whether a particular lesson will occur as a large group process, within a set of structured small groups, or as an individually defined task. A multitude of factors comes into play here; for example, the teacher will have to take into account the timing of the lesson, the instructional materials involved, and the grouping arrangements the students have experienced over the past few days. Perhaps the most critical consideration in making this decision, though, is how the teacher can best encourage students to construct deep understanding of important concepts.

Belief 9 Students learn best in a safe and secure environment. This belief was reflected in the very idealistic Goals 2000: Educate America Act passed by Congress in 1989 which stated, "By the year 2000, every school in the United States will be free of drugs, violence, and the unauthorized presence of firearms and alcohol, and will offer a disciplined environment conducive to learning" (in *Expanding Opportunities for Success: Ohio's Fourth Annual Progress Report on Education,* 1994). Achieving this ambitious goal, hopefully during the first decade of this new century, will require much work on the part of policy makers at the state and local levels. The classroom teacher, too, plays a significant role in the making of a safe classroom. Teachers must recognize, assess, and monitor problems associated with at-risk behaviors in students. Interacting and networking with the whole community, including parents, social service agencies, medical professionals, and law enforcement agencies, are becoming professional responsibilities for current educators. The realm of teacher decision making extends beyond the classroom walls. An effective teacher acknowledges the existence of a world beyond subject matter, the classroom, and the school. To that end, an effective teacher knows that she or he does not "teach third grade," nor does she or he "teach science." An effective teacher teaches human beings, and whether those human beings are 5 years old or 18 years old, they deserve to learn in safe places.

It is informed decision making that is the most credible plank in the argument for teaching as a profession.

■ PEDAGOGY: THE DISCIPLINE OF TEACHING

Pedagogy, like mathematics, music, or philosophy, is a discipline, that is, a recognized area of academic study and practice. The term *pedagogy* itself has Greek and Latin origins and is a reminder of all that was excellent in classical education. In current use, it likewise connotes all that is best in modern education. Whereas educators more commonly use the broader term *education, pedagogy* has the advantage of defining more precisely a rational approach to teaching, the opposite of anti-intellectualism. *Pedagogy* is understood to refer to the discipline of education and not necessarily to all practices that in some way might be associated with teaching. *Pedagogy,* therefore, defined as an extensive body of knowledge that incorporates those principles and practices that have been validated by research and scholarly scrutiny, is a term that will be used often in this book to convey the ideal of enlightened teaching.

Pedagogy as a formal discipline is not always enthusiastically embraced by teachers. Attitudes range from unconcern through condescension to distrust. When teachers are suspicious of pedagogy or associate it primarily with scholarly papers and textbooks, they consider the literature to have little relationship to what really happens in schools. Teachers sometimes remark that a particular idea seems "okay in theory, but won't work in the classroom." Such a position reflects a misunderstanding of theory and of pedagogy.

The authors do not maintain that pedagogy implies absolute certainty, but rather that it is currently the most accurate theory known about education. To reject it or to ignore it and be guided primarily by individual personal experience is to assume a patently anti-intellectual posture. In doing so, one is in essence saying, "Don't confuse me with the facts."

If theory is to reach its fullest potential, teacher decision making—the link between theory and practice—must be guided by pedagogy. Darling-Hammond and Goodwin (1993) propose that for teaching to be viewed as a profession, teachers must view their work as "knowledge based" and must develop habits of deep thinking and reflectiveness. According to Darling-Hammond and Goodwin, "Professionals not only know whether and when to choose particular courses of action according to general principles, but they can also evaluate multifaceted situations in which many variables intersect" (p. 25).

■ THE BASIC DIMENSIONS OF PEDAGOGY

Two generalizations emerge from the previous commentary. First, teaching involves a high order of human functioning. The most effective teachers are well informed regarding modern pedagogical principles and are able to translate those principles of teaching and learning into effective practice. Furthermore, teaching behaviors have many purposes: academic, social, personal, and behavioral. Teachers need a repertoire of skills and methods that will enable them to accommodate a host of instructional demands.

Second, teaching may usefully be conceived as a science that is implemented by artists. Automobile racing serves as an apt analogy. The sophisticated technology involved in modern automotive engineering achieves its potential only in the hands of a talented and skilled driver. Likewise, state-of-the-art pedagogy remains only a promise until it is made functional by competent teachers whose own personalities and perceptions provide the dynamic dimension of pedagogy.

This book uses as its point of departure the beliefs and generalizations presented in this section. The authors have attempted to collect and organize theories, principles, research findings, and practices that usefully elaborate these selected beliefs and generalizations. Again, there is no possible prescription for effective teaching in a direct, one-to-one fashion. However, the authors believe that teachers—and teacher-education students—will benefit from giving careful consideration to the ideas and examples in this book and from translating them within the context of their respective teaching styles and settings.

SCENARIO

Ms. Knettel was listening as her ninth-grade students read aloud from "The Rime of the Ancient Mariner," one verse per student in succession. The reading was expressionless and halting. Students paid little attention as other classmates read. Squirming and fidgeting created a minor disruption.

In planning this lesson a few days earlier, Ms. Knettel speculated that this poem, in particular, was one to which students could relate. It involves a fierce storm at sea, the curse of a so-called Spirit, shipmates who become zombies, and other miraculous events. The poem has vivid imagery and a readily perceived moral. Although some feel it is not the best of Romantic poetry, it seemed well suited to acquaint students with the Romantic style.

As she conducted the lesson, Ms. Knettel realized she had overestimated the potential of the poem to capture the students' imagination. She occasionally interspersed questions like, "Why did Coleridge choose an albatross as the bird that was shot?" and "Why was the ancient mariner telling this tale to the wedding guest, who was a complete stranger?" But the class sat dumbfounded. To continue, she realized, was pointless. Yet, what could she do?

An actual crisis had not yet occurred. The students were not out of hand, even though they were restless. She could momentarily continue with the present activity and buy a little time to think about it.

One alternative, she thought, was for students to read silently and write answers to questions she put on the board. Meanwhile, she could circulate throughout the room helping students individually because many hesitated to ask questions aloud. Another alternative might be

to appoint the best readers as small-group leaders, and each group could read through the assignment together. This would provide active involvement of a greater number of students. A third alternative was for students to act out scenes from the poem: shooting the albatross, the vehemence of the crew, zombies sailing the ship, and confronting the wedding guest. For the poor readers, this would be a particularly useful way of presenting the substance of the poem, and everyone would enjoy the poem more.

Ms. Knettel considered the likely consequence of each alternative, but none of them seemed quite right. Then a fourth alternative occurred to her that was even more appealing. Why not have a class meeting to give the students the opportunity to express their perceptions and opinions and to help her think through the situation? Her long-range intention for the class was that the students become increasingly empowered and responsible, and she was consciously aware that her decision at this point was influenced by that goal.

"Class," she said, "we seem to have gotten bogged down. Do you think it would help if we talked about it? Let's spend the 25 minutes we have remaining in a class meeting. Move your chairs into a circle, like we did the last time, but lift them so we're not too noisy."

Ms. Knettel sat in as a member of the circle but asked Marge if she would chair the meeting. A lively discussion ensued. Some students felt that "The Rime of the Ancient Mariner" was "boring them to death" (their expression), and they didn't see the point in studying it. Other students said they enjoyed the poem, even though they had difficulty expressing a rationale for their position. Finally, Geri asked, "Do you really think this stuff does us any good, Ms. Knettel? How can we ever use it?"

Ms. Knettel had taken the opportunity to reflect and to formulate the outline of her response while the students discussed their views for nearly 20 minutes. Now Geri provided the opportunity to comment.

"As a matter of fact," Ms. Knettel said, "there are few things you learn in school that you use directly. Everything you learn becomes part of what you are and contributes to broad understandings and appreciations. Remember that 'The Rime of the Ancient Mariner' was written about 200 years ago. Many thousands of poems have been written since; yet few of them are known or read today. This poem is still popular, mainly because it tells us with beauty and grace something important about the human condition. For example, we now sometimes use the expression 'a person has an albatross around his neck,' and it has a useful meaning because of the legacy Coleridge left us in his poem. Along with other great literature, this poem has made our thinking and expression much richer."

The students were quiet for several moments. Then Geri and several others agreed that they hadn't thought of it that way before. Tyler commented that he still didn't like poetry, in general, but that he could see how somebody might. The bell rang at that point, and the students left the room still talking about the possible merits of good poetry.

Ms. Knettel now sensed more interest from the students. The likelihood existed that, for the moment, they were willing to give the poem the benefit of the doubt. She realized that her job was to try to get them to the point of making a reasonable commitment. By tomorrow, she thought, I've got to use a little imagination and come up with a plan that utilizes the students' own experiences as a point of departure for further reading of the poem.

■ RESEARCH AND THEORETICAL BASE

General Perspectives

Ms. Knettel made a timely decision that redirected the activity in her class. She did, in fact, employ a systematic approach to decision making that may not be apparent to a person unfamiliar with the dynamics of the process. These dynamics have their basis, in part, in the knowledge base related to decision making.

Perhaps the single most significant statement in the literature related to decision making was made by Shavelson (1973); he pronounced decision making to be *the* basic teaching skill. It is a statement that stands unchallenged because it is self-evident. Support for the statement is founded in logic and experience, not in research. In this same vein, Hunter (1984) defined teaching as "the constant stream of professional decisions that affects the probability of learning: decisions that are made and implemented before, during, and after interaction with the students" (pp. 169–170).

Research on teacher decision making reflects the highly contextual nature of teaching; for instance, the research has addressed such related topics as teacher decision making regarding content structure (Klimczak, Balli, and Wedman, 1995), learning activities (Parker and Gehrke, 1986), classroom management (Emmer, 1982), planning (Borko and Livingston, 1989), curriculum deliberation (McCutcheon, 1995), content (Mahood, Biemer, and Lowe, 1991), and assessment (Nickell, 1999). In a very recent review of research on instructional decision making within the field of social studies, Kirkwood (2002) found additional internal and external contextual factors influencing teacher decision making: availability of materials such as textbooks, methods best suited for students, what their peers value, and community influence. Other influences on their instructional decisions were their personal and professional experiences.

Perhaps it is the fragmented nature of the research on teacher decision making or the intimate nature of decision making itself that limits the degree to which teachers utilize deeper, more reflective levels of decision making. Shavelson (1983) expressed his concern in his review of the research that, although teachers made about 10 interactive (i.e., during instruction) decisions per hour, they tended to consider few alternatives. They were more concerned with justifying their choices than in examining them critically. In other words, the potential for decision-making skills to contribute to effective teaching is being only marginally realized. While Shavelson reported 10 interactive decisions an hour—one every six minutes—Clark (1988) claimed from his review of the literature that teachers made an interactive decision every two minutes. These researchers may differ somewhat in their perception of interactive decisions, but we can assume from their informed estimates that teachers average an interactive decision every two to six minutes. Therefore, teaching is affected for better or worse by an interactive decision 50 to 100 times each day. Clark said further, "The research on teaching has made an empirical case that the practice of teaching is complex, uncertain, and dilemma riddled" (p. 10). This is a compelling reason to encourage rational and effective decision making as part of professional development in both preservice and in-service programs; informed decision making by teachers is the most credible plank in the argument that teaching be considered a profession.

The decision making of novice teachers has been examined, and the results are not unexpected. Nagel and Driscoll (1992) found in a study of student teachers that the novices had little commitment to practices they had learned in university coursework. Their more important concern was acceptance within the school culture. "Teaching decisions were influenced by field experiences, peers, personal experience in the schools, and the relationship with the cooperating teacher. There was a significant lack of mention of university coursework" (p. 8). Westerman (1991) found that, "In contrast to the model for expert teachers, decision making for novices seems more linear than dynamic . . . " (p. 300). In another review of research, problem-solving facility was also a difference between experts and novices. Experts spend more time analyzing a problem, understand it at a deeper level than novices, and are faster and more accurate at solving problems (Hmelo-Silver, Nagarajan, and Day, 2002). Mohlman Sparks-Langer and Colton (1991), in reviewing the literature on reflective teaching, concluded that experience was the reason experts had rich schemata as compared with the novices, who had less developed schemata. All of these findings remind us that novice teachers present a special case in our efforts to understand teacher decision making.

Decision making undoubtedly is a basic teaching skill, but educators are left essentially to their own devices regarding its application. Evidence of the direct impact of theory and research on teacher decision making is minimal. However, each contribution to the literature on decision making expands our knowledge of it. A critical mass of knowledge may one day exist, signifying a major breakthrough in the skill and application of decision making.

Instructional Perspectives

During the 1970s and early 1980s, process-outcome studies contributed in an important way to the knowledge base of teaching. Generally speaking, this empirical research measured correlations between teacher behavior and student achievement to identify effective teacher practices. Rosenshine (1983) listed some of these effective practices: "structur[e] the learning; proceed in small steps . . . ; provide many examples; ask a large number of questions . . . ; provide feedback and corrections . . . ; have a student success rate of 80% or higher . . . ; provide for continued practice" (p. 336). These kinds of practices were organized into a structured set of functions that provided guidelines for effective teaching:

1. Review, checking the previous day's work.
2. Present new content/skills.
3. Provide for initial student practice.
4. Provide for feedback and correctives.
5. Provide for student independent practice.
6. Provide weekly and monthly reviews. (p. 337)

Much of the research done on effective teaching used population samples from urban elementary school settings. The outcomes were measured by standardized tests. Even though the findings were variably generalizable to other school populations and were important in the development of pedagogy, the limitations of the research became increasingly apparent to educators. The outcomes that were sought and measured involved two factors: essentially convergent thinking that yielded right answers, and acquisition of basic learning skills. Chapter 2 includes an expanded commentary on several aspects of effective teaching and its applicability to secondary classrooms. The authors acknowledge in this edition, as we did in previous editions of this book, that structured and directive teaching—sometimes called active teaching—such as lectures and recitation is an essential set of skills for the fully functioning teacher.

As scholars during the latter half of the 1980s, through the 1990s, and into the beginning of the new century have proclaimed, another important dimension of learning—students' personal meaning making—is not sufficiently addressed with direct-teaching approaches. National curriculum reports from subject-area learned societies began to appear in the late 1980s, the first from the National Council of Teachers of Mathematics. These reports, while they address their respective disciplines, have many common features, which include (Zemelman, Daniels, and Hyde, 2000, pp. 4–6):

- Less whole-class, teacher-directed instruction
- Less student passivity: sitting, listening, receiving, and absorbing information
- Less presentational, one-way transmission of information from teacher to student
- Less classroom time devoted to fill-in-the blank worksheets and other "seat work"
- Less attempt by teachers to thinly "cover" large amounts of material
- Less rote memorization of acts and details
- Less emphasis on competition and grades in school

- Less use of and reliance on standardized tests
- More experiential, inductive, hands-on learning
- More active learning in the classroom
- More emphasis on higher-order learning
- More deep study of a smaller number of topics
- More responsibility transferred to students for their work
- More choice for students
- More enacting and modeling of the principles of democracy
- More cooperative, collaborative activity

The teaching approach that incorporates many of these features has come to be called constructivist teaching. The term is a fairly recent one, but this student-centered approach has its roots in the work of philosopher John Dewey and cognitive/developmental psychologist Jean Piaget, two of the seminal educational theorists of the twentieth century. In this mode, students become active searchers into knowledge rather than passive receivers of it. They are encouraged to discover their own meanings and to develop new understandings through inquiring, reflecting, problem solving, and applying. Brooks and Brooks (1993) listed several characteristics of learning settings that encouraged constructivist learning:

> *They free students from the dreariness of fact-driven curriculum and allow them to focus on large ideas. They place in students' hands the exhilarating power to follow trails of interest, to make connections, reformulate ideas, and to reach unique conclusions. They share with students the important message that the world is a complex place in which multiple perspectives exist and truth is often a matter of interpretation. They acknowledge that learning, and the process of assessing learning, are, at best, elusive and messy endeavors that are not easily managed. (p. 21)*

We include this commentary on effective teaching and constructivist teaching in this chapter because they are two major sources within the pedagogical knowledge base that inform teachers' decision making. This is becoming even more apparent at the beginning of the new century, considering the extensive supportive commentary in the literature. Throughout this book, repeated reference will be made to practices that emerge from these two perspectives on teaching—and learning. We assert in the following section that rational bases for decision making, when they apply, are professionally preferable to intuitive bases. Effective teaching research and constructivist teaching theory are two of these rational bases that will serve reflective teachers well. The two bases are not polar opposites, nor are they mutually exclusive. Darling-Hammond and McLaughlin (1995) believe that what should be emphasized in the professional development of teachers is "the appropriateness (their emphasis) of teaching decisions to the goals and contexts of instruction and the needs of students" (p. 603). The authors would extend this sage advice to include all aspects of teaching, including instructional planning, classroom interactions, and evaluation of student learning.

■ APPLICATION TO PRACTICE

The Process of Decision Making

As cited, a persuasive argument has been made for designating decision making as the basic teaching skill. Indeed, effective decisions inevitably precede effective teaching. This is a compelling rationale for both examining decision making and striving to become proficient in its essential skills. But decision making is a subtle concept and involves skills that are not directly acquired. Instead, as shown in Figure 1.1, the teacher must acquire certain predisposing awarenesses and attitudes, after which an improved decision-making capability is possible and probable.

Impact of Belief System

Teachers accumulate teaching-related ideas over time. Generalized information, attitudes, and assumptions are internalized and constitute the teacher's belief system. In the classroom scenario, Ms. Knettel wanted her students to be interested in lesson content and was disturbed that her lesson was proceeding mechanically. She needed to make a decision. But the decision she ultimately

Assumptions	and	Beliefs

Intuitive Bases
(unexamined beliefs & practices)
   Experience
   Tradition
   Personal Needs
		Rational Bases
		(informed beliefs & practices)
		   Pedagogical Principles
		   Constructivism Principles
		   Teacher Effectiveness
		   Research
		   Scholarly Contributions
		   Examined Practice

Absence of Choice	*Conscious Nonreflection*	*Deliberate Reflection*
Planning Decisions	Interactive Decisions	Evaluation Decisions

Figure 1.1   Components of Teacher Decison Making

made, like most thoughtful decisions, was not based on one identifiable principle or idea but was the product of a belief system consisting of many integrated ideas. If the ideas from which a belief system is developed are judiciously selected, the decisions that emanate from it will be generally sound. Unfortunately, the judicious selection of ideas is not an easily monitored process, and it requires knowledge and experience.

Part of the skill of decision making, therefore, involves an astute selection of ideas that will predispose subsequent decisions. One can assume that there existed within Ms. Knettel's belief system regard for the democratic process and respect for her students' perceptions and opinions.

Some teacher beliefs are fairly simple: Homework should be assigned routinely, for example, or, conversely, routine homework is an unproductive use of students' time. Other beliefs are more elaborate and far-reaching. Some teachers subscribe to the proposition that learning occurs most effectively when the teacher is authoritarian or, again conversely, when the teacher is minimally directive. Such beliefs—some soundly conceived, some only superficially; some clearly defined, some vaguely—characterize individual teaching styles.

Some further examples of teachers' beliefs will help clarify the pervasive, although sometimes subtle, influence of those beliefs on teacher decisions. Some teachers consider punishment to be a deterrent to future misbehavior; others contend that punishment is a negative influence on the classroom climate that increases the potential for misbehavior. Some teachers also believe that meticulous planning contributes to effective instruction; others believe that structured plans inhibit spontaneity. Moreover, some teachers think of grades as ends in themselves; others consider grades to be means for providing feedback and correction. Which beliefs in each of these pairs—and the many more that might be listed—are right? Which can we say with confidence will result in more effective learning? Which may actually undermine students' learning? The task of every teacher is to develop a belief system that is pedagogically sound and personally comfortable. Teachers are more or less successful because of a variety of factors, some of which they cannot personally control. Fortunately, the belief system, one of the most powerful of these factors, can be directly controlled.

The belief system is itself informed from two bases, the intuitive and the rational. Each is comprised of several components. The intuitive components include the following:

Experience-based impressions: Teachers' personal judgment regarding what is appropriate or useful practice. Examples: "After 10 years of teaching, I know that I must get students' total attention before I begin class." "When I send a student to the office, I don't have any more trouble in that class the rest of the day."

Traditional practices: Common strategies and techniques that are widely accepted in schools and that have a rationale rooted in conventional wisdom. Examples: Friday is test day. Students write out the answers to the questions at the end of the chapter. Reading is taught in the morning.

Personal needs: Personality-related and mental-health-related factors that precondition the teacher's perception and behavior. Examples: Students' desks are arranged in rows so that the teacher can control the noise level and direct lessons from the front of the room. All students in industrial technology work on the same project at the same time.

Rational components include the following:

Pedagogical principles: Those well-established and extensively documented tenets that often have a basis in related areas of study such as psychology, sociology, communication, leadership, organization, and group process. Examples: Positive reinforcement promotes the highest level of student achievement. Students learn best when they perceive meaning and relevance in a topic.

Constructivist approaches: Emphasis on the student as meaning maker. Example: Students are actively engaged more in inquiry and the discovery of personal meaning than in being receivers of preorganized knowledge.

"Teacher effectiveness" practices: Effective teachers were found to employ in common certain techniques in their teaching. Example: When the teacher initially poses a question to the entire group and pauses, and then calls on an individual student, the probability that nearly all the students are cognitively involved is increased.

Research findings: Discoveries through systematic methods of research into content of education, instructional approaches, and learning effectiveness. Examples: Low-ability students learn best from concrete approaches. Task time correlates positively with student achievement.

Scholarly contributions: Those essays, models, theories, and judgments of learned academicians that are an essential source of intellectual vigor and developmental thrust. Examples: Gardner's (1983) *Frames of Mind: The Theory of Multiple Intelligences* and the work on best practice and new standards (Zemelman, Daniels, and Hyde, 1998).

Examined practice: The strategies and techniques that have been determined through experience to be effective and consistent with professionally endorsed principles of pedagogy. Examples: A variety of activities that show concern for students' span of attention result in effective teaching. Treating students with respect and sensitivity contributes to the quality of classroom life.

Importance of Using Examined Beliefs and Practices

Even in our modern schools, it is not unusual to find teachers whose practice is shaped primarily from their past experiences. Some teachers (also counselors and administrators) are unquestionably effective simply because of their ample intuitive grasp of what their role demands and their talent for responding to students. These naturally gifted teachers are often referred to as "artist teachers." Less gifted teachers are obviously less effective.

To the extent that teachers operate primarily on the basis of experience, they perform analogously to the tribal medicine man. Through his use of both mystique and proficiency with primitive medicines, he may actually perform a valuable service for his tribespeople. His practice, however, lacks a rationally developed base. Little change occurs in his practice from generation to generation because there is, essentially, no understanding of causes and, instead, simply a recognition and treatment of symptoms. This is a casual analogy and, in all fairness, should not be overstated. Changes have obviously occurred in education over any recent period of time one chooses to examine.

The fact remains that the gap between what is and what might be (real–ideal discrepancy) is a serious professional concern, evident by the 1980s reports on the condition of schooling: *A Nation at Risk* (National Commission on Excellence in Education, 1983) as reported on by Goldberg and Harvey (1983) and "A Study of Schooling" (Goodlad, 1983). The former study stated that inferior education is one reason for lack of competitiveness with other nations, and that even though mediocrity is the norm rather than the exception, we can—and must—do better. In a discussion of the latter study, Goodlad stated, "The most striking discovery to emerge from the data is what might be called sameness of form in the substance and design of the curriculum whether the subject is English Language Arts, Mathematics, Science or Social Studies" (p. 467). More recently, Sarason (1990) described contemporary schools as "intellectually boring places" (p. 111) with "one-size-fits-all delivery systems" (p. 114).

There are many reasons for the real–ideal discrepancy in the schools, and teachers' use of unexamined beliefs and practices contributes to that discrepancy. Unexamined practice encases our professional feet in blocks of anti-intellectual cement and makes moving forward both as individual teachers and as a profession very sluggish. If the recommendations in all of the studies of schooling were implemented but some critical mass of teachers continued to use primarily experienced-based approaches, a real–ideal discrepancy would continue to exist.

APPLICATION for DIVERSE CLASSROOMS

Teachers must examine carefully their beliefs concerning students' ability to learn. If teachers hold lesser expectations of students' potential or place students in ability groups that are maintained throughout the year, student achievement is negatively affected. Research shows that beliefs about the lower intellectual ability of students from certain minority groups or socioeconomic levels lead to a disproportionately high percentage of these students being placed in lower level groups and classes (Good and Brophy, 2000).

■ INFORMED DECISION MAKING

A science of education emerges from rational sources. Intuitive sources will inevitably remain as a factor in decision making, but practices based on rational sources should take precedence in any case in which they are available and applicable.

Intuitive sources are, in particular, inclined to reflect bias and self-service. Consider, for example, the case of students in class who make minimal efforts to perform assigned learning tasks. The teacher who makes a superficial evaluation of students may consider them to be lazy. That judgment places the fault—and therefore the responsibility—entirely on the students. The teacher may nag and occasionally reprimand students or may simply ignore them except to assign low marks.

On the other hand, a teacher using a rational perspective is more likely to infer that they lack sufficient motivation, a factor for which the teacher shares responsibility, and may look for causes and solutions to the motivation problem. In Ms. Knettel's scenario, she began to search for causes rather than to assume that students would take an interest in Romantic poetry. Teachers who acknowledge their responsibility in a situation are more likely to take initiatives to improve the conditions for learning.

If educators were to relate their informed beliefs to their practice, changes would occur in their practice. The following are some possible areas of potential change:

Discipline practices: The recent outpouring of professional literature on the management of student behavior signals a heightened awareness of past inadequacies and provides direction in the development of more enlightened approaches; approaches include the use of reasonable consequences, conflict management, and student self-management.

Individualization: New understanding through cognitive-style studies and left brain–right brain experimentation raises expectations regarding the compatibility of teacher strategies with learner assimilation. Recent research on multiple intelligences (Gardner, 1983) and its application to classroom teaching (Armstrong, 2000) provide the teacher with extensive information on the learner as an individual.

Higher-level thinking: Modern techniques of questioning can significantly raise the quality of students' thinking and increase the potential for a lasting impact. Bloom's taxonomy (1956) stimulated efforts of scholars and practitioners to emphasize the use of information as a means to an end, not as an end itself.

Instruction: Discriminating and imaginative use of a variety of strategies, such as those suggested in *Models of Teaching* (Joyce, Weil, and Calhoun, 2000) and in *Cooperative Learning: Theory, Research, and Practice* (Slavin, 1990), extend the purpose and range of instruction. Meaningful use of constructivist teaching—for example, the pursuit of student questions and the posing of critical problems—and of concepts such as time-on-task, direct teaching, instructional cues, and others popularized by research on effective teaching contribute to effective instruction.

Evaluation: Concepts such as nongraded classrooms, mastery-level learning, authentic and alternative assessment, contract grading, diagnosis and prescription, rubrics, portfolios, and criterion-/norm-referenced considerations can help integrate evaluation with instruction.

The previous examples include both some older, familiar ideas and some recent ones. A teacher whose belief system and, therefore, whose practice is informed by such constructs is one for whom theory is—as Dewey (1929) insisted—the most practical of all things. Dewey meant simply that, as a practical matter in effective teaching, a sound conceptual framework (i.e., an informed belief system) is necessary. Without it, teaching is likely to be superficial and lacking in clear purpose.

Hints for the Beginning Teacher

Consider keeping a journal during your first year of teaching. Entries could include reflections on key decisions that you made during the course of the day. What were the decisions you made? What were the outcomes? What changes would you now make in these decisions?

Clark and Peterson (1986) captured the spirit of informed decision making as it contributes to reflective teaching when they wrote, "The maturing professional teacher is one who has taken some steps toward making explicit his or her implicit theories and beliefs about learners, curriculum, subject matter, and the teacher's role" (p. 292). These experienced teachers have become "researchers on their own teaching effectiveness" (p. 293).

■ THE DECISION-MAKING CONTINUUM

Virtually all teacher behavior involves choice, including the choice not to make a choice! By the idea of choice, we mean that the possibility of alternatives exists, the simplest of which is whether to act. Some actions are characterized by the absence of any conscious choice; they represent unconscious behaviors on the part of teachers. Conditioned responses and unconscious knee-jerk or habitual behaviors exemplify teacher behaviors at the absence-of-choice end of the continuum. The repeated use of certain words or phrases (especially *okay* and *you know*), rolling the chalk in a hand, and raising the voice to talk over student noise are examples of this behavior. These examples and several other kinds of behavior from this end of the continuum are such a constant part of a teacher's pattern that they help define a teaching style and in some cases are recognized as a teacher's idiosyncrasies.

At the middle range of the continuum, behavior contains a conscious dimension, with some degree of spontaneity as well. Perhaps it is best described as conscious, nonreflective behavior. Examples of this sort of behavior often fall into the category of routine behavior such as seating students in alphabetical rows, using the textbook as virtually the sole resource in a course, and starting lessons regularly by reading the answers to the homework.

At the deliberation end of the continuum, decision making is characterized by reflection. If one assumes that some degree of decision making has occurred all along the continuum—any teaching-related action is, by definition, preceded by a decision—the term *purposeful reflection* best describes the mental operation at this far end. Examples of this behavior are unit planning, offering enrichment or remediation to particular students, and using a balance of lower- and higher-order questions in classroom discussions.

Teachers make hundreds of habitual responses and spontaneous choices in the course of a teaching day. For the sake of their sanity, they must. Practicing teachers may remember the mental fatigue they felt at the end of the day before they established a repertoire of effective responses and techniques. On the other hand, teachers must not take their habitual choices for granted and thereby engage in glib decision making. To do so inclines them toward the "mindlessness" syndrome observed by Silberman (1970) in so many classrooms in the late 1960s or the "monotonous sameness" reported by Goodlad (1983) in describing classrooms of the late 1970s. These findings of mindlessness and monotony are, in part, due to superficial attention to decisions. Teachers should remain aware of the consequences of their decisions as reflected in their emerging teaching styles.

Some situations arise that are unfamiliar and present momentary uncertainty—even for an experienced teacher such as Ms. Knettel. Like Ms. Knettel, a teacher must consider the alternatives, weigh the likely outcomes, and select a course of action. This sequence of mental activities extends beyond spontaneous choice and requires decision making based on principles of education, research findings, and examined practice—the core of pedagogy.

A teacher may encounter the same situation in the future and, having previously made a personally acceptable response, may readily do it again. Therefore, the same teacher behavior (response) that once required reflective decision making may become, at a later date, a simple matter of spontaneous choice.

In the process of teacher development, both of these types of teacher responses—thoughtful and spontaneous—deserve consideration. If the teacher should develop a set of automatic behaviors that are counterproductive, then teacher effectiveness is diminished; for example, a teacher may habitually lecture as a means of covering content and may exceed student attention span, or a teacher may frequently threaten students whose behavior is considered inappropriate. These approaches may contribute to the teacher's momentary comfort as a means of responding to the immediate demands of teaching, but the long-term effects on students are contrary to the conditions of productive learning. Continual repetition of such practices can only result in mindless and monotonous teaching.

Choice patterns or sets of responses result from prior decision making, so reflective decision making as the basis for these patterns is an essential step toward successful teaching. It is important to look at the sources from which these first-encounter decisions are made.

■ THE LOCUS OF DECISIONS

Decisions occur in three different aspects of teaching: planning and preparing for instruction, the interaction phase, and evaluating learning outcomes. Each of these aspects involves different kinds of considerations.

Planning Decisions   Decisions made prior to instruction can be made without haste or a sense of immediacy, and can be made after lengthy reflection. In the process, the teacher has time to pose some searching questions and to make use of those educational principles, research findings, and theories that relate to the intent of the instruction. Some of these broad questions include: Is this the most worthwhile topic or activity for these students at this time? Do the students have the knowledge and skills necessary to handle the content? How does this topic or activity relate to the objectives of the course? Other more specific questions that should also be posed include: What are some key questions that will direct students' thinking toward the lesson objectives? What sort of entry will most effectively initiate learning?

Interactive Decisions　Teachers make an average of one interactive decision every two to six minutes (Clark, 1988; Clark and Peterson, 1986; Shavelson, 1983). Furthermore, decisions made during the interactive phase of instruction often must occur rapidly, for time is severely limited. Yet, one's success as a teacher clearly is contingent on the quality of these decisions. The seasoned teacher who has encountered a wide variety of conditions and who has learned appropriate responses by some means—even trial and error—is surely at an advantage. Ms. Knettel made the decision to use a classroom meeting based on prior experience with the activity.

A less experienced, but alert, teacher may speculate about possible situations that will require decisions and will think them through beforehand. As situations arise, they will not be quite so strange or puzzling and can be taken in stride. For example, a teacher may be planning a small-group activity for the following day's lesson. The class has not participated in small-group activities as yet, so the teacher does not know how students will respond. Therefore, the teacher could make an alternative plan, such as an appropriate seat-work assignment, as a contingency.

But no amount of preparation can help the teacher predict every situation that will occur. What then does the teacher do? Several nonspecific strategies are applicable in these cases:

- Simply pause and take a moment to reflect, even at the risk of momentary awkwardness.
- Admit honestly to the class that the situation requires some time to think through.
- Make a decision, if the consequences are not irreversible, with the intent of reviewing it later.

Any teacher who has a well-informed belief system and who is in touch with that belief system has an important advantage in this interactive phase of instruction. When sound educational principles that can be quickly called to use populate the belief system, effective decisions are the probable outcome. Fewer off-the-top-of-the-head judgments will occur. The teacher whose belief system is more intuitively based rather than rationally based or who simply does not make sufficient effort to act rationally will make a large proportion of suspect decisions while teaching that can cause problems for both the teacher and the students.

Evaluation Decisions   Finally, decisions are made about evaluating student progress before, during, and following instruction. The teacher must determine the extent to which students have performed according to some standard. The more explicit both the initial objectives for learning and the criteria for evaluation are, the more clear and valid are the decisions regarding students' performance. The teacher who has thoughtfully developed objectives and criteria beforehand will find the formative and summative evaluation decisions simpler to make. On the other hand, a teacher whose evaluation decisions are largely after the fact fails initially to provide students with a clear idea of expectations and is likely to engage in arbitrary, expedient means of assessing achievement. The consequences are predictable: Validity of the evaluation is marginal, and the very purpose of evaluation is compromised.

■ SUMMARY POINT ■

Being aware of decision making as a process and understanding the dynamics of the process does not exhaust the potential of this concept to contribute to effective teaching. Decision making is the professional orientation and a pattern of thinking that undergirds one's instructional style and ensures that teaching will be conducted as a thoughtful practice. To the extent that this occurs, a teacher cannot be comfortable employing unwitting, intuitive responses to the demands of teaching; rather, rational sources become the only acceptable basis for decisions and for subsequent related choices. Rational, reflective decision making is the basic teaching skill that, fully developed, is essential to optimally effective teaching.

■ QUESTIONS FOR REFLECTION ■

1. Nine general beliefs are included in this chapter, but these represent only the beginning of a much longer possible list. What are some other teaching-related beliefs that you currently hold?

2. The assertion is made in Chapter 1 that decision making is the basic teaching skill. What arguments might be made to support or refute that statement? What, in fact, are the subskills that comprise rational decision making?

3. Teachers make decisions about all the aspects of teaching, including physical arrangement of the classroom, climate, lesson planning, instructional style and strategies, testing and evaluation, classroom management rules and routines, and student behavior. What are some typical decisions you as a teacher might make in these contexts, and, importantly, what are your beliefs and motives that underlie them?

4. Personal needs are included in the list of intuitive (unexamined) bases for teacher decisions. What is your own needs profile that is likely to predispose, for better or for worse, decisions you will make as a teacher?

■ REFERENCES ■

Armstrong, T. (2000). *Multiple Intelligences in the Classroom* (2nd ed.). Alexandria, VA: Association for Supervision and Curriculum Development.

Bloom, B. (Ed.). (1956). *A Taxonomy of Educational Objectives, Handbook I: Cognitive Domain.* New York: McKay.

Borko, H., and Livingston, C. (1989). "Cognition and improvisation: Differences in mathematics instruction by expert and novice teachers." *American Educational Research Journal, 26,* 473–498.

Brooks, J., and Brooks, M. (1993). *The Case for Constructivist Classrooms.* Alexandria, VA: Association for Supervision and Curriculum Development.

Brophy, J., and Good, T. (1986). "Research on early childhood and elementary school teaching programs." In M. Wittrock (Ed.), *Handbook of Research on Teaching* (3rd ed.). New York: Macmillan.

Clark, C. (1988). "Asking the right questions about teacher preparation: Contributions of research on teacher thinking." *Educational Researcher, 17*(2), 5–12.

Clark, C., and Peterson, P. (1976). "Teacher stimulated recall of interactive decisions." Paper presented at the annual meeting of the American Educational Research Association, San Francisco.

Clark, C., and Peterson, P. (1986). "Teachers' thought processes." In M. Wittrock (Ed.), *Handbook of Research on Teaching* (3rd ed.). New York: Macmillan.

Darling-Hammond, L., and Goodwin, A. L. (1993). "Progress toward professionalism in teaching." In G. Cawelti (Ed.), *Challenges and Achievements of American Education.* Alexandria, VA: Association for Supervision and Curriculum Development.

Darling-Hammond, L., and McLaughlin, M. W. (1995). "Policies that support professional development in an era of reform." *Phi Delta Kappan, 76*(8), 597–604.

Dewey, J. (1929). *The Sources of a Science of Education.* New York: Liveright.

Emmer, E. T. (1982). *Management Strategies in the Elementary School Classroom* (Tech. Rep. 6052). Austin, TX: University of Texas, Research and Development Center for Teacher Education.

Expanding Opportunities for Success: Ohio's Fourth Annual Progress Report on Education (1994). Columbus, OH: Office of the Governor.

Gardner, H. (1983). *Frames of Mind: The Theory of Multiple Intelligences.* New York: Basic Books.

Goldberg, M., and Harvey, J. (1983). "A Nation at Risk: The report of the National Commission on Excellence in Education." *Phi Delta Kappan, 65*(1), 14–18.

Good, T., and Brophy, J. (2000). *Looking in Classrooms* (8th ed.). New York: Addison Wesley Longman.

Goodlad, J. (1983). "A study of schooling: Some findings and hypotheses." *Phi Delta Kappan, 64*(7), 465–470.

Hmelo-Silver, C., Nagarajan, A., and Day, R. (2002). " 'It's harder than we thought it would be': A comparative case study of expert–novice experimentation strategies." *Science Education, 86*(2), 219–243.

Hunter, M. (1979). "Teaching is decision making." *Educational Leadership, 37*(1), 62–64, 67.

Hunter, M. (1984). "Knowing, teaching, and supervising." In P. Hosford (Ed.), *Using What We Know About Teaching.* Alexandria, VA: Association for Supervision and Curriculum Development.

Jackson, P. (1968). *Life in Classrooms.* New York: Holt, Rinehart & Winston.

Joyce, B., Weil, M., with Calhoun, E. (2000). *Models of Teaching* (6th ed.). Boston: Allyn & Bacon.

Kirkwood, T. F. (2002). "Teaching about Japan: Global perspectives in teacher decision making, context, and practice." *Theory and Research in Social Education, 30*(1), 88–115.

Klimczak, A. K., Balli, S. J., and Wedman, J. F. (1995). "Teacher decision making regarding content structure: A study of novice and experienced teachers." *Journal of Instructional Psychology, 22*(4), 330–340.

Mahood, W., Biemer, L., and Lowe, W. T. (1991). *Teaching Social Studies in Middle and Senior High Schools: Decisions! Decisions!* New York: Merrill.

McCutcheon, G. (1995). *Developing the Curriculum: Solo and Group Deliberation.* White Plains, NY: Longman.

Mohlman Sparks-Langer, G., and Colton, A. (1991). "Synthesis of research on teachers' reflective thinking." *Educational Leadership, 48*(6), 37–44.

Nagel, N., and Driscoll, A. (1992). "Dilemmas caused by discrepancies between what they learn and what they see: Thinking and decision-making of preservice teachers." Paper presented at the annual meeting of the American Educational Research Association, San Francisco.

National Commission on Excellence in Education (1983). *A Nation at Risk.* Washington, DC: U.S. Department of Education.

Nickell, P. (Ed.) (1999). "Authentic assessment in social studies." *Social Education, 63*(6), 326–381.

Parker, W. C., and Gehrke, N. J. (1986). "Learning activities and teachers' decision making: Some grounded hypotheses." *American Educational Research Journal, 23,* 227–242.

Rosenshine, B. (1983). "Teaching functions in instructional programs." *Elementary School Journal, 83*(4), 335–351.

Sarason, S. (1990). *The Predictable Failure of Educational Reform.* San Francisco: Jossey-Bass.

Shavelson, R. J. (1973). "What is the basic teaching skill?" *Journal of Teacher Education, 24,* 144–151.

Shavelson, R. J. (1983). "Review of research on teachers' pedagogical judgments, plans, and decisions." *Elementary School Journal, 83*(4), 392–413.

Silberman, C. E. (1970). *Crisis in the Classroom.* New York: Random House.

Slavin, R. (1990). *Cooperative Learning: Theory, Research, and Practice.* Upper Saddle River, NJ: Prenctice Hall.

Westerman, D. (1991). "Expert and novice teacher decision making." *Journal of Teacher Education, 42*(4), 292–305.

Zemelman, S., Daniels, H., and Hyde, A. (1998). *Best Practice: New Standards for Teaching and Learning in America's Schools* (2nd ed.). Portsmouth, NH: Heinemann.

2

Building a Climate for Learning

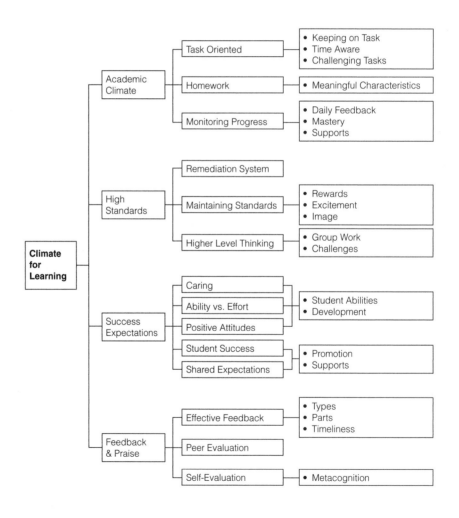

■ OVERVIEW

You are about to meet Tom Baldino, a master teacher who knows that teaching is more than lesson plans and tests. He will demonstrate his approach to building an effective classroom climate that encourages student learning.

Building a supportive learning environment to increase student success continues to be an important goal for all teachers. Teachers exercise minimal control over many environmental factors. However, beginning teachers can develop an understanding of how the learning environment they are creating contributes to the success of students or negatively impacts certain types of students. Beginning teachers can learn to develop practices that are supportive of each learner. These practices must be compatible with teachers' knowledge of their students and of themselves as teachers, knowledge of the curriculum, and understanding of the influence of the context in which they are working. Considering all these factors, effective teachers can monitor their own behaviors to establish classroom conditions that encourage each learner.

Many studies have examined effective teaching through the process–product (input–output) research of the 1970s and 1980s. Schools and teachers that were especially successful in promoting student achievement have been studied, and investigations have been made to identify the factors leading to that success. Although we recognize today that the teaching behavior of successful teachers is only one dimension of the complex spectrum that influences student learning, we still need to consider certain elements of effective teaching that have been repeatedly identified through classroom research and practice over the years as having considerable impact on learning.

This chapter will focus on some of the characteristics of classrooms and teacher behaviors that build a positive climate for learning—an academic climate, promotion of high standards, expectation for success, and provision of feedback and praise that encourages the development of metacognitive skills.

The key to instructional effectiveness is, as ever, a wise and informed teacher–decision maker who considers the school context (setting), student needs, and curricular goals. The complexity of the instructional process is such that no teacher can plug in certain practices and achieve guaranteed success; rather, this chapter emphasizes the importance of understanding the interaction between teacher and students and the impact that the teacher's behavior and decisions about instruction have on student success within the sphere of influence of the classroom and the school.

A climate for learning is the sum of all the students' perceptions and predispositions to their association with schools. Climate refers to the affective aspects of the classroom—such as feelings generated by and about the teachers, the students, the subject matter, and the school—that contribute positively or negatively to the learning environment. Teachers exercise some control over environmental factors. Beginning teachers need to pay attention to factors that affect classroom climate and to notice these factors' impact on students.

SCENARIO

Tom Baldino was meeting his math class for the fourth time in the first week of school. It was a diverse group, with a mix of white students (mainly males), a number of African Americans, several Latinos, and two Native Americans. He knew that a cooperative-learning approach would be important to help this group become cohesive. He had his work cut out for him in addressing their math needs as well. The diagnostic tests he administered during the first class sessions revealed that his students were not up to grade level in their math skills. Basic skills seemed to be in place, but analytical-reasoning skills registered low, as did problem-solving skills. Most of the class had obtained a sixth-grade achievement level, putting them two years behind in math proficiency.

Mr. Baldino smiled at the students as they entered the room. He stood in front of the desks, seating chart in hand, trying to match names with faces. The halls emptied and became quiet as students found their seats.

Chatter subsided because he was standing in front of the class looking at the students. He had explained on the first day that students could talk until he stood in front of the class, ready to start the lesson. Though still unfamiliar with him and with some of the other students, the class was following his rules. He had shared only three rules with them, and he intended to enforce them.

"I've been putting you through your paces the last few days so that I could get an idea of your math skills and your knowledge," he said. The class let out a subdued groan and waited expectantly. "Now it's time to get started and to use that ability you show to do well in math. How many of you want to do better in math this year?" About half of the class slowly raised their hands. "Well, you've come to the right place. All of you. Baldino-the-Wizard is going to start working

his wonders on you—even on those of you who didn't raise your hands. Right here in this room, before your very eyes, and with considerable help from you, you are all going to become good math students. It won't happen overnight, but with some help from both you and the magic hat, it will happen."

Students giggled as Mr. Baldino reached under his desk and pulled out a magician's wand and a tall, black silk hat. Occasionally, he had fun hamming it up for the classes and being an amateur magician helped. All eyes were on him as he stood in front of them, waving his hand over the hat as if he were going to pull out a rabbit. He couldn't help doing a few simple, sleight-of-hand tricks with chalk and pencils, such as pulling a pencil out of the ear of a student sitting in the front row. Everyone laughed and seemed to relax as math class took a turn toward the unexpected.

"Now that I've got your attention, let's see what mysteries the hat holds that are going to turn you into good math students. First, let me check again to make sure I know which students are going to use this magic this year." He peered carefully at the class, trying to contact every eye. "Let's see again those hands of people who want to become good math students this year." This time more hands went up. Only about five remained down—those of five boys in the back. He made a mental note of the boys' reluctance to be involved and chose one of them to come forward to be an assistant. The student reluctantly agreed and ambled to the front.

"Okay, now that I have some assistance, let's check the magic hat for ways to make our math powers stronger." He had the assistant hold the hat and tap it with the wand as he pulled out a rubber chicken. The class laughed politely.

Baldino admitted to himself the act had gone over much better for the seventh grade, but he was determined to start them on a higher note. After next instructing the aide to tap the hat twice, Mr. Baldino pulled out a slip of paper that, he explained, contained a magic, coded message. He went to the board, scribbled down some mathematical symbols, and then wrote on the board, "Math Magic. You become a math whiz by doing the following." He did more hamming by chanting mysteriously and waving his arms, and then he plunged into the hat for another magic message. This one read: "Homework papers turned in every day Monday through Thursday. On Mondays and Tuesdays, students will be responsible to determine their own homework assignments. Homework ideas will be available in the Math Wizard Mystery Book on the teacher's desk. Those who complete the week's assignments receive a magic award of no homework on Fridays." The proclamation was received with some groans and some cheers.

With a flourish, Mr. Baldino pulled out another slip. "All tests will be graded pass or take over. No numerical grade will be given. Students will continue to work on difficult material until able to pass a test."

The list went on to include the following, which were written on the board:

"All students will bring magic tools to class: books, pencils and papers, calculators, and thinking caps."

"Students will develop a goal plan for themselves to chart their progress over the next three months."

"Students will be expected to work in small groups of two or three during weekly practice times."

"Students will be responsible for bringing in once a week for the next month real-life problems that require math problem solving."

When he was finished, the students looked subdued, but they were all watching him. He described the magic fun corner of the room that would be filled with math games and math puzzles to be used for relaxation time after work was completed or if a special award was given. (He hoped to add a computer to the room the next year. It would be excellent for practice exercises and individual instruction.)

He ended with a pep talk on class attitude, saying that for the magic to work, everyone had to keep believing that they could handle the material. The tests showed they had the ability; now they had to prove it to themselves and to everyone else by following the magic plan.

Mr. Baldino thought through his additional plans. He expected to give a feedback quiz once a week and an exam as students finished units of work. The units would be focused on the topics in the NCTM curriculum (National Council of Teachers of Mathematics). Units would be built around problem solving and inquiry projects that would be interdisciplinary in nature. He would hold periodic review lessons and include items from past units in his tests. He would continually convey to the class and to each individual student his belief in everyone's ability to become a math wizard. He planned to have all students develop math portfolios of their work so that their success profiles could be easily seen. This visible feedback about progress was to be an important part of the magic to make students feel successful. He explained aloud that his magic—and the students' magic—would work together to achieve success.

After emptying the hat, he asked the class if they knew of any other magic formulas to promote success. One boy from the unreceptive group suggested that the teacher teach them how to pull money from people's ears. The class nodded approval. Mr. Baldino located a quarter in his pocket and then seemingly pulled it from the ear of the girl in the front seat while he talked about the introduction to the lesson.

A teacher's decisions about behavior and academic standards contribute to classroom climate and influence students' attitudes toward learning.

"To solve a problem or to create magic, we must use good thinking. How would you think about solving the problem of how high the ceiling would have to be in a room that contains a stack of 1 million quarters?" The class started to buzz as students got out paper and quarters and began to discuss the problem with each other.

TOPIC 1: ESTABLISHING AN ACADEMIC CLIMATE

■ RESEARCH AND THEORETICAL BASE

When examining the research on climates that encourage student learning, several factors surface from the effective-schools research (Lezotte, 1984.) One of the factors that has implications for decision making about curriculum and in-struction encourages the teacher to focus class activities on the completion of meaningful academic objectives. The teacher presents the learning objectives to the class and helps students reach those objectives to the best of their ability. The issue is not completion of material but of holding students accountable, to demonstrate understanding of the key concepts so that they can use the knowledge in mean-ingful ways. Students are not motivated to learn when they are required to mem-orize material that they can't apply.

In a research summary of teacher effects on student achievement in urban schools, Brophy (1982) listed emphasis on cognitive objectives within a warm, supportive climate as a key teacher behavior. In another study, Rosenshine (1979) cited a major focus on challenging academic goals as a characteristic of teachers in effective classrooms. He indicated that students learn best in classrooms in which there is both academic emphasis and teacher-directed instruction. The direct-teaching model (teacher interacting with total class) that he observed being employed in effective schools included two practices related to emphasis on aca-demics: (1) teachers placed a clear focus on academic goals, and (2) teachers made an effort to promote extensive content coverage and high levels of student in-volvement. Today's teachers are advised through findings of recent research and in the standards work of national groups such as the NCTM to reduce content coverage and focus on key concepts in more depth. Less and in-depth is the adage. Deep understanding is the goal (Brooks and Brooks, 1993).

Another factor that contributes to the establishment of an academic climate is the amount of time that the student is involved with the content. The teacher must consider three aspects of the involvement behavior: (1) how much time is pro-vided by the teacher (allocated time), (2) to what degree students are engaged dur-ing the time provided (engagement rate or time-on-task), and (3) how successfully students are involved (academic learning time and processing time, that high-quality time in which students devote themselves to processing meaning through a question period or discussion, or through doing meaningful tasks) (Fisher et al., 1978; Jensen, 1998).

The importance of on-task time is supported consistently in the 1970s teacher behavior research. In their review of research on teacher behavior and student achievement, Good and Brophy (2000) cited studies showing that academic learn-ing was influenced by the amount of time students spent engaged in appropriate academic tasks. Studies comparing the amount of time low-achieving students and high-achieving students spend actively working with content have revealed that students with more involvement time also have a higher achievement level (Good and Beckerman, 1978; Perkins, 1965). Presently, researchers have turned to other issues; however, time allocation issues remain a pressing agenda given de-clining national test scores in eight key subject areas when compared internation-ally (Good and Brophy, 1996).

In the past few years, educators have begun to employ learning strategies that are compatible with principles about learning and the brain. These principles add another dimension to consider in the use of time in the classroom. Jensen in *Teach-ing with the Brain in Mind* (1998) reminds us that the brain has difficulty maintain-ing a high level of attention beyond 10 or 15 minutes. The teacher can keep students involved by changing stimuli, such as using a variety of teaching techniques, but the brain needs time to process what it is learning. After a presentation of new content, students will need processing time to internalize meaning. Processing time can be done in small-group discussions on the new learning, by writing in journals about the learning, in question time with the teacher, or by independent practice. The amount of this personal processing time depends on the difficulty of the material and the background of the student. Jensen warns that "you can either have your learners' attention or they can be making meaning, but never both at the same time" (1998, p. 46). The key point here is that teachers must allow for and encourage personal processing time after new learning has been introduced.

■ APPLICATION TO PRACTICE

The following practices are recommended to the teacher for generating an academic climate in the classroom.

1. Be task oriented and time aware.
2. Keep students on-task and involved with challenging tasks.
3. Give limited and purposeful homework.
4. Monitor progress for student success.

Be Task Oriented and Time Aware

A task-oriented teacher is aware of the use of time spent on a lesson, the purpose of the lesson, and the students' need to process the lesson's new information. A major effort is made to keep students productively involved throughout the lesson in a variety of ways. The teacher starts class promptly by indicating to the class what needs to be accomplished during a specific time period and the purpose for the day's learning activities. This establishing-set technique is advocated by both Hunter (1994) and Rosenshine (1979). Rosenshine included it as part of the first function—structuring the lesson—in his direct-teaching strategy (see Chapter 8). By way of this introduction, the students know what is expected of them and that the teacher will make sure the tasks are accomplished. The instruction portion of the lesson will center on the planned objective(s) and the learning activities (including practice time) that will be used to accomplish the objective. The teacher monitors the students' progress in accomplishing the lesson's objective through feedback; circulating around the room to check on their progress; collecting, checking, and recording their completed assignments; or informal assessments.

Teachers need to become aware of their use of time during the instructional day. Much instructional time is wasted in the classroom by such practices as allocating 20 to 30 minutes in class for students to work on homework, excessive viewing of films, class announcements, attendance routines, and starting class (Lowe and Gervais, 1988). McGreal (1994) reported recent studies showing that the time between the bell ringing in high schools and instruction beginning averaged about 9 minutes out of the 50-minute period.

The National Education Commission on Time and Learning (1994) conducted a 24-month investigation and concluded that the academic-learning unit had been stolen to make room for a host of nonacademic activities. The commission recommended that the academic day needed to provide at least 5.5 hours of core academic instructional time. The expectation was that within those hours teachers should engage students in activities that increase their quality academic learning time.

These time studies make it clear that teachers need to know how time is being used in their classrooms. Through conscious clock watching for several days or by using a student observer, a fellow teacher, or the principal, teachers will be able to gather information that informs them about their use of time. How much time is spent on the opening of class? When do students stop working? Is the time spent on a task in proportion to the importance of the task? How much time do the students spend on teacher materials in contrast to working with the teacher or their peers? How much individual attention does a student receive each week from the teacher? How much time during each class period does the teacher spend interacting with the class? How much time does the class actually spend actively involved with the lesson or doing reflection on the lesson?

Trying to find the answers to these questions through the analysis of the instructional pattern of one's own teaching helps develop a sense of time awareness for the teacher. Teacher and classroom observers can determine the amount of students' engagement time by using uncomplicated observational instruments. Percentages can be determined for students' time-on-task during the observation period. Student-engagement time—another term used to describe student on-task time—takes into consideration both time and "engaged time," which is the amount of time the students actually spend working on content during that period. Other methods that can be used to gather time-related information could include the use of Flanders interaction analysis for quantitative time analysis of classroom interaction, time-on-task instruments, teacher notation of time at beginning and end of instruction segments, student notation of time, or the teacher noting in the plan book the amount of time for each phase of instruction or time spent with certain students for several class periods. Observing academic learning time (high-quality involvement) is difficult unless the observer moves around the room and examines the students' output.

The authors have observed that beginning teachers may spend too little time developing concepts or explaining processes. A typical approach by a novice teacher is to explain the material once, then move to limited class discussion or practice, and then quickly move to independent practice. The checking for understanding function of direct instruction is done minimally, resulting in the teacher's having to provide much individualized instruction and/or in students' showing poor performance. Allowing time for the teacher to ask questions to see how students understand the material or time to encourage student questions is essential for students' processing and clarifying information.

An important aspect for teachers to consider when making decisions about use of time to promote a climate for learning is that of the differences in student learning rates. Teachers must make careful instructional decisions about the use of time, informed by their knowledge of students' learning rates and styles, the background of their students' knowledge of the content, and the complexity of the material. Berliner and Biddle (1995) pointed out the significance of the students' "opportunity to learn" factor, calling it the single most important predictor of student achievement. Therefore, teachers must be aware of their use of time in providing students their opportunity to learn.

Keep Students On-Task and Involved with Challenging Tasks

Moreover, to establish a climate for learning and to keep students motivated and on-task, the teacher must be aware of the class's engagement time and of each student's academic learning time. Academic learning time, as defined from the research done in the 1970s (Berliner, 1979), is that high-quality time when the student is involved with the content and is succeeding. The teacher may have to use a variety of methods to help certain students increase their on-task time, such as calling on students by name, busying students with an activity, encouraging group work, having students present their learning to each other, focusing on students by moving around the room and checking their papers, interacting with students about the content rather than other distracting topics, and spending little time on organizational and management tasks such as setting up equipment or handing out materials. Today, with the increased emphasis on students working in groups, the teacher needs to be monitoring group progress by listening carefully to groups' discussions and by asking questions about students' understanding of their work as well as requiring informal assessment techniques such as student logs. Use of discipline measures should be limited and employed only to maintain an orderly environment for learning (see Chapter 3). For example, we sense that Mr. Baldino was task oriented even while maintaining a sense of humor.

Jensen (1998) lists factors that influence attention for learning. He emphasizes (1) giving students choices on content, amount of time on work, work partners, projects, arrangement of environment, process, or resources; (2) making material relevant—personal, related to family, their town or city, or adolescent life stage; and (3) making it engaging through such approaches as using emotions or physical activities (p. 48).

It is also essential to provide students with meaningful activities that offer academic challenges. A teacher plans activities that involve students with application, analysis, and synthesis experiences as well as with practice with lower-level knowledge and comprehension tasks. Learning activities should be examined to see if they encourage students to use higher-level thinking skills and problem-solving techniques. Challenging unit projects can be developed such as involving students in working on community issues—for example, conducting a community survey to focus the town's attention on the recreational needs of youths and senior citizens. Students may do research on school or community environmental problems. Other activities could include such tasks as setting up a computer home page on which to display a class newsletter highlighting projects such as the writing and producing of creative publications or videotapes. The students need to have choice and input into formulating such activities.

How students are reacting to classroom activities is important for teachers to sense. Individual students will react differently depending on their view of the teacher's perception of them as learners and depending on their own interest in the curriculum and the tasks. Therefore, the teacher needs to be listening, observing, and questioning students to determine students' perceptions that may influence their responsiveness to learning.

Give Limited and Purposeful Homework

The third practice is assigning homework. Homework received national attention when reports on schools in the early 1980s revealed that little homework was being assigned in U.S. schools and that even less was being completed. The importance of homework was documented in a U.S. Department of Education study (1985) entitled *What Works,* which cited research showing the beneficial effects of homework on learning. In response, some school districts around the country passed mandatory homework laws that pressured teachers to assign homework four or five times a week; for example, in 1986 the Chicago Board of Education adopted a policy across all grade levels that homework was to be assigned every night, from 15 minutes of work for kindergarten to 2½ hours of work for high school students (Snider, 1986).

Such actions necessitate caution. Assigning homework will not in itself guarantee academic achievement. Homework activities must be carefully selected by the teacher to accomplish a specific purpose and should be limited in quantity and tied to course objectives and student outcomes. Homework is best suited for the following purposes: to provide students with more practice, if needed, after a group practice session in class; to provide students more time to develop a paper or project over a period of several days; and to provide students time to become familiar with concepts or themes presented in reading material prior to discussion in class. Routine homework that has no purpose other than to keep students involved with 20 math problems or 5 pages of history every night will not increase achievement or encourage a climate for learning. This kind of busy work fosters negative attitudes toward homework.

When purposeful homework is assigned, the teacher makes decisions regarding the application of the assignment to the daily lesson and the weight of its evaluation. The teacher needs to go over the work in class to provide immediate feedback to students. Homework should be collected and checked to determine whether it is completed correctly. A teacher's cursory glance over a paper is enough to see if the homework is finished and understood or to check on any problems that a student may have had with the assignment. A check mark in the grade book can indicate that the assignment has been accomplished. Those students who have not turned in homework should be notified they are being held responsible for it. A student's handling of homework assignments should be an appropriately weighted part of the grade-period mark.

A caution to consider on homework is that disadvantaged students—those who are homeless or have no place to study at home or do not have access to a computer with which to work—may be treated inequitably through homework assignments. Don't give homework if students won't be able to complete it.

Monitor Progress for Student Success

An essential element of the academic climate is the nurturing of students' potential and monitoring their progress. The teacher nurtures students, with the intent to encourage the students to keep trying, by making them aware of their individual progress and potential. A model of frequent quizzes and fewer large exams gives more information to the students and their teacher about the students' learning. Encouraging students to keep their own records of their progress builds self-monitoring and student goal setting. The teacher and students can create rubrics for evaluation purposes prior to the start of a unit or project. Then students can more easily self-evaluate using the rubric criteria. Planning conference times with students during the school year or at the end of class several days a month are important ways to support student feelings of success in the class. Results from pre- and posttesting can be shared, along with term grades and samples of student work collected in student portfolios. The emphasis should be placed on the continuous progress of the student toward reaching the learning goals set by the teacher and/or the student.

APPLICATION for DIVERSE CLASSROOMS

In considering the monitoring of time in the classroom, Salend (1998) cautions teachers to realize that different cultural groups have different concepts of time. Some cultures may view student relationships as more important than performance on timed assignments; for example, ". . . helping a friend with a problem may be given priority over completing an assignment by a certain deadline" (p. 391). Also, students with different concepts of time may have difficulty with timed tests.

TOPIC 2: PROMOTING HIGH STANDARDS

■ RESEARCH AND THEORETICAL BASE

The purpose of this section is to emphasize the importance of individual accountability and high standards but not to sacrifice social responsibility and positive interdependence for academic excellence. The message of Mr. Baldino was not one of competition but rather of individual progress and group interaction for learning. Mr. Baldino addressed high standards in his classroom when he announced to the students that all tests had to be passed or taken over until passed. His message was that there would be no failures in the classroom. The goal was understanding and individual progress, not high test scores. If students failed, they would be retaught via programmed materials or through controlled group practice and, later, independent practice (Hunter, 1994). He also stressed the importance of students' goal plans, coming prepared to class with books and paper, and seeking life applications of mathematics. He believed that informing the class of the standards they had to meet was essential.

Mr. Baldino knew that in many groups, including Native American cultures, the achievement of the individual was of less value than the social good of the group. He would emphasize group work frequently and the progress of the whole class as well as of individuals so as not to place Native American students in conflict with the mores of their culture (Swisher, 1990).

The issue of establishing higher standards became a nationwide charge in 1983 following the publication of the findings of numerous national reports on the status of public education. The National Commission on Excellence in Education report *A Nation at Risk* (1983) called for the upgrading of standards by increasing basic academic requirements for graduation. The commission recommended that more rigorous and measurable standards and higher expectations for academic performance and student conduct be adopted by schools and colleges.

Teachers need to establish performance standards that challenge but do not discourage students. Levin and Long (1981) pointed out that most researchers agree a 100 percent mastery standard is neither realistic nor necessary in the classroom. A 70 percent to 80 percent performance level is acceptable if that score indicates that a student has achieved the essential understanding and is prepared to move ahead in the course. The teacher should recycle through the content students who do not meet the acceptable understanding level. Others who have met the acceptable level should move forward.

To summarize the numerous research studies, one can say that setting reasonable standards for performance in the classroom includes maintaining an acceptable level of performance on everything from conduct to homework and tests. The goal of these standards is to create a climate in the classroom that conveys the following message: The business in the classroom is to learn; students can be and are expected to be successful.

Hints for the Beginning Teacher

During your first year of teaching, you will likely establish a formal or informal mentoring relationship with one or more veteran teachers in your building. At least once a month, schedule time to observe these peers teaching in their classrooms. Ask yourself what they do that promotes a positive learning climate.

■ APPLICATION TO PRACTICE

The following practices can convey to students that high standards are maintained in a classroom:

1. Setting an academic performance level that all students must meet.
2. Establishing an organizational system for remediation.

3. Maintaining a standard of performance.

4. Emphasizing higher-level thinking as well as memory-level and comprehension-level cognitive functioning.

5. Encouraging group work, peer tutoring, and group development of performance criteria.

Setting a Mandatory Performance Level

The teacher should set a performance level for each key objective to indicate at what point each objective has been satisfactorily met; for example, a teacher must decide that an objective has been mastered if students are able to pass a test on the information at the 70 percent level and explain key concepts, are able to answer 8 out of 10 problems correctly and explain the process they used, or can write a paragraph with only two errors in sentence construction, spelling, and punctuation. Below-level students would continue to do remediation work and then be retested on an objective until they met the achievement standard.

Deciding the level at which to set performance standards is difficult for teachers, especially for beginning teachers who cannot rely on past experiences. Research does not reveal appropriate performance levels for optimum learning. Each teacher must determine the level appropriate to challenge—but not frustrate—the class or individuals. Also, the teacher may decide to set individual performance levels. These performance levels may be raised or lowered during the year to improve the learning climate and adjust to the needs of students.

Establishing an Organizational System for Remediation

If a teacher defines a performance level for major objectives as recommended in this chapter, an organizational system for remediation will also need to be established. This means that the teacher builds a reserve of additional explanatory materials, practice activities, and tests on key objectives. If some students are unsuccessful in reaching the accepted level of performance, they continue to study and practice until they reach the level or until the teacher decides to move them on to the next phase. (This feature was emphasized in Tom Baldino's approach in the scenario.) A successful remediation program cannot be implemented until the teacher has a supply of materials from reference textbooks, sample texts, and, in those cases when skills and content have not changed, old textbooks from which to draw material and additional practice for the learner.

Using peer tutors (see Chapter 8) and remediation groups is an important part of the remediation system, as well. If this remedial system is in place, the teacher has more time to reinstruct students who have not reached the satisfactory performance level.

The remediation or recycling stage will be most effective if it involves the teacher's controlled practice with a small group or an individual. The teacher conducts the controlled practice to reexplain, model, and illustrate the material. Then the students proceed to small-group practice or independent practice. When this step has been completed successfully, retesting occurs. During those times when the teacher is working with an individual or a small group that needs remediation, the rest of the class can be involved in group work or independent practice to review the objective or to achieve a new objective.

Maintaining a Standard of Performance

Teachers who maintain an academic climate use certain pertinent practices in their instructional and management approaches. Homework is collected and checked so that students know that homework is a required performance standard and that they will receive feedback on it. Not every homework paper must receive a grade. Other practices used by teachers to convey academic standards include assuring that work missed because of absences is made up; that most class time is spent on academic tasks; and that objectives for learning tasks are shared with students and, at times, developed by students. Rewards are handled carefully. Marginal or wrong answers are not rewarded or criticized; rather, the student learns to analyze incorrect answers to see where the problem occurred and why it occurred. The emphasis is on understanding more than correctness. Excellent work and effort are rewarded.

Teacher behavior that reflects high standards may include such practices as lessons prepared in advance, correct use of grammar, correct spelling, legible writing on both the board and papers, prompt return of student work, and good teacher attendance. A teacher's professional commitment to using class time to concentrate on academic tasks and conducting class in a supportive but businesslike manner impresses students. A professional teacher will also encourage students to provide feedback on how the class is functioning for them. In addition, teachers convey their interest in students' progress by supplying frequent feedback through quizzes, tests, comments on assignments, and daily comprehension checks.

Emphasizing Higher-Level Thinking

Encouraging thinking at the higher levels of application, analysis, synthesis, and evaluation as identified in Bloom's *A Taxonomy of Educational Objectives* (1956) is a practice essential to promoting achievement and high academic standards. In their planning and questioning, teachers need to remember that recalling information is a necessary but not sufficient condition for student success. In addition to the establishment of basic knowledge, opportunities for using information through solving problems, generating hypotheses, analyzing alternatives, and creating imaginative solutions should be available. Bloom's taxonomy can be helpful to teachers when developing objectives and learning activities on higher levels of the cognitive domain.

The following list of higher-level thinking skills identified in Donna Walker Tileston's book *10 Best Teaching Practices* (2000, pp. 39–40) can help teachers review which thinking skills they are helping students to develop:

I. Critical Thinking Skills—to analyze, use objective criteria to evaluate data

   A. Inductive Thinking Skills
      seeing cause and effect   identifying relevance
      solving open-ended problems   forming relationships
      making inferences   doing problem solving

   B. Deductive Thinking Skills
      using logic   doing syllogisms
      understanding contradictions   solving spatial problems

   C. Evaluative Thinking Skills
      identifying fact and opinion   predicting consequences
      identifying credibility of   doing sequencing
        a source   using decision-making skills
      identifying central issues   recognizing propaganda
        and problems   noting similarities and differences
      recognizing underlying   evaluating arguments
        assumptions
      detecting bias, stereotypes,
        clichés
      evaluating hypotheses
      classifying data

II. Creative Thinking—ability to produce new and original ideas
      recognizing attributes   elaborating, providing much detail
      having fluency—having   doing synthesis (Bloom's *Taxonomy*)
        many ideas
      having flexibility—seeing
        things in different ways
      demonstrating originality

III. Problem Solving—ability to use complex thinking to solve problems
      identifying the problem   developing alternative solutions
      analyzing the problem   applying the best solution
      formulating a hypothesis   monitoring and evaluating solution
      formulating appropriate   drawing conclusions
        questions
      generating ideas

An academic climate with appropriately high standards can be maintained in any classroom. The climate is promoted by a teacher who conducts class in a businesslike manner—namely, someone who establishes goals and objectives, encourages student goal setting as well, and helps students learn to use higher-level thinking skills.

Encouraging Group Development of Performance Criteria and Group Work

With the emphasis on group work and cooperative learning today, students need to see that high standards can be upheld within the small groups as well as with whole-class work. The quality of the activity that students are doing establishes the performance level to be expected of the group. Authentic cooperative-learning activities that encourage students to demonstrate learning outcomes important to them, with evaluation criteria identified by the group, motivate students and encourage self-directed learning (Putnam, 1993); for example, Putnam reported that students who were learning the scientific method decided to conduct experiments that they devised to investigate a question about a subject important to them. One student investigated various kinds of cat food and the container in which she put the food to see how they affected her cats' eating. The class then evaluated each inquiry project to see whether it followed carefully the designated steps of the scientific method. Group criteria for products often are higher than teacher-established criteria. The teacher will need to work with the students to help them become proficient in setting group standards and standards for individual performance within the group.

TOPIC 3: EXPECTATION FOR SUCCESS

■ RESEARCH AND THEORETICAL BASE

In the opening scenario, Mr. Baldino was well aware that by the time many students reach eighth grade, they have poor self-images in mathematics. He knew that to improve their achievement, he needed to promote a successful image for them all. His expectations for students were positive. He had assessed their potential through diagnostic tests and knew they were capable because they had basic mathematical skills even though they had been mediocre achievers in the past. He had formulated plans about the methods he would use to improve their math images.

As was attested by the classic but controversial *Pygmalion in the Classroom* study by Rosenthal and Jacobson (1968), teachers' attitudes toward students do influence student performance. Students in the study who were identified as having a high potential for success achieved at a higher level than would otherwise be predicted. Purkey (1978) related a student's story concerning his inability to sing: "When I was in the third grade, a choral teacher said that I was a good listener (implying a poor singer). Everyone laughed except me. I've never uttered a musical note in public from that day to this" (p. 33). Purkey's book, *Inviting School Success,* also emphasized the importance of sending students verbal and nonverbal supportive messages that encourage them to learn and to succeed.

Research literature is full of studies that substantiate the effect of teacher expectations on student achievement. Good (1981) reviewed 10 years of research on teacher expectations and concluded that teachers behave differently toward different students and affect student achievement accordingly. Over time, student achievement and behavior will conform more and more closely to the teacher's expectations. One finding from a Brophy and Good study (1970) revealed that students for whom teachers held high expectations gave more correct answers in reading groups and achieved higher average scores on a year-end standard test than did students for whom the teacher held low expectations. Again, this study conducted in an elementary classroom has clear implications for secondary classrooms as well.

Good and Brophy (2000) pointed out that teacher expectations affect teacher perceptions and interpretations. Teachers may observe behaviors that they expect to see from certain students and screen out other behaviors that could cause teachers to question their perceptions. Teachers also may interpret what they see in light of their expectations to justify their view of certain students rather than being open to information that could cause them to change their interpretation.

The self-fulfilling-prophecy studies (Rosenthal, Baratz, and Hall, 1974; Rosenthal and Jacobson, 1968) illustrate the need for teachers to be aware of the effect their perceptions and interpretations may have on student behavior. Students may behave in a particular way because the teacher perceives them behaving in that manner. Thus, students who are considered slow by their teacher might consider themselves poor students regardless of their ability, which may indeed be comparable to that of other classmates.

The effective-schools research conducted by Edmonds (1979), Brookover and Lezotte (1977), and others discovered that raising expectations for success among both teachers and students improved the achievement level of that school. An apparent cause of poor achievement in urban schools is directly related to the low academic expectations teachers tend to hold for pupils in those schools.

An experience illustrating the effect of teacher attitudes on a class was recounted to one of the authors by a friend who was a secondary English teacher. She explained that her third-period class had been giving her headaches because they were not doing their work, talked throughout the class period, and conveyed to her that they did not like English or her. At her wits' end in trying to cope with the situation, she decided to try a positive approach. She began to smile a lot at the class, made positive remarks to individuals, dropped her negative approach to classroom management, praised them for their efforts, and explained that she had been frustrated with them because she knew this class had a high potential but was not reaching it. As a result, the class slowly began to turn around, and within a month she was amazed to find that it was one of her favorite classes. Students were achieving considerably better than in the past. She acknowledged that the experience taught her a valuable lesson in building positive expectations. Clearly, what was operating here was that her attitude about the class had led her to treat the class differently. She had been less able to perceive positive behaviors that she had not expected from them—even to the point of distorting what she did see. When she forced herself to perceive them differently, she began to notice the real abilities of the class for the first time and was more able to address the difficulties she had been having with them.

The research of Salonen, Lehtiner, and Olkinuora (1998) cautions us to consider the complexity of cognitive and motivational factors that influence student success. Be aware that teacher expectations do not have similar effects on all students. Students who are motivated by a task are less concerned with teachers' expectations of them. Teachers' expectations of students with nontask orientation can increase students' negative feelings toward the task, their own abilities, or school in general. The researchers suggest that teachers need to understand their students as individuals and the impact teacher interaction has on them. With better understanding through communication with each student, teachers can help students develop coping strategies and more positive attitudes toward themselves as learners.

■ APPLICATION TO PRACTICE

Effective teachers like Mr. Baldino develop a climate for success in the classroom by doing some or all of the following practices:

1. Having a caring attitude toward all students.
2. Developing positive attitudes concerning students' abilities.
3. Developing positive attitudes in students toward their success in the subjects.
4. Helping students to understand that success can be reached through their efforts.
5. Demonstrating that the teacher and the school are supportive of student success.
6. Using scaffolding.
7. Providing all students with opportunities to be successful by adapting learning activities and materials to fit students' ability and interest.
8. Becoming aware of messages being communicated to students, both verbally and nonverbally.
9. Showing interest in all students.
10. Sharing expectations about learning and school by teachers and students talking together.

Developing an Important Disposition—A Caring Attitude

A success-oriented academic climate for learning does not mean a cold, impersonal, factory-like environment. Students deserve caring teachers, not ones who ignore low achievement or bad behavior to help students feel good, but rather teachers caring in the sense of wanting the best for students and considering their needs to help them grow. Mr. Baldino in the scenario demonstrated caring by bringing his enthusiasm for magic and math into the classroom to make learning more pleasurable while holding students to high standards. His plan was to converse with each student and examine his or her work while sharing his belief that each one could be successful with mathematics.

Professionalism and caring are not inherently in conflict. Being professional does refer to a teacher's trying to do the best possible job for the students. Although the emphasis on good teaching today is often equated with students' high academic achievement, achievement is not the only measure of the effective professional. Dispositions—attitudes and values—play a key role in effective teaching. The standards of the National Council for the Accreditation of Teacher Education and the INTASC (Interstate New Teacher Assessment and Support Consortium) Standards that influence teacher education programs throughout the country require that professional dispositions of the teacher candidate be identified and assessed. The caring disposition is essential for the teacher concerned about building a climate for successful learning. Noddings (1986) and others (Schaps, Lewis, and Watson, 1995) noted that caring contributes to students' development and learning by encouraging a greater level of interaction and a desire to learn to emerge. Productivity increases by changing the climate of the classroom to one focusing on the social organization and individual learning.

Noddings (2001) says caring teachers not only listen to students and respect their legitimate interests but also share their wisdom with students. They are attentive to what students are telling about themselves and their learning. Caring implies a continuous drive for the competence to interact adequately with students and their learning needs. The caring teacher is concerned about the student first and the curriculum second.

Stone (2002) describes a caring teacher as one who deals with the whole student. Students have a variety of problems, some of which may be serious. He suggests getting to know the parents of the students through phone calls home or notes sent to invite them into the school beyond the scheduled conference days. In this manner, through talking with the parents, a teacher can understand the students better and build an association with the parents as team partners.

Developing Positive Attitudes Concerning Students' Abilities

Recent articles (Murphy, 1993) and books (Goodlad and Keating, 1994) have called our attention to a prevailing U.S. attitude that innate ability—rather than effort, as believed in nations with high academic achievement such as Japan—determines school success. Our tracking system sorts students and encourages them and their teachers to consider students as able or "terminally" unable. Schools' failure to provide or encourage different types of intelligence and learning styles often result in prejudicial practices. In junior and senior high schools, the separation of students by curriculum into vocational and academic tracks often results in the vocational group coming from poor and racial minority groups (Goodlad and Keating, 1994). Thus students may decide not to work hard because they and their teachers view their ability to learn as limited rather than capable with ability to make up for the deficits in their experiences and background. The result too often is that students are allowed to waste their time just getting by, to remain unchallenged, and to enter the job market unprepared for meaningful work other than in low-paying service jobs.

Teachers need to have positive attitudes concerning students' abilities. Teachers need to believe in their students regardless of their ability levels, backgrounds, or previous records because students look to them for cues about how teachers assess their abilities. A teacher can trap students in poor achievement if little is expected of them because of their ethnic group, academic labeling, or family background. Research reports (Pang and Sablan, 1998; Ogbu, 1974) reveal that teachers' racial attitudes do affect teachers' beliefs about students' abilities. Average achievement was viewed as acceptable for minority and poor children and unacceptable for middle-class and white children. Even more alarming was the finding that a number of white teachers felt they could not teach African American students. Therefore, teachers must try to keep an open mind and encourage positive behavior in each student. Conveying confidence in students' ability was perhaps the most impressive aspect of Mr. Baldino's class. His so-called magic was his way of convincing students of their eventual success—the self-fulfilling prophecy.

Helping Students Develop Positive Attitudes

Helping students to feel good about themselves, as well as to believe in their ability to be successful in a school subject, is important. The state of low math achievement in the country, as reflected in results of national testing, may be directly linked to the nation's poor self-concept concerning the ability to do well in the subject. Consider how frequently one hears intelligent, successful people admitting in conversations or on late-night talk shows that they were terrible in math. Teachers must help students develop a positive attitude by convincing them of their potential for success through supportive comments, reinforcement, and individual help as needed. Such supportive communications with students may sound like the following:

Your questions during class today were important ones. You asked about key points that were causing others trouble, too. You had more than 70 percent of your homework correct yesterday. Keep up the good work. Remember: I'll be available to answer your questions if you become confused again.

Another approach to helping students develop positive attitudes is to give them opportunities to share their knowledge gained through their experiences and their personal beliefs.

APPLICATION for DIVERSE CLASSROOMS

To help African American and Latino youths to achieve, the teacher must help them believe they can become good students (as Mr. Baldino did in the scenario). Because many of these students suffer from low esteem, it is important to tell them every day that they can do well. Regardless of the subject area, have them research a prominent African American or Latino personality and discuss his or her accomplishments with the class. "Whether a teacher is teaching math, history, or science, approximately 10 to 15 minutes each period must be set aside to inspire, encourage, and motivate inner-city students" (Stone, 2002, p. 7).

Relationship of Success to Feelings of Self-Empowerment

Building expectations for student success means encouraging students to understand that success can be reached through their own efforts. Helping students realize that they control their fortunes in school by the amount of time and effort they are willing to put into their work is an important task. This control principle can be impressed on students by having them keep track of the time they spend on a unit or project, as well as by encouraging them to evaluate their work using criteria developed by the teacher or the class. Making students aware of their progress through the use of charts and graphs helps them observe that they have control over their achievement; they realize that the grades they receive are not given by the teacher but rather result from their own efforts.

The literature reports programs such as the one at Centennial High School in Fort Collins, Colorado (Lamperes, 1994), an alternative school for at-risk students that has turned around a low attendance rate and high dropout rate. The school now boasts that 42 percent of the students have reached the honor roll (with a grade point average of 3.2 or higher) through the teaching of necessary prosocial skills. Teachers create a culture of interaction that stresses cooperation, positive relationship, and noncoercion, and they empower students to determine their own success. The program focuses on positive attending skills, problem solving of critical issues, and promoting the notion that every student can learn. All students are provided with personal knowledge of their learning strengths as well as the teaching styles of their instructors. They are taught how to assess what they need to do to learn and achieve, as well as how to solve their own problems through conflict resolution skills. The success of the school as evidenced by their attendance records and the low number of police visits is attributable to, among several factors, the self-empowerment of the students.

Hints for the Beginning Teacher

A key characteristic in the development of students is the students' increasing ability to self-regulate as they increase their sense of control and sense of self-esteem. Give them many opportunities to build self-control through choices—student-set time limits, student-developed rubrics for assessment, student-set task goals, and so forth.

Support for Student Success

A student needs to feel that the school as well as the teacher supports students and encourages their success. Such conditions as public telephones for student use, an attractive cafeteria setting in which students have access to hot and cold drinks during study hours, and attractively decorated classrooms are all examples of messages sent to students about the concern of the school for their welfare. Display cases filled with academic and extracurricular awards and athletic trophies are important. Displays of student pictures and work convey positive messages. Guidance counselors with doors open to students, a student and teacher tutoring system within the school, and teachers with hours available to help students are important for establishing a support network. Peer support networks for at-risk students are an effective human resource, as well. Many schools are establishing close relationships with social service agencies in the community to help support students and their families who have problems that affect the students' success.

In the opening scenario, Mr. Baldino let all his students know that during his seventh-hour planning period every day, he was available to tutor anyone needing help. He would also arrange tutoring sessions before or after school on request. This type of teacher behavior conveys to students that teachers are concerned about them and are trying to help them.

Scaffolding

An important instructional support that is referred to frequently in the reading area today but has applications for every content area is *scaffolding*. This is a verbal print and nonprint support structure that the teacher uses to help students learn and that can be withdrawn when students have learned the material. It is metaphorically comparable to instructional "training wheels." Examples of scaffolding techniques include questions that guide students to key points or relevant backgrounds, study guides, verbal cues, summaries of important reading material, flowcharts, concept maps, graphic organizers, and task organizers that help students with various parts of a project. These techniques are to encourage students' deeper thinking, expand their perceptions, and help them problem solve.

When at the completion of the unit or the project, scaffolding may be necessary to encourage reflection and processing. Key questions, according to Caine and Caine (1997), that can be used to scaffold students' understanding and processing are the following (p. 185):

What are you doing?

What is the purpose?

Can you explain it?

What would happen if . . . ?

Do you know why . . . ?

The teacher can follow up on the students' responses with a further question or with a more complex problem to challenge them.

Opportunities for Success

To promote success, the teacher needs to structure success experiences so that all students can feel positive about themselves as learners. Students need opportunities to succeed frequently on learning tasks. Teachers must make sure that students achieve success consistently by encouraging them to meet challenging objectives gradually and to prepare students with tutoring, guidance, and feedback. Each student's success rate should be monitored and used as a basis for decision making about that student; for example, a student who may not be able to write an exam, for whatever reasons, may take the test orally, and a student who has poor reading ability in junior high may use a different textbook or do different assignments with fewer pages involved. These are straightforward, even obvious, examples. Imaginative, concerned teachers will find many ways to individualize tasks. The point is that teachers must be flexible and willing to adapt to individual needs if all students are going to be successful in the classroom. Teachers need to individualize learning tasks whenever necessary so that students are engaged with tasks and materials suitable for their success rate.

Teacher Messages

Teachers need to become aware of the messages they send to students through their verbal and nonverbal behavior. These messages may reinforce the more academically able and ignore or criticize the weaker students (Good, 1981). Examples of such debilitating behaviors come from a review of the literature (Good and Brophy, 2000) and include the following:

1. Good students are seated across the front and down the middle of the room.
2. Teacher eye contact is mainly with higher-achieving students.
3. Teacher calls on higher-achieving students much more frequently than lower-achieving students.
4. Teacher punishes off-task behavior in lower-achieving students and more frequently ignores it in higher-achieving students.
5. Teacher communication with lower-achieving students is mainly negative and critical.
6. Teacher gives little wait time to lower-achieving students to answer questions.
7. Teacher praises higher-achieving students more.
8. Teacher displays work of only the higher-achieving students.
9. Teacher gives higher-achieving students more cues with which to respond to questions.
10. Teacher requires less effort and work from lower-achieving students.

Showing Interest in All Students

By changing the seating pattern to meet students' needs, teachers can convey an interest in students. Those who have difficulty paying attention or seeing the board may sit in the front; talkative students may be mixed with quiet students to encourage better attention. Regardless of the seating pattern, teacher eye contact with students—even those in the back of the room and in the far rows by the windows or doors—needs to include all students so that the teacher can send and receive nonverbal feedback.

Verbal and nonverbal behavior that expresses teacher interest, such as speaking to each student at least once in a period and trying to have some individual communication daily, is important for positive classroom climate. Students with more academic weaknesses or quiet students may sit in class without recognition for a week or more at a time. Part of the communication should be positive feedback given at the appropriate time.

An effective teacher does not have to be a magician, although Tom Baldino used this ploy. However, an effective teacher does need to be able to make purposeful decisions that help establish a climate for success in the classroom. The decisions Mr. Baldino made in approaching his class through one of his hobbies were based on his knowledge that students work harder if the climate in the room is interesting to and supportive of students, and if students know what is expected of them. He understood that in achievement, reinforcement can bring results. He planned to use the puzzles and the math games for reinforcement as well as for teaching interested students magic. He would see that students received frequent feedback so that they would know the results of their efforts and the skills they needed to learn. Many math experiences from life situations would be available for group and individual practice. Through practice and self-checking, students would learn at their individual rates.

Students who fell behind would either become a separate group that Mr. Baldino would teach for 10 or 15 minutes each day or be introduced to new material while still being held responsible for learning the material of the previous unit. Promoting student feelings of responsibility to learn the course material was an important goal set by Mr. Baldino. Holding students accountable for practice exercises or for taking tests that would be self-checked encouraged their feelings of responsibility.

Mr. Baldino decided to use much of his class time for working with individuals and small groups on remediation problems as necessary, as well as on enrichment experiences. The beginning of most classes would consist of large-group instruction in which review and introduction of lesson content would occur. Explanation and demonstration would follow, after which groups would work on mathematical problems to demonstrate their understanding. Individual practice would then follow. An important part of the yearly curriculum would be working on problem-solving and analysis skills. He would give frequent quizzes and unit and review tests so that he could monitor class progress. Much feedback and reinforcement would be used to encourage positive feelings toward the subject and to emphasize the standards students should meet. Students would be expected to keep track of their progress in their math portfolios.

Mr. Baldino looked forward to the effect his plan would have on the class. His success rate had been high before. He knew he could encourage success for everyone again, but he knew that for this class, he would have to learn a few new magic tricks himself.

Sharing Expectations

Teachers and students sharing their expectations concerning learning content, achievement, and social behavior can help form bonds and create a positive learning climate. Ennis (1998, p. 177) lists some key factors that can help teachers connect positively with their students and enhance student learning:

1. Understand students' backgrounds and the constraints and opportunities they provide for learning.

2. Provide numerous opportunities for legitimate academic success early in the school year. Focus initially on students' strengths and use those strengths to build student confidence and scaffold later learning tasks.

3. Explain your grading system with concrete examples that demonstrate how students can enhance their grades. Confront the issue of low or failing grades by explaining the situation that led to the grade and providing an alternative or second chance for students to complete the work, emphasizing important study, writing, or test-taking skills useful for future assignments.

4. Construct sequenced learning tasks that facilitate skills acquisition in your subject area, and be willing to remediate skills both within and outside of your subject to promote student success.

5. Focus on the process of how you teach that includes positive, affirming ways of interacting with students, and insist that they treat each other with the same level of courtesy.

6. Provide frequent opportunities for students to express their goals and aspirations for learning. Assist students to set positive, realistic goals and envision a successful future. Use these clues as you work with students to jointly create expectations that you both can share.

TOPIC 4: PROVIDING FEEDBACK AND PRAISE

■ RESEARCH AND THEORETICAL BASE

Teacher feedback also influences student performance and achievement. Teacher feedback has been mentioned briefly in two previous sections dealing with establishing an academic climate and expectation for success. However, it is also necessary to examine feedback and praise in their own right so that the importance of each in contributing to a positive learning environment can be better understood.

Bloom (1976) cited feedback as the teaching behavior most consistently related to student achievement. Feedback commonly means receiving knowledge of results. However, knowing whether the response is right or wrong is not sufficient for learning. Levin and Long (1981) pointed out that many research studies demonstrated that knowledge of right and wrong answers alone had little or no effect on improving learning. In his theory of school learning, Bloom (1976) emphasized that the student needs to know the corrective procedures to be taken. When teachers are able to provide information about what is left to be learned and corrective measures for students' responses, instruction is more effective. Bloom stated that student learning is dependent on knowledge of results when that knowledge can be used for correction.

As Levin and Long (1981) detailed in *Effective Instruction*, effective feedback contains three components: (1) a definition of correctness or standard of performance to be met, (2) evidence indicating whether the standard was or was not achieved, and (3) corrective procedures as to what must be relearned, and how.

A major form of feedback teachers use is grades, but it is important to realize that grades do not provide the student with all the feedback necessary for learning. Grades do indicate a standard of performance and the student's progress relative to that standard, but they do not indicate the kinds of problems students are encountering or the steps being taken to remediate those problems. Therefore, it is advisable for the teacher to provide each student with corrective feedback, as well as to help students increase learning.

Anderson (1989) pointed out that teachers today want students to be able to monitor and regulate their own work. This is a cognitive process called metacognition. Students are taught to analyze where they are having difficulties and what they need to do to move beyond the difficulties. Teachers who encourage students' monitoring themselves plan learning activities that promote student responsibility and less dependency on teacher approval.

■ APPLICATION TO PRACTICE

As research and experience have confirmed, feedback is an essential practice for effective teaching. Anyone who has ever tried to learn a sport, such as golf or tennis, can identify with the frustration one can experience as a learner if the teacher does not give feedback in the practice stage. Learners need to know what they are doing correctly or incorrectly. Otherwise, they may be doomed to repeat the same errors unless they can learn how to make corrections. Feedback that announces that one has missed the golf ball or hit the tennis ball into the net is useless in helping a person achieve goals. One needs to know what corrective procedures to take. Similarly, students who receive a test paper marked 55 percent know that they have not done well, but what to do next remains a mystery. Meanwhile, some of the most useful functions of a test—to correct misunderstandings and guide future learning—are not realized. Thus for several reasons, more informative feedback is necessary.

The following considerations are pertinent regarding the use of feedback and praise:

1. Attend to standards of performance, students' progress, and corrective procedures.
2. Give immediate feedback.
3. Use peer evaluation and self-evaluation as feasible.
4. Use reinforcement, praise, and criticism purposefully.

5. Use students' ideas as reinforcers.

6. Use verbal and nonverbal reinforcers.

7. Develop students' metacognitive abilities so that they can provide their own feedback.

Three Parts of Effective Feedback

As cited previously, effective feedback contains three pieces of information essential to the learner (Levin and Long, 1981): (1) the standard of performance, (2) the student's progress toward meeting that standard, and (3) corrective procedures to be taken, or additional instructive feedback needed to meet the standard or objective. Examples of effective verbal feedback are the following:

Corrective Feedback

John, 75 percent was passing and your paper was graded as 65 because you missed many of the problems with a decimal in the divisor. Let's go over the procedure and principles for working with decimals in the divisor by your explaining to me how you divide with decimals. That way we can see where you ran into problems. After we work out that difficulty, you can try this practice exercise to check on your new understanding.

The teacher will provide corrective feedback after John is able to identify where he has difficulty with the process.

Instructive feedback is another type of feedback that provides students with extra information about the task or content (Salend, 1998) such as in the following example:

Instructive Feedback

Your quiz grade is 32 percent with 70 percent as passing. As you described it, your problem seems to be that you didn't read the chapter carefully. Let's go over your outline of the main ideas and then reread the chapter. Here is a study guide for the chapter that should be a help to you. You can retake the quiz tomorrow.

It is important that students know the standards of performance prior to the evaluated activities. The teacher and students together can develop a rubric to evaluate the project, or the teacher can give examples of acceptable paragraphs or procedures to follow in writing up a lab report, as well as an indication of the level of achievement required for a passing mark.

A teacher using effective practice relates the student's score or performance to the acceptable level of performance to be met. Some examples are: "John, 80 percent is expected; you received 65 percent." "The essay must have four complete paragraphs; you have only three, Betty." "Passing is 70 percent, Tony; you have 75 percent." Teachers generally provide this knowledge of results to their students. However, the next step is the critical one—indicating the problem areas and the practice step to be taken; for example: "Four errors in your paragraphs involved run-together sentences, Carla. I will give you some practice papers on writing and punctuating complete sentences that may help you with the problem. Get together with your study partner and go over the papers together." Now the feedback process is complete and provides the student with information that can promote learning.

Written comments on papers are an important form of feedback and can offer praise or criticism. Using comments to establish communication with individuals can be a valuable technique for the teacher. They communicate to the student that the teacher is concerned enough to write a message. After surveying a number of studies on the effects of written comments, Levin and Long (1981) emphasized the importance of making comments specific so that students know which response to continue and which areas need to be improved or relearned. Example: "This is not one of your better tests, Rosy. You must have been tired. Notice that you missed four questions and you did not appear to know the main points of the chapter. See me and let's schedule a retest."

Give Immediate Feedback

The effective teacher provides regular and immediate feedback; for example, teachers can give oral feedback during recitation and practice. "Everyone close your eyes. Now raise your hand if this response is correct." In her presentations on effective teaching techniques, Madeline Hunter (1994) demonstrated an oral diagnostic technique that gave both the teacher and the students immediate feedback during a lesson. She would ask the audience to raise one finger if they thought the answer to a teacher question were A and two fingers if the answer were B. When more than half the audience would raise the wrong finger to answer a question, she would remark that she would have to give more practice on that phase of class instruction because they had overlooked a key point. She knew they were confused. The audience knew that they had incorrectly interpreted the point that she was making and the situation they were examining on the screen. The immediate feedback let them know the technique they needed to reexamine.

Using a simple oral diagnostic tool such as Hunter's "raising fingers" response method is an example of effective and immediate feedback for both the students and the teacher. The teacher discovers whether the students are comprehending while also involving every student in the activity. Other examples include correcting all important assignments, suggesting corrective procedures, and returning papers promptly. Giving frequent quizzes and tests is an important feedback measure and should be used for remediation. Requiring students to make corrections on graded assignments and to return them to the teacher for correction verification can assure the teacher that the students have examined their problem spots and have made the appropriate modifications. Student errors should be diagnosed as to their cause and the misconceptions should be clarified promptly.

Use Peer Evaluation and Self-Evaluation of Papers

All this feedback can mean mounds of paper for the teacher to examine. Consider self-managed feedback that students can receive through work with computers, rubrics, peer editing, and group work. Having students engage in peer evaluation and self-evaluation of their papers can be an effective technique as long as the students understand the evaluation criteria. Putting students into small groups of two or three and encouraging them to evaluate each other's work can be valuable for all concerned if students have learned how to handle that responsibility. Teachers can teach their students the procedures for peer evaluation and self-evaluation. Students from the fourth grade upward should be able to handle this type of group learning experience well as long as the teacher has indicated precisely what is required of the group. The teacher or the students can identify the evaluation criteria. The teacher can provide examples to illustrate the standard for each criterion. Students can then examine each other's work and give each other feedback on how well the papers meet the criteria.

Having a chance to examine each other's work and receive help from peers can be beneficial and effective teaching tools. Teachers can use small groups for peer instruction as well as for feedback. Students can teach each other the main ideas or check each other on vocabulary words, compare responses with the teacher's answer sheet, and help each other with corrections and remediation practice.

Teachers play a facilitator role during this experience by moving among the groups and keeping them on-task, assessing how productively the groups are working, answering questions, and giving judgments when the groups are confused and request teacher input.

Allowing students to check their own papers is a good device to promote independence in the students and to free the teacher to work with individuals. The teacher must learn quickly by observation which students abuse the privilege of marking their own papers and which ones can handle the task responsibly. Self-checking supplies students with immediate feedback from which they can decide whether to proceed or to continue on the current topic or skill.

Student checking does not relieve the teacher entirely from the responsibility of examining student papers, however. The teacher needs to check student papers to learn where errors are occurring. On the basis of that information, the teacher then makes decisions concerning reteaching, regrouping, or moving the class along to the next unit.

Use Reinforcement, Praise, and Criticism Purposefully

Other forms of feedback used by teachers are praise and reinforcement (the rewarding of desired student performance) and criticism (the reprimanding or correcting of student performance). The use of praise and criticism should be considered carefully by the teacher as factors having an effect on the climate of the classroom and the self-concept of the individual student. The amount of praise used by the average teacher is between 1 percent and 2 percent of total classroom interaction time. Criticism is used twice as much as praise (Amidon and Flanders, 1967). Reinforced feedback is important for the development of student self-confidence and motivation. Criticism is linked negatively to these learning factors. Studies describe criticism as impairing learning because it decreases motivation and damages self-esteem (Levin and Long, 1981). Brookover, Beady,

Flood, Schweitzer, and Wisenbaker (1979) found that teachers in effective class-rooms used more positive reinforcement to encourage student achievement and used it on a consistent basis. In summarizing the research on effective schools, the *Encyclopedia of Educational Research* (Mitzel, 1982) pointed out that in the more effective classrooms, pupils received more praise and less criticism.

In summarizing research on academic praise, Brophy and Good (1986) found weak but positive correlations tying praise to achievement, particularly for younger and lower-ability students. A caution needs to be raised here because researchers have discovered that teachers can use reinforcement and praise to control students' behavior. Students can be made to feel insecure and dependent on the teacher's feedback if the praise becomes necessary for every student action to assure students they are progressing satisfactorily. Therefore, teachers should understand their use of reinforcement and its intended result. Also, if teachers reinforce by praising every student response, participation is rewarded but encouragement for quality of response is neglected.

Two major points that come from the literature concerning reinforcement and criticism emphasize that students should understand the reason for any given rein-forcement and know when and how to modify behavior where appropriate (Levin and Long, 1981). Stallings's (1983) research showed that effective teaching behaviors are those that acknowledge or praise correct responses and probe to help the stu-dents examine incorrect responses. The research also pointed out that praise was not necessarily beneficial and more was not necessarily better. It may even be intrusive. Much teacher praise is used as a controlling device rather than expressing admira-tion for students' accomplishments. Judicious and informed use of praise is recom-mended (Brophy and Good, 1986). Positive reinforcement tied to students' beliefs about themselves and learning can help promote intrinsic motivation (Jensen, 1998).

When giving feedback to students, teachers are likely to include words of praise and reinforcement or criticism. All are important psychological tools and must be used carefully by the effective teacher. Praise can encourage the develop-ment of a positive self-concept, which should increase a student's motivation to learn, to participate, and to become more self-directed. Reinforcement can take on many forms. It can range from praise using one word such as *good* or *great*, to us-ing student ideas, to nonverbal types such as a smile or pats on the back. Similarly, criticism, ranging from verbal chastisement because of failure to perform well, to nonverbal looks of disgust and annoyance should be avoided to encourage stu-dents to learn from their mistakes and problems. Suggestions on how to use both reinforcers and criticism more effectively to encourage student progress are of-fered in the following paragraphs.

Reinforcement and praise that benefit the student the most are referenced specifically to the condition or product of merit. One example is, "Good work in our discussion today, Jim. Your comments related very well to last night's reading assignment and to the international trade question I asked today. You provided a good model for the other students to follow in the way you handled the question." Another is, "Sally has an excellent picture here because she kept the outline of the tree but within the tree drew a number of different scenes telling a story. She was very creative."

Use Student Ideas as Reinforcers

Effective praise also includes use of students' ideas. This type of reinforcement acknowledges that a student's contribution is important, thus encouraging more student involvement. Use of a student's comments signals acceptance by the teacher and can give the student a stronger feeling of self-worth. Example: "Good idea, Carlos. Carlos calls our attention to the fact that Mrs. Bennett may not have wanted to accept the money at first. Is there any evidence of her reluctance that you can find in the story, class?" (The teacher restates Carlos's response, and then asks a question built on the student's idea.)

In his work on analyzing classroom behavior, Flanders (1970) listed seven categories of teacher behavior, one of which was acknowledging the use of student ideas. He found that this reinforcing behavior conveys to students that their ideas are important enough to be given further consideration. The positive impact of this is greater than that of a one-word reinforcer such as *good.*

Rosenshine and Furst (1971) indicated five ways teachers can use student ideas when verbal interaction is taking place in class.

1. *Acknowledging* a student's contribution by repeating the response aloud to the class with the student's name. Example: "Sue said the number is brought to the right-hand side."
2. *Modifying* a student's contribution by putting it into different words to make it more understandable without changing the student's ideas. Example: "I believe you implied, Barry, that the gross national product is not an accurate measure of the economy's health. Is that right?"
3. *Applying* the student's response to some situation, or using it as an explanation for some event. Example: "Remember when Carmen told us that Jack's decision to leave before Todd came home with the news could get Jack into some trouble? Well, here is the trouble."
4. *Comparing* the student's response to something in the text or the lesson or to a similar event. Example: "Julie said the word was used as an adverb. Let's look in our books on page 37 to see how an adverb can be used and to see if we agree with Julie."
5. *Summarizing* students' contributions and using them to make a point. Example: "After examining the comments that Jack, Della, and Maurice just made, I think they may be saying essentially the same thing—that nuclear disarmament plans are meaningless unless they include all nations with nuclear capabilities. This is an important point to consider. Let's examine what it means."

Use Verbal and Nonverbal Reinforcers

Teachers need to guard against the overuse of certain words for praise, which thereby lose their impact. Teachers need to plan a list of reinforcement words they can use and also to plan nonverbal reinforcers such as displaying student work, smiling, nodding, and patting on the back. Both aspects of praise, verbal and nonverbal, need to be used purposefully by teachers.

A note of warning is in order concerning nonverbal feedback. Many studies of nonverbal behavior have substantiated that nonverbal communication "speaks" louder than verbal. A student will acknowledge messages from a teacher's facial expressions over any spoken messages. Therefore, it is important for teachers to be aware of the use of nonverbal feedback for praise or criticism because a teacher's body language is sending out evaluative nonverbal messages much of the time. Examples of nonverbal behavior that send negative messages to students can include those such as an unwillingness to touch a student of a different race, not making eye contact with certain students, sending only scowling messages to selected students, seldom calling on certain students, not bending over a desk or moving to a student's desk to offer help, and looking at the clock or watch while a student is commenting.

Use Feedback to Develop Students' Metacognition Abilities

Helping students become aware of their own thinking processes and working with them to acquire specific learning skills is an important goal for teachers. Then the feedback the teacher gives is not focused on the "right" answer but rather on helping students to analyze what they are thinking, to make comparisons and distinctions to models that the teacher or they may have in mind, to see errors that are occurring in their thinking, and to make self-corrections (Ornstein, 1990). This type of feedback is called metacognition.

Metacognition is a cognitive process whereby students are taught specific learning strategies so that they can sense when they are not learning or are having trouble learning and when they may be able to review where problems seem to be occurring. For students to be able to function metacognitively, teachers need to train students to be aware of the objective or goal during a learning activity, to monitor the strategies they are using to reach those goals, to analyze the effects of the strategies they are using, and to decide if they are satisfied with their responses based on the goals they are trying to accomplish (Pressly, Johnson, Symons, McGoldrick, and Kurita, 1989).

The development of metacognition takes time. Students need to develop certain thinking skills and to understand clearly what is expected of them. They need to be able to sense when they are getting close to the answer or to reaching the goal or when they are moving farther away. Students need to be able to analyze what part of a problem needs more work and what additional information is needed to solve the problem (Weinstein and Mayer, 1989).

Much information exists on thinking skills. It is important for the teacher to know how to incorporate these skills into students' learning strategies. Teachers can give feedback on how effectively students are applying these skills in their daily work. For example, Charles Letteri (1985) has formed the following list of thinking skills that students need to process and use information:

1. *Analysis*—The ability to break down complex information into component parts for the purpose of identification and categorization.
2. *Focusing-scanning*—The ability to select relevant or important information without being confused by irrelevant or secondary information.

3. *Comparative analysis*—The ability to select a correct item from among several alternatives and to compare information and make proper choices.

4. *Narrowing*—The ability to identify and place new information into categories through its attributes: physical characteristics, principles, or functions.

5. *Complex cognitive*—The ability to integrate complex information into existing cognitive structures and long-term memory.

6. *Sharpening*—The ability to maintain distinctions between cognitive structures (including old and new information) and to avoid confusion or overlap.

7. *Tolerance*—The ability to monitor and modify thinking, to deal with ambiguous or unclear information without getting frustrated.

Feedback that specifically encourages students to use these and other skills to examine areas they do not understand or errors they have made helps them become independent learners. The most effective academic climate teachers can promote in their classrooms is one that challenges students to take charge of their own learning.

■ SUMMARY POINT ■

Teachers play a key role in shaping the classroom learning environment. Teachers and students create the classroom environment by their verbal and nonverbal behavior displayed toward each other and by their execution of teaching and learning responsibilities. The decisions teachers make regarding the treatment of students and the standards of the classroom, including behavior and academic standards, contribute to the classroom climate. Within this climate each student's self-image is influenced positively or negatively toward learning.

This chapter on climate included many practices teachers may use to promote a positive learning environment. These practices were detailed to enable beginning teachers to recognize the choices available to them when making decisions about their teaching behaviors. Classroom practices need to be considered in light of the effect they have on creating a favorable learning climate. They need to be kept in mind when planning instruction. Chapter 5 discusses other considerations to keep in mind when planning lessons.

■ POSTSCRIPT: SCHOOL CLIMATE ■

This chapter has addressed the classroom climate that promotes student learning. However, the classroom climate is influenced by the school environment to a considerable degree. School environments for learning differ considerably across the country. Different communities with diverse socioeconomic groups in various geographic regions of the country have schools that look and operate differently from other schools. Even within a school district, schools may differ in terms of their facilities and learning climate.

In *Savage Inequalities,* Jonathan Kozol (1991) vividly depicted the squalid conditions that exist in some of our urban schools: plumbing that does not work, broken windows, and drug pushers hanging around the school grounds. Yet in other city schools, despite the age of the buildings, the facilities are well maintained and well equipped. The physical condition of schools sends a message to the students as to whether they—the students—are important to their community and to society. The conditions create a positive or negative image concerning the value of learning. Unfortunately, many factors, such as segregated housing, low incomes, and school attendance policies, often segregate students so that children who are African American, Hispanic, or recent immigrants from Asia may attend schools with substandard conditions. Teachers within these classrooms have to overcome the climate set by poor conditions and work harder to create a positive learning environment. Federal money was earmarked in 1994 for school improvement and staff development, particularly for those states with a larger percentage of at-risk children in deteriorating school facilities. Cuts in the federal budget in 1995 and 1996 reduced that aid considerably.

Each school has its own culture that shapes the climate of the building and sends messages to students about what is important in that environment. Ryan and Cooper in *Those Who Can, Teach* (1995) point out that schools most often are concerned with efficiency and economy and are less able to accommodate arrangements for privacy or small groups to work together. Through architecture, rules, and schedules, to mention only a few aspects of the institution, the school sends messages as to what is valued that influences the learning climate.

A recent research study (Plucker, 1998) reported that high schools with environments that promoted academic achievement obtained higher student aspirations ratings than the majority of schools that did little to nothing to promote academic achievement. Students reporting high inspiration and ambition perceived their school climates to foster student self-confidence, mentoring, excitement, and belonging, as well.

Douglas Heath (1986) has formulated the following questions about the school environment that may help you examine the learning climate of schools you are observing or may be considering for employment purposes:

1. Is this school so big I'd feel lost in it?

2. How proud are the faculty and students about the school?

3. What are the conditions of the bathrooms?

4. Are students I see in the halls aloof, sullen, cheerful, effervescent?

5. Does the principal call students by name? Do any stop to ask him or her a question?

6. Do faculty greet me warmly in the teachers' room, or do they ignore me?

7. How flexibly, imaginatively, or colorfully have teachers created their work space?

8. How do I feel when I walk into a classroom I am to observe?

9. What do the arrangement of desks, presence of plants, orderliness of the room, and comments on the chalkboard tell me about this teacher's assumptions concerning how students are to behave and learn in the classroom?

10. What does the room tell me about the teacher?

■ WEBSITE RESOURCE ■

 The Responsive Classroom website has been developed by the the Northeast Foundation for Children (NEFC), whose goal is to help K–8 teachers create teaching and learning classroom environments that are safe, challenging, and joyful:

www.responsiveclassroom.org.

It has been developed by teachers and consists of practical strategies for social and academic learning. The primary strategies are morning meeting, rules and logical consequences, guided discovery, academic choice, classroom organization, and family communication.

There is a new research section on applying responsive classroom principles and practices. A professional development section provides opportunities for instructional improvement such as through workshops. A search process enables users to get to books and resources in its archives.

■ QUESTIONS FOR REFLECTION ■

1. How important is the teacher's role in making a difference in student achievement?

2. What approaches would you use starting the first day of school to build a positive learning climate?

3. On a typical school day how would you plan the use of time in a 50-minute class period?

4. What attitudes do you need to develop toward children, the curriculum, the school, parents, the community, and yourself as teacher to foster a positive learning climate?

5. Can you recall classrooms that you were a student in or that you visited in which the climate was strongly positive for learning? What did the teacher and students do to promote that positive climate?

6. Have you experienced or observed teacher or student behaviors that created a negative classroom climate? What were these behaviors and conditions that created a poor learning environment?

7. In your teaching experiences, what have you observed about your interaction with aggressive male students, quiet and docile female students, minority students, students for whom English is a second language, and students who don't follow directions? (Continue identifying different types of students one would expect to find in the classroom. Consider carefully how you as teacher react or might react to each type of student.) Would your reactions and interactions support or threaten the positive learning climate?

8. How would you demonstrate in your classroom that you are a caring and professional teacher? Do you see problem areas in the clash between professionalism and caring? How would you handle these problem areas?

	ANALYSIS SCALE

TEACHER _____

OBSERVER _____

CLASS _____

DATE _____

ANALYSIS SCALE

OCCURRENCE

1. Not evident
2. Slightly evident
3. Moderately evident
4. Quite evident
N Not applicable

CATEGORIES	OCCURRENCE	COMMENTS

1. ACADEMIC CLIMATE: TEACHER . . .
  a. Makes students aware of lesson's objective or task.
  b. Is aware of how time is spent during class period.
  c. Provides academic challenges.
  d. Monitors student progress.		

2. HIGH STANDARDS: TEACHER . . .
  a. Sets a performance level for each objective and/or task.
  b. Encourages group development of performance criteria.
  c. Establishes a system for remediation.
  d. Promotes higher-level thinking and problem solving.		

3. EXPECTATION FOR SUCCESS: TEACHER . . .
  a. Has a positive attitude; encourages a positive attitude in students.
  b. Adapts learning activities for increased possibility for student success.
  c. Shows interest in and cares for all students.
  d. Shares expectations and encourages students to share their expectations.		

4. FEEDBACK AND PRAISE: TEACHER . . .
  a. Provides feedback on standard of performance, student's progress, corrective procedures.
  b. Provides timely feedback.
  c. Employs student self-managed feedback devices.
  d. Uses praise and criticism sparingly and judiciously.
  e. Encourages student self-monitoring.		

■ REFERENCES ■

American Association of University Women. (1992). *How Schools Short Change Girls.* Washington, DC: AAUW Educational Foundation.

Amidon, E., and Flanders, N. (1967). *The Role of the Teacher in the Classroom.* Minneapolis, MN: Association for Productive Teaching.

Anderson, L. (1989). "Learners and learning." In M. Reynolds (Ed.), *Knowledge Base for the Beginning Teacher.* New York: Pergamon Press.

Berliner, D. (1979). "Tempus educare." In P. Peterson and H. Walberg (Eds.), *Research on Teaching.* Berkeley, CA: McCutchan.

Berliner, D. (1992). "Educational reform in an era of disinformation." Paper presented at the American Association of Colleges for Teacher Education Annual Conference. San Antonio, Texas.

Berliner, D., and Biddle, B. (1995). *The Manufactured Crisis: Myth, Fraud, and the Attack on America's Public Schools.* New York: Addison-Wesley.

Bloom, B. (Ed.). (1956). *A Taxonomy of Educational Objectives: Handbook I. Cognitive Domain.* New York: McKay.

Bloom, B. (1976). *Human Characteristics and Student Learning.* New York: McGraw-Hill.

Brookover, W., Beady, C., Flood, P., Schweitzer, J., and Wisenbaker, J. (1979). *School Social Systems and Student Achievement: Schools Can Make a Difference.* New York: Praeger.

Brookover, W., and Lezotte, L. (1977). *Changes in School Characteristics Coincident with Changes in Student Achievement.* East Lansing: Michigan State University, College of Urban Development.

Brooks, J., and Brooks, M. (2001). *The Case for Constructivist Classrooms.* Alexandria, VA: Association for Supervision and Curriculum Development.

Brophy, J. (1982). "Successful teaching strategies for the inner-city child." *Phi Delta Kappan, 63*(8), 527–530.

Brophy, J., and Good, T. (1970). "Teacher communication of differential expectation for children's classroom performance: Some behavioral data." *Journal of Educational Psychology, 61*(5), 365–374.

Brophy, J., and Good, T. (1986). "Teacher behavior and student achievement." In M. Wittrock (Ed.), *Handbook of Research on Teaching* (3rd ed.). New York: Macmillan.

Caine, R., and Caine, G. (1997). *Education on the Edge of Possibility.* Alexandria, VA: Association for Supervision and Curriculum Development.

Delpit, L. (1995). *Other People's Children: Cultural Conflict in the Classroom.* New York: New Press.

Edmonds, E. (1979). "Effective schools for the urban poor." *Educational Leadership, 37*(1), 15–24.

Ennis, C. (1998). "Shared expectations." In J. Brophy (Ed.), *Advances in Research on Teaching.* Greenwich, CT: JAI Press.

Ericsson, K., and Charles, N. (1994). "Expert performance: Its structure and acquisition." *American Psychologist, 49,* 725–747.

Evertson, C. (1982). "Differences in instructional activities in higher and lower achieving junior high English and math classes." *Elementary School Journal, 82,* 329–350.

Fisher, C. W., Felby, W., Marliane, R., Cahen, L., Dishaw, M., Moore, J., and Berliner, D. (1978). *Teaching Behaviors, Academic Learning Time and Student Achievement: Final Report of Phase 111–13. Beginning Teacher Evaluation Study.* San Francisco: Far West Laboratory for Educational Research and Development.

Flanders, N. (1970). *Analyzing Teaching Behavior.* Reading, MA: Addison-Wesley.

Good, T. (1981). "Teacher expectations and student perceptions: A decade of research." *Educational Leadership, 38*(5), 415–422.

Good, T., and Beckerman, T. (1978). "Time on task: A naturalistic study in the sixth-grade classroom." *The Elementary School Journal, 78*(3), 193–201.

Good, T., and Brophy, J. (1996). "Teaching effects and teacher evaluation." In J. Sikula (Ed.), *Handbook of Research on Teacher Education* (2nd ed.). New York: Macmillan.

Good, T., and Brophy, J. (2000). *Looking in Classrooms* (8th ed.). New York: Addison Wesley Longman.

Goodlad, J., and Keating, P. (Eds.). (1994). *Access to Knowledge: The Continuing Agenda for Our Nation's Schools.* New York: College Entrance Examination Board.

Hale-Benson, J. (1986). *Black Children: Their Roots, Culture, and Learning Styles.* Baltimore: Johns Hopkins University Press.

Heath, D. (1986). "Developing teachers, not just techniques." In K. Zumwalt (Ed.), *Improving Teaching.* Alexandria, VA: Association for Supervision and Curriculum Development.

Houser, N. (1996). "Climate for diversity." *Urban Education, 136.*

Hunter, M. (1994). *Enhancing Teaching.* New York: Macmillan.

Jensen, E. (1998). *Teaching with the Brain in Mind.* Alexandria, VA: Association for Supervision and Curriculum Development.

Kozol, J. (1991). *Savage Inequalities.* New York: Crown.

Lamperes, B. (1994). "Empowering at-risk students to succeed." *Educational Leadership, 52*(3), 67–70.

Letteri, C. (1985). "Teaching students how to learn." *Theory into Practice* (spring), 112–122.

Levin, T., and Long, R. (1981). *Effective Instruction.* Alexandria, VA: Association for Supervision and Curriculum Development.

Lezotte, L. (Ed.). (1984). "Conducting an effective school program." *The Effective School Report, 2*(10), 1.

Lowe, R., and Gervais, R. (1988). "Increasing instructional time in today's classroom." *National Association of Secondary Principals* (February), 19–22.

McGreal, T. (1994, December 2). "The research on good teaching: A practical update on what works and what's new." Speech given at the Kaleidoscope of Learning Conference, Cedar Rapids, IA.

Mitzel, H. (Ed.). (1982). *Encyclopedia of Educational Research* (5th ed.). New York: Free Press (division of Macmillan), American Educational Research Association.

Moyers, B. (1994). *Healing and the Mind.* New York: Doubleday.

Murphy, J. (1993). "What's in? What's out? American education in the nineties." *Phi Delta Kappan 74*(8), 641–646.

National Commission on Excellence in Education (1983). *A Nation at Risk.* Washington, DC: U.S. Department of Education.

National Education Commission on Time and Learning Fact Sheet (1994). Washington, DC: Department of Education.

Noddings, N. (1986). "Fidelity in teaching, teacher education, and research for teaching." *Harvard Educational Review, 56*(4), 496–510.

Noddings, N. (2001). "The caring teacher." In V. Richardson (Ed.), *Handbook of Research on Teaching* (4th ed.). Washington, DC: American Educational Research Association.

Ogbu, J. (1974). *The Next Generation: An Ethnography of Education in an Urban Neighborhood.* New York: Academic Press.

Ornstein, A. (1990). *Strategies for Effective Teaching.* New York: Harper & Row.

Pang, V., and Sablan, V. (1998). "Teacher efficacy: How do teachers feel about their ability to teach African-American students?" In M. Dilworth, (Ed.), *Being Responsive to Cultural Differences: How Teachers Learn.* Thousand Oaks, CA: Corwin Press.

Perkins, H. (1965). "Classroom behavior and underachievement." *American Educational Research Journal, 2*(1), 1–12.

Plucker, J. (1998). "The relationship between school climate conditions and student aspirations." *Journal of Educational Research, 91*(4), 240–246.

Pressley, M., Johnson, C., Symons, S., McGoldrick, J., and Kurita, J. (1989). "Strategies that improve children's memory and comprehension of text." *Elementary School Journal, 90,* 3–32.

Purkey, W. (1978). *Inviting School Success.* Belmont, CA: Wadsworth.

Putnam, J. (Ed.). (1993). *Cooperative Learning and Strategies for Inclusion.* Baltimore: Paul H. Brooks.

Rosenshine, B. (1979), "Content, time, and direct instruction." In P. Peterson and H. Walberg (Eds.), *Research on Teaching: Concepts, Findings, and Implications.* Berkeley, CA: McCutchan.

Rosenshine, B., and Furst, N. (1971)."Research on teacher performance criteria." In B. O. Smith (Ed.), *Research in Teacher Education: A Symposium.* Upper Saddle River, NJ: Prentice Hall.

Rosenthal, R., Baratz, S., and Hall, C. (1974). "Teacher behavior, teacher expectation, and gains in pupils' rated creativity." *Journal of Genetic Psychology, 124*(March), 115–122.

Rosenthal, R., and Jacobson, L. (1968). *Pygmalion in the Classroom: Teacher Expectation and Pupils' Intellectual Development.* New York: Holt, Rinehart & Winston.

Ryan, K., and Cooper, J. (1995). *Those Who Can, Teach* (7th ed.). Boston: Houghton Mifflin.

Sadker, M., and Sadker, D. (1985, March). "Sexism in the Schoolroom of the 80s." *Psychology Today,* 54–57.

Salend, S. (1998). *Effective Mainstreaming: Creating Inclusive Classrooms* (3rd ed.) Upper Saddle River, New Jersey: Merrill.

Salonen, P., Lehtiner, E., and Olkinuora, E. (1998). "Expectations and beyond: The development of motivation and learning in a classroom context." In J. Brophy (Ed.), *Advances in Research on Teaching.* Greenwich, CT: JAI Press.

Schaps, E., Lewis, C., and Watson, M. (1995). "Schools as caring communities." In National Center for Restructuring Education, Schools, and Teaching, *Resources for Restructuring.* New York: Author.

Snider, W. (1986, June 11). "Chicago board adopts strict homework policy." *Educational Week, 38*(3), 1.

Stallings, J. (1983, June). *Findings from the Research on Teaching: What We Have Learned.* Charleston, WV: West Virginia Department of Education.

"Status of black children." (1989). *Black Child Advocate, 15*(4).

Stone, Randi. (2002). *Best Practices for High School Classrooms.* Thousand Oaks, CA: Corwin Press.

Swisher, K. (1990). "Cooperative learning and the education of American Indian/Alaskan native students: A review of the literature and suggestions for implementation." *Journal of American Indian Education, 29*(2), 36–43.

Tiedt, P., and Tiedt, I. (1995). *Multicultural Teaching* (4th ed.). Boston: Allyn & Bacon.

Tileston, D. (2000). *10 Best Teaching Practices.* Thousand Oaks, CA: Corwin Press.

U.S. Department of Education (1985). *What Works.* Washington, DC: U.S. Government Printing Office.

Weinstein, C., and Mayer, R. (1989). "The teaching of learning strategies." In J. Sheinker and A. Sheinker (Eds.), *Metacognitive Approach to Study Strategies.* Rockville, MD: Aspen.

3

Democratic Classroom Discipline

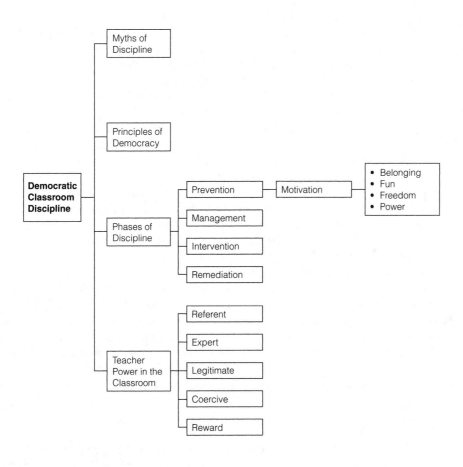

Discipline typically has an ominous connotation for the teacher. The term conjures up an image of misbehaving students frustrating the teacher's sincere instructional efforts. One may be left with the impression that teaching would be more appealing if it were not for discipline. However, this perception takes into account only a narrow—but highly visible—band within the wide spectrum of discipline.

In a more dispassionate and broad-based perspective, discipline is neither good nor bad. It is a necessary and pervasive dimension of every classroom. Within that setting, discipline refers to the inclination of students to comply with the teacher's expectations. Discipline, then, is comprised of factors both external and internal to the student. Understanding discipline and dealing with it require that both aspects be addressed.

When collective student behavior is "good"—that is, when students behave in an orderly and responsible manner—discipline is a tacit matter. Classroom activities proceed in a manner that is satisfying to the teacher and, we usually assume, to the students as well. Little overt attention is given to the subtle factors that result in orderly and cooperative behaviors. But when "bad" behavior occurs, whether due to ineffective teacher actions or to conditions internal to students that lie beyond the teacher's immediate control, that behavior calls attention to itself. Dealing with it becomes a matter of urgency on the teacher's part. At the very least, it is annoying; it may even be threatening to the teacher and cause an uncomfortable emotional state. Impulsive or irrational discipline-related decisions are likely to occur when a teacher experiences this condition.

When teachers think of discipline, this uncomfortable "bad" condition usually comes to mind. Yet the "good" condition, during which students behave within the limits of expectations agreed upon by the teacher and students, is also a part of discipline. Establishing in the classroom these conditions to which students respond positively is as much a part of discipline as the monitoring, controlling, and intervening behaviors more commonly associated with it. Discipline, in this teacher-oriented sense, refers both to the structure—especially the explicit limits placed on student behavior—intended to produce an optimum learning setting and to the manner in which the teacher's authority will be used.

Perhaps mastering the subject matter is not the most difficult aspect of teaching. Most new teachers and veteran teachers admit that managing the classroom is the hardest part of the job. Teachers *should* be concerned about classroom management for a number of reasons, and DiGiulio (2000) provides five of them: (1) Learning and achievement are at stake. (2) "A well-run classroom makes your job easier and it makes teaching possible" (p. 5). (3) A teacher's effectiveness is largely determined by how well the classroom is managed. (4) Litigation against teachers often centers around management issues. (5) "Our society needs it desperately" (p. 6).

■ OVERVIEW

An informed belief system is the basis for sound teaching decisions, including discipline-related decisions. Common sense or conventional wisdom for addressing the concerns of discipline is not adequate in the modern secondary classroom. The first step in developing a personal plan for classroom discipline is to become informed regarding professionally endorsed principles of discipline. The second step is to develop a comprehensive set of practices that attends to all four phases of discipline: prevention, management, intervention, and remediation. Finally, acquiring an understanding of the teacher's social power in the classroom is useful in implementing the intended practices. The ideas previously presented on classroom climate (Chapter 2) focus on producing the conditions of productive learning, particularly Topic 3—Expectation for Success—and Topic 4—Providing Feedback and Praise. Essentially, they form the foundation of sound discipline. The thrust of this chapter is to help new teachers acquire a framework for decision making about discipline. It stops short of providing prescriptions because these are situational and would require more elaboration than space allows. Many sources in the literature describe practices in detail, and the reader is encouraged to seek those that are compatible with individual needs and preferences.

SCENARIO

Jane DeFederico—"Mrs. D" to her students—was trying some new ideas in managing her general-science class this third year of her teaching. Her first two years had not been all that bad, but she felt that the class could have accomplished much more if she had not had to spend so much time and energy maintaining a reasonable semblance of order. She had attended a course on discipline during the summer and had written a term paper describing a personal discipline strategy based on her new understanding of promoting student responsibility. She would find out whether theory was helpful in addressing her concerns.

She had done some things the first few days of class that she had not done in the past. She established a seating arrangement that provided ready access to all the students but that gave special consideration to students who might need the greatest attention. Expectations, just a few in number and positively stated, had been written on the board, discussed at length, revised with student input, and left there as a continuing reminder. Students were given the opportunity to express what they expected from her. Class routines and signals had been established and practiced. With these done, she felt more comfortable and ready to begin to move ahead.

Now the class was in the third week, and Mrs. D was beginning a unit on chemistry. As the bell rang, she stood at the front of the classroom affecting a businesslike demeanor. To her satisfaction, the class came quickly to order. As an advance organizer for the day's lesson, she was using the concept of bonding. The class was asked to think of instances that involved an attraction between two things.

Claire called out almost immediately upon hearing the activity described, "My mom and dad."

Mrs. D moved a few steps to the board and tapped purposefully on rule number 3 referring to raising one's hand to be called on by the teacher. Claire raised her hand somewhat sheepishly. "All right, Claire, that certainly is one kind of bond. What are some more, class?" Several hands went up. Mrs. D pointed to Anita.

"People and dogs," answered Anita.

"Well, yes, bonds often exist between people and animals; emotional bonds, I suppose we would call them. Why do these kinds of bonds exist?" Several hands that had been up went down as this higher-level question was posed. Mrs. D used this change in momentum as an opportunity for student decision making. "I see that several of you are not sure how to answer that last question," she stated and then repeated the question. "What would it take for nearly all of you to answer the question?" she asked. After a brief discussion about using the textbook and working in small groups of two or three students, Mrs. D said they should go ahead and do either or both of these things. After less than five minutes, the class reassembled and hands were raised around the room to answer the question. The key term the students agreed to use in their response was *attraction.*

During the next phase of the class discussion about attraction, Mrs. D noticed Andrew and Leslie on the opposite side of the room begin a whispered conversation. She looked in their direction as she continued the discussion. "Yes, attraction is a key idea, and it applies to things other than people and animals. Leslie, can you think of an example of inanimate things?"

Leslie's attention was quickly drawn back to the class discussion, and she remarked, "Magnets stick to our refrigerator door at home. That seems like a bond."

In response to Leslie's example, Ronnie exclaimed in a low but audible voice, "That's dumb." Mrs. D acknowledged Leslie's answer and called on Jerome for his idea. Meanwhile, she arrived at Ronnie's seat and looked sternly at him for a few moments until his eyes dropped. He had gotten the message. This discussion in the class proceeded for several minutes as many examples were shared. Finally, Aaron observed that it seemed as though bonding was everywhere.

"Exactly," Mrs. D responded enthusiastically, "and that is just the point. Now we're going to be studying chemistry for the next two weeks. What sort of bonds do you think we are going to be especially thinking about?"

> Throughout the class Mrs. D recognized that there was some fidgeting and straying of attention. She had hoped to continue the discussion for a few more minutes but realized now that a change of pace and activity was in order to regain students' attention and avoid possible disruptions. She proceeded to answer her own question about the bonds they would be thinking about and then pulled down a periodic table chart as a reference for the class. A more direct-teaching mode would help, she reasoned; they need some information about the elements so that they can begin to understand how chemical bonding creates all the kinds of matter we know. She began a minilecture about the electrical charges associated with protons and electrons that establish the basis for bonding.

This brief glimpse into Jane DeFederico's classroom illustrates her informed, systematic approach to discipline. Jane was aided by her term paper that we may assume contained her carefully thought-out design for discipline and the identification of underlying principles that had been shared with and critiqued by other knowledgeable educators. She quickly implemented her plan at the beginning of the year by conducting several activities intended to clarify expectations and to invite student input into establishing the classroom climate. When inevitable misbehavior did occur, she was ready to respond. Meanwhile, she would do what she could within the instructional mode to prevent most of the incidental misbehavior.

Jane indicated that she was realistic in her expectations for student behavior and was willing to accommodate as necessary. As a sensitive teacher she became aware during the episode that the class was nearing the end of its tolerance for the discussion mode, even though her plan had been for further use of discussion. A likely response to students' waning attention might have been an expression of dissatisfaction with their off-task behavior. Jane's more enlightened response was to change the pace and shift to a more promising mode. Her informed belief system served her well in this instance of midlesson decision making.

When minor lapses in student compliance occurred, Jane took immediate but judicious action. In each case, the lesson proceeded smoothly while Jane dealt unobtrusively with the target student or students. Students received the message that learning was important in this classroom but that their dignity was important, too. They had probably begun to sense by this third week of class that Mrs. D "had her act together." No serious problem occurred in this episode, and this classroom seemed to have been an unlikely place to expect it. It could happen, of course, but Jane DeFederico seemed prepared to deal competently with it if and when she had to.

■ RESEARCH AND THEORETICAL BASE

Discipline, as a general aspect of every classroom, is difficult to study. Discipline does not exist as a discrete entity but rather as a collection of many factors. Much of the research that is helpful in understanding discipline is more specifically focused on such factors as reinforcement, span of attention, or teacher transitions.

Furthermore, this sort of research has as much implication for instruction as it does for discipline.

Clarification of the relationship between instruction and discipline is helpful in understanding the research in areas that affect both. Many of the teacher strategies and behaviors that are intended as effective instruction operate simultaneously, but tacitly, to diminish misbehavior. Some teacher behaviors are specifically instructional; others are specifically disciplinary. Between these two extremes is an overlapping area referred to as classroom management. Prevention and management strategies such as clearly stating expectations and establishing efficient classroom routines fall within this area. In Chapter 2, these strategies are addressed as they relate to classroom management; for example, a teacher's expectations for success during instructional planning and during instruction are intricately linked to classroom management; also, a teacher's use of praise and feedback during instruction will directly affect classroom management.

In earlier editions of this textbook, the literature on classroom management that was reviewed tended to focus on teacher control of group dynamics. For example, Kounin (1970) described how effective classroom managers control groups of learners through a "scientific approach to discipline" including the use of intervention techniques such as "withitness" (p. 80) and "overlapping" (p. 85). Doyle (1986) concluded that effective classroom managers, like effective managers in any workplace, develop and maintain work systems. The recommended strategies for effective classroom management were formal and prescriptive in nature.

Perhaps the best known of the formal discipline strategies is Canter's (1976) *Assertive Discipline.* The bases for the model are the teacher-centered premises that the teacher must be in charge in the classroom and that no student has the right to interfere with the classroom instruction. Assertive discipline provides for predetermined rewards for compliant behavior and penalties for misbehavior. This model is popular with many teachers because it presents a definitive set of procedures that the teacher controls. A certain amount of controversy attends the assertive discipline model, as described in a series of 1989 articles (Canter; Render, Padilla, and Krank; McCormack; McDaniel; Curwin and Mendler). Emmer and Aussiker (1989) concluded after reviewing the studies on assertive discipline that "in spite of teacher and administrator perceptions that are often positive, there is not evidence that Assertive Discipline training results in improved student behavior" (p. 119). Brophy and McCaslin (1992) are more favorable in their assessment in that they conclude that assertive discipline

> *can be helpful for teachers who are notably lacking in both confidence and viable strategies for dealing with problem students, and it is an improvement on earlier developed control methods that placed even more emphasis on reward and punishment and less emphasis on helping students to understand the rationales underlying rules in addition to the rules themselves. However, the program emphasizes establishing externally enforced control over problem behavior rather than diagnosis of causes and treatment through long-term change strategies. (p. 61)*

Much of the attention to discipline in the past has focused on control aspects. However, Gettinger (1988) emphasized that prevention in the form of proactive classroom management had greater potential than remediation for effecting optimum classroom conditions. Proactive management relies on the teacher's use of his or her social power in the classroom. Because the act of teaching is a form of influencing others, the topic of teacher power in the classroom appears in much literature on learning climate and classroom management. Perhaps an alternative conception of teacher power that emerged in the professional literature on learning climates over the past decade is the defining feature of current research and theories on discipline. With the shift in instruction from direct teaching to constructivist approaches has come a commensurate shift in discipline strategies, from teacher-centered, authoritarian approaches to student-centered approaches aimed at fostering respect and collaboration within a "community of learners." These approaches necessitated a reconceptualization of power. In more authoritarian classrooms, power is viewed and used in what Kreisberg (1992) calls a "power over" sense. This use of power is characterized by control and competition for scarce goods like A and B grades and teacher approval. According to Kohn (1996), Hoover and Kindsvatter (1997), and Wood (1992), teachers whose aim is to develop democratic communities within the classroom find themselves embracing an alternative view of power that moves from a use of *power over* to a use of *power with*. Kreisberg proposes that, as the teacher develops an understanding of power with, the process of empowering others begins:

> Power with *is manifest in* relationships of co-agency. *These relationships are characterized by people finding ways to satisfy their desires and to fulfill their interests without imposing on one another. The relationship of co-agency is one in which there is equality; situations in which individuals and groups fulfill their desires by acting together. It is jointly developing capacity. The possibility for* power with *lies in the reality of human inter-connectedness within communities. . . . (emphasis in original; pp. 85–86)*

The relationship of constructivist discipline approaches to the fostering of democracy is emphasized by Aronowitz and Giroux (1985) who wrote, "It is a contradiction to envision a democratic society when its inheritors, the kids, are forced to live under conditions of unrelieved subordination" (p. xi). Kreisberg (1992) recommends, "In order to develop people who are committed and capable of democratic participation, we must create communities, bit by bit, in which democracy is increasingly learned and practiced every day. This is a democratic dynamic; the ongoing interactions between people and the institutions they create and that create them" (p. 207).

The notion of classroom democracy and related emphases on student dignity and self-reliance are reflected in recent research on classroom discipline. A shift away from generalized, teacher-centered approaches to classroom management has occurred over the past five years in the literature. Instead of a broad set of directives aimed at controlling students and maintaining "work systems," approaches to classroom management in recent years have tended to be more student centered and more concerned with teaching students to manage themselves. DiGiulio's (2000) work on "positive classroom management" provides a "step-by-step guide to successfully running the show without destroying student dignity." Burden (2000) describes how understanding the multifaceted nature of student motivation can lead to effective classroom management. Campbell (1999) also focuses on student motivation and self-esteem as the core issues of classroom management. Raffini (1996) suggests ways that teachers can become successful classroom managers by enhancing student autonomy and by increasing belonging and relatedness in the classroom. Student self-reliance should be the goal of classroom management according to Norton (1995), who elaborates on Glasser's (1992) work on quality schools. In order to create a climate in which students manage themselves, teachers must encourage student self-assessment of their work. Lewis (2001) examines the role of classroom discipline in promoting student responsibility whereas Savage (1999) focuses on teaching students self-control through management and discipline. Involving students in the creation of the classroom discipline program is a recurring theme in this recent research on "the moral dimensions of teaching and classroom discipline" (Edwards, 2000). Character education and classroom management appear in the literature under the headings of "judicious discipline" (Gathercoal and Crowell, 2000) and "caring" in the classroom (Pena and Amrein, 1999). Other writers have deconstructed the broad topic of classroom management into singular topics such as "emotional intelligence and behavior management" (Bodine and Crawford, 1999), "middle school classroom management" (Bucher and Manning, 2001–2002), and classroom management in urban schools (Matus, 2001). Three works that review this recent research on management are *Classroom Management for Secondary Teachers* (Emmer, Evertson, and Worsham, 2000), *Beyond Behaviorism: Changing the Classroom Management Paradigm* (Freiberg, 1999), and *Solving Discipline Problems: Methods and Models for Today's Teachers* (Wolfgang, 1999).

> *Prospective teachers should recognize the value of being well informed, but that their personal interaction style and level of social development are critical factors as well.*

■ APPLICATION TO PRACTICE

Classrooms characterized by a positive climate and academically motivated students are those in which misbehavior of consequence occurs infrequently. Realizing this, however, is of little help to those preservice or in-service teachers who feel the need to understand the dynamics of discipline and who want to both acquire confidence in their ability to establish order and decorum and deal effectively with misbehavior when it occurs. Important purposes of this chapter are to contribute to the understanding of discipline and to make realistic suggestions regarding discipline-related approaches.

One may wonder why concern with discipline should still be prevalent after so many years of being recognized as a school problem. Writings from ancient Egyptian, Greek, and Roman societies inform us of the recalcitrant nature of students from those eras; for example, an elderly Socrates stated in the fourth century B.C.:

> *From the day your baby is born to you must teach him to do things. Children today love luxury too much. They have detestable manners, flout authority, have no respect for their elders. They no longer rise when their parents and teachers enter the room. What kind of awful creatures will they be when they grow up?*

The question regarding the concern with discipline has no easy response, or it would have been answered long ago. The nature of discipline is such that a final solution is not even possible. Only the sound principles of discipline will remain constant; the application of those principles will vary as the factors and conditions in classrooms vary. The commentary in this chapter is essentially a rationale for this statement.

The professional literature presents a wide array of definitions of discipline, which may in itself be testimony to the misunderstanding that often attends it. As was previously stated, discipline for the purposes of this book refers to the inclination of the students to work with the teacher to establish a climate conducive to learning. Discipline, therefore, is a dynamic set of conditions that exists within students, individually and collectively, the effect of which is revealed in the classroom in terms of order and decorum. Direct implications for the structure established in the classroom and the use of teacher authority stem from these conditions. Discipline is not something a teacher does in the sense that a teacher "disciplines" students. To use *discipline* as a verb is to confuse it with a teacher's controlling or punishing acts. Discipline recognized as a dynamic set of conditions affecting the pertinent causes, not just the visible symptoms, is clearly the basis for an informed approach.

Addressing the conditions related to discipline greatly complicates the task of the teacher in achieving a desirable level of classroom decorum. It is one thing to tell the class to be quiet, or to confiscate a squirt gun, or to ask inattentive students to participate in a group discussion; it is quite another to create the conditions within which these behaviors are neither attractive nor feasible alternatives in the students' view. The relationship of climate and motivation to discipline becomes clearer when one considers that student behavior is in large measure influenced by the quality of the climate and the level of their motivation.

The educational practices associated with effective classroom management are sophisticated. This fact has not been fully appreciated by educators. As a result, personal experience and intuition—sometimes generally referred to as "common sense"—are the basis of many teachers' discipline-related decisions; for example, the widespread use of punishment, when defined as retribution involving physical pain or mental discomfiture, is not defensible in a democratically oriented environment (though one must be careful in generalizing out of context). Yet, new teachers entering the classroom are socialized compellingly into the use of retributive punishment. (Consider the frequent use of detention.)

Discipline commonly involves decision making that involves several variables. In a classroom of 20 to 30 students, each a separate personality with unique perceptions and needs and all involved with the many academic, social, and psychological factors indigenous to that setting, the complexity of achieving and maintaining order is apparent. Gage (1978) pointed to the futility of depending on preconceived prescriptions such as those often included in lists of "teacher shoulds." He contended that effective functioning at this level requires an artistic dimension, or a level of performance that transcends routine or mechanistic applications. This is not to say that teachers do not have much to learn from the professional literature about discipline, but in fact just the opposite. An informed belief system is essential for being aware of—let alone achieving—the desirable outcomes of effective discipline. Prospective teachers should recognize the value of being well informed, but should realize that their own personal interactive style and level of social development are critical factors as well. "Withitness," in other words, is a matter both of possessing social competence and of being well informed.

Dealing with discipline is further complicated by its emotional aspects, especially in the case of teacher interventions with noncompliant students. When students misbehave in classrooms in obvious violation of the teacher's expectations, it may be sensed by the teacher as an affront. Self-esteem is in large measure a function of the teacher's own perceived competence; students' misbehavior signals the teacher's impotence at that given moment. By undermining a teacher's perception of personal competence, students trigger what psychologically are instinctive acts of self-preservation by the teacher (i.e., preservation of the self-concept). Meanwhile, those pedagogical principles relevant to such situations are likely to be ignored in the urgency to restore psychological comfort. Teachers are swept up in a tide of events of which they have only tenuous control and limited understanding—fertile conditions for nurturing a mystique. A succession of these events in the classroom can be devastating to the teacher.

Hints for the Beginning Teacher

Student perceptions into how a sense of community is being established in your classroom can provide powerful insights for you. After a unit of instruction, a group project, and so on, have your students complete a "Climate Survey" with questions that cause students to assess how they have or have not contributed to the climate and to reflect on how they can continue to support each other's learning.

■ THE MYTHS OF DISCIPLINE

The mystique of discipline resulting from the conditions described has deterred teachers from seeking rational—or pedagogical, if you will—approaches. Some of the expedient approaches that have been devised deserve to be considered as the myths of discipline. The myths are widely accepted and form the basis for many teachers' discipline-related decisions. But these myths simply do not stand up to scrutiny; they are not pedagogically valid. Taken collectively they violate several generally accepted, virtually self-evident classroom principles: Students' worth and dignity must be respected in accordance with democratic ideals; teachers should structure classrooms with the needs and natural inclinations of students clearly in mind; teachers should use authority judiciously in the classrooms;

and teachers have a major responsibility for students' motivation. Recognizing the myths for what they are and rejecting them as the basis for one's discipline decisions is necessary for the development of a defensible approach to discipline. Fifteen common myths are listed here (adapted from Hoover and Kindsvatter, 1997), each followed by a statement that is the pedagogically endorsed counterpart of the myth. These may be helpful in screening new ideas encountered about discipline or in purging ideas that are not sound.

Myth 1: Student misbehavior is self-evidently the student's fault.
Endorsed Principle: Misbehavior may have multiple causes, one of which may include teacher characteristics and/or practices.

Myth 2: Discipline implies an adversarial situation that involves a power struggle between the teacher and the students.
Endorsed Principle: Reason rather than coercion is the basis of sound discipline; discipline involves doing something for or with students more than doing something to students.

Myth 3: Good control depends on finding the right gimmick.
Endorsed Principle: Good control is achieved through sound judgment grounded in an informed belief system.

Myth 4: Every teacher can become highly competent in creating the conditions of good discipline.
Endorsed Principle: Teachers will inevitably vary in their potential to become effective classroom managers, especially as their personalities and belief systems vary.

Myth 5: The best teachers are those in whose classrooms students dare not misbehave.
Endorsed Principle: Intimidation is at cross-purposes with humaneness; it only signals the teacher's lack of interpersonal skills or social maturity.

Myth 6: A good classroom is a quiet classroom.
Endorsed Principle: The nature of the learning activity should determine the nature of students' participation, and sometimes participation noise—while it must be held to a reasonable level—is desirable.

Myth 7: The teacher should not smile before Christmas.
Endorsed Principle: A teaching style devoid of a sense of humor and grounded in an adversarial posture is bankrupt.

Myth 8: Punishment is educational.
Endorsed Principle: A reasonable consequence is focused on the student's best interest; punishment serves mainly the punisher. The only certain outcome of punishment is that the person being punished suffers. Respect and worthwhile learning, not fear, should be instilled through discipline; the mindless use of punishment is a travesty in education.

Myth 9: The behavior of teachers can be understood only in terms of their instructional role.

Endorsed Principle: From a personal, human-needs point of view, teaching is an important means in the teacher's life of satisfying certain basic psychological needs such as power, security, and self-esteem.

Myth 10: Students deliberately test the teacher to find out what they can get away with.

Endorsed Principle: There is no insidious conspiracy on students' part to test the teacher, but students are not psychologically comfortable until they know the limits—de facto, not just de jure—of their freedom in the classroom.

Myth 11: To remain unprejudiced, teachers should not examine students' records.

Endorsed Principle: Teachers should know as much as possible about their students to make decisions about them that are in the students' best interest.

Myth 12: Being consistent should take precedence over all other considerations.

Endorsed Principle: Teachers' informed and judicious judgment should take precedence over thoughtless consistency.

Myth 13: Keeping students occupied will prevent misbehavior.

Endorsed Principle: Keeping students on-task with thoughtful assignments is vitally important for both classroom order and productive learning, but mindless busywork is never justified. Further, busywork induces boredom, which in turn predisposes misbehavior.

Myth 14: Students will behave for the teacher if they consider the teacher to be one of the gang.

Endorsed Principle: The teacher's rightful role involves authority and leadership, and the teacher's credibility and effectiveness are undermined by most behaviors that have teacher popularity as their major intent.

Myth 15: All misbehavior should be dealt with swiftly.

Endorsed Principle: Misbehavior that disrupts learning must obviously be terminated when it is detected. However, some misbehavior alerts the sensitive teacher to the student's need for help, so the teacher should not too quickly default to expedient, self-serving measures that may exacerbate the problem.

Teachers have the responsibility to provide every student with the realistic opportunity for emotional comfort and personal success. It is unrealistic, possibly unethical, to force students to fit the school without regard for any other concerns; to do so is not only self-serving, but the discipline problems that result from this approach underscore its inadequacy.

In the scenario at the beginning of the chapter, Jane DiFederico was depicted as using appropriate approaches to address the disciplinary aspects of her classroom. If she had subscribed to myth number 1 (misbehavior is self-evidently the student's fault), she may simply have proceeded with her lesson as originally planned even as students grew restive. Then, when misbehavior occurred on the part of the students whose attention spans had been exceeded, she may have acted in terms of myth number 3 (good control depends on finding the right gimmick) and myth number 8 (punishment is educational). In so doing, she could have assigned a detention to offending students with the rationalization that they deserved it and would know better next time. One does not need to proceed very far with this type of scenario to realize what sort of climate is being created in such a classroom and that a self-serving teacher is exploiting teacher authority.

Students should be expected to cope with reasonable conditions and responsibilities and to be dealt with firmly when they do not conform with the necessary expectations of a democratic institution. Even more important is that children need the guidance of enlightened teachers who are free of the shackles of the myths of discipline and who employ practices that reflect the best of both the art and science of teaching.

■ THE PRINCIPLES OF DEMOCRACY

Discipline is sometimes thought of essentially as reacting to misbehavior and restoring classroom order. When this is the case, the ends may be considered to justify the means, which gives rise to misguided and punitive control techniques. However, an educationally sound approach to discipline has its basis in humane, democratically oriented principles. They function both as a guide and a check in teachers' discipline-related decisions. As examples, therefore, teachers' democratic discipline approaches should have the following characteristics:

1. Be conceived on the basis of pedagogical and human-relations principles and in all cases preserve the dignity and personal integrity of students.
2. Have a developmental thrust that democratically produces important personal and social-learning outcomes.
3. Reflect the belief that promoting self-control in students is at least as important as procuring their compliance.
4. Have the intent of doing something for or with students more than doing something to them.
5. Avoid aggravating the problem of an already troubled student.

Democratic discipline approaches are described in great depth in *Democratic Discipline: Foundation and Practice* by Hoover and Kindsvatter (1997). This work provides an expanded treatment of democratic discipline including an extensive background, philosophical discussion, and practical suggestions for classroom use.

■ SUMMARY POINT ■

Teachers' discipline-related decisions are influenced by philosophical considerations, pedagogical principles, and teacher personality. Purposeful reference to each of these sources is necessary for teachers in the development of their informed approach to discipline.

REVIEW

Important Considerations Regarding Discipline

1. Discipline is usefully considered to be the level of students' support of classroom guidelines for orderly and respectful behavior.

2. Refer to the myths of discipline as an aid in scrutinizing current ideas and selecting new practices.

3. Keep the faith; expedients may seem to serve the moment but they undermine the quality of discipline.

■ THE PHASES OF DISCIPLINE

While becoming aware of the myths and developing an informed belief system, teachers must also acquire a clear understanding of the concept of discipline. As implied by the definition of discipline in terms of student predispositions, it is a neutral concept, a means of categorizing certain factors related to interaction in the classroom. Realistically, however, discipline often has a negative connotation for practitioners because it conjures images of misbehavior, the primary source of teachers' apprehension. Developing an informed, practical approach to discipline requires that one transcend the intuitive, often negative and simplistic, view that frequently exists and acquire a comprehensive awareness of the several interrelated components. A straightforward approach to acquiring a comprehensive view of discipline is to consider in order the nature and implications of its four phases: prevention, management, intervention, and remediation.

Prevention   This phase is first, both logically and intuitively, in the process. The chapters on classroom climate, planning, and instruction address this phase of discipline in important ways. The climate developed over time through the cumulative interactions of teacher and students establishes the social norms that both define and limit appropriate student behavior. The motivation, especially intrinsic motivation, associated with the learning activities energizes both the substance and direction of students' behavior. When this motivation is strong, students' immediate basic drives are satisfied, or at least sublimated, and misbehavior is not an attractive alternative. Thus it is obvious that teachers need to be well prepared, to try to make the topic somehow relevant, to provide for variety and individual differences, and to be enthusiastic, fair-minded, and good-humored. Cooperating with these conditions is the most crucial aspect of discipline; paradoxically, these conditions do not readily come to teachers' minds when concerns about discipline arise. Rather, teachers are more likely to think of discipline in terms of authority and control.

Motivation.   Motivation is so important to prevention, and therefore to positive discipline, that it is given special attention in this section. Glasser's (1992) theory of motivation provides a useful perspective on the role of the teacher in establishing positive conditions for learning. He postulated that human beings have five basic psychological needs: survival, belonging, fun, freedom, and power. Like Glasser, we believe that, in most cases, survival needs are not dominant in typical classrooms, so the following discussion about student motivation will address the last four needs. When these needs are not sufficiently met, deficiency conditions such as anonymity, boredom, anxiety, and impotence occur. If one were to design a situation in which the deficiency conditions were the intention, it is likely that something that looks like a typical classroom would result! Consider the possibilities for relative anonymity in a classroom of 20 to 30 students; for boredom when physically and socially active adolescents are rendered mostly passive and quiet for extended periods of time while they study material about which they have limited innate interest; for anxiety in a setting in which their academic achievement is incessantly tested and their social status is tentative; and for impotence as they are manipulated without personal recourse by the whim of the teacher.

This obviously is a pessimistic view of the classroom, and yet Schlechty (2001) reported that "ritual engagement," "passive compliance," "retreatism," and "rebellion" were all too common in U.S. classrooms. Kohn (1996) believes that many of the behavior problems described by teachers are due to student boredom, resulting when students were "acting up mostly to make time pass faster" (p. 19). That is the bad news; the good news is that teachers can do much to provide for the basic needs of students in the classroom setting in the four critical areas of belonging, fun, freedom, and power. In the organization of secondary schools, teachers are inclined to view themselves as purveyors of their subjects. Teachers need to sense what lies beyond that narrow interpretation of their role. Preferably, they should conceive of themselves as agents for enriching their students' lives in many dimensions.

Belonging.   Can you remember the feeling of being "faceless" when you were a secondary student? Do you recall hours going by with the sensation of being lost in a sea of students? Teachers can give straightforward help to students in the area of belonging by knowing their names and using them outside as well as inside the classroom. A greeting by name from the teacher can be very satisfying to a student. Beyond that, knowing students more personally provides opportunities to refer to them in the course of learning activities. Bill is a fine pianist; Jennifer is an avid soccer player; Danny, who is disfigured from a childhood burn accident, skydives on weekends; Allyson has lived in seven different states. Teachers may make special efforts to talk with students, especially shy or unpopular ones. Eating lunch with students occasionally could be effective as could attending co-curricular activities such as athletic events or drama productions.

By using praise judiciously, a teacher can make a student's day. Supportive notes on students' papers are also helpful. As these suggestions indicate, providing students with evidence of their worth as human beings basically involves the application of effective human relations principles.

Fun.   Stimulation, engagement, and fun are factors that are most readily associated with motivation. Learning without fun is difficult. Teaching approaches in meeting this need make up much of the commentary on effective teaching. In a sense, one can consider the instructional ideas presented in other chapters in this book as the basis for promoting cooperative student behavior. More specifically, teacher enthusiasm and liveliness contribute to a sense of play in the classroom. Providing students with a credible rationale for learning activities and convincing students of the relevance of a topic is helpful. In the course of instruction, teachers should plan for "peak experiences" that will be remembered when the French and Indian War, quadratic equations, gerunds, and sporophytes are forgotten. These might include preparing an ethnic meal, a three-day backpacking expedition, being a quasi-official city or county officeholder for a day, or developing a mural for the cafeteria wall.

Finally, teachers gain credibility by modeling their academic discipline for students: math teachers who are computer specialists, English teachers who publish poetry, or technology teachers who design a simulated automobile electrical system. Being a showman in the classroom helps, but over time being a scholar of substance may be more valuable in stimulating students to achieve academically. Playing with interesting people is, after all, more fun than playing alone.

Freedom.   Students' needs for freedom essentially require that the teacher give students a voice in classroom decision making. Providing every student with a variety of options is most important in this regard. This involves recognizing individual differences among students and accommodating them in appropriate— even creative—ways. Such strategies as variable grouping, differentiated expectations and assignments, individual projects and independent learning, peer tutoring, and cooperative-learning arrangements, and grade contracts with stress on personal goals and personal improvement may be employed. A realistic view of meeting this need for freedom means that the teacher begins to use a *power with* approach with students.

Power.   Power, like freedom, is a need with implications throughout the needs categories, but it has a particular focus that is useful for teachers. By power, we mean that people have the need to exert reasonable control over their own lives and to have influence among associates. Two strategies previously cited regarding the freedom need—independent learning and grade contracts—are pertinent to satisfying the power need, as well. Students' perceptions and opinions should be sought when feasible and acted on when possible. The classroom should be established as a participatory democracy but with the necessary limitations imposed by the school organization. Classroom meetings are a common and useful mode for addressing classroom concerns. Within this setting, the students are encouraged to own the learning objectives established within the class. Having access to power through these means diminishes students' needs to seek power in less desirable, possibly disruptive ways, or worse, to experience anxiety from feelings of frustration and develop increasingly negative attitudes over time.

The commentary regarding the four basic needs makes little reference to discipline as such. However, in the classroom, as in a football game, the best defense is a good offense. The teacher who maintains an effective discipline offensive based on the motivation that results from effective instructional practices will engage infrequently in defensive reactions to student noncompliance.

In the scenario, we find Jane—Mrs. D—attending to prevention by developing a comprehensive approach to discipline and clearly establishing regularities to facilitate the classroom operation. However, the effect of prevention measures tends to be pervasive rather than specific, and establishes the norm of democratic classroom discipline. We can infer from the quality of the interaction that prevention, as defined in terms of classroom climate and student cooperation, was acceptably evident; yet it did not totally prevent instances of minor deviation.

Although preventive approaches to discipline occur continuously, they are most essential at the beginning of the year. DiGiulio (2000) outlines early preparation tasks related to the physical setup of the classroom (e.g., storage space, safety concerns, furniture arrangement); instructional concerns (e.g., curriculum guides, class participation expectations, late work); and managerial duties (e.g., absences, record keeping).

The concern for clear expectations deserves elaboration because of its special importance. Classroom order depends on clear, explicit rules. The students may be involved as much as possible in developing these rules to promote ownership of them. Most recommendations in the literature are for a few general rules stated in a positive way rather than a lengthy list. Such rules might include: respect the property of others; help maintain a quiet and orderly classroom; and be responsible for keeping your own work space neat. Once developed, the rules should be permanently displayed in full view. Most importantly, perhaps, students should be taught what the implications of the rules are for their behavior in an initial discussion and, in later discussions, as behavior warrants. When all this has been done, the teacher must be consistent in enforcing cooperation and dealing with noncompliance.

Management routines are closely associated with rules. These involve establishing early and clearly procedures for such things as accomplishing routine tasks, speaking to the teacher or other students, going to the rest room or library, using learning centers and classroom technology, and then carefully monitoring implementation of the procedures. Students' awareness of guidelines for operating an efficient classroom contributes to their sense of well-being.

Management   The demarcation between prevention of misbehavior and maintenance of acceptable behavior is hazy at best. However, management behaviors of the teacher are generally those things a teacher does in addition to instructional behaviors and are intended to keep students on-task. As a first order of concern, this requires having a businesslike, purposeful (although certainly not humorless) approach to learning activities. Furthermore, it involves moving around the room during the course of the lesson, maintaining eye contact with students, noting any occurrences of incipient misbehavior, citing instances of exemplary behavior, actively involving as many students as possible in the learning activity, and stating expectations as appropriate. These behaviors reflect the teacher's "withitness." Monitoring students' behaviors and conducting classroom meetings, referred to as prevention practices, would in some instances be more appropriately considered as management activities.

The managing behaviors a teacher engages in are in essence a combination of instructing and discipline behaviors. Figure 3.1 depicts management as a roughly defined area in the middle of a continuum between instruction and discipline. This indicates that a classroom can be managed using strong, authoritarian discipline, much as we would expect in the military. Control problems are minimal and are handled quickly and efficiently. This figure also suggests that a classroom can be managed using instructional practices. We can envision an industrial technology class where all the students are busy working on their individual projects at their stations while the teacher confers with a small group of students needing assistance. In the real world of the classroom, though, students are managed through a combination of a teacher's instructional and discipline-related behaviors. According to the research, effective teachers rely more on instructional behaviors to manage the classroom. This can be accomplished by creating the conditions for a good learning environment and thereby increasing the probability that discipline problems will be prevented. Effective teachers are effective managers; effective managers prevent potential problems.

The learning environment requires purposeful attention. The effective manager physically organizes the classroom to implement learning activities efficiently; for example, desks are arranged appropriately for discussion, lectures, and small-group work. The learning environment can also be structured psychologically by setting expectations for student learning and behavior. As an illustration, the teacher might say, "Today we are going to do some role-playing to try to understand how teenagers make decisions about their social lives. To be able to accomplish this, I will need your cooperation." Role-playing is a very effective method to learn and feel what others are experiencing—but only if everyone is listening and paying attention. Rules can be set and routines can be established to help guide students as they go about their learning tasks.

The effective managing teacher has planned to vary instruction to achieve learning objectives in different ways and for the purpose of stimulating students' interest and involvement. When students are faced with the same instructional method or strategy each day in one class, they become bored. Boredom provides opportunities for students' minds to wander and become preoccupied with other students and nonacademic activities. Teachers need to master a repertoire of methods and strategies to provide a stimulating instructional environment. The great variety of techniques, methods, and strategies presented in Chapters 6 through 8 should contribute significantly to a teacher's repertoire of instructional approaches. Teaching must also be focused to maintain students' attention and in-

Figure 3.1 Classroom Management as a Function of Instruction and Discipline

volvement. Preplanned specific objectives are essential to provide instructional direction and focus.

There is a concern with the management phase because teachers tend to take students' behavior for granted by shifting the major responsibility for behavior to the students. Students should be responsible up to a reasonable point and should be given as much responsibility (and corresponding freedom) as they can manage. However, the students deserve the teachers' systematic attention to management tasks to diminish the temptation of and opportunity for misbehavior. Therefore, teachers should develop complementary instructional and managerial strategies designed to promote a smooth-running, orderly, productive classroom (Burden, 2000; DiGiulio, 2000); for example, teachers should move about the classroom and have intermittent eye contact with every student while they conduct an interactive lecture, a recitation, or a guided or reflective discussion. The teacher should move to a distant point of the room as a student responds or comments so the student will speak loudly and the teacher will be able to view most of the class. If the teacher is incompetent in this regard, should students nevertheless be expected to remain continuously forgiving and compliant? Only if they are zombies! The most important day of class in terms of its potential impact is the first day of school. Students acquire their first impressions at this meeting, the tenor of the class is established, and momentum is initiated. This day should be more carefully and purposefully planned than any other. Although no formula exists for conducting this meeting, a likely sequence of events might be the following:

1. Conduct introductions, beginning with the teacher's, in which some appropriate bit of personal information is shared.
2. Present a course overview and rationale, highlighting interesting and relevant activities.
3. Present academic expectations and the grading policy, accompanied by a rationale.
4. Present expectations for classroom routines, including a brief list of general rules, and directions regarding how to enter and leave class, obtain a pass, be recognized to speak, use classroom technology, pass papers in, obtain materials— whatever a comprehensive classroom-management plan requires. This may extend over a number of days.
5. Provide an opportunity for students to express their expectations for the teacher, with the possibility of mutual verbal contracting.
6. Assure students they will be successful learners in your class.
7. Begin studies during the first meeting. The students will get the message that you consider class time to be precious and irretrievable, that it must be protected and used purposefully.
8. Attend to filling in seating charts, handing out textbooks, and making an initial study assignment. More than one period may be needed to complete the entire agenda, but it will be well worth whatever time it takes.
9. Begin the first of many discussions about democratic discipline principles. Discussion topics may include the meaning of individual dignity, student responsibility, classroom community, personal empowerment, and self-management.

In Mrs. D's room, the management phase of discipline was readily evident. She commenced class in a businesslike way as she assumed a posture that clearly communicated her expectations and yet invited student input. Students' participation was encouraged and supported so that they would stay with the lesson. Through alert monitoring, two instances of incipient misbehavior were detected and quickly defused. Meanwhile, she enforced the rule about the raising of hands. She changed the mode when restlessness occurred but did not chide the students about it. She displayed the all-important quality of "withitness" to an admirable degree.

Tips for Democratic Classroom Discipline—Prevention. Two general approaches to keep in mind that can help prevent management problems are *know yourself* and *know your students.* Specific tips that classroom teachers may want to use include:

Know Yourself

1. Examine any feedback about your classroom management skills that you have received from cooperating teachers, mentors, university or school district supervisors, and so forth. What strengths have they identified? What weaknesses have they pointed out? Be honest in this review of feedback. Every teacher, regardless of years of experience, has room to grow. Based on the feedback you have received from other educators, what are two things that you can do to improve in the area of classroom management?

2. Think about some of your teacher behaviors that may impact classroom management.
   - Do you talk too much?
   - Do you talk privately with students about their behaviors?
   - Do you threaten students about possible consequences and not follow through (e.g., "If you keep whispering back there, I'll give a detention.")?
   - Are you too flexible with assignment due dates?
   - Do you get to know your students on an individual level?
   - Do you use sarcasm with students?

   Consider one or two of these behaviors that you would like to decrease and one or two that you would like to increase. Then be specific about *how* you plan to change your behavior. For example, write down two ways that you plan to firm up due dates of assignments.

3. Consider asking your students for feedback about your management skills. An anonymous survey helps to ensure honest responses. Of course, some students may not be comfortable giving a teacher their opinions while others may use the opportunity to "get back." Still, when students see that you are willing to act on their suggestions, they can be reliable "mirrors" of how you manage their classes. Ask open-ended questions such as, "In what ways does my behavior affect your behavior in this classroom?" "What are some things I can do to help you become more attentive (engaged, motivated, etc.)?"

Know Your Students

1. Use student information cards to help you get to know some things about your students outside of class. For instance, at the beginning of the term, ask the students to complete one side of an index card with such information as their names, telephone numbers, parents' names, address(es), last year's English (or math or science, etc.) teachers' names, work schedules, club/sport commitments, and so forth. On the other side of the card, ask the students to write down their schedules so you can see what other classes they are taking (and so you can find them quickly).

2. Some teachers use these card to keep track of home contacts. These teachers make it a practice to call homes and speak to parents in the evenings. These conversations are positive in nature. (Many parents report that the only time a teacher calls is when he or she has bad news.) The teachers may call about good test grades or improved behavior. The topics and dates of the conversations are recorded on the cards for future reference.

3. Other teachers use a phone log to keep track of telephone calls made to students' homes. This log is simply a list of students' names, dates of calls, and conversation topics.

4. Consider going to students' after-school activities. Let them know that you are interested in their basketball games, their concerts, even their jobs. When students see that you take a genuine interest in them, their relationship with you can take on a more genuine, caring tone. Adolescents (people in general) usually do not want to hurt people who care about them.

5. Talk to students in the halls, in the cafeteria, before and after class. Let them know that you are interested in them as people and not only as your math (history, health, etc.) students.

6. Laugh with them. Humor, laughter, and fun help create a sense of community. Classrooms in which students feel they belong are often places with few discipline problems.

Intervention   This is the phase generally associated with discipline by teachers. New teachers frequently ask: "What can I do when these kids won't be quiet, or are insolent, or are always fooling around?" Some colleagues respond with their favorite approaches, although sometimes these have a basis in conventional wisdom. Better-informed colleagues tend to hedge their answers, realizing there are no guaranteed effective approaches. They leave the new teacher not only frustrated but also questioning the credibility of pedagogy in the area of discipline. The problem does not necessarily lie in the colleagues' practices, which seem to work for them, nor in the pedagogy. The problem is in the question itself, for it essentially addresses symptoms rather than causes. A more appropriate question, at least to begin what could be an extended process, is: "What are the conditions, internal and external, that are causing this situation?" When the question is thus posed, productive problem solving can begin.

More than a score of books and many dozens of articles have been written focusing on this particular phase of discipline. We could hardly do justice to the topic if it were our intention to pass along all the sound advice and suggestions included in the literature. A few important considerations are presented here, but wider reading on the topic is necessary to supplement this commentary for the reader who has a special interest in this area.

When the indirect and tacit techniques of the prevention and management phases are insufficient to preserve order, intervention is necessary. Preservice teachers often have difficulty in learning about appropriate interventions from effective teachers because effective teachers only occasionally need to use them. The teachers who need to use them frequently, on the other hand, are not the preferable role models. Therein lies a paradox: Interventions, or overt teacher intrusions, are least well learned from the most effective practitioners. So whereas judiciously selected intervention techniques should be part of every teacher's repertoire, they are always expedients and not the definitive aspects of a teacher's style.

By definition, interventions, or teachers' efforts to stop disruptive behavior, are expedients, so they should be used frugally and with discretion. An important consideration should be initially to use the mildest form of intervention that is likely to be effective and to resort to more stringent forms only as necessary. It is useful to consider the more seriously misbehaving student to be a troubled child who is exhibiting the symptoms of a personal problem rather than a bad kid who needs to be straightened out. The teacher then approaches the situation as a "therapist" rather than a "disciplinarian" and uses as a matter of personal style the science and art of pedagogy instead of the raw power with which the teacher role is endowed. Teachers in these circumstances might share the oath of the physician: *Primum non nocere,* or "The first thing (is) to do no harm." We affirm, however, that firmness is an essential quality for effective discipline.

Teachers need to have skill in applying a graduated set of interventions. But remember that clear rules and expectations must already be in place so that the errant student may be referred to them. The preferable approach to dealing with a nonattentive or mildly disruptive student is to use a question or some other instructional cue to enlist the student's active involvement in the lesson. This may be considered as much a management activity as an intervention. If this is not possible, and the teacher notices incipient misbehavior, nonverbal interventions such as eye contact and a "teacher look" should be used. If a look doesn't suffice, then moving to the target area in the room provides a stronger signal. The proximity of the teacher to restive students is usually sufficient to quell a minor disturbance. When these means have not been sufficient, the teacher may catch the student's eye and gesture with the head or hand, indicating that a particular behavior is inappropriate, or, if the teacher is in the immediate vicinity of the misbehavior, touching the student lightly but meaningfully or opening the book on the student's desk sends an unmistakable signal.

When these unobtrusive, nonverbal approaches fail or are not feasible, a verbal reminder is necessary. Initially, just saying the student's name, perhaps accompanied by shaking the head, should be employed. If the misbehavior is moderately disruptive or persistent, using the student's name followed by a redirecting statement may be effective. If these approaches are unsuccessful, the teacher should approach the disrupter and quietly but firmly direct the student to another seat, a time-out site, or whatever else is appropriate under the circumstances. This is the point at which the teacher may feel anger at having been affronted by the student. Resist it! Remain calm and in control. Above all, avoid a confrontation of any sort. It is a no-win situation for the teacher and for the student.

Teachers' responses to student misbehavior must qualify as reasonable consequences related to the behavior. Arbitrary punishments, such as remaining standing, writing a phrase repeatedly, serving a detention, or receiving an angry reprimand, rarely if ever meet the test. They tend to be retributive and have no redeeming social or educational value. Despite teachers' common belief, research shows that such punishments are largely ineffective as deterrents of future misbehavior. On the other hand, reasonable consequences sometimes appear superficially to be similar to a punishment (i.e., mild reproval may be appropriate or a student may be directed to take another seat). The difference lies in whether the student recognizes the consequence as being directly and logically related to the misbehavior and whether it is a potential learning experience for the student. Furthermore, punishment tends to satisfy the needs of the teacher, but a reasonable consequence attends to the needs—at least the predicated needs—of the student. Glasser's (1992) work on managing students without coercion provides an alternative to traditional forms of retribution. Called restitution, this form of intervention provides opportunities to the misbehaving student to make natural amends to people who may have been offended or property that may have been damaged. For instance, a student who has disrupted the teacher's closing remarks over a text chapter may be required to present a detailed summary of the chapter to the class. For a detailed description of restitution, see Glasser's work.

Many kinds of misbehavior obviously have no readily conceivable direct and reasonable consequence; for example, a student may have a habit of calling out, using profanity, or intimidating other students. A more generalized and systematic teacher response is useful for such behavior. A program using behavior citations might be established. Such notices serve as a record of the incident and incorporate a graduated set of consequences. The first might involve a brief conference in which the teacher tries to help students develop insight into their behavior and make a commitment to more appropriate conduct. The second citation would repeat the procedure and intent of the first, but involve a more extensive conference and possibly a written contract as well. A third citation would build on the first two, and perhaps involve a third party—parent, administrator, counselor—as appropriate. A fourth citation would signal a serious behavior problem and involve referral to a specialist. If this approach is adopted schoolwide, especially at the secondary level, it should involve in-school suspension. Any teacher—or school—that adopts a program based on these general guidelines has to work out the specifics accordingly. The advantages are that it does qualify as a reasonable set of consequences for misbehavior, emphasizes the developmental thrust of democratic discipline, and is consistent with the humane, democratic principles espoused by modern-thinking educators.

To implement a graduated set of interventions, the teacher must decide what is important in the classroom. For instance, is it important that students bring writing materials to class? Why? Is it important that students refrain from talking with each other? Why? When? Deciding what is important is, in essence, determining what is valued when it comes to learning.

Mrs. D had generally cooperative students in her classroom, better this year than in her first two years because of her new, well-planned approach to discipline. Nevertheless she did use several nonverbal interventions. When Claire called out an answer, Mrs. D tapped rule number 3 on the board specifying that students should seek permission by raising a hand. A question addressed to Leslie on the topic was, in fact, an intervention into Leslie's whispered conversation. Ronnie received a "visit" from Mrs. D as she strategically positioned herself at his desk and caught his eye. All of these unobtrusive interventions occurred without missing an academic beat. Mrs. D had become proficient in using nonverbal measures. Inevitably, verbal reminders will be required on occasion and sometimes even stronger measures. Hopefully, she will employ these with the same measured restraint and judgment.

Tips for Democratic Classroom Discipline—Intervention.   While it is impossible to predict management/discipline problems that could occur at any time in the classroom, some specific techniques that could help you intervene include:

1. Try to say "Yes" more often. Glasser (1992) suggests that teachers may say "No" too often to the hundreds of questions fired at them daily. We hear questions such as, "May I go to the rest room?" "Can we work together on this assignment?" "May I finish this reading at home?" A democratic classroom management outlook means that the teacher aims to teach students to control themselves. Glasser advises us to substitute many of our "No" responses with "No, because . . . ," "Yes, if," or "Yes." There is a continuum to these teacher responses that shifts the responsibility of control from the teacher to the student. For example, if a student asks to use the rest room, the teacher can, of course, say, "No." A response such as, "No, because you have left the room three times this week," gives the student a reason and a hint at a possible future course of action. A response such as, "Yes, if you wait until we are finished with this board work" places the responsibility on the student.

2. Try a version of "My job is. . . . Your job is. . . ." If a student continues talking to another classmate after you have asked him or her to be quiet, you can stop your lesson and say, in a polite tone, "Right now my job is to teach this material on vocabulary. I need to review three more words and explain some derivatives. Your job is to copy this material on the board into your notebook and participate in the class discussion. Let me know when you're ready for both of us to do our jobs." This democratic approach adds a sense of community to the classroom dynamic.

3. When student behavior becomes disruptive and emotions become heated, try to carry on conversations with the disruptive student in private. It is certainly appropriate to ask the student to wait in the hall until you can take a break from the lesson to meet with him or her. These few minutes also give both you and the student some time to cool off and let you come up with a plan. Once you are able to join the student in the hall, use a calm voice and try to establish eye contact. Invite the student to work with you to come up with some kind of solution to the problem.

4. In private or in front of the class, ask a rule breaker, "What is the rule here?" If, for example, a student continues to work on math homework in your history class, ask him about the class rule. (Of course, this is assuming you and the students have established a class rule about staying on task in the room.) If the student does not know or will not state the rule, repeat it yourself, then ask, "Can you do that?" Respond by saying, "Thank you, we all appreciate it."

5. Some adolescents can be especially sarcastic. Smart aleck comments in the classroom often lead to tension and ill feelings. The teacher has several options when confronted with this kind of student behavior. For instance, the teacher can respond by saying, "I don't talk to you like that. Please don't talk to *me* like that." The teacher can be even more direct by saying, "I don't like comments like that. I'd like you to either keep them to yourself or share your concerns with me privately."

6. The teacher who is consistent tends to have fewer discipline problems. Students feel insecure and resentful with a teacher who suppresses student actions one day and tolerates them the next.

7. Teachers who teach well have fewer discipline problems than teachers who do not take the time to plan interesting lessons with meaningful opportunities for student engagement.

Remediation   The purpose of behavior remediation is to diminish—and ideally eliminate—a student's disposition to the disruption of learning. As was noted earlier, it may begin as an extension of the teacher's intervention and incorporate follow-up as the consequences of the citations are applied. This is the phase of discipline within which important student-learning outcomes may occur. Teachers are not trained therapists, and they must recognize their limitations in dealing with pathologically induced behavior. Nevertheless, as well-informed, compassionate adults, teachers have the potential to affect students' attitudes and behaviors in beneficial ways. Teachers can help students realize that behaviors have reasonable consequences. They may also help students gain insights into the underlying reasons for their behavior and thus be better able to control their own lives. Furthermore, for the remedial aspect of the behavior-related contracts, teachers can help students consider alternative behaviors and monitor their compliance to the contract. How much time can a teacher spend in this sort of activity? It is a matter each teacher must work out individually. But it is a means of effective change in the lives of some students who greatly need to change.

APPLICATION for DIVERSE CLASSROOMS

Jere Brophy in his book *Teaching Problem Students* (1996) explains that modeling is essential when working with problem students. The teacher can use thinking aloud and self-talk to explain modeling behaviors. Instruction on coping strategies and social skills may be necessary. Students need to know why the skill is desirable, how to implement the skill, and when and why to implement it. Such

(continued)

instruction may be necessary with students regardless of race, ethnic background, or socioeconomic level.

Teachers must be careful not to let students with behavior problems or attention deficits influence teachers' behavior so that they begin to treat students inappropriately. Teachers can help students to gain better self-control by teaching them coping strategies, and then using cues, reminders, praises, and recognition to reinforce positive behaviors.

■ WEBSITE RESOURCE ■

 The the National Education Association website

www.nea.org

contains much current information on key topics impacting teachers: boosting student learning and achievement, building better learning environments, growing in my job, and connecting schools, families, and communities.

The NEA Works 4 Me website at

www.nea.org/helpfrom/growing/works4me/library.html

contains tips from teachers offering ideas and solutions that you can use in your classroom immediately. Tips center on the following topics: teaching techniques, content, managing your classroom, relationships, getting organized, and using technology.

■ TEACHER POWER IN THE CLASSROOM

The commentary in the previous section described classroom conditions and teacher behaviors associated with a comprehensive approach to discipline. The final section of this chapter presents another perspective on teachers' discipline-related behaviors. In any social situation in which a leader exerts influence on the other members of the group, power is involved. As noted in the research section, power and democratic classroom management are closely linked. Five kinds of power are possible: referent (personality), expert, legitimate, coercive, and reward (French and Raven, 1968). Each of these dimensions of power has implications for the teacher (Richmond and McCroskey, 1983). Students' behavior can be related to their perception of the teacher's use of these different types of power. The teacher who is aware of the uses and possible pitfalls in the application of each type of power has, therefore, a cogent decision-making rationale for selecting appropriate discipline-related practices.

The concept of power does not itself constitute an approach to discipline; rather, power is a dynamic within the process. Understanding its role and effect helps the teacher acquire a more in-depth understanding of discipline. With this understanding, the teacher can more knowledgeably recognize optimum and inferior models of discipline-related interactions and establish teacher-behavior goals accordingly. Any approach to discipline will be enhanced when the teacher refines discipline decisions by using insights into the power dynamic and moves from a *power over* interpretation to a *power with* interpretation of the power dynamic. Kreisberg (1992) views the shift from power over others to power with others as a move toward empowerment and self-discipline.

Referent Power   This is probably more readily understood if it is thought of as the influence one has through personality. Referent power is especially related to the interpersonal and communication dimensions of the classroom and thus can be termed *relation power*. A teacher who is endowed with or acquires a generous measure of referent power may be expected to have a high degree of social poise, exhibit a healthy sense of humor, maintain a respect for the feelings and rights of students, and be reasonably stable and consistent in demeanor. The teacher remains aware of the impact of each verbal interchange and demonstrates to the students sincere concern for their best interests. The outcome of these characteristics is a comfortable classroom climate and students who identify with and even sincerely want to be good for the teacher.

In the scenario, Mrs. D can be assumed to have relied to some extent on referent power as she took a position at the front of the room to begin the class session. The students' respect was implied as they quickly came to order. As we get a sense of the kind of teacher she is in the remainder of the scenario, there is no hint that other kinds of power are necessary. Referent power, however, is often subtle in its effect.

Expert Power   The competence of the teacher in conducting the tasks of managing the classroom and guiding learning is the basis for this power. The teacher, therefore, must be an informed scholar who is an advocate of the subject and is able to select aspects of it that are appropriate for the students to bring it alive, flesh it out, and help students recognize its relevance and possibilities. Another way of saying this is that the teacher must possess, in Shulman's (1987) words, pedagogical content knowledge.

Other aspects of expertise are manifest in the teacher's classroom-management practices. Systematic approaches are evident in much of what routinely occurs, such as making seating arrangements, establishing expectations, keeping records, marking and evaluating students' work, and passing out papers. The teacher's instruction is characterized by variety and student involvement. Students sense a certain ownership in the learning objectives and activities. In addition to the typical teacher-dominated presentations, one might also expect to find role-playing and simulations, projects, learning centers, hands-on opportunities, and independent study. Higher-level thinking will occur as students reflect on important ideas. The concept of individualization will be applied as special-purpose groups form and disband and enrichment and remediation are available to students as needed. Motivation will be an overriding concern of the teacher, who realizes that instruction without motivation is bankrupt. In describing expert power, we are, in effect, describing effective instruction. The implication is not that a teacher must be unusually talented to be reasonably successful. We do believe, however, that a mediocre teacher cannot depend on control measures to compensate for an inability or unwillingness to provide effective instruction.

Even in expert teachers' classrooms, misbehavior occasionally occurs. Expert teachers maintain a calm demeanor, quickly evaluate the situation and decide what approach will interfere least with the ongoing learning activity, and then respond firmly yet respectfully to the student. When students realize that the teacher is purposeful, assured, and unflappable (getting to be this way should be every teacher's developmental goal), they are less inclined to misbehave.

Mrs. D displayed her expertise in the instructional dimension as she began the chemistry unit with an advance organizer, then proceeded to develop the topic using the students' ideas. Later in the class she changed instructional modes as some students' span of attention ran out. These are expert instructional behaviors that have a positive impact on students' behavior, as well. As a competent classroom manager, she attended to seating arrangements, classroom expectations, class routines, and a systematic plan to cope with serious misbehavior. Her students undoubtedly—albeit tacitly—recognized Mrs. D's competence and considered her acceptable in the teacher role. This positive attitude, in turn, inclined them to generally cooperative behavior.

Referent power and expert power together create a charisma that endows the teacher with virtually all the power to manage successfully in the classroom. Achieving some degree of charisma might well be a goal of every teacher and, in this fashion, operate as a general guide for the teacher's professional growth.

Legitimate Power   As far as misbehavior is concerned, charisma operates primarily as a preventive influence. Realistically, however, the teacher must expect that misbehavior will occur and intervention will be necessary. In such cases, other types of power are available. One of these is legitimate power. This power is inherent in the teacher role, just as it for a police officer, a lifeguard, or a military officer, and it is the basis for their authority.

Students ordinarily submit to legitimate power and respond to it readily. For this reason, legitimate power is attractive to people with a special need to wield power. It could become, in effect, an end in itself and result in abuse of power. The existence of this condition may be inferred from an inordinate number of rules, unreasonable expectations for decorum, rigid classroom structure, gimmicky means of control, or teacher nagging about student behavior.

Legitimate power used appropriately involves establishing reasonable, minimal expectations for order and procedure, monitoring student behavior, and keeping students on-task through nonverbal cues and mild verbal reminders or restraint. In cases of serious misbehavior or persistent disruptive behavior, the wise use of legitimate power involves follow-up in determining causes and using well-thought-out behavior-remediation techniques with the student.

Mrs. D used legitimate power when the indirect influence of referent and expert powers was not a sufficient deterrent. She did diligently monitor the classroom and used unobtrusive reminders as appropriate. On the other hand, she was careful not to use legitimate power injudiciously. She seemed to recognize the point at which its use was counterproductive, that is, when students would feel a loss of dignity or a sense of their own powerlessness.

Coercive Power   The point where legitimate power ends and coercive power begins is not clearly discernible. In practice it can be the point at which the teacher's voice rises from normal volume to louder than normal or when the teacher asks the class in an exasperated tone for the third time to be more quiet. If teachers make direct reference to their authority or threaten or use punishment, coercive power is clearly being used.

Coercive power is necessary on rare occasions in the classroom. When students are fighting, are openly defiant, or are endangering themselves or others, the teacher must take appropriate coercive action because the time for reason and mild authoritarian action has passed. The intervention should employ the minimum force necessary to restore normal conditions—for example, separating the fighting students, requesting that a defiant student go to a designated place, or insisting that firecrackers be relinquished.

Coercive power, as an extension of legitimate power, is highly subject to abuse in the hands of teachers with personalities that incline them to its use. Punishment is the means such teachers use to attempt to gain control over students' behavior. But coercive power, in general, and punishment, in particular, are far less effective than conventional wisdom would suggest. Teachers who are routinely dependent on punishment to achieve a semblance of order are essentially failing in their instructional or managerial performance. On the other hand, when students do misbehave they should expect to confront the reasonable consequences of their behavior. The astute teacher recognizes the difference, which is sometimes subtle, between punishment and reasonable consequences and between measures that are merely self-serving and those that are educationally sound.

Reward Power   The use of rewards is the final application of power. Rewards are actually an integral part of expert or referent power as a teacher approves students' commendable performance. Reward in the form of deserved praise or other appropriate recognition of achievement has a positive overall effect and, in fact, is probably necessary for optimum teaching effectiveness.

Although rewards properly employed are recommended, incentives—rewards not intrinsically related to performance—should be used with discretion. They may serve to initiate student efforts toward achieving some performance goal, but at some point internal sources of motivation should supersede. Otherwise, the performance remains only a means toward an end and learning is incidental rather than purposeful. The use of grades as incentives is probably the most common form of this type of suspect practice.

Rewards can take the form of a bribe or bargain, particularly in regard to discipline. For example, a teacher might offer to let students go to lunch early if they are quiet during the lesson. In this case, they are being quiet for the wrong reason, and a reward is used as a substitute for effective teaching. The insecure teacher who runs a popularity contest with students is especially prone to misuse rewards. In general, when rewards are used to manipulate students or for any other ulterior motives, it is a misuse of this type of power. Furthermore, incentives diminish in effectiveness over time, and ultimately impede learning.

Mrs. D limited her use of reward power in the scenario to praising the ideas presented by two students. In each case, the praise was low-key and emerged as a natural part of the interaction in the class. These instances are examples of the appropriate use of extrinsic reward. Such thoughtful use of reward power contributes over time to students' inclination to be active participants and contributors.

■ SUMMARY POINT ■

The complex nature of discipline may be readily inferred from this chapter. Some teachers have a naturally occurring, mature interaction style that serves them well in the discipline aspects of teaching. Although these teachers may acquire useful insights and skills from experience, much remains to be learned about discipline by any teacher. Anti-intellectualism, more pervasive within discipline than any other aspect of teaching, has inhibited the attainment of a norm condition characterized by fully professional practice. The ideas presented in this chapter can be helpful in transcending the empirical level that is characteristic of current practice and in convincing educators that discipline is not a dirty word.

REVIEW

Important Considerations Regarding Discipline

1. Effective discipline and effective instruction are inseparable.

2. Democratic discipline principles promote not only a sense of classroom community but the democratic process itself.

3. Plan a comprehensive, pedagogically sound approach to discipline addressing, in particular, the four phases: prevention, management, intervention, and remediation.

4. Use the five types of power as a means to select appropriate power with behavior modes within the broad strategies employed.

5. Nothing is so strong as gentleness, nothing so gentle as real strength (Indian proverb).

■ QUESTIONS FOR REFLECTION ■

1. What instances of misbehavior do you recall from your own classroom experience that were well handled and poorly handled by the teacher? Evaluate the respective behaviors based on the principles and approaches in this chapter.

2. The personality of the teacher is identified as a major factor in a teacher's ability to be an effective classroom leader, especially regarding discipline-related matters. Evaluate your own personality as you project yourself into the managing role of the teacher.

3. The literature presenting the theory and research on discipline was described as being informative at the policies/program/principles level, but rarely prescriptive at the incident-by-incident level. How will you use the literature in your development as a classroom

manager? What are the limitations of the literature for that purpose?

4. List the five propositions in the order of their importance that will form the foundation of your philosophy of discipline.

5. As you anticipate developing a plan for having positive and effective discipline in your prospective classroom, what will be its major features in the areas of prevention, management, intervention, and remediation?

■ REFERENCES ■

Aronowitz, S., and Giroux, H. (1985). *Education Under Siege: The Conservative, Liberal, and Radical Debate over Schooling.* Hadley, MA: Bergin & Garvey.

Bodine, R. J., and Crawford, D. K. (1999). *Developing Emotional Intelligence: A Guide to Behavior Management and Conflict Resolution in Schools.* Champaign, IL: Research Press.

Brophy, J. (1996). *Teaching Problem Students.* New York: Guilford Press.

Brophy, J., and McCaslin, M. (1992). "Teachers' reports of how they perceive and cope with problem students." *Elementary School Journal, 93*(1), 3–68.

Bucher, K. T., and Manning, M. L. (2001–2002). "Exploring the foundations of middle school classroom management." *Childhood Education, 78*(2), 84–90.

Burden, P. R. (2000). *Powerful Classroom Management Strategies: Motivating Students to Learn.* Thousand Oaks, CA: Corwin Press.

Campbell, J. (1999). *Student Discipline and Classroom Management: Preventing and Managing Discipline in the Classroom.* Springfield, IL: C. C. Thomas Publisher.

Canter, L. (1976). *Assertive Discipline: A Take Charge Approach for Today's Educator.* Seal Beach, CA: Canter and Associates.

Canter, L. (1989). "Assertive discipline: More than names on the board and marbles in a jar." *Phi Delta Kappan, 71,* 57–61.

Curwin, R. and Mendler, A. (1989). "We repeat, let the buyer beware: A response to Canter." *Educational Leadership, 46*(6), 72–75.

DiGiulio, R. (2000). *Positive Classroom Management,* (2nd ed.). Thousand Oaks, CA: Corwin Press.

Doyle, W. (1986). "Classroom organization and management." In M. Wittrock (Ed.), *Handbook of Research on Teaching* (3rd ed.). New York: Macmillan.

Edwards, C. H. (2000). "The moral dimensions of teaching and classroom discipline." *American Secondary Education, 28*(3), 20–25.

Emmer, E., and Aussiker, A. (1989). "School and classroom discipline programs: How well do they work?" In O. Moles (Ed.), *Strategies to Reduce Student Misbehavior.* Washington DC: U.S. Department of Education, Office of Educational Research and Improvement.

Emmer, E., Evertson, C., and Anderson, L. (1980). "Effective classroom management at the beginning of the school year." *Elementary School Journal, 80,* 219–231.

Emmer, E. T., Evertson, C. M., and Worsham, M. E. (2000). *Classroom Management for Secondary Teachers.* Boston: Allyn & Bacon.

Freiberg, H. J. (1999). *Beyond Behaviorism: Changing the Classroom Management Paradigm.* Boston: Allyn & Bacon.

French, J., and Raven, B. (1968). "The bases of social power." In D. Cartwright and A. F. Zander (Eds.), *Group Dynamics: Research and Theory* (2nd ed.). Evanston, IL: Row Peterson.

Gage, N. L. (1978). *The Scientific Basis of the Art of Teaching.* New York: Teachers College Press.

Gathercoal, P., and Crowell, R. (2000). "Judicious discipline." *Kappa Delta Pi Record, 36*(4), 173–177.

Gettinger, M. (1988). "Methods of proactive classroom management." *School Psychology Review, 17*(2), 227–242.

Glasser, W. (1992). *The Quality School: Managing Students Without Coercion.* New York: Harper Perennial.

Hoover, R. L., and Kindsvatter, R. (1997). *Democratic Discipline: Foundation and Practice.* Upper Saddle River, NJ: Merrill.

Kohn, A. (1996). *Beyond Discipline: From Compliance to Community.* Alexandria, VA: Association for Supervision and Curriculum Development.

Kounin, J. (1970). *Discipline and Group Management.* New York: Holt, Rinehart Winston.

Kreisberg, S. (1992). *Transforming Power: Domination, Empowerment, and Education.* Albany, NY: State University of New York.

Lewis, R. (2001). "Classroom discipline and student responsibility: The students' view." *Teaching and Teacher Education, 17*(3), 307–319.

Matus, D. E. (2001). "Traditional classroom management revisited in the urban school." *American Secondary Education, 30*(1), 46–57.

McCormack, S. (1989). "Response to Render, Padilla, and Krank: But practitioners say it works!" *Educational Leadership, 46*(6), 77–79.

McDaniel, T. (1989). "The discipline debate: A road through the thicket." *Educational Leadership, 46*(6), 81–82.

Norton, B. (1995). *The Quality Classroom Manager.* Amityville, NY: Baywood.

Pena, R. A., and Amrein, A. (1999). "Classroom management and caring." *Teaching Education, 10*(2), 169–179.

Raffini, J. P. (1996). *150 Ways to Increase Intrinsic Motivation in the Classroom.* Boston: Allyn & Bacon.

Render, G., Padilla, N., and Krank, M. (1989). "What research really shows about assertive discipline." *Educational Leadership, 46*(6), 72–75.

Richmond, V., and McCroskey, J. (1983). "Power in the classroom: Two studies." Paper presented at the annual meeting of the Association for Teacher Education, Orlando, FL.

Savage, T. V. (1999). *Teaching Self-Control through Management and Discipline.* Boston: Allyn & Bacon.

Schlechty, P. C. (2001). *Shaking Up the Schoolhouse: How to Support and Sustain Education Innovation.* San Francisco: Jossey-Bass.

Shulman, L. (1987). "Knowledge and teaching: Foundations of the new reform." *Harvard Educational Review, 57*, 1–22.

Wolfgang, C. H. (1999). *Solving Discipline Problems: Methods and Models for Today's Teachers.* Boston: Allyn & Bacon.

Wood, G. H. (1992). *Schools That Work: America's Most Innovative Public Education Programs.* New York: Plume.

4

Curriculum Considerations

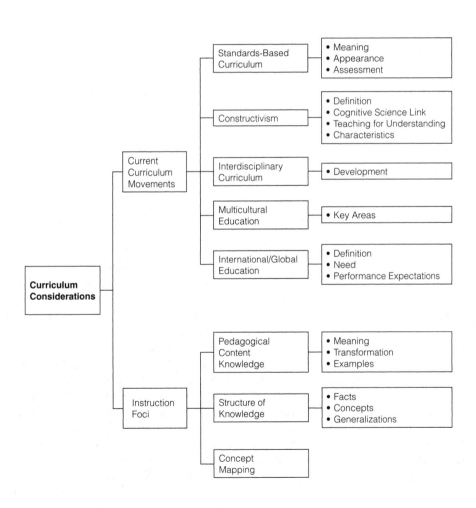

■ OVERVIEW

Planning for teaching necessarily involves curriculum; that is, one must plan to teach *something* for some *purpose.* Both the "something" and the "purpose" are the curriculum; the "something" part is the most obvious. A popular view of curriculum is that it is a plan for learning selected by a school district, that "focuses on goals, objectives, subject matter, and organization of instruction" (Moore, 2001, p. 18). The plan is a linear view that defines *curriculum* as a sequence or progression of content-learning goals and activities that move toward an end. The purpose often remains tacit in teachers' minds, with curriculum guides and textbooks uncritically accepted as the content to be taught. Curriculum in this view is specific, externally imposed, and prescriptive.

Another, broader view of curriculum, based on John Dewey's thoughts in *Experience and Education,* is that it is the *experiences* of the learner that comprise the curriculum. This definition describes curriculum as "all the experiences children have under the guidance of teachers" (Caswell and Campbell, 1935). This definition is one that elementary teachers and middle school teachers may find more comfortable because it emphasizes the importance of the total school environment and the role of the teacher in planning active participation for the students.

In considering the purpose of curriculum, Eisner (1990) takes the broadest view of curriculum and defines the purpose idealistically as "to free the mind from certainty, to liberate children and adolescents so that they can consider options not entertained by their parents . . . to help children become what we are not" (p. 62). In this view, the purpose of prime importance and the role of the teacher is to uncover, as much as it is to cover, the curriculum. The teacher is not just a conduit and a guide to students' discovery; the teacher helps students explore experience and search for personal meanings within and beyond the curriculum.

Eisner's view of curriculum encourages the constructivist approach to instruction: "to have students take responsibility for their own learning, to be autonomous thinkers, to develop integrated understanding of concepts, and to pose—and seek to answer—important questions" (Brooks and Brooks, 1993, p. 13). This textbook supports that view of curriculum and teaching, yet recognizes that national curriculum standards, state curriculum frameworks, and local scrutiny of curriculum may make teachers feel locked in to a curriculum that is assessment driven for high achievement. Indeed, Chapter 8 (on teaching strategies) identifies strategies that increase achievement and learning. However, the authors acknowledge the discrepancy and respond that our approach to instruction, in keeping with the reform movement in education, is a transitional move from behaviorist certainty to emphasis on personal meaning through curriculum built on large concepts, interdisciplinary exploration, scope and sequence that acknowledge children's developmental level, and interactive teaching. The text informs teachers of theories, research, and principles of instruction, with the understanding that interpretation into teaching approaches and student-learning activities is the essence of teaching. In the final analysis, the success of any teacher is determined by the teacher's ability to involve students in learning activities that they perceive to be meaningful and that result in high achievement for the students.

Most of us are far more familiar with a teacher's performance than with the performance of a symphony conductor. Yet, the symphony conductor's performance is more readily visible, more cleanly articulated. As such it provides a useful analogy for understanding the relationship of the teacher and the curriculum.

Can a conductor of a symphony who has been given a detailed score function creatively? It doesn't take much reflection to recognize that conductors not only can, but do. A score is a set of directions subject to the conductor's interpretation. The length of time that notes are held, the dynamics the conductor directs the symphony to create, the tempo used in particular symphonic sections, the balance between sections of the orchestra, the color and timbre created, and the general mood within the movements of the symphony are all subject to the conductor's control. Composers provide scores; conductors amplify the material received and in the process put their own imprint on the work. Making the judgments necessary to create a musically important rendition of a score requires a musical imagination, the ability to hear in one's auditory memory what the music might become, and an ear to know if and when it has been attained. The conductor is the first listener (Eisner, 1990, p. 64).

In some regards, the curriculum is similar to the musical score. However, the curriculum that defines a unit of study is much less precise and confining than a musical score. Teachers have far more latitude in interpreting the intent of the curriculum and having their individual impact on it. When teachers understand curriculum as a *referent*—not the whole plan—they are less intent to be bound to a textbook or a feeling of being manipulated. Their approach can be proactive rather than reactive, developmental rather than technical. The teacher's ear, like the conductor's, becomes attuned to listening for the meanings being generated by the learner. These understandings are the basis on which more complex meanings and interrelationships are built—and on which one's personal curriculum grows.

For the beginning teacher we describe formal curriculum as based on the values and needs of society, adhering to state standards and district guides, with a scope and sequence attuned to learner development. Within that framework, the teacher and the students can develop curriculum together as the students construct their own meanings.

A number of curricular movements that started in the 1980s are continuing in the country today. Teachers need to have some knowledge of these movements so that if their district is making a decision to adopt a particular approach, they have some familiarity with the movement and the possible impact it may have on curriculum and instruction. Several of these important movements are examined in this chapter including standards-based curriculum, constructivism, interdisciplinary curriculum, and multicultural and international/global education. The second part of the chapter discusses aspects of curriculum that need to be considered in instruction today, such as pedagogical content knowledge, the structure of knowledge, and concept mapping.

SCENARIO

Rebecca Hager and Al Marzano were looking over the material on national curriculum standards in the professional library corner of the teachers' lounge. Al was examining the *NCSS Social Studies Curriculum Guidelines* because he taught eighth-grade social studies. Rebecca, a science teacher, was interested in *Project 2061 Benchmarks for Science Literacy*. They were waiting for the arrival of Angeletta Rodrigo, the eighth- and tenth-grade English teacher, to make plans for an interdisciplinary unit they wanted to try to develop on cultures.

The idea to try an interdisciplinary approach to a unit grew out of an excellent in-service workshop they had attended right after the Christmas break. With the Martin Luther King, Jr. celebration occurring in January, they had been expressing their disgruntled feelings that the middle-level curriculum gave only superficial treatment to multicultural foci, and that was done mainly through the social studies. At that point, they decided that, given the information from the workshop and their present concerns about the lack of multicultural treatment within their curriculum guide, they would try to develop a new unit with a multicultural theme to follow their state curriculum framework and their district curriculum guide. The state framework was built on national curriculum standards, and their district guide had been updated in 2000 as part of the district's school improvement plan. They both worked on the revision so they were knowledgeable about the various curriculum standards. Angeletta, the English teacher, had shared with them that she was planning a poetry unit on voices from various cultures that might fit in well with their plans.

Another factor that encouraged them was that basically the same group of students were in Rebecca's second period and Al's third period, so they could try

to do some team teaching. Unfortunately, Angeletta did not have the eighth graders until fifth period, but she would integrate the information or projects into her class whenever possible.

Building on Angeletta's unit on poetry voices, Rebecca and Al were thinking of taking the theme—Voices from the Culture—and examining the culture of various countries through the people of those cultures. As represented in the stories, music, historical reports, case studies, and leaders' speeches, students could examine cultural patterns in use of land, settlement patterns, customs and ideas, and ecosystem changes. A chapter on Human Social Benchmarks for Science Libraries would supply some ideas concerning cultural effects on behavior and the impact landforms, weather, and climate have on human life and the shaping of cultures. Genetic inheritance, social inheritance, and life experience could be examined. Rebecca told Al she would like to have students examine census reports and do some data gathering and analysis, as well. She needed to speak with Carl Bowdin in mathematics.

Both Al and Rebecca agreed that technology would be important in the unit. Students would need to talk with other students in other places and, through the Internet, perhaps speak with a state university sociologist and a poet in residence. The World Wide Web could take them into communities around the country and the world to visit museums, even to see images of famous paintings and sites, as could programs on videodiscs.

Ideas were beginning to flow rapidly. Rebecca cautioned them to keep the unit flexible so that students would interact and ideas could be plugged in. For now, they needed to start to identify the key concepts they wanted to cover.

Rebecca and Al looked at each other, pondering whether they could get the unit ready by April. They'd have to see if Angeletta would delay her unit until . . . .

Rebecca looked at her watch. Fourth period was about over.

Al, Rebecca, Angeletta, and Carl Bowdin would need to spend much planning time together. She looked up to see Angeletta coming through the door. Perhaps they should start with a smaller two-week unit. . . .

Well-informed teachers know about the curriculum changes taking place today and examine those changes as to how they can help students' learning.

PART I: UPDATE ON CURRICULAR MOVEMENTS

Over the past two decades educational reform, starting with the National Commission on Excellence in Education's 1983 report *A Nation at Risk,* has been rampant and continues to be a major political thrust for control of schools at the national and state levels in order to improve national testing results (Orlich, 2000). From these reform pressures have surfaced major curriculum movements that continue to influence curriculum and instruction. These curricular movements include standards-based curriculum, constructivism, interdisciplinary curriculum, multicultural curriculum, and international global education. This chapter will examine each of these movements for the purpose of making teachers and prospective teachers more knowledgeable about them and to feel more comfortable in working within them.

Although this book concentrates on instruction, one cannot teach in isolation from content or curriculum. Every teacher, as does every curriculum developer, must wrestle with the basic questions of what knowledge is important for all to know, what the purpose is of the curriculum, how we can ensure that the curriculum is equitable, and how appropriate the curriculum is for our students' needs. Every teacher must answer these questions, or someone else will provide answers for them. These questions feature largely in teacher decision making: What should students learn? What is the purpose of our school? How do my beliefs about education influence my instruction? Educators continually search for the curriculum that responds to society's expectations to ensure that all students meet district and state standards and grow into productive, well-balanced individuals. The following curriculum movements are providing their own answers to these questions. Teachers need to develop a critical sense as to the effectiveness of these curricular movements in helping the students in their classrooms learn. Educational reform is only as effective as teachers' informed implementation of reform initiatives in their classrooms. Beginning teachers need to examine the movements' influences on their district's educational plan and staff-development initiatives—and, most importantly on their own instructional decisions.

■ STANDARDS-BASED AND ASSESSMENT-DRIVEN CURRICULUM

In the past, teachers made decisions on the important content to teach based on their textbooks and knowledge examined in standardized tests. Presently, with the knowledge explosion and public demand for education accountability, it has become apparent that there needs to be a clearer identification for the country as to those knowledge and skills essential for an educated citizen and that those knowledge and skills need to be assessed.

With the exception of mathematics, in the late 1980s, no national standards had been identified to guide curriculum planning in determining what students should know and be able to do by the time they graduate from high school. In 1992, the National Council on Educational Standards and Testing, a group authorized by the U.S. Congress to help move the national reform forward to accomplish the Goals 2000 mandate (eight education goals set by Congress to meet by 2000), recommended that voluntary national content standards and a national system of assessment be implemented. Since that time, most major discipline-based professional associations have developed content guidelines formed by scholars, researchers, and teachers. A national system of assessment is not in place over these guidelines or standards. However, all of the state education agencies have developed state curriculum guidelines or standards that call for changes in the teaching and focus of education. In Iowa, the only state not to have state standards, local districts are mandated to develop and assess their own district standards.

Today, a school district may be implementing and assessing national, state, or local standards, or a combination of these. The decision rests at the state level. The teacher needs to know which standards are the ones to focus on for curriculum planning. The essential question is the following: What are the standards, evidence, and learning opportunities to which the district is committed (Carr and Harris, 2001)?

National Standards

The national content standards movement started with the National Council of Teachers of Mathematics (NCTM) leading the way by releasing its content standards in 1989. The NCTM has also published Professional Standards for Teaching Mathematics, its vision of the direction mathematics instruction should take. Its publications have served as models for other subject area associations and councils such as the National Council of Geographic Education, National Council for the Social Studies, National Council of Teachers of English, and International Reading Association to develop their content guidelines. In the science area, the National Science Teachers Association, the American Association for the Advancement of Science, and the National Committee on Science Education Standards all developed standards, guidelines, and/or goals in separate publications. Standards for the arts as well as for physical education and foreign languages were generated also. Standards or guidelines are available in most subject areas, including the world of work (Kendall and Marzano, 1996). This means that in all likelihood, the district that employs you now or in the future may be implementing new curriculum based on the national content standards or your state's revised curriculum framework that has been influenced by these voluntary standards. (Check the websites of the cited associations to obtain copies of their standards).

To complete our view of this major curriculum effort, let's examine three key questions about the movement. What is meant by national standards? What do these standards look like? How should these standards be assessed?

First, what is meant by national standards? Again it must be stressed that these standards and/or guidelines are not mandated nationally. Each state and local school district can decide if it will use these content standards. The purpose of the standards is to have experts and practitioners in each content area identify the essential knowledge and skills all students need to know and be able to use.

What do these standards look like? They take various forms. Some of the standards take what is called a literacy model with the intent of identifying basic understandings of knowledge and skills that a literate, educated adult should be able to use. Another model is the academic model that identifies knowledge for those who plan to do advanced study in the field (Kendall and Marzano, 1996). All of the standards acknowledge the importance of emphasizing thinking and reasoning, of emphasizing students' understanding of key concepts and of developing dispositions and practice in constructing one's own understanding through inquiry, and of making connections between what is being learned in school and being used in everyday life (Wiske, 1998).

There is no common format for the standards; however, two prominent types have emerged: content standards and performance standards. Content standards specify what a student should know and be able to do. Performance standards specify assessment and the level at which the student is to demonstrate the knowledge or skill. They often identify the developmental level at which the knowledge and skills should be expected to be learned. These statements of expected knowledge and skills are called benchmarks. An example taken from a valuable reference work on the standards—Kendall and Marzano's *Content Knowledge: A Compendium of Standards and Benchmarks for K–12 Education*—cites the following standard and benchmark:

> *Standard—"Understands basic features of the Earth." (p. 75)*
>
> *Benchmark for grades 6–8 concerning that standard—"Knows that the Earth is the only body in our solar system that appears able to support life." (p. 75)*
>
> *A Level IV—grades 9–12 benchmark for that standard—"Knows that Earth systems have both internal and external sources of energy, both of which create heat: although the Sun is the major external source of energy, the decay of radioactive isotopes and gravitational energy from the Earth's original formation are primary sources of internal heat." (p. 76)*

Differences are apparent among the various efforts. Mathematics delineated 40 curriculum standards for grades K–12. History standards included many more. Social studies standards (National Council for the Social Studies, 1994) were developed around 110 themes and 10 skill areas. Also, on the issue of standards' performance, there is considerable difference among the projects. Standards in history and science identified one set of performance criteria for all; other standards identified two or more levels for performance criteria (O'Neil, 1993).

How should these standards be assessed? Congress has made it plain that at this time it has no desire to pass legislation requiring a national curriculum, thus leaving it up to the states to set their own standards' framework and assessments. However, in 2002, President George Bush signed a school reform bill that required standardized testing of every pupil in the United States in mathematics and reading every year in grades 3 through 8 (Stiggins, 2002). One national venture in assessment—the New Standards Project (2002), a joint venture of the Learning Research and Development Center at the University of Pittsburgh and the National Center on Education and the Economy—was launched in 1990 with 17 states and 6 school districts enrolled. The project, an outgrowth of the 1991 report *America's Choice: High Skills or Low Wages,* has concentrated on changing the way students are assessed by using tests that include performance tasks, projects, and portfolios. The project is a system of internationally benchmarked standards for student performance and an assessment system that measures student performance against the standards. The New Standards Project indicates the level of performance students should demonstrate based on the benchmarks of those countries with the highest student performance in the world. This system permits states and districts to determine whether their students meet national and international standards of performance. In December 1996, the New Standards Project released a set of performance standards in mathematics, English, language arts, science, and applied learning at the elementary, middle, and high schools levels (New Standards Project, 2002).

These national standards pose more challenges for teacher decision making as teachers deliberate in so many subject areas the essential knowledge to be learned. There simply is not enough time to teach all the knowledge identified in these standards. In addition, the content standards are criticized as being a collection of outcomes or performance standards assembled in a nonsystematic manner and without hierarchies clearly shown (Orlich, 2000). The result could be a fragmented curriculum.

■ APPLICATION TO PRACTICE

As part of the educational reform and accountability movement of the 1990s and continuing in this decade, states have been pushing for higher standards and more testing of students at specific grade levels in the major subject areas. Many state standards include content standards and performance standards that identify what students need to know and be able to do. The standards formed at the state level are general, giving local districts more freedom in designing the specifics to accomplish the standards.

You will need to be conversant with the district standards and the assessments you will be using. You will need to analyze the standards and your students to learn the following (Solomon, 1998, p. 175):

- What specific things do these standards require the students to know?
- What specific things do these standards require the students to be able to do?
- How will the students be assessed on these standards?
- What will be the consequences of poor performance on these standards?
- What are the students' present levels of development?
- What are the students' present levels of knowledge?
- Which of these standards can we help them achieve at this grade level?
- How will the students' cultural differences, goals, and interests affect their ability to achieve the standards?
- What are our resources of time, space, human energies, and materials?

As results from assessments give you data on the progress of your students, you will need to reflect on your curriculum and make changes in your objectives and learning experiences. Standards-based curriculum, as with all curriculum, demands continual assessment, reflection, and redesign. The curriculum will require all teachers to be better prepared in the areas of concept learning, multidisciplinary curriculum, problem solving, inquiry, and thinking skills. You must be able to use alternative forms of assessment, such as performance tasks and portfolios. You will need to be able to make careful decisions about content that support your district's goals and curriculum framework. You will guide students in studying content more in depth, in making connections across many subjects, and in relating the knowledge to their own lives. Your decisions will be informed by the information you are able to obtain concerning students' prior knowledge, their level of understanding, and their motivation to learn. The school district must be held accountable to help you help all students accomplish the goals of the school.

Hints for the Beginning Teacher

Take time to familiarize yourself with your district's course(s) of study for your subject area and grade level. The more knowledgeable you are about the expectations of your district the more confident you will feel in developing your long-range year plan. Examine the major objectives in your lesson plans and unit plans to see how they align with the objectives in the course(s) of study. Think about what changes you can make to ensure that you teach the objectives deemed essential for students at your grade level.

Constructivism Movement

When we study reforms in education through the curriculum standards established by national professional organizations such as the National Council for Teachers of Mathematics and the National Science Teachers Association, we encounter a student-centered view of learning approach to instruction that some educators refer to as constructivism, or the teaching for understanding perspective to curriculum and instruction. This perspective, identified by Thomas Good in the Handbook of Research on Teacher Education (1996) as "the most powerful integrative tradition for influencing classroom practice" (p. 629) deals with student learning and outcomes. Constructivism is influencing the teaching of reading and writing (Tierney, 1990) and other subject areas (Newman, Griffin, and Cole, 1989). Constructivist teaching and learning, introduced in Chapter 1 in this text, recognize that knowledge is created in the mind of each learner and that effective teaching approaches delve into the learner's mind through active learning; learner-generated inquiry; concrete, authentic experiences; collaborative investigations and discussions and reflection; and structuring learning around primary concepts. Much of the change initiatives taking place in school reform advocate practices that are considered constructivist teaching practices.

Constructivism is not a method or a strategy as defined in these chapters, but rather a theory about knowledge and learning that is changing how teachers perceive their instructional roles and their students' roles. Teachers are to help students relate new content to the knowledge they already know, as well as to have them process and apply the new knowledge (Good and Brophy, 2000). Before students can solve problems and generate fresh approaches, they must examine the new content in relation to what they already know and build new knowledge structures (Resnick and Klopfer, 1989). "Subject matter topics are not something to be covered by the teachers and passed to students, but areas of experience and ideas to which students relate their own associations and concepts for these topics" (McNeil, 1995, p. 4). Students build their own unique understandings of the content, which may or may not be accurate understanding. If the students simply memorize the information without giving it their own meaning, it will be difficult to recall and to use.

■ RESEARCH AND THEORETICAL BASE

The research and theory base of the constructivist approach is not about teaching but rather about knowledge and learning (Marlowe and Page, 1998). It has its roots in the work of Jean Piaget, a Swiss scholar concerned with cognitive development and the formation of knowledge. He examined how people came to know their world.

As explained by Brooks and Brooks (1993), Piaget (1952) saw the "human mind as a dynamic set of cognitive structures that help us make sense of what we perceive. These structures grow in intellectual complexity as we mature and as we interact with the world . . . through maturation and experience, the groundwork for new structure is laid" (p. 26). A number of cognitive theorists have built on Piaget's work to explain how learners actively construct their world (Bruner, 1964; Siegel and Cocking, 1977; Von Glasersfeld, 1981; Wigginton, 1989). These emergent theories from cognitive psychology about how we learn to recognize that knowledge is not a substance that can be transferred from the teacher's head to the students'; rather, knowledge must be constructed individually by every student (Lockhead, 1985). From this view of learning comes the term *constructivism*.

Recently, studies from cognitive science, particularly cognitive psychology, are informing educators about cognitive development and students' construction of knowledge. This information is not brain research that is popular to talk about today. Many teachers feel they are up-to-date if they verify their practices as influenced by "brain research." However, John Bruer (1997) cautions us that brain research is still in its infancy and "has little to offer teachers in terms of informing classroom practice" (p. 4). It is the field of cognitive science, mainly cognitive psychology, from which we can obtain some useful insights into student learning that can influence instructional decisions.

The American Psychological Association in 1993 published the Learner-Centered Psychological Principles: Guidelines for School Redesign and Reform. These twelve principles have been generalized into five statements (Alexander and Murphy, 1994) that are keys to effective teaching today:

1. Students' prior knowledge influences learning.
2. Students need to think about their own learning strategies.
3. Motivation has a powerful effect on learning.
4. Development and individual differences influence learning.
5. The classroom's social context influences learning.

■ APPLICATION TO PRACTICE

These five generalizations from cognitive science taken separately have been known by teachers for a long time. However, when considered together as a view of learning that influences student learning, they encourage changes in teaching. Students' prior knowledge becomes the starting point from which instruction helps either to change prior misconceptions and/or to build broader and deeper understanding. The student's role is not one of receiving knowledge but of being an active participant in constructing meaning and engaging in self-reflection on one's learning. Student motivation builds as students see connections in concepts and application of knowledge to real-life situations. Teachers must be aware of and able to accommodate developmental and individual differences to assure that learning is possible for each individual. For these generalizations to impact learning within the classroom, the teacher must create a social environment that promotes a learning community that is interactive, challenging, and supportive of each student.

Some educators call this constructivist approach a paradigm shift or a new mental model of learning that is more effective because it corresponds to how human beings learn (Caine and Caine, 1997). In methods texts, it may be referred to as the constructivist approach or teaching for understanding or active learning. The knowledge base is constructivist with a broad view of learning centered on cognitive science principles.

Constructivism presents a dilemma in decision making for the teacher who has been schooled with a behavioral orientation and is comfortable in the role of the teacher as the deliverer of knowledge. It raises questions such as "How does the teacher assess students' prior knowledge and then build on their current understanding?" "Wouldn't it be more time effective to present the information in a direct-teaching approach and expect students to be able to follow the lesson's development?" "If learning is facilitated by social interaction how much control can the teacher exert to determine if the interaction is on-task and learning is actually taking place?" "How productive can a noisy classroom be?" "How does one come up with authentic learning tasks for class activities if the course is determined by the text and lab manuals that the district has bought?" "Is the teacher seen as less competent and less prepared if one is not 'delivering' content?" "How much direction should the teacher provide without interfering with students' exploration?"

Such questions need to be studied through one's professional reading and discussed with colleagues, especially those presently teaching. The decisions to be made generating from the above questions require much reflective thinking about one's view of learning.

Constructivist teachers' view of learning causes them to expect their students to be able to explain, find evidence and examples, generalize, apply, and represent the concept or principle in a new way (Perkins and Blythe, 1994). They give assignments that push students to use in life applications or situations what they have learned. Such assignments are called authentic tasks. An example of an authentic activity is planning a playground for a new neighborhood apartment complex. This assignment challenges students to use their knowledge in geometry, health and human development, general mathematics, design, and science. Other examples of constructivist or authentic tasks for science require students to use scientific principles to solve household problems such as spot removing or appliance troubleshooting (Good and Brophy, 2000).

The Association for Supervision and Development reported in the February 1994 issue of *Educational Leadership* about the Teaching for Understanding Project, a five-year study conducted by the Harvard Graduate School of Education and teachers in the Boston area (Perkins and Blythe, 1994). Researchers developed a four-part framework to encourage teaching for understanding in a constructivist way (pp. 6–7):

1. *Use generative topics*—Teachers and students generate topics that are essential to a discipline, meaningful to the students, and connectable to topics inside and outside the discipline. These might include patterns in art, mathematics, and poetry, or conflicts of people against themselves in literature.

2. *Develop understanding goals*—Teachers and students need to identify a few key goals for a topic, such as that the students will understand the responsibility of the individual in a democracy, that students will be able to understand several points of view, or that students will appreciate the power of the individual in a democracy. The purpose of the goals is to focus instruction. Within these goals teachers may ask students to formulate more specific learning objectives for themselves or their group.

3. *Plan active experiences that build understanding performances*—Teachers design experiences that support their knowledge of understanding goals. The experiences may culminate in a final challenging performance of understanding, such as a project demonstration or an original skit presented to the class. The experiences should be active and interactive and should involve inquiry prompted by students' questions and research activities using primary sources of data. For example, Robin Woods (1994) explained how he taught a unit on electricity using student predictions and conductivity laboratory experiences to test their predictions and review their initial theories. Teachers also must be sensitive to student responses that can create new performances in different directions than planned.

4. *Conduct ongoing assessment*—In constructivist classrooms with emphasis on understanding, students need regular feedback and opportunity for reflection on their progress in learning. Teachers will either encourage students to develop the criteria that can measure their learning progress or develop the criteria themselves.

The experiences of one English teacher in the Teaching for Understanding Project were described by Rebecca Simmons (1994). The teacher was working in the unit Trials and Literature: Who Determines Justice and How? Students read such books as *To Kill a Mockingbird, Mutiny on the Bounty, Inherit the Wind,* and *Twelve Angry Men.* As students read, they kept charts to identify justice themes. They used the charts in their papers and in debates held near the unit's end. They also kept journals with their responses to higher-order questions, as well as to their own questions and reflections. The teachers ask such questions as the following: "Which of your questions can be answered definitely? Which might have several answers? Were some answers better than others?" (Simmons, 1994, p. 22). A final paper on justice using two or three of the books students had chosen was the culminating performance. (For more in-depth treatment of constructivism, see Brooks and Brooks, 1993, and Good and Brophy, 2000.)

Another example of this student-centered active-learning approach is Doreen Nelson's "modern city building" (1985) curriculum that requires the students to learn content and skills from different subject areas as they develop a scale-model city. Students start off studying their own community, drawing scale maps of the major features—streets, main buildings, parks, and so on. From these maps, students draw up plans for a new city and form a city council that will hear the plans for city development and handle questions such as: Where should the industrial park go in relation to environmental factors? Will there be a transport system and where will it be located? What park areas will be planned? Questions such as these require students to learn much about city government, ecology, landscaping, and city aesthetics. Math skills are important when students build their city to scale. This approach uses an integrated curriculum and cooperative learning with students divided into groups to build the various sections of the city.

Teaching for understanding in a constructivist classroom means helping students make connections of new knowledge with prior knowledge. These patterns of prior knowledge on which students build new knowledge are called *schemas* (Anderson, 1984). The schemas provide a context for new information and help students better understand content. The KWL approach is an effective tool to activate prior knowledge. What do you already *know* about this topic? What do you *want* to know? What did you *learn*? (Asked after exploration and instruction.)

Teaching for understanding in a constructivist classroom means using instructional strategies that move learners from rotely giving "information" to reaching deeper understanding through their own questioning, exploration, testing out of ideas, making connections among content areas, and working cooperatively with peers and adults to prepare to be lifelong learners (Brooks and Brooks, 1993). Some constructivist strategies include cooperative learning, conflict resolution, thinking and process writing, integrated and interdisciplinary approaches, portfolios, and performance-based assessment practices (Hyerle, 1996).

Additional characteristics of constructivist classrooms are as follows (Brooks and Brooks, 1993, p. 17; Good, 1996, p. 630; Good and Brophy, 2000, p. 427):

1. Curriculum is presented with emphasis on big concepts.
2. Students construct networks of connected knowledge by linking new content to existing knowledge.
3. Pursuit of student questions is highly valued.
4. Curricular activities rely heavily on primary sources of data and manipulative materials, and focus on authentic issues and problems.
5. Students are viewed as thinkers with emerging theories about the world.
6. Teachers behave in an interactive manner, mediating the environment for students.
7. Teachers seek students' points of view to base future lessons on student conceptions.
8. Assessment is interwoven with teaching and occurs through student exhibits and portfolios.
9. Students work primarily in groups.

A teacher needs to think about constructivism as helping students to construct usable knowledge (Good and Brophy, 2000) by encouraging inquiry, problem solving, reflective thinking, and group activity to apply new learning.

Three books with many helpful suggestions for instruction in constructivist classrooms are Brown and Adams (2001), *Constructivist Teaching Strategies;* Marlowe and Page (1998), *Creating and Sustaining the Constructivist Classroom;* and Gagnon and Collay (2001), *Designing for Learning.* (Also, see the lesson plan for constructivist teaching in Chapter 5 of this text.)

■ INTERDISCIPLINARY CURRICULUM

Another curriculum movement in educational reform is the implementing of interdisciplinary curriculum or integrated curriculum, either through teams in high school, such as in the scenario, or through the planning by one middle school or subject teacher of interdisciplinary units. This interdisciplinary curriculum fits well into the constructivist classroom. By having subjects combined around themes, problems, or issues, wherein the subjects are connected rather than studied in isolation, students can begin to see meaningful relationships. These themes enable students to delve into concepts and generalizations that have been identified in subject standards, to deal with big questions and larger perspectives, and to develop their ability to learn through exploration. The learning rather than the subject matter becomes the center of attention (Martinello and Cook, 1994). The learners' questions, activities, and projects become more important than internalizing facts from one discipline area at a time. Too frequently the separate subject approach to curriculum leads to a "disconnected and incoherent assortment of facts and skills" (Beane, 1995, p. 618).

Students may study a unit on a topic such as the prairie, if they live in the Midwest, and become very involved in examining the history of the land in their area, efforts to restore or safeguard prairie land, and the grasses and wildflowers of the prairie. They may read books, visit museums, and talk to grandparents about life on the prairie. They may analyze prairie soil, chart the amount of original prairie left in their area of the state, graph the amount of rainfall in comparison to a mountainous region, and collect varieties of prairie grass and wild flowers. With a theme topic, students can decide what subtopics they want to know about, and the academic disciplines can be the sources and tools for learning with content, skills, and processes integrated into the curriculum. Their textbooks become reference sources. The curriculum may be built around themes, problems, or local issues that are important to that particular site and group of students; hence, it has high interest for the students.

■ RESEARCH AND THEORETICAL BASE

The theoretical base for interdisciplinary curriculum comes from the works of John Dewey and other educators whose writings were part of a reform movement in educational, social, and political affairs during the early part of the twentieth century called the progressive movement. The early progressive thinkers placed heavy emphasis on *how* to think rather than on *what* to think. The curriculum was interdisciplinary in nature, with subject matter as part of the learning process rather than the source of ultimate knowledge. The teacher's role was to guide students in their problem solving and scientific inquiry (Ornstein and Hunkins, 1993).

The other research base is in constructivist theory, which maintains that students construct their own understanding of the world. Experience is the key, and learners understand according to analysis of their own experiences. Self or personal concerns can be the focus of interdisciplinary curriculum as well as larger issues and problems (Beane, 1995).

The major research study that examines the results of interdisciplinary curriculum is the famous "eight-year study" (1932–1940) that researched the effect of a nontraditional education in progressive schools with largely interdisciplinary curriculum on education in traditional subject-centered programs. The findings of the study were that students in the progressive schools were as well prepared for college as those prepared in traditional schools (Aiken, 1942).

For a current report on the effectiveness of interdisciplinary curriculum, one can read descriptions of programs in education journals such as the following from Aleknagik School in Southwest Alaska. All classes in this K–8 school revolve around a theme with a science or social studies emphasis. The interdisciplinary focus has produced favorable results with reports of "good intellectual growth," students able to make connections, and teachers demonstrating a cooperative spirit (Peters, Schubeck, and Hopkins, 1995, p. 636). A recent research study (Hargreaves and Moore, 2000) comes from Toronto, Canada, where 29 seventh- and eighth-grade teachers implemented a common curriculum in the major subject areas of language arts, social studies, mathematics, science, and technology. They developed integrated units on such themes as conflict and change, life cycles and relationships, global perspectives, the impact of advertising, and constructing bridges. They organized units to make connections with real issues in students' lives and with people, ideas, and events beyond the classroom. They emphasized "higher-order thinking, problem solving, application of knowledge to real problems, creativity and invention, and the embedding of learning in real life and real time" (p. 89). The results of the study showed curriculum integration to be intellectually demanding but rewarding. The teachers found the approach brought more relevance and rigor into classroom learning.

■ WEBSITE RESOURCE ■

National Standards and Professional Education Associations

To read or order a copy of the national standards for the major secondary academic areas, check out the websites of the national professional associations:

www.ncss.org (National Council for the Social Studies)

www.nctm.org (National Council of Teachers of Mathematics)

www.ncte.org (National Council of Teachers of English)

www.nsta.org (National Science Teachers Association)

www.actfl.org (American Council on the Teaching of Foreign Languages)

The national standards in most cases are current or in the process of being revised. You can reach the standards either by clicking directly on specific links through pull-down menus or by typing in Standards in a search box.

Information is also readily available on membership, conferences, and resources for teachers, including teaching ideas, related to the professional association.

■ APPLICATION TO PRACTICE

The interdisciplinary approach is popular today, particularly in the middle school curriculum because of the success of the middle school movement over the past 40 years; the diversity of children in the regular classroom; the needs of the workplace for the skills emphasized in interdisciplinary curriculum; and the recent research in cognitive science demonstrating the necessity of helping learners establish bridges between school and life, between knowing and doing (Roberts and Kellough, 2000). Some schools, as part of their reform, have implemented interdisciplinary team teaching such as called for in New York State's "Compact for Learning" (Darling-Hammond, 1993).

Jacobs (1989) identified four steps for developing integrated interdisciplinary units. They involve: (1) selecting an organizing center, such as a theme, topic, problem, or concept; (2) brainstorming associations from the perspective of different fields, with the graphic representation of the brainstorming depicted with a *webbing*—a wheel with spokes and subspokes—on which topics or information related to the center hub are written; (3) establishing guiding questions to provide a framework; and (4) designing activities to explore the questions.

Martinello and Cook (1994, p. 60) gave a longer list of steps to designing theme studies that may prove useful as teachers attempt this innovation to curriculum and teaching. Their guidelines for designing interdisciplinary theme studies are as follows:

1. Select a theme or problem as the organizing center.
2. Develop a web, or build other designs to generate a wealth of ideas.
3. Identify questions through the lens of different disciplines.
4. Identify concepts; formulate generalizations within the theme.
5. Meet local curriculum requirements and the framework of the district and the state.
6. Map out or draw the general sequence.
7. Formulate with the students the questions to explore that guide the unit.
8. Develop ideas for a learning activity—clusters of ideas around concepts.
9. Identify content and process objectives.
10. Design learning activities.
11. Choose culminating projects.

12. Use resources to explore questions.

13. Decide on record-keeping, reporting, and assessment measures.

Other instructional issues that need to be considered when planning and implementing integrated or interdisciplinary curriculum include the following (Adams, 2001):

groupings: how and why

exceptional learners

early and late finishers

high- and low-ability learners

multiple intelligences, learning styles

The above issues need to be considered in all curriculum planning because they will impact the effectiveness of the unit for different learners.

For more information on interdisciplinary resources, visit the National Center for Cross Disciplinary Teaching and Learning at the following website: www.iisgp. ubc.ca/interdisciplinary/bridges.html.

An example of a unit is shown in Figure 4.1 to suggest how a teacher might develop a web with the students to examine the scope of an interdisciplinary unit. A

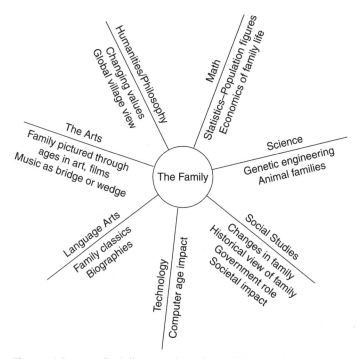

Figure 4.1 Interdisciplinary Unit Web on "The Family"

step-by-step approach to the development of integrated units is available in Roberts and Kellough's book, *A Guide for Developing Interdisciplinary Thematic Units* (2000), and in Mallery's *Creating a Catalyst for Thinking—The Integrated Curriculum* (2000).

The topic can be shaped in many different directions but needs to be focused around key questions such as those below:

1. What is the family body?
2. How did the family change over the ages?
3. What were the major impacts on the family over the last several centuries?
4. Is the family solely a human phenomenon?
5. How does the family influence society and vice versa?
6. What will the family look like in the future?

■ MULTICULTURAL EDUCATION

Another major curriculum movement in the educational reform era is the multicultural curriculum. With approximately 9 percent of the U.S. population today foreign born, the highest percentage since before World War II, we are aware that our cultural diversity continues to grow. Indeed, diversity can be viewed as one of our country's defining characteristics (Fuchs, Fuchs, Mathes, and Simmons, 1995). As James Banks (1996) points out to us, our democratic way of life is dependent on our ability to "create and maintain a civic community that works for the common good" (p. 75). Students must acquire the knowledge, skills, and attitudes that will make our pluralistic society equitable and just and will preserve our democracy. Therefore, when planning curriculum units as well as daily lessons, it is important to integrate intercultural concepts and values to prepare students to live in and protect our society of interdependent cultures.

Consider these statistics describing the changing face of our country:

In the year 2010, the number of children of immigrants will rise to 9 million, representing over one-fifth of the school-age population. Four states—California, Florida, New York, and Texas—will account for a third of the nation's youth, and a majority of these young people will be ethnic minorities. (Washington and Andrews, 1998, p. 9)

In many districts and in the entire states of California, Texas, Arizona, New Mexico, and Florida, minority students will be the majority. Minorities already constitute a majority of students in 23 of the 25 largest districts. (Haberman and Post, 1990, p. 32)

Estimates are that children of color will eclipse the number of children of Caucasian ancestry before the middle of this century (Dilworth and Brown, 2001).

The state of California serves as a good illustration of our intercultural era. In California, approximately 40 percent of all students speak a language other than English as their primary language. More than one hundred languages are spoken in school systems of New York City, Chicago, Los Angeles, and Fairfax County, Virginia (McDonnell and Hill, 1993). In addition, over 20 percent of U.S. children are being raised below the poverty line, the highest percentage of all NATO Western nations (Washington and Andrews, 1998).

■ RESEARCH AND THEORETICAL BASE

The essence of understanding multiculturalism and internationalism is understanding the concept of *culture.* In their review of the literature, Cushner, McClelland, and Safford (2000) examined many definitions and identified three major themes: "culture as a socially constructed and dynamic phenomenon, culture as shared by a group which decided through a process of interaction what ideas, attitudes, meanings and hierarchy of values belong to that group, and culture as a set of ideas which is passed on to the young as a means of nourishing the next generation" (p. 56).

Although all cultures from different parts of the world share common characteristics including language, communication patterns, forms of aesthetic expression, and social, political, economic, and religious systems, there are many cultures within each major culture. Pasch, Sparks-Langer, Gardner, Starko, and Moody (1991) distinguished between *macrocultures* and *microcultures.* Whereas the dominant culture, or macroculture, of the United States is Anglo–Western European, many microcultures, or groups of people having unique cultural patterns, exist within the country. Ethnic groups, made up of people from the same race, religion, or nationality with the same culture, are microcultures. Examples include African Americans, Jewish Americans, and Latinos. People incorrectly often use the terms *culture* and *ethnicity* interchangeably.

The United States is a culturally pluralistic, or multicultural, society in which different racial and ethnic groups are encouraged to maintain their individual cultures within the broader culture. It was not always this way. During the great immigration period of the late nineteenth and early twentieth centuries, an assimilationist philosophy prevailed. Schools were expected to assimilate immigrant children into the mainstream U.S. culture as quickly as possible. The term *melting pot* was used to describe the process of different ethnic groups giving up their cultural characteristics to become new Americans.

More appropriate as an analogy for cultural pluralism is a salad bowl. Cultural pluralism accepts, encourages, and celebrates cultural diversity. While people maintain their unique identities, they also adopt traits of the broader U.S. culture. There is a balance between cultural similarities and differences, and heritage is seen as a source of the nation's strength. Regarding the role of education in this process, Banks (1993) suggested that the major goal needed to be to change the entire educational environment so that it promoted a respect for a wide range of cultural groups and assured equal educational opportunity for all. Cushner and colleagues (2000) elaborated on the school's role:

> *The children of diversity who are coming into our schools are unlike any previous generation of students seen in American public education. Today, more than ever before, we have the obligation and responsibility to address the needs of children and*

youth from a variety of backgrounds. At the same time, we must begin to prepare the youth in our charge with the perspectives, attitudes, knowledge, and skills which will enable them to interact effectively, satisfy their own needs, as well as work with others to solve the common problems which face a global, interdependent society. (p. 23)

The multicultural education research shows that five areas matter a great deal in the education of multicultural students (Ladson-Billings, 1994). Area 1 is teachers' beliefs about students. Winfield (1986) pointed out that teachers often perceive African American students as incapable of meeting high academic standards. Such negative attitudes lower teacher expectations and, in turn, lower the achievement of minority students and their educational opportunities (Lipman, 1993).

Area 2, which is crucial in multicultural education, is the content and materials used. Superficial celebration of ethnic holidays and heroes trivializes multicultural education. Instead, multicultural emphasis needs to be an ongoing part of the regular curriculum (Ladson-Billings, 1994). Also, "a realistic image of ethnic and racial groups should be included in teaching materials in a consistent, natural, and integrated fashion" (Banks, 1993, p. 253).

Area 3 addresses instructional approaches that ensure equitable pedagogy. Teachers need to examine their instruction to use the best instructional methods that will not handicap or discriminate against any group. Equitable pedagogy may mean using peer tutors for all students or cooperative learning groups. Learning to speak to children in their own language could be a powerful learning tool as well.

Area 4 is educational settings. This area refers to the fact that even though schools are desegregated today, most students of color attend segregated schools. Even if they are in desegregated settings, tracking practices often put them in low-ability groups (Oakes, 1985).

Area 5 is teacher education, crucial in multicultural education and cultural variations in teachers' preservice preparation (Zeichner, 1992). Research shows that many teachers receive little information about multicultural education. Therefore, they may express their biases in discriminatory ways through the handling of or perceptions they have about their students without realizing their practices may be causing differences in student performance and achievement.

Hints for the Beginning Teacher

A good source for ideas on how to integrate multicultural themes into the curriculum can be found in the *Teaching Tolerance* magazine mailed twice a year to educators at no cost. Get on the mailing list at Teaching Tolerance, 400 Washington Avenue, Montgomery, Alabama 36104, or order through fax (334) 956-8486. The Internet address is www.teachingtolerance.org.

■ APPLICATION TO PRACTICE

Dilworth and Brown (2001) identified the following as essential practices for teaching in multicultural classrooms:

1. Build on the cultural wisdom and experience of the students by incorporating these into the daily educational process.
2. Collaborate with parents and the community.
3. Become knowledgeable of cultural learning styles theory.
4. Build the disposition of appreciation for the richness that diversity brings into the classroom.
5. Help students learn how to participate within the power structure of the classroom, school, and community to meet their needs.
6. Encourage group activities where appropriate to increase emphasis on the group rather than the individual.
7. Arrange the curriculum so that students have choices about how they will use their learning time and include many opportunities for experiential learning.

Here are examples of classroom objectives and activities useful in different subject areas to infuse a multicultural emphasis (Iowa Department of Education, 1989):

Language Arts

Objective: Examine how group membership helps determine roles, rights, values, attitudes, and behaviors.

Activity: Students do writing projects on themes such as sisterhood, brotherhood, experiences of acceptance and rejection, belonging to groups, values, and attitudes shaped by their culture.

English

Objective: Same as for language arts.

Activity: Students will do some supplemental reading such as African American historical documents and literature, for example, *The Perils of a Slave Woman's Life,* while studying classic American literature such as *The Scarlet Letter.*

Mathematics

Objective: Demonstrate skills for effective social action across racial, ethnic, sex, culture, and ability groups.

Activity: Students will compete in groups to see which group can build the tallest structure using only paper, tape, scissors, and paper clips. Groups on completion will analyze the team process and examine the amount of cooperation as well as the application of mathematical principles.

Science

Objective: Examine how group membership helps determine values, attitudes, and behaviors.

Activity: Students will compare and contrast attitudes of various groups toward the environment—American Indian, Asians, Hispanics, and so on.

Social Studies

Objective: Describe self and others as cultural beings shaped by a cultural context.

Activity: Students will trace on the U.S. map the movements of their parents, grandparents, and so forth, and write as to who went where, why they moved, and what they did in each place.

The Arts

Objective: Investigate the influence of the cultural perspective in understanding self and others.

Activity: Students will examine various forms of artistic expression of cultural groups in this country, noting similarities and differences of artistic style such as use of color, symbol, texture, line form, and material.

■ INTERNATIONAL/GLOBAL EDUCATION

Along with the multicultural movement in the curriculum, one needs to include international education or global education to expand the world view of students. Although all subject areas of the school curriculum will need to be involved in international, or global, education for a more realistic perspective of the world, by the nature of its content the social studies area has demonstrated the most commitment to achieving this goal. Therefore, it seems fitting to start with a definition of global education by the National Council for the Social Studies (1981):

> *Global education refers to efforts to cultivate in young people a perspective of the world which emphasizes the interconnections among cultures, species, and the planet. The purpose of global education is to develop in youth the knowledge, skills, and attitudes needed to live effectively in a world possessing limited natural resources and characterized by ethnic diversity, cultural pluralism, and increasing interdependence. (p. 1)*

Another narrower, but more publicized, definition of global education that focuses on global economic interdependence can be found in the report of the National Governors' Association (Fleming, 1991). The report advocated an education much more in tune with global changes because "world trade and financial, economic, and political developments have transformed disparate economic systems into a highly interdependent global market place. Today, the nations that inhabit the planet are often more closely linked than neighboring states or villages were at the turn of the century" (p. 11).

■ APPLICATION TO PRACTICE

What should be the content of global education? The National Council for the Social Studies (1994) identified the importance of "global connections and interdependence" as strand 9 of the 10-strand standards network. The council's curriculum standards recommended the following:

> *that students in early grades examine global connections and basic issues and concerns, suggesting and initiating action plans. In the middle years, learners can analyze interactions among states and nations and their cultural complexities as the response to global events and changes. At the high school level, students can think systematically about personal, national, and global decisions, interactions, and consequences, including addressing critical issues such as peace, human rights, trade, and global ecology. (p. 29)*

The Council's study included the following performance expectations for global study:

1. Explore ways that language, art, music, belief systems, and other cultural elements may facilitate global understanding or lead to misunderstanding.
2. Give examples of conflict, cooperation, and interdependence among individuals, groups, and nations.
3. Examine the effects of changing technologies on the global community.
4. Explore causes, consequences, and possible solutions to persistent, contemporary, and emerging global issues, such as pollution and endangered species.
5. Examine the relationships and tensions between personal wants and needs and various global concerns such as use of imported oil, land use, and environmental protection.
6. Investigate concerns, issues, standards, and conflicts related to universal human rights, such as the treatment of children, religious groups, and effects of war. (National Council for the Social Studies, 1994, p. 70)

The following unit idea is an example of incorporating an international focus into the high school social studies curriculum. This unit can be planned to use cooperative-learning groups of three or four students. The Internet can be utilized in the research as well as community resources.

Trading Partners (Gagnon and Collay, 2001, p. 23)

Objective: To examine how global connections affect us, even to the jobs we will hold.

Tasks: Students will investigate how global trade will influence their future employment. Students will explore international trade between continents and determine how it might affect their future jobs. Teachers can specify regions, goods, or services, and jobs, depending on the curriculum. Students list jobs of family and friends and then review the want ads to see the kinds of positions that employers are seeking to fill. Students choose an occupation and a company for the duration of the unit and then list ways the company is linked to international trade.

| APPLICATION for DIVERSE CLASSROOMS |

Teaching multiculturalism and global education involve identifying the pertinent concepts and generalizations to be incorporated within units and lessons, devising and selecting appropriate instructional methods and strategies to teach them, and planning for their use. Effective short- and long-term planning with an emphasis on students' thinking about what they are learning and making personal connections with the content increases the probability that they will be better prepared to assume an informed and active role in our modern multicultural, global society.

■ SUMMARY POINT ■

Effective teachers are familiar with the national curriculum standards developed through the early 1990s. These standards can be a guide to identify key concepts to teach.

Constructivist teaching, a learner-centered approach, emphasizes teaching for understanding and acknowledges that students construct knowledge for themselves based on the knowledge they already have.

Interdisciplinary curriculum is important today because it connects knowledge and builds relationships rather than having knowledge learned in isolation.

Multicultural and international education must be an essential part of the curriculum because our country has many diverse cultures and ethnic groups.

International education emphasizes the interconnectedness among cultures throughout the globe.

PART II: VIEWING CURRICULUM THROUGH INSTRUCTIONAL EYES

■ PEDAGOGICAL CONTENT KNOWLEDGE

Curriculum and instruction are separate entities, but there is a necessary relationship between them. They have been studied and described separately perhaps more than any other elements of the teaching process. However, the relationships between them have not received nearly as much attention. Shulman (1987) used the phrase *pedagogical content knowledge*—a jargony-sounding but usefully descriptive phrase that refers to the linkage between content and delivery. It implies a teacher's in-depth grasp of the subject matter, sensitivity to the possibilities and limitations of the students as learners, and skill in the use of a variety of teaching modes. With the concept of pedagogical content knowledge, we may envision the fully functioning teacher who senses the potential within the subject matter for students' optimal learning, who knows the key concepts and how to develop those concepts in a variety of approaches, and who is able to follow through in designing pertinent learning activities.

■ RESEARCH AND THEORETICAL BASE

Recent research shows that beginning teachers have incomplete and superficial levels of pedagogical content knowledge (Feiman-Nemser and Parker, 1990; Gudmundsdottir and Shulman, 1987; Shulman, 1987). Grossman (1989) found that first-year teachers who had master's degrees but no teacher-education training were less prepared to handle student needs than beginning teachers who had completed teacher training. The former teachers, unable to decide what instructional practices to use, attributed students' lack of understanding to inattentiveness or lack of motivation.

Hashweh (1987) investigated three experienced physics teachers and three experienced biology teachers as to the impact their subject knowledge had on their teaching. When teaching in their field they knew the problems learners had with the content and were more able to provide a variety of accurate examples, analogies, and demonstrations than when they taught outside their field.

Although this research is new and limited, it does show that pedagogical content knowledge is related to knowledge of the content. But it is much more than that: It is knowing how to teach the content in a manner compatible with the subject area (Cochran, DeRuiter, and King, 1993).

■ APPLICATION TO PRACTICE

The assumptions of pedagogical content knowledge may at first be discouraging to the prospective or novice teacher. A bachelor's degree preparation for teaching is obviously not sufficient to prepare one to comply fully with the expectations implied by pedagogical content knowledge. However, it suggests a direction for the continuing development of every teacher, that is, the acquisition of increasingly effective ways of contributing to students' intellectual maturation. Fenstermacher (1986) made the point that teacher education is not intended to prescribe ways of teaching as such but more importantly to show prospective teachers how to think about teaching.

Shulman maintained that how teachers developed examples and models affected how students understand subject matter (1986). He suggested a process that he called *transformation*, whereby teachers would address the task of transferring the learning possibilities they conceived to the minds of the learners. He stated that transformation occurred through some combinations of the following steps rather than rigid adherence to an explicit ordering (p. 16):

1. Preparation (of the given text materials) including the process of critical interpretation.

2. Representation of the new ideas in the form of new analogies, metaphors, and so forth.

3. Instructional selections from among an array of teaching methods and models.

4. Adaptation of these representations to the general characteristics of the children.

5. Tailoring the adaptations to the specific youngsters in the classroom.

He added that "these forms of transformation, these aspects of the process wherein one moves from personal comprehension to preparing for the comprehension of others, are the essence of the act of pedagogical reasoning, of teaching as thinking, and of planning—whether explicitly or implicitly—the performance of teaching" (p. 16).

Some examples of pedagogical content knowledge will be helpful in further understanding the concept. Consider Sally, a seventh-grade mathematics teacher, who became aware that many students were experiencing difficulty with understanding the concept of percent. After talking with several students who were having difficulty, she realized that to them percent represented a new level of abstraction in mathematics. Percent did not refer to absolute quantities like all the mathematical constructs they had studied up to that time, but rather to an implied ratio that had meaning only as it was applied (usually) as a multiplication factor. Repeating "percent means hundredths" many times during each class meeting proved to be ineffective. What, wondered Sally, existed in their experience that would help them make a connection with percent? It occurred to her that the idea of 100 cents to a dollar would be familiar to them. Sally provided those students who continued to have problems with packets of pennies and gave them the tactile and visual experience of manipulating the pennies as she guided them in thinking in terms of percent. As a result, all her students achieved the mastery-level working knowledge of percent. Meanwhile, the remainder of the class had gone on to work with decimal percents and finding a number when a percent of it is given, based on problems the students cooperatively made up.

In this relatively simple example, Sally used her understanding of percent and her ability to think from her students' perspective to create an effective learning activity. The idea for the activity emerged from the combination of the topic and a relevant learning principle—using past learning as a connector to new learning—to create a bridge to students' new learning. Further, Sally did not feel constrained to keep the class together, which would have resulted in either the quicker students becoming bored or the slower ones being left behind.

Another example (Parrish, 1991) involves a case in which Clark, a social studies teacher, wanted his students to comprehend the concept of invention and the role of inventions in contributing to the evolution of a society. He asked the class members to play a mind game and invent something that would make life easier. As an example, he suggested a machine that would grade essay tests. The students responded with ideas such as a time machine that would allow one to go back and undo the effects of bad decisions, a golf club that eliminated hooks and slices, a three-dimensional television, and a fold-up parking meter that could be used anyplace free of charge. Clark selected two of them to discuss in terms of their advantages and disadvantages. It came as a surprise to the students that seemingly desirable inventions had a negative side, as well. When this had been established, the students were prepared to understand the effect of the cotton gin on the South at the turn of the nineteenth century. Along with the effect of bringing high profits to the plantation owners, it raised the value of slaves and stimulated the slave trade, and because cotton is hard on the land, much land was depleted by overgrowing cotton. In subsequent units, when such inventions as the steam engine and sewing machine were important topics, the students would better understand their effects.

Clark might simply have had the students read about these events in their history books, or he might have talked about them in a lecture. But allowing the students to "develop" their own inventions and determine their effects lent a dimension of personal meaning that would otherwise not have existed. Clark understood his topic well and realized that a powerful insight lay beyond the fact of the cotton gin, so he employed a method that tapped into the potential of the topic. This, indeed, is an application of pedagogical content knowledge.

A final example of this bridge between content and instructions is of Judy's general science class. In a unit on astronomy, Judy wanted students to acquire an elementary understanding of the relationship of Earth with the visible bodies in the universe. One of the bodies that has special significance is Polaris, the North Star. It would have been a simple matter to explain the facts related to Polaris, but as she considered her objective, she felt it might be more effective if she presented it as a discrepant event that needed to be investigated further. So she told the class that of the 6,000 visible objects in the sky, only one appeared not to move, that it was always in the same position when we looked for it. She told the class that they could ask questions, but she would answer only yes or no until they could determine the reason for this discrepant event and identify the particular body.

The process of inquiry is used all too rarely in classrooms. Yet, it is a powerful mode of thinking and learning that contributes to students' reasoning powers. When the nature of the content is such that it lends itself to inquiry, the teacher who has a sufficient measure of pedagogical content knowledge will recognize it and conduct the inquiry that will be both motivating and useful to the class.

Pedagogical content knowledge is a powerful concept in the interest of educators as they aspire to move education to the status of a major profession. According to Shulman (1987),

> *Pedagogical content knowledge is the category most likely to distinguish the understanding of the content specialist from that of the pedagogue. . . . We expect a math major to understand mathematics or a history specialist to comprehend history. But the key to distinguishing the knowledge base of teaching lies at the intersection of content and pedagogy, in the capacity of a teacher to transform the content knowledge he or she possesses into forms that are pedagogically powerful and yet adaptive to the variations in ability and background presented by the students. (pp. 8–15)*

Building on the research and writing of Shulman, Grossman and Stodolsky (1994) point out that knowing the content and knowing methods are not enough. The teacher must take into account ". . . the specific grade level . . . the school's organization, mission, culture, and location, and the district, state, and national contexts in which teaching and learning occur" (p. 180).

Therefore, as you plan for instruction, to translate your discipline into powerful learning experiences for your students and make the curriculum come alive in young minds, you will need a generous measure of pedagogical content knowledge—knowing what strategies are most effective for encouraging student learning—and taking into consideration the students' development, school's mission, and local and state environments. All these and more impact the teacher's decision making.

■ STRUCTURE OF KNOWLEDGE

To be an effective teacher with pedagogical content knowledge, one must have a thorough understanding of one's content area, a knowledge that will keep learners designing or redesigning their cognitive structuring of important content. Gardner (1991) points out that information is transformed into understanding when the mind creates new cognitive structures or reshapes present ones. (Angeletta Rodrigo in the scenario knew the importance of building a knowledge structure for concepts that she taught as she decided to make that structure graphic with a web.)

Traditional education approaches often present broad coverage of subject areas and encourage memorization or repeating of chunks of information. The curriculum is broken down into pieces, and students concentrate on learning these pieces without seeing how the pieces fit together and what the structure of the whole is. Facts remain facts and are not tied into concepts. The emphasis is on basic skills, fact-driven content, and proceeding "part" to "whole." In constructivist classrooms, the curriculum is presented "whole" to "part," with emphasis on big concepts. Constructivist teachers organize information around concepts with conceptual clusters of problems, questions, and discrepant events (Brooks and Brooks, 1993). This approach is consistent with the new findings about learning from cognitive science (Doyle, 1992). "Structuring curriculum around primary concepts is a critical dimension of constructivist pedagogy" (Brooks and Brooks, 1993, p. 46). When students can break down the concept into parts that they can see and understand, they then can make sense of the concept. Curricular activities designed by both the teacher and the students around broad concepts can help students with understanding.

Whether teachers intend to teach in the constructivist approach or combine traditional and constructivist practices, they must understand the structure of the knowledge that they are teaching to be effective with content pedagogy. In other words, when planning instruction, teachers think about the subject matter they are going to teach. They then are operating in the cognitive domain—the domain of learning that focuses on academic or intellectual content. The structure of that content can be examined as facts, concepts, and generalizations. Forming that content into various intellectual operations from which objectives are formed can be examined using Bloom's taxonomy (see Chapter 5, which deals with planning).

This structure of knowledge can readily be illustrated by a pyramid (Figure 4.2) that visually displays the relationship of facts to concepts and generalizations in terms of quantity and quality.

There are billions of isolated facts, but there are fewer concepts because concepts are formed from facts and serve as their organizers. Generalizations are at the top of the pyramid because there are even fewer generalizations than concepts. Generalizations are statements expressing the relationship of concepts; hence, concepts are embedded in them. Another reason generalizations are at the top is because they are

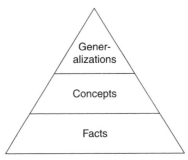

Figure 4.2   Structure of Knowledge

the most abstract form of knowledge generally studied by elementary and secondary students. Formal theories are actually the highest form of knowledge but are not generally studied until the college level. As abstractions, generalizations are more easily transferred to other situations, which makes them more applicable and useful for learning. Whereas facts are specific and have the least generality, concepts involve some degree of generality, and generalizations are compounded concepts. Most of the instructional content taught in elementary and secondary schools is from the factual and conceptual levels.

Facts

A *fact* is a "statement about concepts that is true or verified for a particular case on the basis of the best evidence available" (Martorella, 1991, p. 150). Factual knowledge "consists of specific data about events, objects, people, or other things that can be or have been verified by the senses" (Banks, Banks, and Clegg, 1999, p. 78). In addition, facts are restricted to a particular time and place. There is a major problem with teaching facts as the basis of identifying and organizing content because they have little transfer value from situation to situation. Facts best serve to illustrate concepts and support generalizations. When planning units and lessons, the concern should be to identify those facts that are useful to teach a particular concept or generalization (Armstrong, 1980). This not only suggests that the only worthwhile facts to teach are those that serve as evidence for higher forms of knowledge but also that those taught in isolation of concepts and generalizations will not contribute to meaningful learning. Facts taught in isolation may be memorized and retained for a short time but, without linkages to concepts and generalizations, tend to be forgotten soon after the test.

Concepts

"Concepts are the ideas or abstractions formed as a result of categorizing data from a number of observations" (Gunter, Estes, and Schwab, 1990, p. 98). They are names given to categories formed as factual information is classified. Concepts enable us to group together different things that have some similarities. In a sense, concepts are created to help people be more efficient in their communication. They help us sort out the many events, people, ideas, objects, and other phenomena with which we come in contact daily, formally and informally. Martorella (1990) remarked that "concepts allow us to organize and store similar pieces of information efficiently. Once formed, they eliminate our need to treat each new piece of knowledge as a separate category. In a sense, concepts are hooks on which we can hang new experiences" (p. 190). This sorting-out process, or categorization, helps us reduce the complexity of our environment. Comprehension is enhanced because concepts facilitate communication and, most importantly, they assist in the transfer of learning. This is the primary reason why concepts, as a higher form of learning, should become the basis of the content to be taught and the focus of teaching (along with generalizations).

We now have reached a general consensus through cognitive science that every human being constructs his or her own meanings about knowledge and how things work in the world on the basis of knowledge already possessed. We organize that knowledge into concepts and subconcepts. *Concepts* are labeled events or records of events or objects that we can define and understand because they occur with regularity. They have critical characteristics that help identify them from other concepts. For example, fruits have critical characteristics that distinguish them from vegetables. Within the fruit concept group are subconcepts of different types of fruits. They, too, have critical characteristics of their concept group but also have distinguishing characteristics from others in their groups—differences between apples from oranges.

Acquiring new concepts is done either by *discovery,* the way young children learn, or by *reception learning.* Reception learning is the way many students learn in schools—by memorization of concepts or processes—but students may not see the regularities or critical characteristics in events, objects, or relationships designated by these new concepts (Novak, 1990). This is rote learning without understanding. Understanding enables the student to see the regularity in the event or the activity. Rote learning does not build on prior knowledge and is not influenced by misconceptions that we all hold about how things work. Novak (1991) points out that rote-memory knowledge is usually retained for only two or three weeks and is not stored in long-term memory because it is not attached to our past knowledge structures. Therefore, students who do poorly on science or math achievement tests may not have developed an adequate concept structure. Even repetition of science information from year to year will not help if understanding of concepts is not present.

Hints for the Beginning Teacher

Do not assume that students come to you with a concept structure in place to make the necessary connections to new information. Take the time to find out what students know, what misinformation they have about the content, and where no structure exists, create structures for new information (Jenson, 1998).

TABLE 4.1   FACTS, CONCEPTS, AND GENERALIZATIONS

Generalizations with Embedded Concepts	Examples of Related Facts
All *matter* in the *universe* is affected by *gravity*.	Jupiter's gravitational pull keeps its moons in orbit around it.
Different kinds of *materials* respond differently to *electric forces*.	In metal materials, electric charges flow easily. In glass, electric charges can hardly move at all.
One may divide the category of *motion* into steady motion, speeding up, and slowing down.	Newton developed the laws of motion.
Fundamental forces of nature include *gravitational* and *electromagnetic* forces.	The Earth moves at a rate of 67,000 mph.

Generalizations

Generalizations are broad statements that serve as principles expressing the relationship of two or more concepts. Facts are different because they are based on single events; generalizations emerge from a large body of information. Generalizations are similar to facts in that they "are propositional in nature; that is, they are true only so far as available evidence continues to support their truth" (Armstrong, 1980, p. 31). Like facts, generalizations are verifiable and a doubted generalization becomes a hypothesis to be tested with data. Generalizations hold power for teaching because they are inferences based on large sets of data that can be used to make predictions. Predicting is a higher-level critical-thinking skill. Moreover, because generalizations have predictive qualities, they are easily transferable to other situations. "The synthesis represented by a generalization provides the student with a broad, wide-reaching state that applies to the past and the present and to all cases everywhere" (Martorella, 1991, p. 153).

Table 4.1 shows the relationship of facts, concepts, and generalizations through illustrations adapted from a science curriculum.

■ WEBSITE RESOURCE ■

The Eisenhower National Clearinghouse for Mathematics and Science Education website has a wide range of information, curriculum resources, web links, professional development opportunities, general topics in science and math, and current events:

Some of the subtopics are free stuff, frequently asked questions, lesson plans and activities, professional resources funding opportunities, standards, equity and diversity, implementing technology, assessment, inquiry, and problem solving.

www.enc.org

■ WEBSITE RESOURCE ■

The ERIC Clearinghouse for Social Studies/Social Science Education contains databases for information about social science content and teaching strategies at

www.indiana.edu/~ssdc/eric_chess.htm.

The ERIC/ChESS database is a component of ERIC, which is supported by the U.S. Depart-ment of Education. The primary database of interest to social studies teachers is the *Digest*, which contains brief introductions to many current topics, plus a bibliography of related resources. Eight or more *Digests* are published each year with full text available.

■ CONCEPT MAPPING

Consider now a technique that enables students to chart the structure of new knowledge for themselves. The technique is called concept mapping. Concept mapping is an educational tool that one of the authors is using in her courses to help students see the structure of key concepts and fields in which they will be teaching. Concept maps can be used with any subject matter. They are two-dimensional representations of cognitive structures that show the hierarchies and the interrelatedness of concepts involved in a discipline or a sub-discipline (Novak and Gowin, 1984). They are most effective when students construct their own personal concept maps for topics they are studying. The practice takes time as students struggle with key ideas and definitions to fit them into what they already know and then begin to see new relationships, new meanings.

The author's experience is that each time she teaches a course she constructs a concept map that continues to change with the added insights gained from the previous teaching experiences. Students are asked to design their own concept maps of the content as the course progresses. A map for a single class session may include many concepts and subscripts. Having students draw the map at the end of a session in which new information is introduced is a good way to check on their understanding.

■ RESEARCH AND THEORETICAL BASE

Concept mapping is based on Ausubel's (1968) assimilation theory that what is most important in learning is what the learner already knows and how the new learning will interface with or relate to previous knowledge.

Joe Novak and associates at Cornell introduced concept mapping in 1972. Since then, it has gained acceptance particularly by science teachers in many parts of the globe. Some of the research claims for the effectiveness of concept mapping in learning science have been reported by Okebukola (1990); Novak (1990); Wandersee (1990); and Rye and Rubba (1998).

■ APPLICATION TO PRACTICE

The pattern to use in making concept maps was originated by Novak (1990) and Wandersee (1990). Okebukola (1992, p. 218) reported the steps the student should take as follows:

- The student notes the key words/concepts, phrases, or ideas that are used during the lesson or read in the text.
- The student arranges the concept and main ideas in a hierarchy from the most general, inclusive, and abstract to the most specific and concrete.
- The student draws circles or ellipses around the concepts.
- The student connects the concepts (in circles) by means of lines or arrows accompanied by linking words so that each branch of the map can be read from the top down.
- The student provides examples, if possible, at the terminus of each branch.
- The student cross-links hierarchies or branching of the map where appropriate.

For a more simplified approach to concept mapping called webbing, try these four generalized steps that are a part of the Novak steps but do not require as much specificity. This approach works well with concepts that are not made up of parts that can be arranged in a hierarchy. Linking words are not used in this approach. The four steps in webbing include the following (Morine-Dershimer, 1990):

1. List all the words or phrases connected with your topic or concept.
2. Group the words or phrases together in an order that makes sense to you.
3. Label your groups according to the characteristics your groups have in common.
4. Draw a web that shows your groups and subgroups in relation to each other and to the major concept or topic (see Figure 4.3).

Our experience has been that when students are required to construct their own personal concept maps for topics they are studying, they find new meanings in the subject and new ways to relate what they already know to the content they are learning. In short, concept maps constructed by students help them to learn meaningfully. Subject matter ceases to be a mass of definitions to be memorized or problems to be solved by the routine plugging in of numbers or symbols into abstract formulas.

Concept maps are no magic bullet. It usually takes several months of regular practice and feedback to teach students how to construct good concept maps; webs are easier to form. The teacher must also take the time to learn how to teach students to do concept maps and to learn to become a constructive critic, allowing students to create maps meaningful to them. Concept maps are to be redrawn as students see and construct new relationships. Students need to be able to talk about their maps and explain their structure.

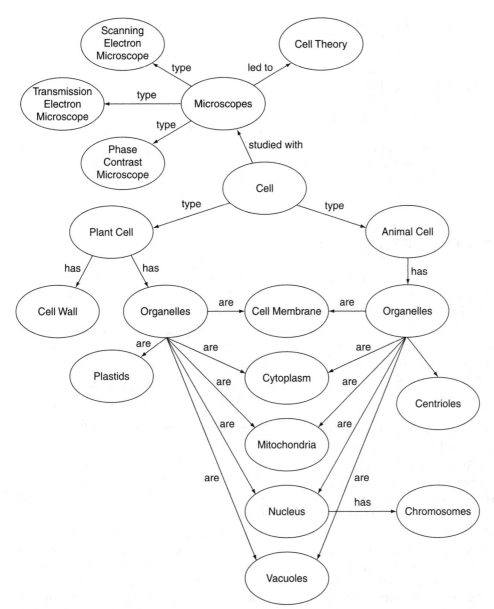

Figure 4.3 Concept Map from a Class Demonstration on Cells

Reprinted by permission from Lynne Anderson-Inman and Leigh Zeitz, "Computer-based concept mapping: Active studying for active learners," *The Computing Teacher,* August–September 1993, 21(1), 8.

■ SUMMARY POINT ■

Pedagogical content knowledge is the intersection of curriculum and instruction wherein teachers use their grasp of content and the students' understanding or misunderstanding to transform the content into forms that are easily learned.

Teachers employ pedagogical content knowledge to present content in suitable classroom representations.

The structure of knowledge in school curriculum is displayed in facts, concepts, and generalizations. A fact is a statement about a concept that present evidence verifies as true. A concept is the key to our understanding. It is the form in which we categorize knowledge. Generalizations are broad statements that express the relationship between two or more concepts.

Concept mapping is an educational tool that helps students see the structure of key concepts and topics. Webbing is a simplified approach to concept mapping conducted by listing key words connected with the concept, grouping words in a sensible order, labeling groups, and drawing a diagram that shows the groups and their relationships to each other.

■ QUESTIONS FOR REFLECTION ■

1. Why do you believe the authors included a chapter on curriculum in a book on effective teaching? What other topics might you have included in the chapter?

2. Do you believe that national curriculum standards and assessment are important for the country as we move into the twenty-first century?

3. If the United States were to adopt a national curriculum, how would the roles of the teacher and the school district change?

4. How do you see the constructivist approach to education differing from the traditional approach? What do you see as advantages and possible disadvantages of the constructivist approach?

5. Do you have to develop an interdisciplinary unit in your methods class? If so, what is the planning procedure you are going through? Do you believe that you are able to address the concepts and skills you consider important as effectively as you could focusing on them in isolation? What do you see as the advantages and disadvantages of interdisciplinary curriculum?

6. Do teachers present subject matter differently to more and less capable students? What have you observed?

7. How are you preparing yourself to address multicultural education in your classroom?

8. What example can you give to demonstrate your understanding of content pedagogy?

9. Have you tried drawing a concept map or web for effective teaching of a unit you are teaching? What big ideas would you include in it?

10. How do you see K–12 textbooks structured? Are they emphasizing concepts and the connection of concepts, or do you get the feeling that they are presenting many facts that are disconnected? Would they be helpful to you if you were teaching for depth rather than breadth?

■ REFERENCES ■

Adams, A. (2001). "Integrated instructional units: Teaching for the real world." In J. Brown and A. Adams (Eds.), *Constructivist Teaching Strategies.* Springfield, IL: Charles C. Thomas.

Aiken, W. (1942). *The Story of an Eight-Year Study.* New York: Harper & Row.

Alexander, P., and Murphy, P. (1994). "The research base for APA's learner-centered psychological principles." Paper presented at American Educational Research Association Meeting, New Orleans.

Anderson, L. F. (1991). "A rationale for global education." In K. Tye (Ed.), *Global Education: 1991 Yearbook of the Association for Supervision and Curriculum Development.* Alexandria, VA: Association for Supervision and Curriculum Development.

Anderson, R. (1984). "Role of the reader's schema in comprehension, learning, and memory." In R. Anderson, J. Osborn, and R. Tierney (Eds.). *Learning to Read in American Schools: Basal Readers and Content Texts.* Hillsdale, NJ: Lawrence Erlbaum.

Anderson-Inman, L., and Zeitz, L. (1993). "Computer-based concept mapping: Active studying for active learners." *The Computing Teacher, 21*(1), 8.

Armstrong, D. (1980). *Social Studies in Secondary Education.* New York: Macmillan.

Ausubel, D. (1968). *Educational Psychology: A Cognitive View.* New York: Holt, Rinehart & Winston.

Banks, J. (1993). "Multicultural education for young children: Racial and ethnic attitudes and their modification." In B. Spodek (Ed.), *Handbook of Research on the Education of Young Children.* New York: Macmillan.

Banks, J. (1996). "Multicultural education: For freedom's sake." In E. Hollins (Ed.), *Transforming Curriculum for a Culturally Diverse Society.* Mahwah, NJ: Lawrence Erlbaum.

Banks, J., Banks, C., and Clegg, A. (1999). *Teaching Strategies for the Social Studies* (5th ed.). New York: Longman.

Beane, J. (1995). "Curriculum integration and the disciplines of knowledge." *Phi Delta Kappan, 76*(8) 616–622.

Brooks, J., and Brooks, M. (1993). *The Case for Constructivist Classrooms.* Alexandria, VA: Association for Supervision and Curriculum Development.

Brown, J., and Adams, A. (Eds.) (2001). *Constructivist Teaching Strategies.* Springfield, IL: Charles C. Thomas.

Bruer, J. (1997). "Education and the brain: A bridge too far." *Educational Researcher, 26*(8), 4–16.

Bruner, J. (1964). "The course of cognitive growth." *American Psychologist, 19,* 1–15.

Caine, R., and Caine, G. (1997). *Education on the Edge of Possibility.* Alexandria, VA: Association for Supervision and Curriculum Development.

Carr, J., and Harris, D. (2001). *Succeeding with Standards.* Alexandria, VA: Association for Supervision and Curriculum Development.

Caswell, H., and Campbell, D. (1935). *Curriculum Development.* New York: American Book.

Cochran, K., DeRuiter, J., and King, R. (1993). "Pedagogical content knowing: An integrative model for teacher preparation." *Journal of Teacher Education, 44*(4), 263–272.

Cushner, K., McClelland, A., and Safford, P. (2000). *Human Diversity and Education: An Integrative Approach* (3rd ed.). New York: McGraw-Hill.

Darling-Hammond, L. (1993). "Reframing the school reform agenda." *Phi Delta Kappan,* (June), 753–761.

Dewey, J. (1938). *Experience and Education.* New York: Macmillan.

Dilworth, M., and Brown, C. (2001). "Consider the difference: Teaching and learning in culturally rich schools." In V. Richardson (Ed.), *The Handbook of Research on Teaching.* Washington, DC: American Educational Research Associates.

Doyle, W. (1992). "Curriculum and pedagogy." In P. Jackson (Ed.), *Handbook of Research on Curriculum.* New York: Macmillan.

Eisner, E. (1990). "Creative curriculum development and practice." *Journal of Curriculum and Supervision, 6*(1), 62–73.

Feiman-Nemser, S., and Parker, M. (1990). "Making subject matter part of the conversation in learning to teach." *Journal of Teacher Education, 41*(3), 32–43.

Fenstermacher, G. (1986). "Philosophy of research on teaching: Three aspects." In M. Wittrock (Ed.), *Handbook of Research on Teaching* (3rd ed.). New York: Macmillan.

Fleming, D. B. (1991). "Social studies reform and global education." *The Social Studies, 82,* 11–15.

Fosnot, C. (1996). *Constructivism: Theory, Perspectives, and Practice.* New York: Teachers College Press.

Fuchs, D., Fuchs, L., Mathes, P., and Simmons, D. (1995). "Peer-assisted learning strategies: Making classrooms more responsive to diversity." *American Educational Research Journal, 34*(1), 176.

Gagnon, G., and Collay, M. (2001). *Designing for Learning: Six Elements in Constructivist Classrooms.* Thousand Oaks, CA: Corwin Press.

Gardner, H. (1991). *The Unschooled Mind: How Children Think and How Schools Should Teach.* New York: Basic Books.

Good, T. (1996). "Teaching effects and teacher evaluation." In J. Sikula (Ed.), *Handbook of Research on Teacher Education* (2nd ed.). New York: Macmillan.

Good, T., and Brophy, J. (2000). *Looking in Classrooms* (8th ed.). New York: Addison Wesley Longman.

Grossman, P. (1989). "A study in contrast: Sources of pedagogical content knowledge for secondary English." *Journal of Teacher Education, 40*(5), 24–31.

Grossman, P., and Stodolsky, S. (1994). "Considerations of content and the circumstances of secondary school teaching." In L. Darling-Hammond (Ed.), *Review of Research in Education* (Vol. 20, pp. 179–221). Washington, DC: American Educational Research Association.

Gudmundsdottir, S., and Shulman, L. (1987). "Pedagogical content knowledge in social studies." *Scandinavian Journal of Educational Research, 31,* 59–70.

Gunter, M., Estes, T., and Schwab, J. (1990). *Instruction: A Models Approach.* Boston: Allyn & Bacon.

Haberman, M., and Post, L. (1990). "Cooperating teachers' perceptions of the goals of multicultural education." *Action in Teacher Education, 12*(3), 31–35.

Hargreaves, A., and Moore, S. (2000). "Curriculum integration and classroom relevance: A study of teachers' practice." *Journal of Curriculum and Supervision, 15*(2), 89–112.

Hashweh, M. (1987). "Effects of subject matter knowledge in the teaching of biology and physics." *Teaching and Teacher Education, 3,* 109–120.

Hyerle, D. (1996). *Visual Tools for Constructing Knowledge.* Alexandria, VA: Association for Supervision and Curriculum Development.

Iowa Department of Education (1989). *A Guide to Developing Multicultural, Nonsexist Education Across the Curriculum.* Des Moines, Iowa: Author.

Jacobs, H. (1989). *Interdisciplinary Curriculum: Design and Implementation.* Alexandria, VA: Association for Supervision and Curriculum Development.

Jenson, E. (1998). *Introduction to Brain Compatible Learning.* Del Mar, CA: Turning Point.

Kendall, J., and Marzano, R. (1996). *Content Knowledge: A Compendium of Standards and Benchmarks for K–12 Education.* Aurora, CO: Mid-continent Regional Educational Laboratory.

Ladson-Billings, G. (1994). "What we can learn from multicultural education research." *Educational Leadership* (April), 22–26.

Lipman, P. (1993). *Teacher Ideology Toward African-American Students in Restructured Schools.* Unpublished doctoral dissertation, University of Wisconsin, Madison.

Lockhead, J. (1985). *New Horizon in Educational Development: Review of Research in Education.* Washington, DC: American Educational Research Association.

Mallery, A. (2000). *Creating a Catalyst for Thinking.* Boston: Allyn & Bacon.

Marlowe, B., and Page, M. (1998). *Creating and Sustaining the Constructivist Classroom.* Thousand Oaks, CA: Corwin Press.

Martinello, M., and Cook, G. (1994). *Interdisciplinary Inquiry in Teaching and Learning.* New York: Macmillan.

Martorella, P. (1990). "Teaching concepts." In J. Cooper (Ed.), *Classroom Teaching Skills* (4th ed.). Lexington, MA: Heath.

Martorella, P. (1991). *Teaching Social Studies in Middle and Secondary Schools.* New York: Macmillan.

McDonnell, L., and Hill, P. (1993). *Newcomers in American Schools: Meeting the Needs of Immigrant Youth.* Santa Monica, CA: Rand Cooperation.

McNeil, J. (1995). *Curriculum: The Teachers' Initiative.* Upper Saddle River, NJ: Prentice Hall.

Moore, K. (2001). *Classroom Teaching Skills.* Boston: McGraw-Hill.

Morine-Dershimer, G. (1990). "Instructional planning." In J. Cooper (Ed.), *Classroom Teaching Skills* (4th ed.). Lexington, MA: Heath.

National Commission on Excellence in Education. (1983). *A Nation At Risk.* Washington, DC: U.S. Department of Education.

National Council for the Social Studies (1981). *Global Education: Position Statement.* Washington, DC: Author.

National Council for the Social Studies (1994). *Expectation of Excellence: Curriculum Standards for Social Studies.* Washington, DC: Author.

National Council of Teachers of Mathematics (1989). *Cumulative and Evaluation Standards for School Mathematics.* Reston, VA: Author.

National Council of Teachers of Mathematics (1991). *Professional Standards for Teaching Mathematics.* Reston, VA: Author.

Nelson, D. (1985). *City Building Education.* Los Angeles: Center for City Building Education Programs.

New Standards Project. (2002). www.ncee.org/OurPrograms/nsPage.html.

Newman, D., Griffin, P., and Cole, M. (1989). *The Construction Zone: Working for Cognitive Change in School.* Cambridge: Cambridge University Press.

Novak, J. (1990). "Concept maps and vee diagrams: Two metacognitive tools to facilitate meaningful learning." *Instructional Science, 19,* 29–52.

Novak, J., and Gowin, D. (1984). *Learning How to Learn.* New York: Cambridge University Press.

Oakes, J. (1985). *Keeping Track: How Schools Structure Inequitably.* New Haven, CT: Yale University Press.

Okebukola, P. (1990). "Attaining meaningful learning of concepts in genetics and ecology: A test of the efficacy of the concept-mapping heuristic." *Journal of Research in Science, 27*(5), 493–504.

Okebukola, P. (1992). "Concept mapping with a cooperative learning flavor." *The American Biology Teacher, 54*(4), 218–221.

O'Neil, J. (1993). "Can national standards make a difference?" *Educational Leadership, 50*(5), 4–8.

O'Neil, J. (1997–1998). "Why are all the black kids sitting together?" *Educational Leadership, 55*(4), 12–17.

Orlich, D. (2000). " Education reform and limits to student achievement," *Phi Delta Kappan, 81*(6), 468–472.

Ornstein, A., and Hunkins, F. (1993). *Curriculum—Foundations, Principles, and Theory* (2nd ed.). Boston: Allyn & Bacon.

Parrish, C. (1991). Unpublished lesson plan, Kent State University, Kent, Ohio.

Pasch, M., Sparks-Langer, G., Gardner, T. G., Starko, A. J., and Moody, C. D. (1991). *Teaching as Decision Making.* New York: Longman.

Perkins, D., and Blythe, T. (1994). "Putting understanding up front." *Educational Leadership, 51*(5), 4–7.

Peters, T., Schubeck, K., and Hopkins, K. (1995). "A thematic approach." *Phi Delta Kappan, 76*(8), 633–636.

Piaget, J. (1952). *The Origins of Intelligence in Children.* New York: International University Press.

Resnick, L., and Klopfer, L. (Eds.). (1989). *Toward the Thinking Curriculum: Current Cognitive Research: 1989 Yearbook of the Association for Supervision and Curriculum Development.* Alexandria, VA: Association for Supervision and Curriculum Development.

Roberts, P., and Kellough, R. (2000). *A Guide for Developing Interdisciplinary Thematic Units.* Upper Saddle River, NJ: Merrill.

Rye, J., and Rubba, P. (1998). "An exploration of the concept map as an interview tool to facilitate the externalization of students' understandings about global atmospheric change." *Journal of Research in Science Teaching, 35*(5) 521–545.

Shulman, L. (1986). "Those who understand: Knowledge growth in teaching." *Educational Researcher, 15*, 4–14.

Shulman, L. (1987). "Knowledge and teaching: Foundations of the new reform." *Harvard Educational Review, 57*, 1–22.

Shulman, L. (1990). *Aristotle Had It Right: On Knowledge and Pedagogy* (Occasional Paper No. 4). East Lansing, MI: Holmes Group.

Siegel, I., and Cocking, R. (1977). *Cognitive Development from Childhood to Adolescence: A Constructivist Perspective.* New York: Holt, Rinehart & Winston.

Simmons, R. (1994). "The horse before the cart: Assessing for understanding." *Educational Leadership, 51*(5), 22–23.

Solomon, P. (1998). *The Curriculum Bridge.* Thousand Oaks, CA: Corwin Press.

Stiggins, R. (2002). "Assessment crisis: The absence of assessment for learning." *Phi Delta Kappan, 83*(10), 758–765.

Tierney, R. (1990). "Redefining reading comprehension." *Educational Leadership, 47*(3), 37–42.

Von Glasersfeld, E. (1981). "The concepts of adaptation and viability in a radical constructivist theory of knowledge." In I. Sigel, B. Brodinsky, and R. Golinkoff (Eds.), *New Directions in Piagetian Theory and Practice.* Hillsdale, NY: Lawrence Erlbaum.

Wandersee, J. (1990). "Concept mapping and the cartography of cognition." *Journal of Research in Science Teaching, 27*(10), 923–936.

Washington, V., and Andrews, J. (1998). *Children of 2010.* Washington, DC: National Association for the Education of Young Children.

Wigginton, E. (1989). "Foxfire grows up." *Harvard Educational Review, 59*(1), 24–49.

Winfield, L. (1986). "Teacher beliefs toward at-risk students in inner-urban schools." *The Urban Review, 18*, 253–267.

Wiske, M. (Ed.). (1998). *Teaching for Understanding.* San Francisco: Jossey-Bass.

Woods, R. (1994). "A close-up look at how children learn science." *Educational Leadership, 519*(5), 33–35.

Zeichner, K. (1992). *Educating Teachers for Cultural Diversity.* East Lansing, MI: National Center for Research in Teacher Learning.

5

Planning for Teaching

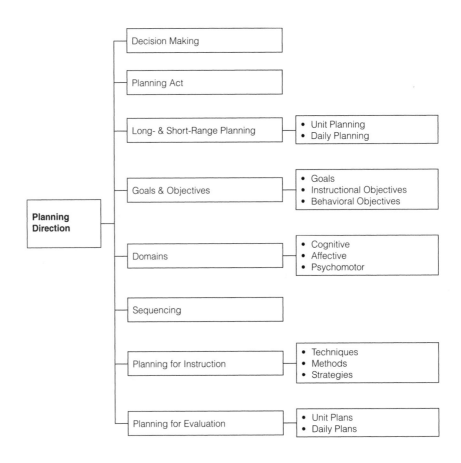

Planning Direction

- Decision Making
- Planning Act
- Long- & Short-Range Planning
  - Unit Planning
  - Daily Planning
- Goals & Objectives
  - Goals
  - Instructional Objectives
  - Behavioral Objectives
- Domains
  - Cognitive
  - Affective
  - Psychomotor
- Sequencing
- Planning for Instruction
  - Techniques
  - Methods
  - Strategies
- Planning for Evaluation
  - Unit Plans
  - Daily Plans

All teachers plan. No teacher enters the classroom without having an idea of what to present (except perhaps those unfortunate substitute teachers who arrive at the school and find that no plans are available for their use). However, the nature of plans differs widely from teacher to teacher. Some plans may be quite structured and comprehensive, such as when a physics teacher prepares students to engage in a complex and intricate laboratory experiment. Others might be less structured, such as when a government teacher prepares questions for guiding a discussion to help students develop meaning about a civic issue. Other plans might exist only as vague intentions in the mind of the teacher. Teachers who are particularly glib may consider winging it without benefit of much deliberate planning to be a sufficient practice. Few conscientious educators would agree.

Sound planning contributes to good teaching. Claims to the contrary are likely to involve self-serving rationalizing, if not outright naiveté. The issue is not whether one should plan but how one should plan. No single answer fits all cases. Some teachers, especially inexperienced teachers, are likely to find rather detailed plans to be beneficial. Other teachers may find that less specific plans, but plans that nevertheless contribute to purpose and direction in the lesson or unit, are more useful.

To some extent, plans are the extension of the teacher's personality and instructional style. As Hoover (1972) observed, they are, in that sense, a personal invention on the part of each teacher. The teacher who is basically a structured person will take a different approach to planning than a free spirit will. One could hardly use the plans of the other effectively, even while covering the same topic. The approach taken in this book attempts to accommodate a wide range of personalities, teaching styles, grade levels, subject areas, and teacher experience, while stressing the necessity for conscientious, soundly conceived planning.

Many different approaches to planning are practiced by teachers. Planning, broadly defined, includes those teacher activities that organize school- and student-related activities (Clark and Yinger, 1980). A general definition such as this takes into account the diversity of teachers' personalities and styles: formal, detailed planning for highly structured teachers and more informal approaches for those who are less structured. From this perspective, it is relatively easy to adapt a broad definition of planning to the more specific task of instructional planning. Within this context, plans are designs for guiding students' involvement in learning activities.

■ OVERVIEW

Starting with the premise that effective teaching in large part reflects careful planning, this chapter endeavors to describe the three major components of plans—objectives, instructional approaches, and evaluation—and to explain the different types of long- and short-range planning. Emphasis is given to how teachers can use this information to make reflective decisions about the plans they design to guide instructional efforts.

SCENARIO

Virginia Grove is a fifth-year social studies teacher at a large suburban high school. It is the last period of the school day. Virginia's study hall is small, and the students are occupying themselves with completing homework assignments. The two students in the back of the room talking quietly are not a disruption, so she has some time to reflect on how she can wrap up the Civil War unit the class has been studying for the past two weeks. For the past several years, she has done this by reviewing the major battles and discussing the surrender of Lee to Grant at Appomattox Courthouse in 1865. Last year, she had enough time to show a short videotape of the war based on original Mathew Brady photographs.

As Virginia reflects on the class's activities up to this point, she is concerned that most of the time has been spent on political and military aspects of the war, such as the causes, elections, comparisons of the North and South, and the battles. She recalls that in a Civil War history course she had in graduate school last year, the instructor, in his lecture on the final campaign, aroused her feelings about the tragedy of war. Her students, she felt, should learn about war in its most basic human terms. Does the school library have a copy of Grant's memoirs and another source documenting common soldiers' experiences and attitudes? Grant's perceptions of the surrender and the soldiers' feelings would help her communicate to students the emotional dimension of war. She makes note of several questions that might serve as the basis of a discussion of feelings about war and to stimulate higher-level thinking about war's futility. Could she use a small-group activity to share feelings and ideas? Why not have the students assume the role of a Southern or a Northern soldier who thinks about returning home after the surrender is announced? The small groups could compose hypothetical letters expressing their feelings about war as related to the feelings the soldiers might have had. Students would certainly find the content more meaningful using this approach. She wonders if the "think-pair-share" cooperative-learning approach would work to structure the sharing a little more.

As the period draws to a close, she recalls that the public library has a large history section. Surely she can find some primary sources there if the school library does not have them. Virginia starts toward the library. Better check whether Wednesday would be okay to have her students in the library to do a short research project comparing the U.S. Civil War with recent civil wars in other countries. Also have to make sure a couple of computers are available so that students have access to the Internet. This will give her two days to have the students explore the concept of *civil war* using several past and present conflicts. Virginia smiles at the thought of this assignment because the in-service-day speaker on the new curriculum standards for social studies had stressed the importance of relating the past to the present to help students construct meaning about the relevance of U.S. history. What was the name of the diary written by a young Bosnian teenager in the siege of Sarajevo? Apparently some reviewers had said it was great insight into the horrors of war. She thinks about seeing Amanda White, the new English teacher, to find out more about this book and to see how it might be integrated into the Civil War lesson. What about the possibility of doing an integrated social studies–English unit with Amanda?

As she says hello to the principal in the hall, it occurs to her that she should check the newly revised U.S. history course of study to be certain that she has fulfilled all of the objectives listed for the Civil War. She begins to feel very good about the upcoming lessons.

■ RESEARCH AND THEORETICAL BASE

Virginia Grove used a systematic approach to planning the end of the Civil War unit. She carefully considered instructional methods used in the past and what the students had learned during the unit to design lessons based on students' needs and interests. Decisions related to planning were made reflectively. In addition, several characteristics of Virginia's approach to planning can be supported by current principles and research on planning.

The precept that effective planning is essential for effective teaching is a familiar one to teachers. In the past, so little research was done on planning that this was a statement of faith rather than certainty. Although a substantial body of research exists relating teacher behaviors and techniques to achievement, it has only been within the last 30 years that significant research has been conducted on planning. Most of it has been descriptive and has been conducted at the elementary school level. Generalizations based on this research must be considered tentative, but they do have implications for teachers preparing unit and daily lessons on the secondary level.

Historically, methods texts have consistently recommended a remarkably similar format for planning unit and daily lesson plans. One universally accepted principle has been that objectives must be specified first to provide direction for the teacher and students as learning activities are implemented. Decisions then need to be made about the content and about which instructional approaches should be used to achieve the objectives.

What does research say about teachers' actual planning practices? In a review of research on planning, Clark and Yinger (1979) found that teachers generally have not faithfully applied the principles advocated by teacher educators. In general, the studies conducted by Peterson, Marx, and Clark (1978) and Morine (1976) in a variety of settings with a range of pupils showed that teachers considered content, learning activities, and instructional strategies before objectives as they planned for classes. Most of the time that teachers spent on planning was used in making decisions about the instructional context; far less time was spent on objectives and evaluation. A recent review of research drawn primarily from U.S. and Spanish sources supports these findings and adds that activities appear to be the most salient feature and they constitute the building blocks of planning although the content is usually the starting point. Unit planning is one of the most frequent and important tasks of teachers. Better learning usually results when teachers plan units carefully with the aim of achieving objectives based on the content and students' needs. Another finding is that knowledge based on previous teaching experience determines how teachers plan their teaching, although most teachers base their lessons on the teacher's book that accompanies the students' textbook. Very importantly, when teachers adjust their plans to the progress made by students, there is a positive effect on learning (Sanchez and Valcarcel, 1999).

Such findings bear careful scrutiny in light of research on effective teaching that has identified a focused approach to instruction as a characteristic of effective teachers. Levin with Long (1981) analyzed a substantial number of studies relating students' knowledge of instructional goals to achievement. Although some disagreement occurred, generally it was found that students achieved more if the teacher had informed them of the objectives in specific terms. It was concluded that instructional objectives facilitated learning when students were shown what was to be accomplished and how they were to do it. Objectives in these studies apparently served to provide students with a sense of direction and security. Research reviewed very recently at Mid-continent Research for Education and Learning supports the positive relationship of establishing objectives and the improvement of student achievement across all content areas and across all grade levels (Varlas, 2002).

Teachers also consider classroom-management approaches when planning. Thornton (1991) found, in his review of research, that teachers planned with multiple goals that were primarily related to subject matter and classroom management/socialization. Sometimes, these goals were competing, and the latter area may have become more influential in determining the direction of planning.

Some other interesting conclusions have been made based on research about teachers' planning practices. Clark and Yinger (1980) found that teachers spent approximately 12 hours per week engaged in instructional planning. The planning process begins with a general idea that moves through phases of continual modification and elaboration. Teachers' written plans reflect only a small portion of the total plan. Most details remain in the teacher's mind. Clark and Peterson (1986) concluded, "Substantial teacher energy is devoted to structuring, organizing information, and managing limited instructional time" (p. 260).

In a study conducted by Earle (1992), experienced elementary and secondary teachers were surveyed and interviewed about their planning practices. One very interesting finding was that many teachers used mental imagery in the planning process. They visualized what the lesson would be like and how it might unfold in practice, including anticipating problems. Consequently, planning goes on more in the mind than on paper for many teachers.

It has also been found that the development of routines in planning increases teacher efficiency and flexibility. To a great degree, routine helps reduce the complexity and unpredictability of teaching, thereby allowing teachers more time and energy to devote to other activities. Beginning teachers in particular should also realize that long-term benefits can be derived from concentrated planning during the first weeks of the school year. During this time, teachers develop a workable system of procedures, time allocations, groupings, schedules, and outlines. For the most part, their established systems remain in effect for the entire school year (Evertson and Emmer, 1982).

Two studies compared the planning habits of novice and experienced elementary teachers. Westerman (1991) analyzed information from five experienced suburban teachers and their student teachers. She found that experienced teachers had a more comprehensive view of the knowledge taught and of the learners. Novices narrowly focused their planning on achieving objectives rather than accommodating student needs by making connections with what they already knew. This instructional component of comprehensively viewing the classroom and integrating new information with old are basics of constructivist pedagogy.

In a second study comparing the planning practices of experienced and novice teachers, Tyson (1991) found that experienced teachers tended to tailor their lessons around important and difficult components of the subject matter, thus giving them greater emphasis. Novice teachers rarely did this. Also, experienced teachers were more willing to check for student understanding of skills that had been previously taught rather than assuming they all learned as novice teachers tended to do.

Another thrust of educational research has been determining which teacher-controlled learning-environment variables have an impact on students' achievement. Weil and Murphy (1982) reviewed teacher-effectiveness research and found that students tended to achieve more in teacher-directed and controlled learning environments. Within these environments, a strong academic focus is evident, students are actively involved in learning with minimal off-task behavior, and the teacher holds students accountable for their work. Brophy and Good's (1986) review of research on teacher behaviors and student achievement supported this closely related finding: Students who achieved most had teachers who planned and organized prior to instruction on a daily basis.

Cooper (1990) defined an effective teacher as "one who is able to bring about intended learning outcomes" (p. 3). Given the current findings from research and the complexity of decisions that must be made anticipating and reacting to the immediate classroom situation, it is extremely difficult to visualize an effective teacher at work in the classroom who has not made careful decisions about evaluation procedures, goals, methods, and strategies.

Plans are the extension of the teacher's personality and instructional style.

■ APPLICATION TO PRACTICE: PLANNING DIRECTION

Decision Making as the Basis for Planning

In one sense, as was implied in Chapter 1, life is inevitably a series of decisions. Every conscious behavior one engages in follows a decision to perform that behavior. But most decisions occur as habit, conditioning, or simple response. In teaching, examples of such habit decisions include calling for order when the bell rings, taking attendance, recognizing students who raise their hands to ask questions, and watching the clock to make sure the lesson is completed in time. None of these decisions requires reflection. At a somewhat higher level, decisions require some reflection and involve making fairly straightforward choices. Some examples of reflective decisions are choosing whom to call on to answer a particular question, determining the point at which a source of disruption requires overt attention, and deciding whether a particular item should be included on the unit test.

At the highest level, decisions require extensive reflection, often involving synthesis and evaluative thinking. The decisions made at lower levels might generally be characterized as process oriented. At the highest level, the decisions are more likely to be purpose oriented. Some examples of this type are determining what seating arrangement best facilitates instruction, choosing the appropriate referent to evaluate particular episodes of learning, and selecting certain remediation activities for children with particular learning difficulties. This level of decision making was evident in the scenario, in Virginia Grove's approach to planning the culmination of the unit.

Planning requires attention at the highest level of decision making. When planning is ineffective or marginally effective, very likely it is because that planning has received perfunctory attention rather than serious reflection. The "mindlessness" that Silberman (1970, p. 10) recognized in classrooms and that Goodlad (1983) implicitly reaffirmed could be due in large measure to the lack of thoughtfulness that teachers have given planning. Therefore, teachers should give deliberate attention to the following questions as they develop their plans.

Planning Act

Planning begins as the teacher initiates thinking about possible learning activities for subsequent classes. The procedure for such planning appears to be straightforward, systematic, and logical. It involves developing objectives, selecting subject matter and associated materials, choosing strategies and methods to be employed, and deciding how to evaluate the achievement of intended outcomes. This approach is typically recommended in textbooks on instruction and by methods-course instructors. Preservice students and student teachers, in particular, are pressured to comply with this rational model.

Ultimately, the plan actually written by the teacher may reflect a format somewhat similar to that already described. But planning is essentially the intellectual process that occurs in the mind of the teacher, more so than the mechanical process of writing it. As previously mentioned, research indicates that teachers rarely plan according to this approach. Objectives, as such, play a very little part in planning (although they are subsequently useful for communicating learning intentions to students). However, they can be a valuable focus for the lesson, particularly for the beginning teacher.

Although textbooks and instructors apparently subscribe to the assumption that planning is self-evidently a logical process, in actual practice planning is more psychological and intuitive. It is more analogous to developing one's own original cocktail sauce than baking a cake from a recipe. Therefore, as one engages in serious planning, it should be done in a natural way, while considering knowledge to be taught, ability and interest of students, time constraints, and materials available.

Multiple Intelligences   Another natural component of serious lesson planning that has gained considerable attention is the theory that students possess varied forms of intelligence, or intellectual abilities or aptitudes as Good and Brophy (2000) referred to them, and that teachers need to take these into account when planning lessons. Howard Gardner's (1983) alternative theory of intelligence hypothesizes that there are six additional independent intelligences in addition to the standard verbal/linguistic and logical/mathematical ones traditionally emphasized in the schools. The additional ones are visual/spatial, musical/rhythmic, bodily/kinesthetic, interpersonal/social, intrapersonal/introspective, and naturalist/physical world (Armstrong, 2000). What does this mean for teachers and the planning process? People learn through their senses and perceptions and have their own preferred ways to learn. Within each of our classrooms, there is a mixture of students with a mixture of learning preferences. Multiple-intelligence theory suggests that content from any discipline can be taught in more than one way and that teachers should design lessons, projects, and assessments with consideration as to how students learn (Campbell, 1997).

The eight intelligences with approaches to teaching adapted from the work of Armstrong (2000) follow.

1. *Linguistic*—Students possess the ability to use words whether in written or spoken form. They think and express themselves in words. This is the most widely used form of intelligence.

   The most appropriate instructional approaches center around reading, writing, speaking, and listening. Methods include formal and interactive lectures, recitations, guided and reflective discussions, and writing activities including journals, debates, playing word games, and so on. *Teacher's planning question*—How can I encourage students to speak and write?

2. *Logical-mathematical*—Students possess the ability to discern logical patterns and relationships. They think by reasoning.

   The most appropriate instructional approaches center around using mathematical computations. Methods include guided inquiry, problem solving, and critical-thinking learning activities including number games, calculating, experimenting, questioning, and so forth. *Teacher's planning question*—How can I encourage students to work with numbers, calculations, and critical-thinking skills?

3. *Visual-spatial*—Students possess the ability to accurately perceive the visual-spatial world; they can navigate through spaces. They think in images and pictures.

    The most appropriate instructional approaches center around using visual presentations, art activities, graphic and artistic representations, drawing, designing, and so on. *Teacher's planning question*—How can I encourage students to use visual media?

4. *Musical-rhythmic*—Students possess the ability to produce rhythm, pitch, melody, and timbre, and appreciate musical expression. They think via sounds, melodies, and rhythms.

    The most appropriate instructional approaches center around singing, rapping, using musical instruments, humming, keeping the beat, and so on. *Teacher's planning question*—How can I encourage students to use music or sound?

5. *Bodily-kinesthetic*—Students possess the ability to control their body movements and express ideas and feelings through movement. They also have a good sense of timing. Students think and feel through bodily movement.

    The most appropriate instructional approaches center around performances (dance, drama, etc.) and sports activities, hands-on learning, and tactile activities, building, and the like. *Teacher's planning question*—How can I encourage students to use bodily movement and involve them in hands-on learning activities?

6. *Interpersonal-social*—Students possess the ability to perceive and discern moods, intentions, motivations, and temperaments in people; they are sensitive to both verbal and nonverbal communication. They think by sharing ideas with one another.

    The most appropriate instructional approaches center around guided and reflective discussion; small-group and cooperative learning, simulations, activities involving collaboration, peer tutoring, and so forth. *Teacher's planning question*—How can I encourage students to share, cooperate and collaborate?

7. *Intrapersonal-introspective*—Students possess self-knowledge and self-awareness, and the ability to express themselves. They understand their own emotive states. They think inside themselves.

    The most appropriate instructional approaches center around reflective discussion, individualized instruction, independent study activities, reflection, journal writing, and so on. *Teacher's planning question*—How can I encourage students to reflect on personal thoughts and feelings?

8. *Naturalist-physical world*—Students possess the ability to observe, categorize, and analyze nature and their environment. They think through organizing themes.

    The most appropriate instructional approaches center around field trips into nature; observation of natural surroundings; collecting, analyzing, and classifying data; working with materials gathered from out-of-doors, and so forth. *Teacher's planning question*—How can I encourage students to use characteristics of the natural world in class?

For example, an Ohio history teacher teaching about the canal era (1800–1860) might traditionally approach this topic by having students supplement the standard text reading with accounts of people working and traveling on the canals from several primary source diary entries from that era (verbal/linguistic). If this teacher were applying the principles of Multiple Intelligences (MI), additionally he or she might involve the students in designing their own canal routes by plotting and calculating the depth, elevation, and miles of their proposed canal route. They then could compare their route with the actual canal routes throughout Ohio (logical/ mathematical). He or she might have them create posters or murals of canal boats, locks, and towns or take a field trip to an actual canal (visual/spatial). Other possibilities are to have the students build replica models of canals or canal boats or even ride a canal boat on the field trip (body/kinesthetic); listen to the Erie Canal Song and write new verses that represent the Ohio canals (musical/rhythmic); form cooperative learning groups to research topics related to Ohio canals and conduct class discussions (interpersonal); reflect upon the narrative readings, projects, and discussions and write diary entries about living near canals and working on canal boats (intrapersonal); and brainstorm and discuss how canals may have negatively impacted the environment (naturalist) (Michael, 1998). The major inference for teachers making planning decisions is that when instructional approaches match learning styles, students' motivation to participate increases significantly.

Consider Virginia Grove's situation described at the opening of this chapter. Virginia had reason to believe that the way she had been teaching the final campaign of the Civil War had been fairly successful. Students had been nominally interested, more so even than with some of the earlier lessons within the unit dealing with the causes, battles, and other aspects of the war.

Nevertheless, Virginia had the nagging sense that somehow this was not enough. The unit had taken on the form of a dispassionate narrative of political and military events rather than a dramatic and dynamic conflict of values. The students had too little realization of the bitterness and agony that had gripped a young, uncertain nation. Unfortunate as the ugly episode was, there were useful insights that the students may have acquired from studying it. As high school students, they were capable of perceiving the Civil War and, as an extension, any war in its tragic human terms. The Civil War may serve better than any other war for this purpose, for it placed Americans in the position of methodically killing other Americans—an unthinkable and outrageous act in conditions other than war.

With this new perspective in mind regarding the potential that the Civil War unit could serve, Virginia realized that the instructional methods she had used previously, primarily involving reading, lecture, recitation, guided discussion, and films, were inadequate to stimulate students' expression of feelings. Students needed to become involved with more than the simple processing of knowledge that had characterized most of the unit. A vicarious association with one who suffered the most from the consequences of war—the common Northern or Southern soldier—had to be established. She chose the small-group method to allow students to express and share feelings elicited by composing a soldier's letter. By varying her instructional approach in this manner she was also tapping into her students' interpersonal and intrapersonal intelligences.

■ WEBSITE RESOURCE ■

Exploring Multiple Intelligences is a site provided by New Dimensions of Learning at

www.multi-intell.com.

This site is chock full of ideas, training opportunities, resources, articles, and many links to other resources on multiple intelligences including ASCD, projects such as New Horizons for Learning and Project Zero at Harvard, where the father of multiple intelligences, Howard Gardner, is on the faculty. Other links include schools that are implementing the theory in many different ways.

The chapter began with the statement, "All teachers plan." By now, it should be apparent that a major requisite for effective teaching is a consistently conscientious effort toward planning. This effort was quite evident in Virginia's preparation for wrapping up the Civil War unit. The decisions she made regarding content and instructional approach for the lesson were based on her judgments about students' progress and the balance of the kinds of learning and experiences they had to date. The result was a dynamic and innovative plan.

> *Effective teachers plan systematically using rational decision making.*

Long- and Short-Range Planning

It is time now to examine more closely the structure of a typical lesson plan. The format is easily recognized by teachers. Following it as one plans will greatly increase the probability of a beneficial learning experience for students.

A useful way of analyzing teacher plans is initially to separate them into three broad categories: long-range plans, unit plans, and daily lessons. Each has a different purpose, a different level of generality, and covers a different time span.

Long-range plans are generally developed for a semester, a year, or perhaps longer. They are called by various names such as course of study, syllabus, or curriculum guide. They usually include global course or program goals, a content or topic outline, major concepts and generalizations, and a proposed weekly time schedule. In Virginia Grove's case, the curriculum guide is for eleventh-grade U.S. history.

Unit Plans   Unit plans are the intermediate stage of planning. They reflect several long-range course goals and are the means of organizing a discrete aspect of the course of study. Unit plans serve as a basis for developing a set of related daily teaching plans and may extend from one to six weeks or longer. Unit plans can include general goals, a rationale, major generalizations and concepts, diagnostic tests, instructional methods and strategies, evaluation procedures, and learning resources. At the middle or junior high school level, an example unit is Uses of Fractions; a high school example is The Legacy of the Transcendentalists. Titles for interdisciplinary units might be Changes, Sports in Society, or Homelessness. The title of Virginia Grove's unit was The Civil War.

Some teachers simply plan day-to-day without first developing a unit plan. Too often the textbook is the only source for these plans. Textbooks, though, are generally sources for content information, not sources for instructional approaches or learning activities. Teacher's editions of textbooks and resource kits publishers provide contain valuable supplementary materials but typically do not provide specific plans. Without the unit plan to aid in organizing ideas and approaches, teaching is likely to lack cohesiveness, continuity, and relevance. A unit plan is essential to maximize a teacher's—particularly a beginning teacher's—influence as a facilitator of students' learning and experiencing. Table 5.1 shows a sample unit plan, adapted from one developed by Nona Chambers of Anaconda, Montana.

TABLE 5.1   EXAMPLE UNIT PLAN

Unit Focus: Aging   Subject: Multidisciplinary, with emphasis on reading

Grade: 6   Unit Duration: 2 weeks

I. **Goals**

The students will:

Become familiar with the variety of personalities of the elderly.
Infer the importance of art as a means to bring together the older and younger generations.
Understand the role advertisements play in stereotyping the elderly.
Determine how current music has depicted the elderly.
Analyze the ways in which the elderly interact with other members of the family.
Realize the possibilities for a productive life in old age.
Understand the contributions of the elderly from a historical perspective.
Realize how young and old people can relate socially.
Become aware of how people deal with the death of a loved one and one's own dying.
Speculate about how people in their homes and community can help and learn from the elderly.

II. **Topics**

Different kinds of grandparents	Creativity in old age
Art as a bridge to understanding being old	Famous oldsters
Stereotyping of the elderly through advertising	Relating to the elderly
Elderly in today's music	Death and dying
Elderly in family settings	Helping the elderly

III. **Instructional procedures**

A. Discussion based on students' differing perceptions, ideas, and feelings related to the issues and personalities in the book *Grandpa*.

(continued)

TABLE 5.1   EXAMPLE UNIT PLAN (CONTINUED)

B. Students create their own self-portraits using a variety of art mediums and draw pictures of what they expect to look like when they are about 70 years of age. Individual discussions with students on differences between portraits.

C. Students locate advertisements that show how society depicts the elderly, share the advertisements with the group, make judgments about stereotyping, and speculate how the advertisements could be changed to a more positive view of the elderly.

D. A variety of songs will be played related to the elderly ("When I'm 64"—Beatles; "Old Folks"—from *Jacques Brel Is Alive and Well and Living in Paris*; "It Was a Very Good Year"—Sinatra; etc.). Students will share their opinions through discussion about the meanings of the words and how the elderly are depicted.

E. Role-playing will be used to depict the elderly and analyze how the elderly interact with members of the family. Several reenactments will take place based on students' impressions, opinions, positive and negative stereotypes, and perceptions of reality.

F. Individual student reports on famous oldsters including inferences about their motivations to be productive and creative beyond 70 years of age. Optional activity is student sharing of reports with class.

G. Students will view the film *Peege* about an elderly woman experiencing isolation in a nursing home. After students respond individually to questions in written form about the film, small groups will be formed for students to share responses, experiences, and attitudes.

H. Students read the book *About Dying*. Discussion on the feelings about the characters, their opinion about the book, and their own personal experiences with death such as with a relative, friend, or pet.

I. Oral history interview with senior citizens invited to class. Cooperative groups of students will plan questions and interview narrators about their lives with an emphasis on life as a senior. Group will write a report summarizing their narrators' life stories, accomplishments, problems and opinions.

J. Unit culmination: Review of students' learnings and appeal to students to become actively involved in activities and programs related to the elderly in the community. Perhaps the inquiry method can be used if the class perceives an issue that they care to investigate formally or a problem they wish to attempt to solve.

IV. **Evaluation**

Informal observation of students within large- and small-group discussions and during listening (records), viewing (film), and doing (art) activities using observation forms.

TABLE 5.1   EXAMPLE UNIT PLAN (CONTINUED)

Formal evaluation of students' written reports on famous oldsters based on a provided rubric. Students' advertisements brought to school will also be assessed.

Formal evaluation of the oral history interview group report based on a provided rubric.

V.   Resources

A. Books. *Grandpa,* Barbara Borack; *About Dying,* Sara Bonnett Stein; *The Family at Sunday Dinner,* Marcia Cameron; *Age and Youth in Action,* Gray Panthers; *Getting Beyond Stereotypes,* George Maddox
B. Records. "When I'm 64," Beatles; "Old Folks," from *Jacques Brel Is Alive and Well and Living in Paris;* "Hello in There," Bette Midler; "Old Friends," Simon and Garfunkel; "No Time at All," from *Pippin;* "And When I Die," Blood, Sweat, and Tears; "It Was a Very Good Year," Frank Sinatra
C. Film. *Peege,* Phoenix Films

Daily Plans   The daily teaching plan takes as its point of departure the general goals and broadly defined instructional strategies of the unit plan. In effect, it is a schedule of teacher approaches and student learning activities described in some detail. The lesson plan provides the teacher with organization and specific direction daily. The daily teaching plan includes one or more specific objectives, a sequential arrangement of instructional methods and strategies, and a procedure for evaluation.

Widespread differences occur among teachers regarding the exact form and degree of detail in daily planning. Experienced teachers generally do not need to prepare extensive daily lessons because they have taught similar lessons previously. Their daily plans may be brief outlines of objectives, methods, and evaluation and can be recorded in a typical lesson-plan book. The beginning teacher, however, has very little experience on which to draw for effective instructional approaches. For this teacher, thorough planning must compensate for experience, suggesting that the beginning teacher needs more than a brief outline. Plans developed in some detail— and this will vary from teacher to teacher—are necessary to increase the probability of effectiveness. Examples of daily lesson-plan formats are included in Table 5.2, and two illustrative secondary lesson plans are included in Table 5.3.

Goals and Objectives in Planning

As has been stated, goals and objectives tend to come after the fact, even though they are usually incorporated as the first section of a formally written plan. As investigation of teachers' planning habits reveals, if objectives are not usually used as a basis for developing learning activities, they are helpful later in making

---

TABLE 5.2   EXAMPLES OF DAILY LESSON-PLAN FORMATS

These formats are designed particularly for planning the use of the four primary instructional methods presented in Chapter 7.

FORM 1 (LECTURE):

   I. Objectives
  II. Instructional Approach
     A. Entry: Preparation for Learning
     B. Presentation
     C. Closure: Review of Learning
  III. Evaluation

FORM 2 (INQUIRY):

   I. Objectives
  II. Instructional Approach
     A. Entry: Preparation and Clarification of a Problem, Issue, or Query
     B. Formation of Hypotheses
     C. Collection of Data
     D. Test Hypotheses
     E. Closure: Drawing Conclusions
  III. Evaluation

FORM 3 (DISCUSSION):

   I. Objectives
  II. Instructional Approach
     A. Entry: Identification of Problem, Issue, or Topic
     B. Clarification
     C. Investigation
     D. Closure: Summary, Integration, Application
  III. Evaluation

FORM 4 (SIMULATION GAMING):

   I. Objectives
  II. Instructional Approach
     A. Entry: Orientation
     B. Participant Preparation
     C. Simulation/Enactment Operations
     D. Closure: Debriefing Discussion
  III. Evaluation

TABLE 5.3   EXAMPLE LESSON PLAN (REFLECTIVE DISCUSSION)

SECONDARY SCIENCE

I. Objectives
A. The students will suggest solutions to a hypothetical community-pollution problem.
B. The students will appraise the proposed solutions and select the most feasible one.

II. Instructional Methods and Learning Activities
A. *Entry: Identification of Problem, Issue, or Topic*—Students read a hypothetical account of a local gas station owner who knowingly pollutes the stream flowing behind the station by emptying gas and oil wastes into it daily.
B. *Clarification*—Ask questions to have students review the facts of the hypothetical account. What wastes were dumped into the stream? How much was being dumped daily? What was the noticeable effect on water life? How did the owner rationalize his actions?
C. *Investigation*—Ask questions to have students speculate about possible solutions to the problem: If you were a member of the community and knew that the owner was violating the law, what could you do about it? What are the alternatives? What might be some consequences of the alternatives? Do the consequences conflict with your values? What might be some legal implications?
D. *Closure: Summary, Integration, Application*—Have students appraise the suggested alternative solutions and decide on one approach: Which do you consider the best and why?

III. Evaluation
Students write a brief paragraph summarizing their selection of a problem solution and providing support.

MIDDLE SCHOOL READING

I. Objectives
A. The students will explain why moral issues are difficult to resolve.
B. The students will evaluate Joey's circumstances and decide whether they would keep the $5 he found or return it to the stranger who lost it.

II. Instructional Methods and Learning Activities
A. *Entry: Identification of Problem, Issue, or Topic*—Students read the short story (or teacher reads the story), "Finders Keepers?"
B. *Clarification*—Ask questions to have students review the facts of the hypothetical account of a stranger who unknowingly drops a $5 bill out of his pocket. Joey notices. Does he have a dilemma? If so, what is it?

(continued)

TABLE 5.3   EXAMPLE LESSON PLAN (CONTINUED)

    C. *Investigation*—Ask questions to have the students determine alternatives open to Joey: What could Joey do? What might the man say to Joey if he returned the $5? What could Joey buy with it?

    D. *Closure: Summary, Integration, Application*—Ask questions to have students decide what they would have done in the same situation: What would you do? Why do you feel that way? Has this ever happened to you?

III. Evaluation

The thoughtfulness of the students' answers will indicate the extent to which they can deal effectively with the moral issue.

---

explicit what otherwise are only implicit intended outcomes from studying a given topic or unit. Writing objectives after determining what subject matter is to be dealt with helps teachers clarify in their own minds the most appropriate outcomes of a unit or lesson. When these objectives are in turn communicated to the students, they provide a focus for their learning. Research on effective teaching verifies that incisively stated and clearly communicated objectives function as useful cues for students.

Program Goals   Those broad and general objectives written to cover units of instruction are often termed *goals*. Very often they incorporate verbs such as *understand, comprehend, know, realize, appreciate*, and *create*. Goals often deal with the intended learning at the level of concepts to be acquired. For example:

The students will know the parts and operation of five power woodworking machines (technology education).

The students will realize the purpose for conducting lab experiments using a systematic-analytical approach (science).

The students will understand how values are formed (social studies).

The students will perceive how the concept of role is used to create credible and consistent characterization in a story (English).

Although there is no research that supports one preferable style of expressing goals, the convention adopted by most authors in the professional literature is useful. If nothing else, it tends to lend credibility to the objectives as they are reviewed by other knowledgeable educators (e.g., the principal or supervisor who has occasion to examine the teacher's plans).

The convention involves simply (1) using "students" as the subject of the statement, that is, posing the students as the actors rather than those acted on; (2) having each goal statement express just one broad outcome or learning task; and

(3) keeping this statement as brief and precise as possible. Although at first glance this may seem simple enough, some practice is necessary to master the skill. A friendly, knowledgeable critic can be helpful in this regard. The following is a list of several social studies goals that might have been presented in Virginia Grove's U.S. history curriculum guide for the Civil War:

> The students will experience the feelings soldiers have about war.
>
> The students will know the major issues and events that led the United States into the Civil War and other wars.
>
> The students will become familiar with the major historical schools of thought and their interpretations related to the causes of wars in which the United States participated.
>
> The students will know the strategies, leaders, and outcomes of major battles of wars.

Goals are a generally accepted part of a unit plan. No particular controversy exists over whether they should be used or how they should be stated. The situation is not so placid with objectives, which are more explicit statements of outcomes of particular lessons. For years, a major controversy has existed over whether objectives must be stated behaviorally. The argument is made that learning is defined as a change in behavior; objectives, therefore, should describe the expected change in observable terms. Only when this approach occurs can teacher accountability be straightforwardly assessed. Opponents of behavioral objectives contend that many important learning outcomes cannot feasibly be measured, that many learning outcomes cannot even be anticipated, and, in any event, that learning is highly individual.

The authors have no final resolution for this long-standing controversy, and research provides no definitive answer. Any answers, it seems, are likely to be more related to individual choice than to general consensus. Nevertheless, the authors offer some suggestions for consideration in the matter of writing objectives.

Instructional Objectives   Objectives at higher levels of thinking are more difficult to specify in precise form. Making overly precise statements in these instances is a forced, artificial task for the teacher. Furthermore, learning at these levels becomes more individualized. Working routine mathematics problems produces a similar skill in each of the students involved; deriving meaning from a story has as many outcomes as there are students reading it. Therefore, where the learning experience provides for a range of outcomes or variability based on the perceptions of the learners, instructional objectives are most appropriate. They are also more consistent with a constructivist perspective, meaning that their use is predicated on the assumption that the act of engaging in certain learning experiences is important even though the outcome is not specifically predictable. The degree of achievement of these objectives is difficult to measure, as pointed out by proponents of behavioral objectives. However, the value of an objective is not so much whether it can be measured as whether it guides students toward worthwhile learning and informs students of the teacher's intent for their learning. The instructional objective is specific and relates to singular subjects and grade levels. It includes the following parts:

1. *Audience*—Who is to do the task?
2. *Behavior*—What is the task to be completed?

The parts can easily be identified in an example instructional objective:

Students will write their own ending to the story "The Lady and the Tiger."

Some additional examples of these objectives are listed here:

(Audience) (Behavior)

Students will summarize the meaning of "The Fox and the Grapes" in two or three sentences.

Students will state one example different from any previously given about how they have applied math in an important way for personal purposes.

Students will defend a position they take on dealing with illegal aliens in the United States.

Virginia Grove might have used the following instructional objectives in her planning:

(Audience) (Behavior)

Students will compare the role of women in new fields during the Civil War with their role during World War II.

Students will write a soldier's hypothetical letter home after Lee's surrender to Grant based on accounts of the Civil War recorded by common soldiers.

Students will explain why the Civil War strengthened the national government.

Note that instructional objectives often may be read as activities as much as outcomes. There is less precision, and even the possibility of ambiguity, in such statements. However, some kinds of activities may be considered ends in themselves. To have simply attempted to find a personal meaning or develop a sound position on an issue is a worthwhile intellectual activity.

Behavioral Objectives In instructional instances in which the outcomes are clearly observable and quantifiable, objectives written in terms of pupil performance provide the clearest possible learning cues for students. These are called behavioral objectives and are sometimes referred to as pupil-performance objectives. When the learning involves, for example, working mathematics problems correctly, identifying direct objects, placing living organisms in appropriate taxonomic categories, or typing some average number of words per minute, specific statements of competency levels are especially useful. Behavioral objectives include the following parts:

1. *Audience*—Who is to accomplish the task?
2. *Behavior*—What is the task to be accomplished?
3. *Condition*—What are the circumstances for performing the task?
4. *Degree*—At what level of proficiency is the task to be accomplished?

The parts can easily be identified in an example objective:

(Audience) (Behavior and Degree) (Condition)

Students will correctly complete eight addition problems on a quiz that includes ten problems.

The following are several other examples of specific behavioral objectives:

Students will correctly identify at least four direct objects in context given a news item from their *Scholastic* magazine.

Given a list of five living organisms, students will key them into the appropriate family.

Students will type copy in standard form at 40 words per minute with a maximum of two errors per minute of typing.

Virginia Grove might have used these if she had been using the behavioral format for objectives:

Students will identify four of the five provisions of the Compromise of 1850.

Students will write a 500-word essay comparing the Civil War with one civil war in a foreign country since 1945, incorporating within the narrative at least four similarities.

Hints for the Beginning Teacher

Planning a lesson or a unit can be like entering a dark forest. One way to cast some light on the journey is to work with a partner. Consider "planning out loud" with another teacher or having a peer review your plans for missing objectives, material recommendations, and so on.

Domains and Levels

As teachers devise goals and objectives for their unit and daily teaching plans, another fundamental consideration must be addressed: What level of student learning will be targeted? In other words, will the information, attitudes, or skills to be learned be offered at introductory and basic levels, at more advanced and abstract levels, or, more likely, somewhere in between? Goals and objectives can be classified by areas or domains. Each domain reflects a particular set of beliefs and assumptions about how students learn and behave:

Cognitive domain—Objectives that have as their purpose the development of students' intellectual abilities and skills.

Affective domain—Objectives that have as their purpose the development of students' emotional growth and values development and clarification.

Psychomotor domain—Objectives that have as their purpose the development of students' motor and coordination abilities and skills.

Each domain consists of a hierarchy of levels that reflects a range of student behaviors from simple to complex. As objectives are devised, knowledge of the domains and levels are useful in providing students with opportunities to engage in a wide variety of behaviors to accommodate their diverse interests, needs, and abilities. Knowledge of the levels also assists teachers in making decisions about individualizing instruction. The three domains and their hierarchies of levels are presented with an emphasis on the cognitive domain because of its wide acceptance and application. Examples of educational goals and objectives are provided.

Cognitive Domain   Bloom (1956) provided teachers with a taxonomy, or hierarchy, of objectives appropriate for classifying behaviors in the cognitive domain. The taxonomy consists of six levels ranging from knowledge, with a focus on eliciting facts-oriented reproductive thinking, to evaluation, which represents sophisticated, high-level productive thinking. The levels, which all relate to developing students' intellectual abilities and skills, are as follows:

1. *Knowledge*—Emphasis on remembering information. Characteristic student behaviors include: define, state, name, recall, identify. Examples:

   The students will know the characteristics of Impressionistic paintings (program goal).

   The students will correctly identify 45 out of the 50 state capitals (behavioral objective).

2. *Comprehension*—Emphasis on understanding and organizing previously learned information. Characteristic student behaviors include: relate, describe, rephrase, compare, summarize, interpret, translate, explain. Examples:

   The students will understand the rules of soccer (program goal).

   The students will translate the given paragraph from English into French (instructional objective).

3. *Application*—Emphasis on using information in pertinent situations. Characteristic student behaviors include: give an example, apply, solve, demonstrate, compute, prepare, classify, use. Examples:

> The students will solve two-digit-by-three-digit addition problems (program goal).

> The students will write 200-word essays on the topic of the role of the modern woman, applying the pertinent rules of grammar and logical sentence structure (behavioral objective).

4. *Analysis*—Emphasis on thinking critically about information by studying its parts. Characteristic student behaviors include: give a reason, analyze, conclude, infer, generalize, identify causes and motives, support, provide evidence. Examples:

> The students will distinguish between the use of melody and harmony in musical pieces (instructional objective).

> The students will analyze the secretary of the interior's two motives in leasing federal government lands to the oil companies from the documents presented to show their understanding of the influence of the business community (instructional objective).

5. *Synthesis*—Emphasis on original thinking about information by putting its parts into a new whole. Characteristic student behaviors include: develop, predict, create, synthesize, compose, devise, build, solve, write, paint, produce, speculate, hypothesize. Examples:

> The students will propose a plan to support the development of a new recycling center in the community (instructional objective).

> The students will design a solar home that includes the three essential factors to demonstrate their understanding of the application of passive solar energy principles (behavioral objective).

6. *Evaluation*—Emphasis on making judgments about information based on identified standards. Characteristic student behaviors include: decide, opine, evaluate, appraise, judge, assess, select, agree/disagree, take a position for/against. Examples:

> The students will evaluate the contribution of selected books to the development of American fictional literature (program goal).

> The students will express reasons for their choice of a favorite color from the chart to demonstrate the range of preferences (instructional objective).

Affective Domain Although the primary emphasis in the schools has traditionally been on the development of students' cognitive learning, attempts have been made to balance intellectual learning with affective learning. Krathwohl, Bloom, and Masia (1964) classified students' attitudes, feelings, interests, and values into five levels of affectivity. The range of behaviors is from simple awareness or perception of something to internalizing a phenomenon so that it becomes a part of one's lifestyle. All the levels relate to developing students' emotional learning.

Only the first three levels are presented because of their potential to be practically applied in planning for classroom instruction.

1. *Receiving*—Emphasis on becoming aware of some communication or phenomenon from the environment. Characteristic student behaviors include: attend, listen, describe, identify. Examples:

    The students will acquire an awareness of different artistic expressions ranging from realism to surrealism (program goal).

    The students will listen for the different sounds characteristic of the season of spring so they may develop an awareness of sound as a form of communication (instructional objective).

2. *Responding*—Emphasis on reacting to a communication or phenomenon. Characteristic student behaviors include: read, write, tell, practice. Examples:

    The students will show interest in mystery stories (program goal).

    The students will participate in a community action project to demonstrate their commitment to active citizenship (instructional objective).

3. *Valuing*—Emphasis on attaching worth to something from the environment. Characteristic student behaviors include: appreciate, follow, form, justify, choose, demonstrate, show, value. Examples:

    The students will demonstrate respect for other students' property in school (program goal).

    The students will police their own and others' laboratory behaviors to show they value safety (instructional objective).

The remaining two levels of the affective domain are generally not associated with realistic goals and objectives in the secondary classroom. They involve very high-level affective structure and internalization: organization, or emphasis on organizing values into a system, and characterization, or emphasis on developing an internally consistent system by which one lives.

Psychomotor Domain   Classification of goals and objectives in the psychomotor domain is especially appropriate for the objectives generally associated with motor- and muscular-skill development at the elementary and secondary levels: art, music, physical education, business, industrial arts. Specific units within language arts (writing skills), mathematics (computers), and science (microscopes) also might emphasize the development of student behaviors in this domain.

Several approaches have been developed to classify goals and objectives in the psychomotor domain. One taxonomy has been developed by the American Alliance for Health, Physical Education, and Recreation (Jewett and Mullan, 1977). The three major levels are (1) generic movement—emphasis on becoming aware of and displaying basic movements; (2) ordinative movement—emphasis on organizing perceptual-motor abilities to accomplish particular physical tasks; and (3) creative movement—emphasis on creating physical movement in personally unique ways. Another taxonomy was developed by Harrow (1972) that focuses on observable behaviors ranging from simple to complex: reflex movement, basic fundamental movement, perceptual abilities, physical abilities, skilled movements, and nondiscursive communication.

Applying a taxonomical, hierarchical approach to classifying goals and objectives when preparing units and daily lessons enhances teacher decision making. The nature of three different but related domains, each with many levels, suggests alternatives from which teachers can choose. Choice also increases the probability of variety in teaching and thereby the accommodation of a wide range of students' abilities, interests, and needs. Meeting individual differences in the classroom results in more effective teaching.

Sequencing of Instruction

The instructional sequence is closely related to the student learning level to be targeted during the planning stage. At this stage the teacher's concern is how the content and methods should be optimally organized to achieve the objectives established for the lesson. Another concern is arranging the objectives themselves to increase the probability that the unit goals will be attained.

Designing a logical sequence of instruction involves an analysis of the content to be taught, whether it is representative of the cognitive, affective, or psychomotor domains. The process for the teacher in teaching a generalization, for example, is to build the simpler facts and concepts into more complex relationships to enhance students' comprehension. The same process would also apply to a skill. As an illustration, social studies students would not be expected to engage in decision making that might lead to social action without first understanding and practicing the skills associated with the decision-making process. Those skills would include defining the decision to be made, identifying alternatives, examining their possible outcomes, evaluating alternative decisions, selecting the best alternative, implementing the decision, and assessing results of the action. In summary, the skill of effective decision making is complex, and for students to learn it, the teacher needs to determine the subskills involved and to sequence them in a logical order.

■ SUMMARY POINT ■

Effective teachers approach planning systematically using rational decision making. Research supports the relationship of student achievement and teachers who have planned and were organized. Planning is also essential to achieving constructivist-oriented goals and objectives. Selecting and devising goals and objectives are important parts of planning. Goals and objectives serve as student learning outcomes necessary to provide instructional direction for the teacher.

■ APPLICATION TO PRACTICE: PLANNING FOR INSTRUCTION AND EVALUATION

The primary role of teachers in the schools is instructional, whatever form that may take. What is instruction? In its broadest definition, it is the systematic use of selected techniques, methods, and strategies to create a dynamic interface between the curriculum and the students.

Research has demonstrated that teachers generally think of the content of the lesson and the learning activities before forming objectives when making decisions about lesson planning. In general, they consider the instructional context to be the most important part of planning. This section will examine the instructional and evaluation components in the decision-making process.

Techniques, Methods, and Strategies

A major component of the instructional context is the act of instructing. The curriculum component answers the question, What shall be taught? The instructional component answers the question, How shall it be taught? They are complementary; teaching would not be possible without both of these components.

Decisions about the instructional approach involve a consideration of three major, closely related components: techniques, methods, and strategies. As a teacher plans a lesson, these components are generally considered together. Instructional techniques are a part of every method, and methods are combined to form strategies. The question confronting every teacher planning a lesson is: Which technique(s), method(s), or strategy(ies) will enable me to achieve my instructional objectives?

Techniques   Instructional techniques are combinations of teacher behaviors and skills essential for the implementation of methods and strategies. The teacher behaviors comprising techniques are relatively specific in that each one can generally be observed and analyzed in the classroom setting. Behaviors are the focus if the teacher intends to engage in a self-analysis or shared analysis of performance so as to gather systematic information to use as a basis for improving instruction. Examples of the more widely applied techniques include:

1. *Entry*—The teacher uses an entry to focus students' attention on the lesson and the content to be learned. Skills include using a springboard and/or attention getter and reviewing and previewing content, skills, and/or learnings.

2. *Closure*—The teacher uses closure to wrap up the lesson with the intention of reinforcing key elements of the lesson and helping students transfer what has been learned to the next lesson. Skills include summarizing, integrating, applying and making transitions.

3. *Information giving*—The teacher verbally provides students with explanations and directions necessary to conduct the activities of the lesson. Skills include clarifying, providing student feedback, and using audiovisual aids.

4. *Motivating*—Those verbal and nonverbal teacher behaviors that stimulate students' attention, interaction, and participation. Skills include physical movement, voice, pacing, and body language—that is, gestures, posture, facial expression, and eye contact.

5. *Supporting*—Teacher uses verbal and nonverbal reinforcement and encouragement of acceptable student behaviors. Skills include the use of praise, words of courtesy, acceptance, and use of feelings and ideas.

6. *Listening*—Teacher uses primarily nonverbal behaviors communicating to students that the teacher is attending to what is being said. Skills include physical distance, eye contact, silence, and facial expressions.

7. *Questioning*—Teacher use of verbal statements that have an interrogative function that generally requires students to engage in specific levels of thinking. Skills include formulating convergent and divergent questions, probing, wait time, and phrasing.

Although these techniques are applied by teachers as instructional methods in the classroom, not all need to be directly considered each time a lesson is planned. The extent to which techniques need to be planned will depend on the objectives of the lesson. Instructional techniques are presented in depth in the next chapter.

Methods   An instructional method is an organized arrangement of instructional techniques that is intended to achieve a discrete learning outcome. Examples of primary methods used by many teachers at all levels include:

Formal lecture	Small-group discussion
Interactive lecture	Guided inquiry
Demonstration	Open inquiry
Recitation	Individualized inquiry
Guided discussion	Simulation
Reflective discussion	Role-playing

Although instructional methods are presented in more depth in Chapter 7, several implications for planning are noted here. Methods are the backbone of instruction because they are the most basic way students have traditionally been taught. Teachers understand the nature of methods and can anticipate their positive and negative impact on students. Teachers have a preference for a method(s) most suited to their classroom situation and personality. Although teachers have specific preferences for particular methods, the variety of students' learning styles, interests, and needs within any one class suggest very strongly that they should plan to use a variety of methods. This will increase the probability of holding students' interest and attention and accommodating their multiple intelligences. Teachers should also consider the different methods that can be used to attain the same objective.

Strategies   An instructional strategy is a sequential combination of methods designed to accomplish learning objectives. The methods that Virginia employed to achieve the objectives associated with expressing and sharing feelings are activities that could also be considered part of a strategy. This relationship of methods and strategies is illustrated in the introductory scenario. For the past several years, Virginia Grove employed a general strategy consisting of a combination of several methods to review the final phase of the Civil War. From what can be inferred, recitation was used to review the major battles, followed by discussion to involve students in higher-level thinking about the surrender at the Appomattox Courthouse. This strategy incorporated a videotape that probably served the purposes of information giving and enrichment.

This year, Virginia is planning to alter her approach because her objectives have changed, partially as a result of the above-average level of the students. She has tentatively decided to employ another strategy to achieve her goal of helping students to understand war in its most basic terms. First, she intends to read selections from several primary Civil War sources. This is to be followed by a discussion to stimulate students' feelings about war. An alternative that she is considering is to have the students form small groups in which to conduct their discussions. As a follow-up, she also thought of having each small group write a hypothetical letter that they would then share and discuss. As she employs the discussion method, we can envision a natural emphasis on the use of the techniques of questioning and listening. If she decides to form the students into small groups, we can envision her relying on the techniques of information giving to provide students with structure and direction for the small-group task and managing in an effort to keep students on-task. In summary, the strategy that Virginia was planning to use consists of several methods sequentially arranged: teacher reading, large- or small-group discussion, student group writing, student reporting, and follow-up discussion.

Virginia had also begun to plan an instructional approach to achieve a follow-up objective of the students examining the concept of *civil war* by relating causes and results of the U.S. Civil War with causes and results of civil wars occurring during the past decade. We can imagine a strategy centering on the use of inquiry in which students hypothesize commonalities of civil wars, with small groups carrying out their investigations in the library. She might then use a cooperative-learning approach to have students socially transmit knowledge as they teach each other about the different civil wars they investigated. Perhaps a guided discussion, during which students predict countries and ethnic/racial groups of people that are potentially headed for civil war based on their findings, might wrap up the two days' work. Virginia's instructional strategy for this final phase of the Civil War unit consisted of the use of the inquiry and guided-discussion methods and the cooperative-learning strategy.

Although most strategies are devised by teachers in this manner, a number of strategies have been formally designed and labeled by educators. Joyce, Weil, and Calhoun (2000) identified a variety of teaching models drawn from the work of educators, sociologists, psychologists, and curriculum specialists. They have assigned the models into different groups characterized by a different genre of learning goals.

This book focuses on another group of more formal strategies that have evolved from the effective-teaching research and emphasize higher student achievement. They are as follows:

1. *Direct teaching*—Academically focused, teacher-directed classroom instruction using sequenced and structured materials.

2. *Cooperative learning*—The use of peer tutoring, group instruction, and cooperation to encourage student learning.

All this implies that teachers involved in daily and long-term planning need to be aware that a variety of instructional strategies exist that they can use to meet their objectives, classroom situations, and students' abilities, interests, and needs. These strategies can be informal or formal. (Additional commentary on techniques, methods, and strategies and their relationship can be found in Chapters 6, 7, and 8.)

Given the wide variety of techniques, methods, and strategies from which to choose when planning a unit or daily lesson, beginning and experienced teachers should be able to understand why decision making is so important. A systematic approach to decision making becomes more valuable as the choices in a situation increase. The following are some of the questions a teacher needs to consider when choosing the instructional approach:

1. Which combination of methods and/or strategies is best to achieve the objectives of the lesson?
2. How much time is available during class for implementation of a particular method and/or strategy?
3. To what extent should the methods and/or strategies be adapted to individual students or small groups of students?
4. How can transitions between the use of methods and strategies be made smoothly and beneficially to enhance students' understanding?
5. To what extent will students be actively and passively involved during the implementation of a particular method and/or strategy?

APPLICATION for DIVERSE CLASSROOMS

One can expect that in an average heterogeneously grouped classroom, intelligence test scores can show a range from 60 or 70 to 130 to 140 (Hardman, Drew, and Egan, 1996). This means that the teacher must make plans that deal with intellectual diversity in the classroom. The plan could include such approaches as designing learning activities that enable students to use multiple intelligences as identified by Howard Gardner (1983) such as musical intelligence or spatial, bodily kinesthetic, interpersonal, or intrapersonal intelligences rather than the dominant linguistic and logical mathematical intelligences traditionally emphasized.

■ SUMMARY POINT ■

Planning for instruction involves making decisions about the selection of an appropriate variety of techniques, methods, and strategies to achieve the goals and objectives of units and lessons. Research reveals that teachers actually consider instructional approaches and content before objectives when planning lessons. An appropriate sequence of planning events is: (1) consider the content to be taught and the objective(s) to be achieved simultaneously; (2) establish the method(s) necessary and the resources available to achieve the objective and teach the content; (3) if appropriate, devise or select the strategy(ies) within which the methods are subsumed; and (4) consider the techniques necessary to implement the methods/strategies successfully.

■ PLANNING FOR EVALUATION

Another major planning component is evaluation. As we move into the twenty-first century, evaluation is assuming a more important role in the instructional process. Instead of an emphasis of evaluating students after instruction, determining student progress during instruction is becoming more important. In many ways, instruction and evaluation are becoming more intricately related, and because of this, careful planning becomes even more essential. Teachers need to give as careful consideration to this area as to the formation of objectives and selection of instructional approaches. Evaluation is the process of forming judgments about student progress. These judgments collectively serve as a basis for making decisions. The question facing teachers daily is the extent to which students attained the objectives set for the lesson. Over a longer period of time, teachers are concerned with achieving broader unit goals. Evaluative data gathered in response to these questions are determined by the appropriateness and specificity of the objectives and the quality of instructional methods and strategies employed. In many respects, the outcomes of student evaluation can be a direct reflection on the teacher's effectiveness in the classroom. Consequently, the evaluation component deserves considerable attention.

Evaluation involves making judgments in the form of reflective decisions about instruction. To make decisions to redirect instruction, data need to be gathered during and after instruction. The major part of the evaluation process and the most time-consuming element is gathering information about student performance and progress. The decisions a teacher makes based on the data gathered are reflected in both short- and long-term planning. Planning for evaluation is primarily conducted at the unit-plan and daily-lesson levels. The major concerns teachers have while planning units are determining the time when assessments of student progress should take place, the nature of the evaluation instruments, and how to interpret and represent student progress. At the daily-lesson level, teachers are primarily concerned with how data regarding student progress should be collected.

Unit Evaluation   One of the first concerns teachers have while planning for evaluation at the unit level is incorporating diagnostic and summative evaluation. Diagnostic evaluation is the formation of judgments about a student's learning potential prior to instruction. The data gathered at this preinstructional stage can be useful in helping a teacher plan to meet students' varying abilities.

Although formative evaluation is becoming more important, summative evaluation is the most common approach used by teachers in assessing students' performance. It is generally conducted when the students have completed an instructional unit. The most common form of summative evaluation is a written test. Other alternative assessments might include student projects, performances, or portfolios. We can imagine Virginia Grove's two-week unit test on the Civil War consisting of a mixture of objective and subjective (essay) items. (Diagnostic and summative evaluation are further explained in Chapter 10.)

Judgments resulting from summative evaluation assess the degree to which students have attained the learning objectives of the unit. Postinstructional decisions have a direct bearing on the objectives and instructional approaches to be used in the next unit. Other important decisions relate to how this same unit will be taught even more effectively in the future.

Another major concern teachers have about the evaluation process when designing a unit plan is interpreting and representing the information gathered about student performance. Interpretation is necessary to make judgments about the assignment of values (generally in the form of grades) that are representative of students' levels of progress over a specified period of time or unit of study. The teacher's basic responsibility is to decide whether to assign marks based on a comparison of individual student performance to group performance, a comparison of progress to a predetermined standard, or a comparison to past individual performance. Although the first approach has deeper historical roots and is prevalent in standardized testing, the other two approaches have had important applications over the years. (These approaches—norm-referenced and criterion-referenced, respectively—are described more fully in Chapter 10; see pp. 361–362.)

Daily Evaluation   Daily judgments made by the teacher during instruction are part of formative evaluation. These judgments serve as a basis to make decisions about the objectives and instructional approach guiding students' learning. Daily evaluation conducted during the midinstructional phase is important so that modifications can be made in the program to increase the probability that the objectives will be achieved by the students. The major concern teachers have while planning for daily evaluation is how the student progress data should be collected.

Appropriate techniques must be selected or devised to determine whether students have achieved lesson objectives. A wide range of techniques are available for teachers to use formally or informally. When daily lesson plans are made, evaluation can be formal or informal, depending on the means used to gather data. Informal approaches might include observations of student behavior, analysis of students' contributions to group discussions, conferences with individual students, brief reviews of written homework assignments, impressions of performance, and perusal of student journals. Formal techniques might range from a test to a checklist used to judge students' contributions in a class debate. Other formal approaches might include quizzes, rating scales, and attitude-measuring instruments. However, despite these numerous choices, what is essential when evaluating students' progress is for the technique employed to provide data directly related to the objective being evaluated. Thus, evaluation, like instruction, must be planned.

◼ WEBSITE RESOURCE ◼

A large collection of lesson plans created by teachers to help teachers, especially new teachers, is of great benefit. The plans on pacificnet represent all levels and the major academic subject areas, including the arts and special education. There's even a section with lesson plans that are oriented to managing the classroom. Teachers are encouraged to communicate with other teachers from around the world and to submit plans at

www.pacificnet.net/~mandel.

◼ SUMMARY POINT ◼

The decisions teachers make about planning for the evaluation of students' progress are important and require thoughtful consideration. The evaluation component of planning exists as a means to determine if the goals of the unit or the objectives of the lesson were achieved. As such, the outcomes of student evaluation are a direct reflection on the effectiveness of teachers. Decisions need to be made about the timing of evaluation, the techniques used to gather information on student progress, and how to interpret and represent student progress. Each component needs considerable thought and expression in sufficient detail to be beneficial to students and teachers.

◼ QUESTIONS FOR REFLECTION ◼

1. Based on what you have learned about the scenario teacher, Virginia Grove, and her plans for the upcoming lessons ending the Civil War unit, do you think she is a good teacher? Why?

2. Locate a methods text that represents your major certification area. How does what it recommends in terms of planning units and daily lessons compare with the research findings reported in this chapter?

3. How does the content of the textbook you use in one of your preparations compare with the content listed in the department's curriculum guide or course of study? What content do you teach and why?

4. Think about teaching a concept or generalization in your subject area at the grade level of your choice. To what extent can you visualize the lesson unfolding in your mind's eye as you teach it in your classroom?

5. How well do you know your subject matter? Do you have to rely on the text or do you incorporate information from a variety of additional sources as you plan lessons?

6. Do you agree that effective teaching is based on effective planning, or are there more influential practices contributing to good teaching? If so, what are they?

7. Assume that you agree with the assertion that motivation is the most basic factor in students' learning. What might you do during planning to ensure that students' motivation will be accommodated?

8. Can you recall a peak experience for you during your years in school? Why do you consider it a peak experience, and how might you adapt it for use in your own classroom?

9. To what extent is the planning process logical and to what extent is it intuitive based on your own frame of reference and experience?

10. Secure a copy of a teacher's unit plan. How does it compare with the format suggested in the chapter? What improvements to the unit-planning format can you suggest?

11. What instructional approach might you build into the example unit plan on aging that would encourage sixth graders to construct meaning about what it is like to grow old?

12. Which of the two forms of objectives suggested in the chapter, instructional objectives and behavioral objectives, is most appropriate for your teaching area? Or will you use both? Why?

13. Why does education seem to emphasize achieving goals and objectives representative of the cognitive domain over those of the other domains?

14. How much time should you plan to achieve objectives representing each of the domains (cognitive, affective, and psychomotor domains)?

15. Think of instruction as you experienced it throughout your schooling. What kind of definition of instruction might you synthesize based on your experience? How does it compare with the definition presented in the chapter?

16. Of the instructional techniques presented from which you will draw as you plan to implement lessons, which one do you think is most characteristic of your instructional style or approach? Why? Which one would be a close second?

17. Think of a local, national, or international current event in the papers today. What instructional strategy might you devise to teach it during a 15-minute segment of a lesson? What methods are a part of your strategy and how does each contribute to achieving the objective you have in mind?

18. How important do you consider the entry to a lesson to be? What is one entry to a lesson that you can recall a teacher using from your schooling that grabbed and held your attention? Why was it so effective?

19. Imagine going into class without a plan, without any idea what you are going to do. What problems can you imagine unfolding during the course of the 45 minutes?

20. Suppose you were either student teaching and being observed by the college supervisor or being observed by the principal as a nontenured teacher. What might he or she say in the conference after the observation that is the best evidence that you have planned well for the lesson?

■ REFERENCES ■

Armstrong, T. (2000). *Multiple Intelligences in the Classroom* (2nd ed.). Alexandria, VA: Association for Supervision and Curriculum Development.

Bloom, B. (Ed.). (1956). *A Taxonomy of Educational Objectives: Handbook I. Cognitive Domain.* New York: McKay.

Brophy, J., and Good, T. L. (1986). "Teacher behavior and student achievement." In M. Wittrock (Ed.), *Handbook of Research on Teaching* (3rd ed.). New York: Macmillan.

Campbell, L. (1997). "How teachers interpret MI theory." *Educational Leadership, 55*(1), 14–19.

Clark, C. M., and Peterson, P. L. (1986). "Teachers' thought processes." In M. Wittrock (Ed.), *Handbook of Research on Teaching (3rd ed.).* New York: Macmillan.

Clark, C. M., and Yinger, R. J. (1979)."Teachers' thinking." In P. L. Peterson and H. J. Walberg (Eds.), *Research on Teaching: Concepts, Findings, and Implications.* Berkeley, CA: McCutchan.

Clark, C. M., and Yinger, R. J. (1980). *The Hidden World of Teaching: Implications of Research on Teacher Planning* (Research Series No. 77). East Lansing, MI: Institute for Research on Teaching.

Cooper, J. M. (1990). "The teacher as a decision maker." In J. M. Cooper (Ed.), *Classroom Teaching Skills* (4th ed.). Lexington, MA: Heath.

Earle, R. S. (1992). "The use of instructional design skills in the mental and written planning processes of teachers." Paper presented at the convention of the Association for Educational Communications and Technology, Iowa (ERIC Document ED347 987).

Evertson, C. M., and Emmer, E. T. (1982). "Effective management at the beginning of the school year in junior high classes." *Journal of Educational Psychology, 74*, 485–498.

Gardner, H. (1983). *Frames of Mind: The Theory of Multiple Intelligences*. New York: Basic Books.

Good, T., and Brophy, J. (2000). *Looking in Classrooms* (8th ed.). New York: Addison Wesley Longman.

Goodlad, J. I. (1983). "A study of schooling: Some findings and hypotheses." *Phi Delta Kappan, 64*(7), 465–470.

Hardman, M., Drew C., and Egan, W. (1996). *Human Exceptionality* (5th ed.). Boston: Allyn & Bacon.

Harrow, A. J. (1972). *A Taxonomy of the Psychomotor Domain: A Guide for Developing Behavior Objectives*. New York: McKay.

Hoover, K. H. (1972*). Learning and Teaching in Secondary School*. Boston: Allyn & Bacon.

Jewett, A. E., and Mullan, M. R. (1977). *Curriculum Design: Purposes and Process in Physical Education Teaching-Learning*. Washington, DC: American Alliance for Health, Physical Education, and Recreation.

Joyce, B., Weil, M., with Calhoun, E. (2000). *Models of Teaching* (6th ed.). Boston: Allyn & Bacon.

Krathwohl, D. R., Bloom, B. S., and Masia, B. B. (1964). *A Taxonomy of Educational Objectives: Handbook II. Affective Domain*. New York: McKay.

Levin, T., with Long, R. (1981). *Effective Instruction*. Washington, DC: Association for Supervision and Curriculum Development.

Michael, R. (1998). [Multiple intelligences: Ohio transportation—the canal era.]. Unpublished handout.

Morine, G. (1976). *A Study of Teacher Planning: Beginning Teacher Evaluation Study* (Tech. Rep. No. 76-3-1). San Francisco: Far West Laboratory for Educational Research and Development.

Ohio Department of Education (1994). *Model Competency-Based Social Studies Program* [Draft]. Columbus: Ohio Department of Education.

O'Neil, J. (1994). "Outcomes-based education comes under attack." *Update, 36*(3), 1, 4–5, 8.

Peterson, P. L., Marx, R. W., and Clark, C. M. (1978). "Teacher planning, teacher behavior, and student achievement." *American Educational Research Journal, 15*, 413–432.

Sanchez, G., and Valcarcel, M. (1999). "Science teachers' views and practices in planning for teaching." *Journal of Research in Science Teaching, 36*(4), 493–513.

Shostak, R. (1990). "Lesson presentation skills." In J. M. Cooper (Ed.), *Classroom Teaching Skills* (4th ed.). Lexington, MA: Heath.

Silberman, C. E. (1970). *Crisis in the Classroom*. New York: Random House.

Thornton, S. (1991). "Teacher as curricular-instructional gatekeeper in social studies." In J. Shaver (Ed.), *Handbook of Research on Teaching and Learning in the Social Studies*. New York: Macmillan.

Tyson, P. (1991). "Talking about lesson planning: The use of semi-structured interviews in teacher education." *Teacher Education Quarterly, 18*(3), 87–96.

Weil, M., and Murphy, J. (1982). "Instructional processes." In H. Mitzel (Ed.), *Encyclopedia of Educational Research* (5th ed.). New York: American Educational Research Association.

Westerman, D. A. (1991). "Expert and novice teacher decision making." *Journal of Teacher Education, 42*(4), 292–305.

6

Basic Instructional Techniques

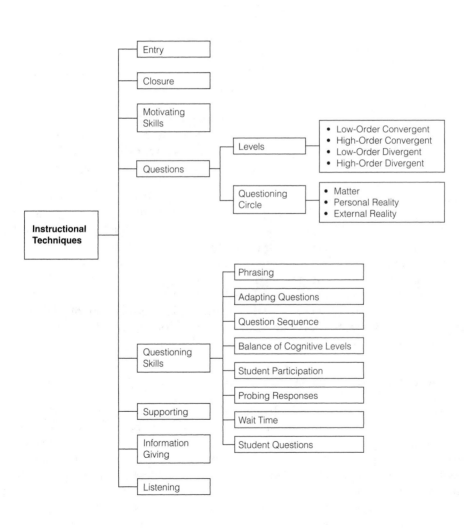

The following three chapters comprise the central focus of the book: instruction. The first several chapters have provided ideas, information, and practice related to those components considered to be the foundation of instruction. Decision making is the most pervasive component of instruction, so much so that effective teaching is inevitably the outcome of effective decision making. Consideration of classroom climate is critical within the instructional process because optimal learning occurs only in a setting of optimal conditions. Optimal conditions also include establishing good classroom discipline for instruction and learning to take place. The foundation also necessarily includes curriculum because instruction is focused on teaching content in one form or another. Planning is essentially a description of the instructional decisions intended to be implemented in the classroom. Instruction, as a logical consequence, is the direct application and testing of the decisions made about students, environment, content, and method.

Instruction has generally been defined as "a process by which knowledge and skills are developed in learners by teachers" (Hawes and Hawes, 1982). Although the proponents of constructivism emphasize the encouragement of students to assume more responsibility for their own learning, clearly the person responsible for initiating, maintaining, and evaluating the instructional process in the school is the teacher. As a process, instruction, in its most basic form, can be depicted as consisting of teacher behaviors, techniques, methods, and strategies. Basic, physical teacher behaviors comprise the primary instructional techniques of informing, motivating, supporting, questioning, and listening. A sampling of these behaviors includes gestures, voice volume, divergent questions, physical movement, and eye contact. Varying degrees of all these techniques are a part of every instructional method teachers employ in classroom settings. Guided discussion, demonstration, recitation, interactive lectures, guided inquiry, and small groups are among the most commonly used methods today. Methods are selected and sequenced by teachers during planning to form strategies that are the most comprehensive forms of instruction. Strategies can be informal and formal. Informal strategies are the most common and are extemporaneously devised during the planning phase of a lesson. Formal strategies are research based and are more highly structured. An example of a formal strategy is cooperative learning. The relationship of all these instructional components is depicted in Figure 6.1. Notice the indication of which chapters in this book provide analyses of each element.

■ OVERVIEW

This chapter focuses on instructional techniques and lesson-presentation components. The research reviewed is drawn, in large part, from the so-called process–product, or process–outcome, research conducted during the past 40 years. This research has focused on determining the effect of specific teacher behaviors and instructional techniques (process variables) on students' learning outcomes (product variables). Most of the research has been concentrated on academic achievement because it is the most obvious and readily measured aspect of learning. The result of researchers' efforts has been the identification of a series of teacher behaviors and techniques that positively correlate with students'

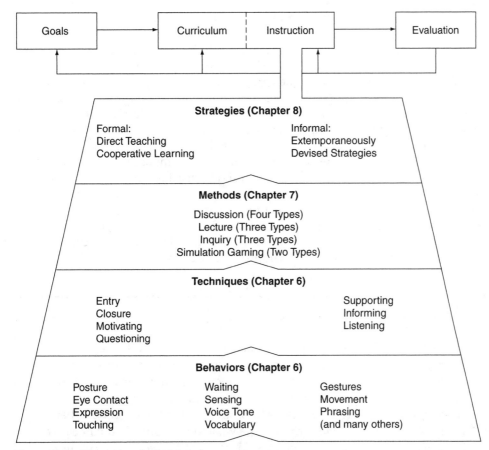

Figure 6.1 Instructional Model

achievement. Good and McCaslin (1992) referred to this form of instruction as "active teaching."

While the instructional techniques that serve as the focus of this chapter are those that research has found to influence students' learning of subject matter significantly, they are also key in enhancing students' understanding of what they have learned. Traditional teaching has emphasized content coverage and learning of basic facts and concepts. Textbooks have been the major source of curriculum, and secondary teachers have relied heavily on interactive lecture and recitation as the primary teaching methods. A more contemporary and constructivist view of teaching is an emphasis on covering less content and exploring topics in greater depth through the use of a variety of teaching techniques, methods, and strategies. The intent is to help students understand what they have learned by processing information at higher cognitive levels and connecting it to their experiences and what they know. It is generally associated with achieving goals related to the constructivist view of learning and teaching.

As teachers move from traditional to active teaching and constructivist approaches, they will need to engage in more extensive decision making, particularly during the planning stage because the constructivist view requires the application of a greater variety of student-oriented instructional approaches and learning activities. The instructional techniques presented in this chapter (entry, closure, motivating, questioning, supporting, listening, and informing) have the potential to contribute toward the teacher's creation of a constructivist classroom environment in which students are challenged to learn through understanding and application.

A series of teaching-analysis instruments is included in this chapter, and in Chapters 7 and 8, on effective teaching techniques, methods, and strategies. These data-gathering forms are intended to be used by teachers and their support personnel (colleagues, team leaders, departmental chairs, and supervisors) as they begin to inquire formally into the nature of their teaching. The purpose of this inquiry is for teachers to become more informed and reflective about their instructional behaviors and approaches. Ultimately, the data gathered can be used effectively to make decisions about improving instruction.

SCENARIO

Richard Taylor wondered how his students would react to the lesson he had planned for the day as they drifted into his seventh-period earth science class. For the past three weeks, they had been studying Earth's environment, particularly its renewable and nonrenewable resources and energy. The focus had been on learning how people depend on the environment and how they can influence it. As a major goal, though, he wanted his students to participate in identifying environmental problems in Norwood, their local community.

Wouldn't it be wonderful if the students actually wanted to make an effort at solving one of the problems they identified?

As the bell signaled the beginning of class, his thoughts drifted to the state science teachers' conference he attended the month before and to the session on encouraging high school–age students to become actively involved in resolving local community environmental problems. Two boys continued talking in loud voices as the period began, and several others still had not taken their seats. Generalizing from this capricious behavior, he realized that his students were probably still too immature to be interested in dealing with community problems.

"Dave and Todd, I would appreciate your attention so that we can get started." Once Mr. Taylor was sure everyone was ready, he told the students, with excitement in his voice, to close their eyes and creatively imagine an environmental crisis taking place in Norwood. After about 20 seconds, he asked students to share their imagined catastrophes with their neighbors in pairs and then with the large group. Barbara described her family receiving a letter from the Environmental Protection Agency (EPA) informing them that their immediate neighborhood was likely to have been built on a toxic waste dump left from an old paint-manufacturing plant that had gone bankrupt 30 years ago. Jim graphically described an imagined killer smog that enveloped their community for five days, killing several older people and a number of animals and making many people sick. It had been caused by an air inversion that created a pocket of trapped waste gases from the steel mill down the river. Shawn talked about not being able to swim in the nearby lake that summer because of the high level of pollution, and Judy thought a crisis for Norwood might be a monstrous trash-and-garbage accumulation caused by a prolonged strike by sanitation workers. Two other students volunteered to share their crises.

As Mr. Taylor slowly moved around the room maintaining eye contact with the participants of the discussion, he noticed that for several students interest was beginning to wane. He commented about the participants' vivid imaginations, thanked them for their contributions, and mentioned that they were going to be focusing on Norwood's environmental problems. "Yesterday, we finished with our discussion of the dangers of nuclear energy and the problems faced by that industry. Now we need to bring our focus down to the community level. Let's leave our imagined crises for the moment and get back to reality by thinking about the present environmental situation in Norwood." He told the students their objective over the next two days was to identify at least three environmental problems that Norwood was facing. "I would like you to take out your journals and take two minutes to write down either one environmental problem that you think Norwood is experiencing right now or one that Norwood could realistically be facing in the near future." When the students began the assignment, Mr. Taylor circulated among them to assist individual students and keep others on-task.

"What are some of the problems you think we have?" he asked. One cited several abandoned houses in the south section of town that looked like they were ready to collapse. Another student added that they were also dangerous because they weren't boarded up. Mary thought Norwood needed to do more to promote solar-energy conservation. "Using solar energy makes so much sense, but we only have one solar home in town," she said. Harold said that he thought there was too much trash on the streets and that maybe the street cleaners were not doing their job. After some further encouragement, several other students volunteered contributions related to the lack of parks, the foul-tasting tap water, and the need for more trees and flowers downtown. Mr. Taylor wrote the last of the students' ideas on the board.

Mr. Taylor complimented the students on how observant they were of the community. "I didn't think you would have come up with the number of problems you did. Well done!" He then asked, "How do we know if these are really problems that Norwood should do something about?" After a sufficiently long pause, he called on Jim, who seemed to be deep in thought. Jim commented that he thought many people in the community would have to consider something a real problem before the city government would do anything about it. "In other words," Mr. Taylor said, "a problem to one person may not be a problem to others. Would you agree?" Jim agreed and Lynn quickly opined that she didn't think a majority of people needed to consider something a problem before the city government did something about it. After all, she couldn't remember Norwood voting on an environmental problem; yet changes seemed to have come about.

Mr. Taylor could hardly contain his enthusiasm for Lynn's insight. "You have just hit on one of the major things I wanted you to learn by the end of the unit! That is the responsibility city government has in dealing with environmental problems." Moving to the side of the room, he then took some time to describe why the city council passed legislation creating the recycling plant the previous year. The point was that the decision was made without initiation from the people and without a vote because the city council, after gathering information from a consultant, was convinced that it was environmentally beneficial to the community. Both individuals and government are responsible for the condition of the environment.

Realizing that several students were either glancing at the clock or gazing out the windows and that there were 20 minutes left in the period, Mr. Taylor decided to quicken the pace of the lesson. "How many remember the definition of a scientist's hypothesis?" Several hands went up and, after pausing, he called on Julie. She replied that it was a solution to a problem. Jim quickly added that it was a guess or proposed solution that needed checking. "How are your ideas about Norwood's environmental problems and hypotheses related?" After getting no responses, Mr. Taylor asked Chris if he had an idea.

Chris, a capable student but mentally lazy at times, responded with, "I don't know."

Mr. Taylor attempted to lead him to the idea he had in mind. "Could the class's thoughts about Norwood's environmental problems be considered hypotheses?"

"I guess so," was the reticent student's response.

Mr. Taylor confirmed his minimal response and asked the class for an explanation. David responded that the problems the class proposed were only guesses at that point because more information and opinions were needed.

"Thanks, David," said Mr. Taylor.

"For homework tonight, I would like you to find out if your parents agree with you." Mr. Taylor explained that the students were going to investigate a problem just like scientists, gathering data to support or refute their hypothesized environmental problems. He passed out a survey rating form for students to write down the proposed environmental problems and record parents' responses. "Tomorrow, with your help, we'll know a little more about our community's environmental condition."

During the remaining 10 minutes, Mr. Taylor had the students read a short article from the *Journal of Environmental Education* on a western community's successful attempt to make its environment safe for its citizens. He thought the article would be appealing to the students because of the dramatic confrontation between the mayor and the representatives of several self-serving special-interest groups at one of the town council meetings.

With one minute left before the bell was to ring, Mr. Taylor asked the students to pass their copies of the article to the front of the room. "Christine, which of the problems we identified do you think your parents will consider the most critical?" She thought the lack of parks and recreation areas was a real concern. Mr. Taylor was able to direct the question to two other students before the bell rang. "I think tomorrow's class will be very interesting because of the information you will be bringing in. See you then."

■ RESEARCH AND THEORETICAL BASE: ENTRY, CLOSURE, MOTIVATING SKILLS

The growing research related to instructional techniques, teacher behaviors, and presentation skills is influential. Attempts to discover factors that constitute effective schools and effective teaching have provided the major impetus for this body of research. School districts and university teacher-education programs have become increasingly aware of these research findings and are incorporating them into in-service and preservice programs to disseminate information on effective teaching skills that enhance students' learning.

Presentation skills are displayed in one form or another in every lesson. Based on his review of the literature, Shostak (1990) found that the entry and closure of the lesson are among the most frequently researched lesson-presentation skills. The entry is the students' first contact with the content and the methods to be used by the teacher. However, teachers infrequently introduce lessons with students' motivation in mind. The majority of teachers' task-presentation statements are neutral, and many are negative (Brophy, Rohrkemper, Rasid, and Goldberger, 1983). In their extensive review of the research, Brophy and Good (1986) concluded that students learn more efficiently and their achievement is maximized when the teacher structures the new information by relating it to what they already know.

This form of entry has been termed *set induction* (Allen and Ryan, 1969). In a series of studies conducted by Schuck (1985), it was found that students achieved and retained more knowledge when their teacher used set-induction techniques. Another consideration in the entry is novelty. Based on his review, DeCecco (1968) suggested teachers should incorporate discrepancies and the element of surprise into lessons to attract and stimulate students' attention and interest. The decisions teachers need to make about the entry to a lesson center on structuring the lesson to relate new information to previous learning and introducing topics and lessons in atypical and interesting ways. Waxman's (1987–1988) review of research on lesson entry strongly supports the positive and influential impact entries have on students' achievement.

All lessons achieve closure by virtue of the fact that finite periods of time govern lesson length. Although logic suggests that a lesson needs a closure to complement the entry, little research has been conducted on the impact of closure on student learning. Based on their review of research, Gage and Berliner (1992) concluded that closure is an important part of an instructional repertoire and teachers need to make decisions regarding how the lesson will be wrapped up and how the bridge to the next lesson will be made.

Of all the major techniques that the teacher uses to teach in a classroom setting, the skills associated with motivation are the most important in terms of encouraging and stimulating students to attain lesson objectives. In an exceptionally extensive meta-analysis of more than 300 research sources, Wang, Haertel, and Walberg (1994) found motivation to be one of the most significant influences on student learning. The research literature on motivation has focused on, among a variety of variables, the teacher's role in projecting an enthusiastic image. Good and Brophy (2000) identified two major aspects of enthusiasm: dynamics in presenting the material—which they called intensity—and interest in the subject matter. Both contribute toward maximizing student achievement, especially for older students (Brophy and Good, 1986). Gage and Berliner (1992) reviewed several major studies demonstrating that student learning is affected positively as teachers employ a variety of expressive behaviors the reviewers labeled as the "teacher's style." Decisions about motivation primarily center on two elements: which verbal and nonverbal behaviors to employ in the classroom to convey enthusiasm for the subject matter being taught, and which behaviors are necessary to maintain student interest and attentiveness throughout the lesson.

Enthusiastic teachers who demonstrate their enjoyment of the subject and teaching have a considerable advantage in attracting student attention and stimulating their involvement.

Motivation can also be gained by varying the instructional approach. Research supports teachers' use of instructional variety and flexibility as a means of maintaining students' attention and increasing achievement (Gage and Berliner, 1992). Based on their review, Good and Brophy (2000) found that in terms of sustaining students' interest, a variety of methods is better than the extended use of one method. Furthermore, research also suggests that the decisions a teacher makes that are related to instructional "activity structures," or methods, also influence students' attitudes and behavior and that this has an impact on instruction (Berliner, 1984). Teachers need to decide how their lessons will vary in terms of the numbers and kinds of instructional methods and strategies to be used and the time necessary to employ them effectively within each class session.

■ APPLICATION TO PRACTICE

Entry

The first few minutes of a class are the most crucial times in relation to teacher impact. The entry to a lesson is generally recognized as the first instructional phase implemented immediately after the teacher has gained the attention of the students. This usually commences at the beginning of the class period. An entry can also occur several times during a lesson as the teacher makes transitions and introductions to discrete segments of any single lesson. Both of these forms of instructional entry share the common purpose of setting the learning process in motion.

The primary purposes of the entry are to focus students' attention on the learning activity, prepare them for what they are going to learn, and encourage them to get involved. Too often classes begin with statements such as, "Okay, take out your homework," or "I'm going to pass out some material I want you to read now," or, "C'mon class, let's get going. We've got a lot of material to cover before the end of the period." Although these statements may accurately inform and direct the students, they quickly become routine and boring to those who may not have a high level of intrinsic motivation. One way to capture students' attention is for the teacher to make casual or personal comments that indicate respect for students or interest in them. A comment of this type contributes toward a positive social-emotional climate and enhances student–teacher relationships. Examples are: "Weren't Chris and Jenny great in the senior play yesterday?" or "I understand that the vocational electronics class needs some broken radios and televisions to repair. How many have one at home they can contribute?"

Another approach to focus students' attention is to use a springboard to induce them to get involved with the objectives of the lesson. This can be accomplished by connecting the content to their lives and experiences, which is a major emphasis of constructivist ideals. Examples include: "How many have seen at least one of the Rocky films and would like to describe a major fight scene?" (springboard for a sociology lesson on violence), or "Who would like to tell about a book you read over Christmas vacation?" (springboard for lesson on reading skills). Springboards such as these serve to focus students' attention and stimulate them to get involved.

A more sensational, and perhaps more effective, way to get students involved with the learning activity is to do something unexpected. This entry can take many forms, such as starting the class by solving a challenging puzzle related to a math concept to be taught during the lesson. Another approach is to play a discovery game such as having students guess what lesson-related object the teacher possesses (perhaps ration stamps as an introduction to the home front during World War II). Occasionally, a shock statement can be used such as, "If you are an average group of students in this school, then two girls in here have had abortions" (as an introduction to a health-class unit on birth control). Anything that stimulates students' curiosity, suspense, or creativity is a possible means to involve students directly or indirectly with the content to be taught.

One approach to lesson entry that many teachers use fairly consistently is preparing students for the upcoming learning activity. The extent to which students are prepared for the ensuing activity directly affects an entry's effectiveness in orienting them and setting the learning process in motion. Ideally this phase of the entry would include a review and preview to prepare students for new learning. The review consists of the important facts, concepts, and skills learned from the previous lesson. In this way, the immediate lesson would be placed into context and cumulative learning would be encouraged. An example is the following statement: "In the last several lessons, we have tried to show how some great thinkers, in speaking to the people of their times, were in fact speaking to people of all times. Today, we shall begin to try to discern that much of their wisdom is still pertinent for us more than a century later."

During the preview, the teacher describes what the class will be engaged in during the period, the objectives pertinent to the lesson, and a rationale. Although it seems that the preview involves extensive teacher commentary, it can be effectively accomplished in a short period of time; for example: "Today if we get through the vocabulary drill and reading section, we can spend the last part of the period playing French bingo to practice these skills. Our primary objective is that you will be able to pronounce correctly the 20 new vocabulary words from the story, 'Jeanne d'Arc.' Although the story is historical, the key words that we will focus on are ones you will find in everyday conversational usage."

It is important to keep in mind that the entry to a lesson is a means to an end, not an end in itself. The effectiveness of the entry is directly dependent on how well the students have been prepared for the upcoming learning activity and how highly motivated they are to pursue the objectives. The decisions a teacher makes during the planning stage are crucial because the impact of the entry will directly affect students' attitude. Their attitude, to a large degree, determines how interested they are in attaining the objectives and how conscientiously they engage in the planned learning activities.

Mr. Taylor, in the illustrative scenario, implemented an interesting and relatively thorough lesson entry. Approximately 10 minutes passed from the time he gained the attention of the students at the beginning of the class session to when he stated the objective. The students certainly did not expect to close their eyes at the beginning of the lesson as Mr. Taylor directed them to do. The effectiveness of this approach was enhanced as the students thought about something quite unusual—a hypothetical environmental crisis in Norwood. Judging from student involvement, the attention getter succeeded. After a brief review to link the previous lesson to the new one, Mr. Taylor mentioned what they would be doing during the day in class. The entry culminated with his statement of the objective: over the next two class sessions, to identify at least three environmental problems Norwood was experiencing. The only phase of the entry lacking in Mr. Taylor's lesson, when comparing his approach to the ideal, was a rationale for the objective. Perhaps he could have mentioned that responsible citizens are aware of current issues and problems and many become actively involved in resolving them for the betterment of the community.

The entry is the initial contact students have with the teacher and the planned learning activity. During these first few minutes teachers have the opportunity to focus students' attention on the learning task in an interesting—and perhaps exciting—way and to prepare them adequately for new learning. In many respects, the entry to a lesson sets the tone for the entire lesson. Because of this, it is important for teachers to take extra care during the planning stage.

Closure

The closure to a lesson is the counterpart to its entry. With a closure, the instructional cycle of a lesson is completed. Whereas the goal of the entry is to focus, prepare, and stimulate the students, the closure serves to reinforce learning outcomes, integrate what has been taught, and make the transition to the next lesson. Unfortunately, classes sometimes stop abruptly without any wrap-up or transition. Teachers who have not planned for closure may stop teaching when the material runs out, then make lame, time-filling comments, or inform students that they may have the rest of the class to start their homework. Occasionally, the bell rings and cuts activities short. Either way, the students are left to tie everything together into something meaningful. This implicit faith in the students' ability or inclination to synthesize information from a presentation meaningfully is largely unfounded.

Usually the closure occurs at the end of the lesson. Yet, often several "mini-closures" are used to terminate segments of a lesson. Just as there can be several entries within any one lesson, there should be complementary closures. The extent to which closure is used will more than likely depend on the ability and interest level of students, the complexity of the content to be covered and the objectives to be achieved, and the time limitations.

One of the major purposes of closure is to reinforce the important learning outcomes that have occurred during the lesson. This can be accomplished by organizing student learning through the use of summary and review. The teacher uses review to reinforce major terms, facts, and concepts. There may be reference to notes on the chalkboard, overhead transparencies, or handouts. Questions are often asked to determine the extent of student knowledge and understanding. Higher-level information and ideas from the lesson are summarized by the teacher or students. During this phase of the closure, teachers begin to determine if their objectives have been attained.

Learning is further reinforced as ideas are integrated within students' cognitive structures. Higher-level ideas are synthesized to clarify relationships, to illustrate concepts and generalizations, or to lead students to insights or self-realizations. New learning also needs to be integrated within the unit. The teacher refers to the overall unit goals in an effort to make the link—for example, "Today we have studied the conditions under which conifers develop. This, then, should help you understand one more factor of the overall ecological development of a free-growth region. We have another factor, deciduous growth, to cover for a complete understanding." The most influential form of integration occurs when students attempt to apply learning. In this case, the teacher provides an incentive by referring to some practical and immediate use of the information or skills learned—for example, "Now that you know the long-range effects of marijuana on your mental and physical well-being, you have evidence for formulating your own attitude about its use," or, "Within a week you should be able to tune up your own car."

The closure to a lesson should also facilitate the transition from one lesson to another. The transition helps students understand the larger picture within which the immediate lesson fits. In terms of lectures, Gage and Berliner (1992) referred to this aspect of closure as *interlecture structuring*. The teacher attempts to build a bridge from one lesson to the next by giving a preview of the next lesson, by asking the students to think over a pertinent issue or problem, or by suggesting an assignment using divergent thinking that will prepare the student for involvement in the next class. This aspect of closure implies more than the routine assignment of homework; for example, "By the next class period, make a note of as many causes of inflation as you can think of and suggest a way that each might be controlled. We can consolidate our ideas and decide what the government should be doing. Then maybe we'll write our congressperson if you like."

Reference to the accomplishments made by the students during a lesson should also be part of the closure, particularly if the lesson was a good one. Comments such as this contribute significantly in producing a positive social-emotional climate in the classroom. The teacher indicates to the class the extent to which the objectives have been achieved or the amount of material that has been covered, especially as this is determined relative to some predetermined guideline; for example, "You people have done nicely to have already gotten through the fourth step of the experiment, and we should have no problem completing the final two steps during the next lab period."

Mr. Taylor used formal and informal approaches to bring closure to the lesson. He began his closure approximately 10 minutes before the end of the period by informing students of the homework assignment that required them to apply in the home setting what they learned. In addition, the assignment helped serve as a bridge to the next day's lesson because of the continuing nature of the students' inquiry. More directly, he indicated that they will know more about their community as a result of the data they gather. Mr. Taylor had the students write the proposed environmental problems on the survey rating form he distributed. This activity seemed to serve as a very informal review of major learnings. In this case, it was the tentative identification of Norwood's environmental problems that related directly to his goal for the lesson. Students' thinking might have been extended with the reading of the article, but there is no evidence that it will be pursued further.

His culminating activity, which involved students in making the transition from class to the home, was particularly effective. Asking them to form judgments about how their parents might react to their tentative list of environmental problems was an excellent way to stimulate higher-level thinking. Mr. Taylor also indicated that he thought the class was interested and that he was looking forward to the next day.

■ SUMMARY POINT ■

The lesson-presentation skills of entry and closure are important instructional components. With the entry, momentum is established with a purposely designed lesson component. With the closure, students are provided with a "kicker" to reinforce the learning that has occurred. Continuity with previous and upcoming lessons is also made during the entry and closure. Research suggests that students learn and achieve more when teachers plan and use entries to lessons. Teachers are also more effective when closures are used. Reflective decisions about each lesson's entry and closure need to be made by the teacher during the planning stage in order to enhance the learning of their students.

Motivating Skills

The conscious attempt by teachers to stimulate students in the classroom to achieve learning goals is a complex process. Students' attitudes and needs are diverse within any one class, and the teacher's attitude and personality have varying effects. It is self-evident that all students are motivated in some way. For the teacher facing 25 to 35 students in five or six classes each day, the question quickly becomes, "Motivated to do what?" It should be obvious that teachers become frustrated when students are motivated into active pursuit of interests unrelated to the lesson's objectives. Enthusiastic teachers who demonstrate their enjoyment of the subject and teaching have a considerable advantage in attracting student attention and stimulating their involvement. Likewise, teachers whose behavior is complacent will probably have problems in encouraging students to become mentally and physically involved.

From an instructional point of view, the effect of the teacher's motivation-related behavior is reflected in the students' inclination to attain the lesson objectives. Motivating behaviors may take many forms. Instructional style determines the motivational techniques that are characteristic of a particular teacher. The most pervasive form of teacher motivational behavior is the use of a variety of verbal and nonverbal behaviors to create a dynamic presence in the classroom. The teacher who purposely uses a wide range of behaviors to display interest in the subject and the students is displaying a certain presence that contributes to enthusiasm.

The range of motivating behaviors displayed by teachers is influenced considerably by their personality and attitude. Another major approach teachers can use to stimulate student interest and involvement is the use of a variety of teaching strategies, methods, and techniques. Although sensitivity to the instructional flow influences the extent to which teachers shift gears within and between lessons, other factors such as knowledge of instructional practices and time for preparation play an important part.

A highly motivating teacher consistently displays dynamic personal behaviors in the classroom. Students and fellow teachers describing that person would probably use descriptors such as enthusiastic, energetic, exciting, and stimulating. The teacher with a high degree of presence is visually and auditorily dynamic. Four major areas that contribute to presence are: physical movement, nonverbal behaviors, lesson pace, and voice quality.

A motivating teacher moves about the classroom during whole-group instruction. This teacher avoids patterned pacing, but moves purposefully about the front and, when possible, to the sides, rear, and through the rows to give students a "moving target." This teacher also remains at a distance from a reciting student to encourage the student to speak loudly. This often requires retreating from a student who is responding. The teacher refrains from sitting on the desk for more than a few minutes at a time and avoids sitting at or standing behind the desk or demonstration table except as necessary. A spatial mapping category system has been devised to help chart patterns of observed teacher classroom travel (Susi, 1985, 1986).

A motivating teacher uses nonverbal behavior to create presence. Research has indicated that nonverbal behaviors have a powerful impact in the classroom. Besides moving about the classroom, this also includes using a variety of facial expressions, maintaining eye contact, using a variety of gestures, using body movements such as nods and head shakes, and placing a hand on a student's shoulder or moving into close proximity to students. The teacher's mode of dress and grooming also send nonverbal messages to students. A neatly dressed and clean teacher will command more respect than one who does not seem to care about appearance. There is an overall impact, a cumulative effect, of the teacher's nonverbal behaviors that will leave students with the impression that their teacher is an enthusiastic and dynamic person who enjoys both the subject and the work.

Motivating teachers also use their voice effectively. The voice is the most obvious instrument with which the teacher conducts the business of teaching. Ideally, the teacher's voice should be strong (not just loud) and have pleasant tonal qualities. The use of inflection should complement the meaning of words being spoken. The voice should not have shrill or strained qualities or obvious impediments that cause the listener to experience discomfort or difficulty. A teacher's vocabulary should be appropriate for the students. The teacher's mode of delivery should be smooth and mature, without the annoying repetition of particular words or phrases or the use of adolescent speech habits (e.g., "like," "you know," "stuff," and "you guys"), and—it should go without saying—the use of correct pronunciation and grammar is essential.

A motivating teacher controls the pace of the lesson. Controlling the pace helps to maintain student attention and to accomplish objectives. Pacing in the classroom results from the teacher's sensitivity to the tenor of student behavior. Although changing mode is a means to control pace, pacing occurs intramodally as well. In a foreign-language drill, for example, students are pushed to the limit they can tolerate; in a discussion in science, patience is exhibited while students reflect on responses. Stepping to the board to write important information is an effective means of adjusting pace because it "freezes" student thought on a point for a few deliberate moments. The teacher moderates the students' excessive exuberance but makes deliberate efforts to provide stimulation when the class lags. The teacher's actual behaviors in the interest of pacing may take many forms; it is important that the teacher behaves deliberately to maintain that optimum learning pace.

A teacher also motivates students by varying the instructional mode. *Instructional mode* refers to the techniques, methods, and strategies used. Just as a teacher commands student attention through personal behaviors, a teacher also sustains attention through instructional behaviors. Attention span is an important consideration, and changing the instructional mode is one means of coping with it. This is most often accomplished by using a particular teaching mode for only a limited period of time and then moving to another mode. There should be at least one major shift during any given class period and possibly as many as three or four depending on the nature and level of the class. This variance in instructional mode is particularly essential in longer, block-scheduled, classes.

The most effective shifts are those that vary the learning stimulus of the students. For example, students in a high school government class might listen to a lecture on the concept *compromise* and how the process connects to their lives and plays a crucial role in government and the formation of laws today. To demonstrate a historical application of the concept, the teacher might then organize students into small groups to read about, discuss, and report on several of the specific compromises of the Constitutional Convention of 1787. A shift from a lecture to small-group interaction is better than a shift from a lecture to a film on the convention, for example, because students move from passive to active involvement. The occasional rearrangement of chairs in the classroom to fit the nature of the learning activity is also involved in changing mode.

As best as we can tell from a written transcript as the only data source, Mr. Taylor seemed to create a relatively stimulating teaching environment through his use of personal and instructional behaviors. At the beginning of the period, he entered the lesson by telling the students "with excitement in his voice" to close their eyes and imagine a crisis taking place in their community. With some imagination, we can almost visualize the altered facial expressions and inflection in his voice on the word *crisis* as one way to depict excitement. Later in the lesson, he complimented the students on their speculations about community problems. Perhaps we can imagine a lowering of the voice for most of the compliment and a louder and inflected voice as he said, "Well done!" We do have a strong indication, though, that Mr. Taylor was concerned about contributing to the students' motivation through varying the pace of the lesson and his physical position in the classroom. He was aware that several students were losing interest at two points during the lesson, and in response to the last observation, he purposely quickened the pace of the lesson to finish what he had planned in the remaining 20 minutes.

A major strength of Mr. Taylor's lesson in terms of the students' motivation that we can determine from the transcript was the significant variety of instructional shifts he employed to sustain students' attention and interest. The lesson was initiated with a brief discussion followed by an equally brief, individually oriented writing exercise that shifted senses. He then continued with discussion involving considerable interaction related to the environmental problems that Norwood was facing. At one point, he incorporated information giving in the form of an extended explanation and then shifted again to discussion. Senses were shifted once more after he presented the assignment and students had to write on their forms. During the closure, he had students read a short article and then wrapped up the lesson with a brief interchange of viewpoints. There were three major instructional patterns: discussion-writing-discussion, explanation-writing-explanation, and a reading-discussion shift. Minor patterns also occurred.

Hints for the Beginning Teacher

Seeing yourself teaching on videotape can be worth at least 1,000 words. Have another teacher or a student videotape you as you teach a typical lesson (i.e., don't put on an act!). As you view the videotape in private, take note of your lesson entry and closure, your wait time, other questioning skills, and so on.

■ RESEARCH AND THEORETICAL BASE: QUESTIONS AND QUESTIONING SKILLS

The most basic way teachers stimulate interaction, thinking, and learning in the classroom is through the use of questions. The research literature on questions and questioning has grown during the past 40 years primarily because of the movement to identify those teacher behaviors and techniques that contribute to students' learning gains. Today, interest in teacher and student questioning continues to grow, particularly within the context of classroom interaction and as a primary means to encourage discussion. Discussion is viewed as an important alternative instructional method to teacher lecture and student recitation because of its potential to promote student understanding of societal issues and problems (in science and social studies classes, for example) and how this might lead to reflective decision making and problem solving. Constructivist teachers encourage active participation during discussions through the use of open-ended questions designed to challenge thinking (Zemelman, Daniels, and Hyde, 1998). Whether they are teacher or student questions, "Asking the right questions can go a long way toward helping teachers and students learn from one another" (Latham, 1997).

The following are generalized research findings drawn from several reviews of research (Wilen, 1991, 1994; Wilen and White, 1991) about teachers' and students' use of questioning in classrooms. The findings support the assertion that questioning is one of the most influential teaching acts because of its potential to stimulate student interaction, thinking, and learning.

1. Questioning can be used to accomplish a wide variety of instructional purposes in the classroom. Purposes include reviewing materials previously read or studied; diagnosing students' abilities, attitudes, and preferences; stimulating critical and creative thinking; arousing interest in a topic; encouraging reflective discussion on an issue or problem; probing students' thoughts and expressions; personalizing subject matter; supporting students' contributions

during a recitation or discussion; assessing progress toward attaining lesson and unit objectives; and even managing and controlling students' behavior.

2. Questioning positively influences students' achievement. Researchers have found that high frequencies of teachers' oral questions correlate with gains in student achievement. Several questioning techniques also positively correlate with students' achievement gains: asking clearly phrased questions, probing students' responses to questions, redirecting questions to other students, balancing the responses of volunteering and nonvolunteering students, using wait time after asking a question and after a student has responded, and providing feedback primarily in the form of acknowledgment after a student responds.

3. Questioning can be used to get students more actively involved in classroom interaction. Researchers recommend that teachers organize the students' seating in a circle or a semicircle to facilitate communication and to create a more student-oriented, conversational atmosphere, one in which the teacher does not dominate the interaction. In a conversational atmosphere the questions are more personal, students' responses are not evaluated, and students have control over speaking turns. Extended wait time increases the quantity and quality of student utterances. Students should be encouraged to ask questions because they respond in more complex ways to each other than to a teacher's questions. Using nonquestioning alternatives—such as different statement forms—during interaction may result in a less-threatening environment and more student participation. (Nonquestioning alternatives are discussed later in this chapter and in Chapter 7 as an important component of the discussion method.)

4. Questioning can be used to encourage students to think. Researchers suggest that recitation is not an appropriate method to encourage students to think because of the emphasis on asking many questions at a low cognitive level within a highly structured interaction pattern that is controlled by the teacher. Students have little opportunity to use language to think and express ideas. Researchers recommend the use of higher-cognitive-level questions if developing critical-thinking skills is an important curricular goal. Researchers also recommend extending wait time after questions because students' responses become more complex and reflective. Use of a variety of teacher and student questioning and of alternative nonquestioning techniques such as the use of statements is also suggested to encourage higher-level thinking. One problem, though, is that there is only an approximate 50 percent congruency between the cognitive level of teacher questions asked and the cognitive level of students' responses. This correspondence can be increased as teachers use cues to clarify expectations for thinking and to reduce ambiguity. Follow-up probing is especially useful for this purpose.

5. Students can ask more and better questions. Researchers have shown that while teachers ask a high frequency of questions (two to four per minute), students ask few information-seeking questions. Researchers recommend that teachers reduce the number of questions they ask and have students formulate more questions. Teachers should share information about their approach to questioning with students to help the students understand the teachers'

expectations regarding the kind of thinking necessary to answer questions. Teachers should consider preparing their students to identify key words within questions that suggest how to process them and the kind of thinking necessary to answer them. Other suggestions center on encouraging students to assume teaching roles. Teachers might train students to generate questions that become the basis of student-led recitations or a part of discussions. Also, teachers might encourage students to engage in reciprocal teaching, or assume the role of teacher, as they formulate and ask questions after reading text sections.

In a case study involving primarily elementary and high school teachers teaching science content, van Zee and her colleagues (2001) found that student questions can occur frequently and spontaneously during student-generated inquiry discussions and peer collaborations in the classroom. In these situations students constructed knowledge with one another as they engaged in independent, yet collaborative thinking. The teacher's role was to facilitate and monitor from afar. Ciardiello (2000) found that when students ask questions of their peers, discussion becomes more frequent, open, egalitarian, and spontaneous. He recommends that teachers should actively prepare students to ask questions of peers and that this might be effective in loosening the teacher's control of questioning.

■ APPLICATION TO PRACTICE: QUESTION LEVELS

Since the time of Socrates, the questions a teacher asks in the classroom and the techniques used to stimulate interaction have been considered essential components of the instructional process. Questions are essential because teachers can conveniently and effectively use them to engage student thinking about issues, problems, and topics under discussion. Although the congruency of the thought level of teachers' questions to students' responses is only around 50 percent, teachers still have considerable impact in their ability to control the thought levels of students in the classroom. As a result, teachers need to pay attention to the questions they ask and the way they ask them. Once the teacher realizes that there are different cognitive levels of questions and that a relationship between questions and student thinking exists, decisions need to be made about the proportion of time students will spend engaged in lower- and higher-level thinking. These decisions will take into account the objectives of the lesson and the method(s) employed to achieve these objectives. Practically every method and strategy that a teacher can employ with individuals or groups of students involves questioning. Two of the most common methods are recitations involving primarily low-level convergent questions to get students to recall important facts and concepts related to an issue or topic and guided discussions that are designed to encourage students to begin thinking as they apply what they have learned. (These forms of discussion and other methods that rely on questioning are presented in Chapter 7.) As teachers plan lesson objectives and the methods and strategies to achieve them, decisions will be made about the balance of thinking levels and the corresponding kinds of questions needed to be asked.

The following classification scheme for identifying and devising cognitive levels of questions is based on Gallagher and Aschner's (1963) well-known adaptation of Guilford's (1956) "structure of intellect" model. The levels have been initially categorized as convergent and divergent to correspond to narrow and broad student thinking and have then subdivided into two additional levels that reflect the hierarchy of thinking levels. Convergent questions serve the important purpose of determining students' basic knowledge and understanding and are the basis for subsequent higher-level thinking. Therefore, lower-level questions should rarely become ends in themselves; they should serve as a means to achieve higher-level thinking. Divergent questions serve the purpose of requiring students to process what they have learned by thinking critically, creatively, and evaluatively. Students need opportunities to practice higher forms of thought if they are expected to become independent and reflective thinkers. Each of the four cognitive levels is accompanied with a definition, example student behaviors, and illustrative questions (Wilen, 1991). In addition, corresponding levels to Bloom's taxonomy (1956) are identified because of teachers' familiarity with this system. Bloom's taxonomy was used as the basis for devising instructional objectives and goals in Chapter 5.

Before proceeding with the introduction of the category system, a word should be said about the importance of identifying example student behaviors, referred to previously in the review-of-research section as "key words" and "clues," and emphasizing the use of these in the planning and asking of questions. Thinking involves the processing of information and questioning helps facilitate this. Costa and Lowery (1989) advocate the use of such clues to communicate to students the type of thinking a teacher wants. Action verbs embedded in the questions can cause students to "use their senses; recall from memory; process the ideas; use or apply the knowledge in some action; and transfer or evaluate those relationships in new or hypothetical situations" (p. 25). The use of questions and related cues have very recently been found to improve student achievement across all content areas and across all grade levels (Varlas, 2002). A conscious use of key words as part of questions increases the probability that a teacher's intention and expectations will be congruent to students' performances as noticed in their responses.

Level I—Low-Order Convergent: Questions requiring students to engage in reproductive thinking. The teacher's intention is to have students recall or recognize information. Emphasis is on memorization and observation, so students' responses can easily be anticipated. Level I corresponds to the "knowledge" level of Bloom's taxonomy.

Example student behaviors (clues): define, recognize, recount, quote, identify, list, recall, answer "yes" or "no."

Example questions: Who invented the sewing machine? How many colors are on the chart? What is the definition given in your book of photosynthesis?

Level II—High-Order Convergent: Questions requiring students to engage in the first level of productive thinking. The teacher's intention is to have students go beyond recall and demonstrate understanding of information by mentally organizing material. Students also apply learned information. Although more thinking is involved at this level, student responses still generally can be anticipated. Level II corresponds to Bloom's "comprehension" and "application" levels.

Example student behaviors (clues): describe, compare, contrast, rephrase, summarize, explain, translate, interpret, relate, apply, use, provide an example, solve.

Example questions: What is an example of cooperation in your home? How are these numbers related? How would you solve this problem using the accounting procedure we just discussed? In your own words, according to the story, how did Tom Sawyer convince his friends to whitewash the fence?

Level III—Low-Order Divergent: Questions requiring students to think critically about information. The teacher's intention is to have students analyze information to discover reasons or causes, draw conclusions or generalizations, or to find evidence in support of opinions. Higher-level productive thinking is involved; thus, students' responses may or may not be anticipated. Level III corresponds to Bloom's "analysis" level.

Example student behaviors (clues): identify motives, reasons, or causes; draw conclusions, inferences, or generalizations; provide evidence; support ideas; analyze information.

Example questions: Now that you have completed the experiment, what is your conclusion about why the substance became denser? Why do you think the girl ran away from home? What evidence can you provide to support your view that the constitutional power of the president has diminished over the years?

Level IV—High-Order Divergent: Higher-order questions requiring students to perform original and evaluative thinking. The teacher's intention is to have students make predictions; solve lifelike problems; produce original communications; and judge ideas, information, actions, and aesthetic expressions based on internal or external criteria. This level represents the highest form of productive thinking; consequently, students' responses generally cannot be anticipated. Level IV corresponds to Bloom's "synthesis" and "evaluation" levels.

Example student behaviors (clues): produce original communications, predict, propose solutions, create, speculate, hypothesize, synthesize, construct, devise, write, design, develop, judge, value, choose, opine.

Example questions: How would you rate the effectiveness of the Environmental Protection Agency? What is a good title for this story? How can we raise money to support the recycling center? What is your favorite orchestral instrument and why? Is the president doing a good job of combatting terrorism?

Questioning Circle

The "questioning-circle" system is a very effective approach to use in planning, observing, and analyzing teachers' and students' classroom questions. Although the previous question-classification system is appropriate for teachers to use when designing constructivist-learning situations, the questioning-circle system may be even better. In addition to encouraging teachers to plan for questions to stimulate students' critical thinking, the questioning-circle approach encourages teachers to personalize subject-matter content. A main tenet of constructivism is that students learn by making connections between new subject matter and their current knowledge and experiences. The more teachers can relate the content to students' lives, the more they will understand it and be able to process and apply it in new situations. Questioning can help accomplish this.

The questioning-circle approach provides a flexible format for questioning by not assuming a sequential and hierarchical thinking pattern. The circles are represented on a plane, with no single type of question "better" or "higher" than another. Christenbury and Kelly (1983) depicted different areas of questioning in the form of overlapping circles, each representing different aspects of reality: (1) the matter—subject of discussion (e.g., topic, concept, issue, problem), (2) personal reality—student's relationship with the subject, and (3) external reality—broader, more worldly view of the subject. Questions are devised based on the circles and their intersections. The most significant question is the central intersection because it requires a synthesis of thinking from all the areas. The questioning circle is shown in Figure 6.2, with sample questions representing the circles and their intersections related to the topic of acid rain*:

1. The matter: What are the causes of acid rain?

2. Personal reality: Have you personally seen acid-rain damage and, if so, how would you describe your experience?

3. External reality: How has the acid-rain problem influenced the policies of other countries?

4. The matter/personal reality: How might you personally be affected by the acid-rain problem?

5. Personal reality/external reality: What could you do to bring the issues and problems associated with acid rain to the attention of other people?

6. The matter/external reality: What are the issues affecting the relationship between Canada and the United States related to the acid-rain problem?

7. The matter/personal reality/external reality: Why should we as citizens of a global society care about acid rain?

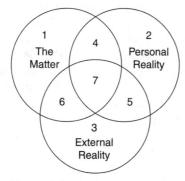

Figure 6.2 Questioning Circle

*Thanks are extended to the teachers participating in William Wilen's thinking-and-questioning workshop (Lake School District, Ohio) for devising these questions.

■ APPLICATION TO PRACTICE: QUESTIONING SKILLS

The formation of questions appropriate to desired objectives is extremely important but no more so than the questioning process. The teacher's effectiveness as a questioner depends not only on devising good questions but also on the way questions are asked. The skillful application of questioning techniques is essential if the questions are to serve the purposes for which they are intended. Effective application of a series of questioning techniques can make the difference between a class of students who are passive, confused, frustrated, and unchallenged and a class of students who are active, stimulated, and reflective. Important to this effective application is a teacher who relies more on current and up-to-date informed sources about questioning techniques than intuitive, or personal, sources for information. If misconceptions about approaches to questioning influence decision making, the effectiveness of the teacher as a questioner will be greatly diminished (Wilen, 2001).

The following is a list of questioning techniques synthesized from a variety of sources on questioning and reported in Wilen (1991). Many of these, based on the effective-teaching research reported previously, are positive correlates with student achievement (Wilen, 1987; Wilen and Clegg, 1986). In addition to the questioning techniques, the nonquestioning alternative of the use of teacher statements has been added. Although there is no research to link the use of statements directly to gains in student achievement, there is a tendency for them to encourage student participation and thinking, particularly during discussion (Dillon, 1988, 1990).

Question Phrasing

Questions need to be phrased clearly to communicate response expectations precisely to students. Vague or ambiguous questions self-evidently lead to student confusion and prolonged frustration if the practice becomes a regular occurrence. A vague question such as "What about the law Congress passed?" forces students to try to guess what the teacher wants rather than thinking of and formulating a direct response to the question. Another source of ambiguity is the run-on question. This occurs as two or more uninterrupted and often incomplete questions are asked in a series. Frustration develops as students try to guess which question to answer. This implies that key questions need to be planned because these are often on a higher cognitive level. Divergent questions need more planning because of their difficulty. This also implies that teachers may need to acquaint students with the different levels of questions to increase the probability that expectations might be communicated more clearly.

Adapting Questions

Questions need to be adapted to the language and ability level of the class and, in many cases, individual students within the class. Most classes are heterogeneously grouped, so questions need to be phrased in natural, simple language to increase the probability that they will be understood by all. Within classes, language will need to be simplified for students who learn at a slower pace or certain inclusion students and made more thought provoking for gifted students. A question for a lower-ability student might be, "From the article you have just read, how does the demand for a product affect its supply?" To higher-ability students, the question might become, "Going beyond the article a little, how does price affect supply and demand, and at what point is market equilibrium reached?" An important implication for teachers is the need to get to know their students to adjust their questions and thereby increase comprehension.

Question Sequence

Asking questions in a planned and patterned sequence, particularly in preparation for guided and reflective discussions, will enhance student thinking, comprehension, and learning. Random questioning rarely communicates a clear focus or intent. The primary factors that influence the choice of question sequence include the objective of the lesson, the ability level of the students, and the prior knowledge and understanding students have of the content being discussed. Some sequences will begin with lower-level questions and will progress to stimulating, higher-level thinking. Others will start with higher-level questions and stay there.

Asking lower-level questions will quickly determine the extent to which students understand the content. For example, consider the following episode: After having the students read an article on proposed changes in immigration laws, the teacher asks the question, "Should the United States permit the immigration of unlimited numbers of refugees from war-torn countries?" Students give minimal support for the opinions they express. The teacher then asks these review-oriented questions: "What is the number-one problem the author associates with immigration?" and "What do the current immigration laws say about refugees from nations involved in war?" Accordingly, if teachers intend to ask questions, they should plan the pattern of those questions, particularly those at the higher cognitive levels.

While planning a sequence of higher-level questions in preparation for a guided discussion is useful and advised, planning such a sequence for an open discussion may not be realistic. Open or reflective discussions are more natural and possess the characteristics of an instructional conversation. This form of discussion, by its very nature, is less structured, with students' responses driving the direction of the inquiry and interaction. The teacher's role is to facilitate and to be responsive to students' comments, questions, and ideas as they develop meaning. Although the teacher certainly has planned one or more objectives to achieve as a result of engaging students in a reflective discussion and has planned a few key, thought-provoking questions, the teacher will need to be more flexible in the sequence of questions and statements to move the students toward understanding.

Balancing Cognitive Levels of Questions

Balancing questions designed to stimulate convergent and divergent thinking will enhance the possibility that a greater range of student cognitive abilities will be developed. Research has demonstrated that teachers at all levels tend to ask predominantly lower-level questions, with an emphasis on Level I convergent questions. Convergent questions should serve the purpose of determining students' basic understanding so that they can apply their knowledge by engaging in subsequent higher-level thinking. Critical and creative thinking is stimulated with divergent questions. Teachers can use information about the levels of questions presented previously to plan an optimal balance of convergent and divergent questions to achieve unit goals and lesson objectives.

Student Participation

Student involvement in classroom interaction can be increased by balancing responses from volunteering and nonvolunteering students, redirecting initially unanswered questions to other students, and encouraging student–student interaction. Too often, only a few students participate in class discussions and recitations and therefore dominate the interaction. Every student can make a contribution to class interaction, and teacher alertness is necessary to perceive verbal and nonverbal cues from reticent students such as a perplexed look or partially raised hand. Discretion should be used regarding the difficulty level and intimacy of the questions when calling on nonvolunteering students. The argument has been made by Kelly (1993), though, that calling on nonvolunteering students is a democratic practice because citizens, just as students, have a democratic responsibility to participate in public talk.

Another useful approach to stimulate a response and thinking is to direct one question to several students. The redirection could be prompted by an unanswered question, an incorrect response, or a desire to get additional responses to the same question. Redirection can involve volunteering and nonvolunteering students. Participation during discussions, particularly, can be stimulated by encouraging students to interact with each other. Sometimes there is a delicate balance between teacher intervention and teacher facilitation. "Jim, how do you react to Mary's point of view that *The Catcher in the Rye* is an example of pornography?" is one way to stimulate student–student interaction. Most interaction is of the teacher–student–teacher type. Student–student interaction involves more students, increasing the probability of a greater diversity of ideas, perspectives, and judgments that are appropriate during a discussion. Small- and cooperative-learning groups are a major means to encourage student–student interaction and are strongly advocated by social constructivists. Thus, the way interaction is encouraged and conducted communicates expectations to the students. More students will become involved in interaction if they are encouraged to do so by the teacher.

Probing Responses

During discussions in which the emphasis is on stimulating more complex student thinking, students sometimes lack skill and confidence to express themselves at the higher cognitive levels. Resulting responses to questions can be ambiguous, incomplete, or superficial. In these cases, teachers need to follow up with probing questions or comments to encourage students to complete, clarify, expand, or support their answers. Probes to encourage students to complete and clarify responses are often necessary with younger learners as they begin to articulate the basics of reflective thinking or with older learners at the upper grades who have not been sufficiently exposed to higher-level questions. Probes are often useful to encourage students to elevate thinking to higher cognitive levels. Comments beginning with such phrases as "What if," "Suppose," or "How about" are common during discussions in which teachers are challenging students' thinking. Probably the most common probes during discussion are those that request learners to support their points of view, opinions, or judgments with evidence from internal or external sources. Comments such as "Why?" "What evidence do you have?" and "How can you support your view?" are common in reflective discussions. This means that learners' initial responses to questions must be heard before probes can be used. Listening skills are very important. Also, to be effective, probes must be nonthreatening and used in a supportive manner.

Wait Time

Students require more time to formulate thoughtful responses, particularly during discussions, because of the complexity of thinking required by teachers' divergent questions. Although students need more time to think, research shows that teachers wait only approximately one second after asking a question before calling on a student and one second after a student responds before probing the response, rephrasing the question, redirecting to another student, or providing the answer (Rowe, 1974).

Teachers can use wait time at least two different ways to increase the probability that students' responses will be more acceptable. The first, postquestion wait time, is the pause after a teacher asks a question and before a student responds, and the second, postresponse wait time, is the pause after a student responds and before the teacher reacts. Waiting three to five seconds improves the quantity and quality of students' responses, thereby increasing the probability of reflective thinking and effective discussion (Atwood and Wilen, 1991). Rowe (1987) found in her research that the lengths of students' responses increased, responses reflected higher-level thought, failures to respond decreased, student–student interaction increased, and the frequency of student questions increased as a result of expanding wait time. Higher-level questions will be minimally effective in stimulating participation and thinking unless students are allowed time to think. Teachers need to remember to pause after asking a question and after a student responds, particularly during reflective discussions.

Student Questions

Students generally expect to answer questions in most classes, not to have to ask them. They rarely ask questions, except when they do not understand something or need more information. Students should be encouraged to formulate questions because they become more actively involved in the learning process.

Just as importantly, as students ask questions at higher cognitive levels, it can be reasonably assumed that corresponding levels of thought are stimulated. For example, suppose students in a Spanish III class have been studying the culture of Latin America. The teacher requests that each student devise two questions to ask a hypothetical visitor from Mexico to acquire a deeper understanding of the lifestyle of Latin Americans. The questions are shared and answered cooperatively by the teacher and students. Teachers should consider whether they have underestimated students' ability to generate thoughtful questions and whether they need to plan ways for students to become more involved in this manner. Two useful sources for approaches that teachers might use to encourage student-generated questions are *Questioning and Teaching: A Manual of Practice* (Dillon, 1988) and *Teaching Thinking Through Effective Questioning* (Hunkins, 1995).

Teacher Statements

It has been only within the last 15 years that nonquestioning alternatives advocated by Dillon (1988, 1994) have seriously been considered as techniques to enhance classroom interaction, particularly during discussions. In addition to wait time, student-generated questions, and signals that teachers communicate to indicate that they are listening to and receiving students' responses, the use of statements by the teacher is suggested. The rationale for using statements is that students respond to them, perhaps more so than to questions. In fact, Dillon urged that nonquestion alternatives be used in place of questions. Among the types of statements that teachers might use to stimulate student participation and thinking are: (1) declarative statement—stating a thought that occurs to you in relation to what the student has been saying; (2) reflective restatement—repeating, paraphrasing, or characterizing what the student has just said; (3) statement of interest—stating that you are interested in hearing more related to what the student has just said; and (4) speaker referral—stating the relationship between what the student has just said and what a previous student has said. Specific examples of different types of statements can be found as part of the commentary on the discussion method in the next chapter. Instead of replacing questions with nonquestioning alternatives, teachers might find it more practical to use them with questioning techniques during recitations and discussions. A further step is to experiment with different combinations of techniques to see which have the most impact on students' involvement and thinking during classroom interaction.

Scenario Analysis

In the illustrative scenario, Mr. Taylor involved his students in several reflective minidiscussions during the course of the class period. The discussions were interspersed with learning activities designed to structure students' critical thinking about their community's environmental problems. The vast majority of questions that he asked were at the divergent level, and the questioning techniques that he

■ WEBSITE RESOURCE ■

The Covington City Schools (Tennessee) have a website for teachers, students, and parents that includes Teacher's Resources at

www.covington.k12.tn.us/resources/ teacher.htm.

Click on Questioning to get information on Socratic questioning, which aims at encouraging critical and evaluative thinking. There are many examples of different types of questions: questions for clarification; questions probing assumptions, reasoning, and evidence; questions encouraging viewpoints or perspectives; and questions about implications and consequences.

employed were realistic and conducive to a reflective discussion. He initiated a discussion at the beginning of the period after having the students imagine an environmental crisis taking place in their community. The question—it is actually an implied question—is classified at Level IV (high divergent), because original thinking was required as students engaged in speculation. Several students responded with their thoughts. Asking students what problems they think their community is facing requires analytical and evaluative thinking. Students are making generalizations based on observations of their surroundings and making a judgment as to which observation is most important. This question could be categorized at Level III (low divergent), although there is no indication that all students supported their responses with evidence.

During the next questioning sequence, Mr. Taylor used several questioning techniques. It was initiated with a Level III (low-divergent) question, "How do we know if these are really problems that Norwood should do something about?" This requires students to draw conclusions, a characteristic of analytical thinking. After using wait time, he called on a nonvolunteer who appeared "deep in thought." Mr. Taylor proceeded to probe Jim's response to expand his thinking on the issue by requiring that he make a judgment. Several other students then offered their points of view. Approximately halfway through the period, Mr. Taylor asked students to recall the definition of *hypothesis*. Defining is a characteristic of Level I (low convergent) thinking. There was also an indication he purposely used wait time. In attempting to have the students relate the definition to their guesses about their community's environmental problems, he called on another nonvolunteer with little success. Even with a probe, the student responded minimally. The question was then redirected to another student who gave a more complete response. After assigning homework and having the students read a brief article, Mr. Taylor directed a Level IV (high-divergent) question to a student. She was asked to make a judgment about her parents' perception of the most critical environmental problem.

In regard to the other questioning techniques, there was evidence that the questions were phrased well and adapted to this average group of students. Although all the questions stimulated primarily divergent thinking, a sequence of questions is evident based on logical thinking about solving problems. Because of the capabilities of the students, Mr. Taylor needed to spend only a minimal amount of time reviewing facts. Therefore, a balance of questions was not necessary. He did not consider it pertinent to have the students devise questions during this lesson.

APPLICATION for DIVERSE CLASSROOMS

Teachers in multicultural classrooms must learn about the cultural backgrounds of their students and the possible impact behaviors representative of their culture and upbringing may have on their behaviors in the classroom; for example, when asking questions, teachers need to know what types of questions are not appropriate for certain students. This account (Heath, 1983) reports that rural African American students in the Piedmont area of the Carolinas had difficulty with the question-and-answer technique used in most lessons. On investigation, it was learned that conversational discussion was appropriate for adults only. Parents gave directions to children rather than asking questions for discussion. When questions were asked by parents, they were convergent questions, asking for knowledge related to the child or young person, such as "What did you do today?" or "Where were you?" Consequently, children were not prepared to respond to convergent questions that focused on knowledge of content.

■ RESEARCH AND THEORETICAL BASE: SUPPORTING SKILLS, INFORMATION-GIVING SKILLS, LISTENING SKILLS

Teachers' display of support for students' responses and activities is primarily noticed in the form of feedback encouraging them to continue their efforts. Support usually takes the form of reinforcement such as praise, acknowledgment of correct responses, and assistance with incorrect answers. Teachers are also supportive when they accept and use students' feelings and ideas. In a very recent review of research, those at Mid-continent Research for Education and Learning identified reinforcing effort and providing recognition as one of nine approaches to improve student achievement across all content areas and levels (Varlas, 2002). Chance (1992), based on his review of research, considered the many different forms of extrinsic reinforcers among the most powerful tools teachers could use. He concluded that teachers must supplement intrinsic rewards with extrinsic rewards to influence student behavior effectively. Brophy (1981), though, found that praise was not always effective in stimulating students' learning gains. A high rate of praise defeats its purpose and therefore does not always serve as reinforcement. Simple use of acknowledgment can often be used to communicate acceptance of students' contributions in place of praise. On the other hand, Gage and Berliner (1992) explained that the discriminating use of praise, the use of corrective feedback, and a teacher's use of student ideas showed a positive relationship with students' achievement and attitudes. Good and Brophy (2000) found that the most effective form of praise is that which specifies to the student the reason for the praise. Teachers should provide feedback to students regarding their performance to encourage them to achieve goals.

Information giving is another technique that teachers regularly employ in the classroom. Teachers generally give information informally over short spans of time, such as when directions are given for an assignment. More formal information giving is used, for example, in the lecture method. Information giving as a technique focuses on short-term purposes—the emphasis in this section.

The available research on information giving centers on the value of structuring new information for students. One of the 14 major findings from the Beginning Teacher Evaluation Study suggested that structuring lessons for the students and giving directions on task procedures were positively correlated with high student success (Fisher et al., 1980). Brophy and Good (1986) found that students learned more efficiently when teachers structured new information for students. The decisions teachers make about the information they will present should address the provision of an appropriate form of structure to enhance students' understanding.

Research supports the important role that teachers' listening behaviors play in interactive learning situations with students in the classroom. Strother (1987) defined listening as "the process by which spoken language is converted to meaning in the mind" (p. 625). In her review of the research, she found that 45 percent of total time devoted to classroom communication was spent on listening, 30 percent for speaking, 16 percent for reading, and another 9 percent for writing. Flanders (1970) found that teacher verbalizations that indicated acceptance of students' feelings and use of their ideas contributed significantly to a positive social-emotional classroom climate. For teachers to express empathy genuinely or paraphrase students' ideas, for example, effective listening behaviors are essential. Garrett, Sadker, and Sadker (1990) further substantiated the need for teachers to display regularly such attending behaviors as eye contact and facial expressions as teachers listen to and communicate with students in group discussions and individual conversations. Furthermore, if teachers expect students to be aware of and regularly display good listening skills, they must also model careful listening behaviors in the classroom (Good and Brophy, 2000).

■ APPLICATION TO PRACTICE: SUPPORTING SKILLS

The extent to which a teacher provides cognitive and emotional support to students in the classroom is based primarily on the kind of climate that has been created. Climate is perceived as "the generalized attitudes, feelings, and actions that prevail in a class" (Levin with Long, 1981, p. 206), resulting from a variety of physical, psychological, social, and intellectual stimuli. A classroom's climate is, in many ways, its character or personality, and climate has an impact on learning in significant ways.

The teacher is primarily responsible for establishing the classroom climate. If a positive social-emotional climate has been created, the students feel supported by their teacher. For example, if the teacher regularly displays behaviors suggestive of a positive attitude toward learning and school in comments to students, promotes cooperation among the students, and is accepting of students' feelings and ideas, students will feel a sense of belonging and will develop respect for the teacher and for each other. In addition, they will be stimulated to participate in class activities.

Several supportive teacher behaviors contribute to the creation of a positive climate. They have been identified by Flanders (1970) as acceptance of students' feelings, praise, encouragement, and use of students' ideas. An additional area of support is the use of courtesy. Teachers can demonstrate acceptance of students' feelings by making those feelings explicit, whether they are positive or negative. Teachers can do this with individual students or with the entire class. For example, imagine a group of excited middle school students returning from a special assembly. To focus them on the task, the teacher might say (with facial expressions depicting enthusiasm), "You must have really enjoyed the presentation. I would like to hear your thoughts before we go back to our work." In this case, the teacher has been supportive by displaying acceptance of students' feelings.

Verbal praise is probably the most commonly and frequently used form of reinforcement and support by teachers in classrooms at all levels. Praise can be expressed as comments ranging from brief expressions such as "good" and "fine" to extended judgments including the specifics of the accomplishment. An example of the latter situation is, "That was an outstanding report, Juan. You not only organized it well and presented it neatly, but also you drew some very interesting conclusions about global warming that we will discuss in class."

Students' contributions and achievements are often taken for granted. Praise has a significant effect on student behavior, so teachers should remain constantly aware of opportunities to praise students in a genuine manner. But keep in mind that the focus must be on the quality of praise; when quantity is the major emphasis, praise does not always have the effect of reinforcement, thereby defeating the teacher's intent. Several rules of thumb have been offered: Deliver praise simply and directly in a natural tone of voice; specify the accomplishment; make sure that nonverbal behaviors are congruent with the verbal praise; and use a variety of expressions (Good and Brophy, 2000).

Encouragement of student behaviors is similar to the use of praise in that it may have the same supportive effect. However, praise is an expression of a teacher's value judgment. The intent of expressions of encouragement is to stimulate a student to initiate or continue with a learning activity or task related to the objectives. Examples include continuing with a response to a question, further pursuit of an investigation in the library, attempting a new skill, and considering a different approach to solve a problem. Expressions such as "you're on the right track," "keep going," "you almost have it," "okay, how about a little more?" are relatively common. Using wait time (pausing) after students have made responses might encourage some to continue their responses with a new perspective at a higher level of cognition. Expressions of encouragement such as eye contact and a hand on a shoulder communicate support for students' efforts and motivate them further.

Moreover, a teacher can create a supportive climate by using students' ideas. The expression of ideas by students is an inevitable occurrence in the classroom and, when feasible, the teacher should capitalize on these ideas. Repeating a student's answer serves to give emphasis to it. When a student has given a somewhat lengthy answer, the teacher may respond with paraphrasing for both clarification and emphasis; for example, "Am I correct that you meant . . . ?" On the occasion when a student has introduced a pertinent idea in the classroom, the teacher may elaborate further, even at some length, as is appropriate. Finally, the teacher may recall students' ideas introduced earlier in the class, giving credit by name when possible, as they pull together ideas into meaningful generalizations.

A teacher's display of courtesy also contributes to creating a positive social-emotional climate in the classroom. It is natural to support students' participation in learning activities and other contributions. The idea is simple: Teachers should be courteous to students because teachers expect courtesy from them. Research reveals that modeling has the potential to influence students markedly. Thanking students for their point of view during a discussion might be more appropriate than using praise, particularly if the teacher did not want to express a judgment on the opinion. By telling a small group of students their effort on a project is appreciated, a teacher can encourage students to repeat the behavior.

While a teacher's use of supporting skills has always been important, it may be even more essential today with the growing emphasis on constructivism and teaching for understanding. Constructivist teachers attempt to create a classroom social environment that encourages sustained dialogue to promote understanding. Discussion becomes a primary method of teachers as they involve students in interaction with them and with each other. Supporting students' contributions to discussion—by accepting and using their ideas and feelings—and using praise are essential to sustain classroom discourse.

Mr. Taylor displayed a variety of supportive behaviors that were conducive to the creation of a positive social-emotional climate. Early in the lesson, there was an indication that he maintained eye contact with students as he listened to and reinforced their contributions. He wrote students' opinions about community environmental problems on the board, a demonstration of support for students' ideas. At one point, he expressed considerable enthusiasm for a student's insight, and one can imagine the animated behaviors accompanying the supportive comment, "You have just hit on one of the major things I wanted you to learn by the end of the unit!" The remaining supportive comments were basically expressions of courtesy. He complimented students on how observant they were of the community, and toward the end of the lesson he thanked David for his opinion.

> *The decisions that a teacher makes regarding the use of instructional techniques are critical because of their resulting impact on classroom climate, learning activities, and student outcomes.*

■ SUMMARY POINT ■

The instructional process consists of techniques, methods, and strategies that teachers have at their disposal as they make decisions about how to plan to meet unit goals and daily objectives in their classrooms. The most basic elements in this process are teacher physical behaviors that, for the most part, can be observed, analyzed, and evaluated. Instructional techniques consist of a series of skills that, in a sense, represent groups of teacher behaviors. Major techniques have been identified and varying degrees of all these techniques are used in each method and strategy teachers employ in the classroom.

Three of these techniques are motivating skills, questions and questioning skills, and supporting skills. Research confirms the importance of these techniques as part of a teacher's instructional repertoire. Student motivation is influenced by the teacher's display of verbal and nonverbal behaviors related to enthusiasm and the use of instructional variety. A teacher's application of a variety of question levels and techniques directly influences the degree of student thinking and participation in the classroom. Support, primarily noticed through the teacher's use of praise, has a significant impact on the classroom's social-emotional climate and student learning.

■ APPLICATION TO PRACTICE: INFORMATION-GIVING SKILLS

Information giving, as a technique that teachers regularly display in the classroom, is basically a shortened and informal form of the lecture. Teachers frequently give information spontaneously—for example, in response to student questions and comments, when presenting an assignment, explaining something, giving short directions, and introducing a video or speaker. Information giving can also be more formal and involve more planning, such as when introducing a unit or summarizing learnings, demonstrating a skill or process, giving involved and extended directions, or presenting a formal explanation. Information giving might last from a brief moment to as long as 10 minutes. The lecture, in contrast to information giving, is generally more highly structured, more formal, and may last from approximately 10 to 45 minutes in a middle school or secondary classroom, depending on the situation.

Although most information giving takes place in unanticipated situations and therefore opportunities for planning are almost nonexistent, several considerations will increase the effectiveness of the communication. Spontaneous responses to questions, explanations, directions, and introductions need to be clearly understood by the students. Approaches to increase the probability of clarity include defining difficult terms and concepts as part of the commentary and providing examples and illustrations to aid comprehension. Feedback should also be solicited from the students. This can be accomplished by simply asking students if they have questions regarding the information given, requesting students to summarize key points, or asking students specific questions as part of a review. Much depends on the ability level of the students, the complexity of the content being presented, and time limitations.

Preparation for more formal information giving is similar to preparing for a lecture. The primary differences are the length of time of the information giving and therefore, ostensibly, the time necessary for planning the presentation. This form of information giving might properly be termed a minilecture involving approximately 5 to 10 minutes. In addition to clarifying the lesson content and obtaining feedback characteristic of spontaneous information giving, additional considerations for formal information giving include, first, providing for an introduction, second, organizing the content, and, third, wrapping up with a brief closure.

The introduction to a minilecture should precisely communicate to students what content will be covered, why it is important to know it, and how it fits into the lesson or unit being studied. This need not take any more than one to two minutes within a brief 10-minute information-giving session.

Organization refers to the presentation of the content in a logical way, moving from simple facts, concepts, skills, or ideas to more complex ones. Starting with what the students know is a logical basis for presenting new information. The intention of closure is to review what has been presented, determine the extent to which students understood what was covered, and make a tie-in to the next learning activity. Clearly the more time devoted to information giving, the more structured and formal the presentation must become to increase the probability that the students will understand what is being taught. Suggestions for conducting effective lectures are presented in Chapter 7.

In addition to the aforementioned skills, other more personally related behaviors and skills influence the effectiveness of information giving. These behaviors have been previously presented and discussed as part of the technique of motivation in this chapter. Mr. Taylor's lesson was primarily discussion and activity oriented. Thus, he engaged in only two instances of information giving. The first time, he reacted spontaneously to a student's insightful comment by providing reasons why their community initiated environmental legislation and how it was done. This took less than five minutes. The second time, he explained their homework assignment. The assignment explanation, including passing out and clarifying the use of the survey form, took no longer than three to four minutes. Minimal information giving was required, primarily because the majority of Mr. Taylor's students had prior knowledge and experiences with their community's environmental problems, and they were interested in the topic.

■ APPLICATION TO PRACTICE: LISTENING SKILLS

Another essential component of classroom interpersonal communication is the regular display of a teacher's listening behaviors. Primarily nonverbal in nature, they influence all forms of teacher–student interaction and contribute to the social-emotional climate of the classroom. As a result of teachers' impact on communication, it is important that they are aware of their use of listening behaviors and model them for students in class. Teacher modeling will also serve to encourage students indirectly to display appropriate listening skills.

The display of effective listening behaviors is dependent on the implementation of a series of skills. Seven behaviors have been identified by Garrett, Sadker, and Sadker (1990): eye contact, facial expressions, body posture, physical space, silence, brief verbal acknowledgments, and subsummaries. Maintaining eye contact with a student who responds to a teacher's question tacitly communicates the teacher's interest in what is being said. Having a personal knowledge of the respondent is important because some are uncomfortable with direct eye contact. A teacher's facial expressions provide the student with feedback about the teacher's reaction to what is being said. A smile as compared with a frown, for example, communicates a different mood and reaction to students. Overdoing facial expressions could also be distracting and hinder communication. Body posture can determine the formality the teacher intends for the situation, and body gestures communicate meaning. Gestures include the position of the arms, hands, and fingers, as well as touching. Communication can be quite varied, depending on how gestures are used, in what classroom situation, and with whom. The physical distance between the teacher and student(s) is also influential in communicating how close a teacher wants to be to the students; close proximity communicates intimacy, whereas distance communicates separateness. All of these nonverbal behaviors need to be closely monitored when working with groups and individual students because of their implicit positive and negative messages and potential impact on students.

The displays of verbal behaviors, particularly in conjunction with the aforementioned nonverbal behaviors, are effective in communicating to students that a teacher wants to hear what is being said and encourages continuance. The behavior most often associated with teacher listening is silence. Silence, or wait time, has already been discussed as an effective teacher questioning technique. It communicates interest and respect for what is being said and stimulates reflection. Too much silence can be awkward and can hinder communication. Brief verbal acknowledgments uttered by the listener during discourse can communicate interest and concern to the speaker. For verbal acknowledgments to be effective, they must be brief and infrequent. Examples include "hmmm," "I understand," and "okay." A brief verbal summary of what has been said may also be useful. Subsummaries are the least used of the listening skills, but occasionally summarizing for the speaker what has been said clarifies the message and supports the speaker (Garrett, Sadker, and Sadker, 1990).

Although we can readily imagine Mr. Taylor engaging in a variety of listening behaviors during the lesson that was depicted in the scenario, there was no direct indication that he used any specific listening skill. Indirect clues are the success he had in stimulating responses to his questions—many at the divergent level—and the respect students apparently had for him as indicated by the lack of classroom management problems.

■ SUMMARY POINT ■

In addition to motivating skills, questions and questioning skills, and supporting skills, two other major instructional techniques are found in every effective teacher's instructional repertoire: information-giving skills and listening skills. Varying degrees of all these techniques can be found in each method and strategy teachers employ in the classroom. Research supports these techniques as effective teaching practices, and because of this, teachers need to consider these techniques carefully while making decisions about instructional variety during the planning stage. Skills associated with information giving have been positively related to students' learning efficiency and success. Listening skills contribute significantly to classroom communication and to a positive classroom climate.

The decisions a teacher makes regarding the use of instructional techniques are critical because of their resulting impact on classroom climate, learning activities, and student outcomes.

■ QUESTIONS FOR REFLECTION ■

1. If you were a science student, would you like to be in the class of Richard Taylor, the scenario teacher? Of the techniques he displayed as he taught the lesson, which appeals to you the most and why?

2. What do you recall from your secondary school days was one of the most influential springboards or attention getters used by your teachers as an entry to a lesson? In what way was it influential?

3. Naturally, it would be ideal if all teachers were motivating in terms of their personal and instructional behaviors. Which of the two, a teacher's dynamic display of verbal and nonverbal behaviors or a teacher's use of a variety of instructional techniques and methods, do you consider more important in terms of motivating students to participate and learn, and why?

4. Do you agree with some that questioning may be the most influential teaching behavior? Why?

5. In what ways might a teacher manage and control students' behavior using his or her questions in class?

6. What are some specific approaches that you might use to encourage students to generate questions that are related to content you might be teaching?

7. When you are involved in a conversation with friends, try using wait time to determine its impact on the interaction. Purposely pause three to five seconds after asking a question (wait time 1) and try pausing after receiving a response (wait time 2). Was there a greater quantity and quality of responses?

8. Do you think that calling on nonvolunteering students is appropriate? Under what circumstances would you call on and not call on nonvolunteering students? Do you agree that this is a democratic practice because all students have a democratic responsibility to participate in public talk? Why?

9. Which type of question do you feel more comfortable asking—closed (low and high convergent) or open ended (low and high divergent)? Under what circumstances might you feel comfortable asking the other type of question?

10. Do you think that your participation in class is influenced by praise from the teacher, or do you prefer another form of reinforcement? To what extent do you need praise? How would you characterize students who are motivated by extrinsic motivation? Intrinsic motivation?

11. Which teacher verbal and nonverbal behaviors have the most impact on you in terms of creating a dynamic teaching image? Why? Which ones, when overdone, turn you off and influence you negatively?

12. Have you noticed the different types of verbal and nonverbal behaviors talk-show hosts engage in to create interest and excitement about the topic for a particular show? In what ways might you and other teachers learn from the approaches that talk-show hosts take to whip up enthusiasm?

13. Suppose you were looking at a videotape of yourself teaching a class of your choice. What would you see in terms of your verbal and nonverbal strengths? What is one area that you would need to develop further? How might you develop it further?

ANALYSIS SCALES

TEACHER _____

OBSERVER _____

CLASS _____

DATE _____

OCCURRENCE	EFFECTIVENESS
1. Not evident	1. Not effective
2. Slightly evident	2. Slightly effective
3. Moderately evident	3. Moderately effective
4. Quite evident	4. Quite effective
N Not applicable	N Not applicable

CATEGORIES (Parts A + B Correspond to Occurrence and Effectiveness in the Analysis Scale)	A. OCCURRENCE	B. EFFECTIVENESS
1. CASUAL OR PERSONAL COMMENTS: A. Teacher makes casual or personal comments intended to affect the lesson entry. B. Teacher establishes a friendly, comfortable climate for learning.		
2. SPRINGBOARD: A. Teacher uses a springboard in the entry. B. Teacher establishes relevance of the content to arouse interest in the current lesson.		
3. ATTENTION GETTER: A. Teacher does something unexpected or sensational in the entry. B. Teacher stimulates students' curiosity, suspense, or creativity to focus attention.		
4. REVIEW: A. Teacher reviews learning from previous lesson. B. Teacher presents a well-organized, succinct review of pertinent learning that provides momentum for the new lesson, or teacher asks incisive review questions to begin the new lesson.		
5. PREVIEW: A. Teacher previews upcoming lesson. B. Teacher states the objectives pertinent to the lesson, presents the rationale, and describes enthusiastically the learning activities that are imminent.		

REFLECTIVE CONSIDERATIONS

Describe the entry used.

How much time was devoted to the entry?

What was the student response to the entry?

Why did you decide on this entry? (self-analysis)

To what extent did you achieve your purpose with this entry? (self-analysis)

ANALYSIS SCALES

TEACHER _____

OBSERVER _____

CLASS _____

DATE _____

	OCCURRENCE	EFFECTIVENESS
1.	Not evident	Not effective
2.	Slightly evident	Slightly effective
3.	Moderately evident	Moderately effective
4.	Quite evident	Quite effective
N	Not applicable	Not applicable

CATEGORIES (Parts A + B Correspond to Occurrence and Effectiveness in the Analysis Scale)	A. OCCURRENCE	B. EFFECTIVENESS
1. SUMMARY: A. Teacher summarizes or causes the lesson to be summarized. B. Teacher and/or students synthesize important points from the lesson; this includes more than only repeating the information in the lesson.		
2. INTEGRATION: A. Teacher cites the broad context within which the lesson is a part. B. Teacher meaningfully relates the lesson to the goals of the unit and to students' previous learning.		
3. APPLICATION: A. Teacher mentions possible uses of the topic/skill learned. B. Teacher makes convincing suggestions regarding the intended immediate or long-range application of the learning outcomes.		
4. TRANSITION: A. Teacher builds a bridge to the next lesson with comments or an assignment. B. Teacher previews coming learnings/activities in a manner that piques student interest; teacher makes a thought-provoking assignment in anticipation of the next class meeting.		
5. REFERENCE TO ACCOMPLISHMENT: A. Teacher comments on accomplishment(s). B. Teacher analyzes the class's progress in terms of the learning objectives; teacher gives specific praise as deserved or encouragement as appropriate.		

REFLECTIVE CONSIDERATIONS

Describe the closure used.

How much time was devoted to the closure?

What was the student response to the closure?

Why did you decide on this closure? (self-analysis)

To what extent did you achieve your purpose with this closure? (self-analysis)

ANALYSIS SCALES

TEACHER _____

OBSERVER _____

CLASS _____

DATE _____

OCCURRENCE	EFFECTIVENESS
1. Not evident	1. Not effective
2. Slightly evident	2. Slightly effective
3. Moderately evident	3. Moderately effective
4. Quite evident	4. Quite effective
N Not applicable	N Not applicable

CATEGORIES (Parts A + B Correspond to Occurrence and Effectiveness in the Analysis Scale)	A. OCCURRENCE	B. EFFECTIVENESS
1. PHYSICAL MOVEMENT: A. Teacher uses movement purposely. B. Teacher successively repositions self in a manner that heightens students' attention and serves the monitoring function; does not pace nervously.		
2. NONVERBAL BEHAVIOR: A. Teacher uses a variety of nonverbal behaviors to create a presence. B. Teacher uses facial expression (laughs, smiles, frowns, scowls, looks inquisitive) for effect and emphasis; gestures, nods, points, touches; creates a dynamic presence.		
3. VOICE: A. Teacher uses voice to attract students' attention. B. Teacher has a pleasant voice with a meaningful tone that expresses confidence and competence; easily heard; inflection evident; speech patter is appropriate for the level of class.		
4. LESSON PACE: A. Teacher varies the lesson pace. B. Teacher moderates or stimulates the flow of activity for optimum learning; adjusts pace in response to evidence of boredom, confusion, or frustration.		
5. INSTRUCTIONAL MODE: A. Teacher varies the instructional approach during the lesson. B. Teacher changes methods and learning activities with appropriate frequency; varies nature of student participation.		
6. ENTHUSIASM: A. Teacher embodies the qualities of liveliness and personal interest. B. Teacher employs a combination of verbal and nonverbal behaviors, lesson pacing, and lesson modes that visibly affect students' attention and participation.		

REFLECTIVE CONSIDERATIONS

What aspect of the lesson created the most motivation within the students?

How do you know?

TEACHER _____   CLASS _____

OBSERVER _____   DATE _____

COGNITIVE LEVELS—	NUMBER OF QUESTIONS ASKED	PERCENTAGE OF TOTAL	ESTIMATED % OF TIME DEVOTED TO EACH LEVEL
LEVEL I—LOW-ORDER CONVERGENT: Requires students to recall or recognize information. Emphasis on memorization and observation. Responses can easily be anticipated. Students define, recognize, quote, identify, recall, and answer "yes" or "no." Corresponds to Bloom's "knowledge" level.		%	%
LEVEL II—HIGH-ORDER CONVERGENT: Requires students to demonstrate understanding and apply information. Students describe, compare, contrast, rephrase, summarize, explain, translate, interpret, relate, apply, use, provide an example, and solve. Corresponds to Bloom's "comprehension" and "application" levels.		%	%
LEVEL III—LOW-ORDER DIVERGENT: Requires student to think critically about information, ideas, and opinions. Students discover motives, reasons, or causes; draw conclusions, inferences, or generalizations; provide evidence or support for conclusions, inferences, or generalizations. Corresponds to Bloom's "analysis" level.		%	%
LEVEL IV—HIGH-ORDER DIVERGENT: Requires students to perform original, creative, and evaluative thinking. Students produce original communications, make predictions, propose solutions, create, solve lifelike problems, speculate, construct, devise, write, design, hypothesize, synthesize, develop/judge ideas and problem solutions, express opinions, and make choices and decisions. Corresponds to Bloom's "synthesis" and "evaluation" levels.		%	%
Totals		%	%

REFLECTIVE CONSIDERATIONS

What indications did you notice that students were engaging in critical thinking?

To what extent were students' responses congruent to the levels of the teacher's questions?

ANALYSIS SCALES

TEACHER _____

OBSERVER _____

CLASS _____

DATE _____

OCCURRENCE	EFFECTIVENESS
1. Not evident	1. Not effective
2. Slightly evident	2. Slightly effective
3. Moderately evident	3. Moderately effective
4. Quite evident	4. Quite effective
N Not applicable	N Not applicable

CATEGORIES (Parts A + B Correspond to Occurrence and Effectiveness in the Analysis Scale)	A. OCCURRENCE	B. EFFECTIVENESS
1. PHRASING: A. Teacher uses questions. B. Teacher phrases questions so that response expectations are clearly communicated to the students; no run-on questions.		
2. ADAPTING QUESTIONS: A. Teacher adapts questions to the class. B. Teacher adjusts questions to the language and ability level of the students.		
3. SEQUENCE: A. Teacher asks questions sequentially. B. Teacher asks questions in a patterned order indicating a purposeful questioning strategy.		
4. BALANCE: A. Teacher balances convergent and divergent questions. B. Teacher uses questions at appropriate levels to achieve the objectives of the lesson.		
5. PARTICIPATION: A. Teacher uses questions to simulate a wide range of student participation. B. Teacher encourages student involvement by balancing responses from volunteering and nonvolunteering students; redirects initially answered questions to other students; encourages student–student interaction particularly appropriate during a discussion.		
6. PROBING: A. Teacher probes initial student responses to questions, particularly during discussions. B. Teacher follows up initial student responses with questions that encourage students to complete, clarify, expand, or support their responses.		
7. WAIT TIME: A. Teacher uses wait time after asking questions and after students' responses, particularly during discussions. B. Teacher pauses a minimum of three seconds after asking divergent questions to allow student thinking; teacher also pauses after students' initial responses to questions to encourage continued commentary.		

continued

8. STUDENT QUESTIONS: A. Teacher requests students to ask questions. B. Teacher encourages students to devise pertinent questions to stimulate thinking at the divergent level; students ask thoughtful questions.		
9. TEACHER STATEMENTS: A. Teacher balances question asking with statement making, particularly during discussions. B. Teacher uses a variety of statement forms (declarative, reflective, interest, speaker referral) to encourage student interaction.		

REFLECTIVE CONSIDERATIONS

Did the questions asked elicit the quality of thinking intended?

How would you describe the questioning strategy (or pattern) used by the teacher?

If the teacher used both questioning and statements, which do you think was more effective in stimulating interaction and thinking? Why?

Of all the questioning techniques used, which do you think was the most influential in encouraging critical thinking?

How do you know?

       SUPPORTING SKILLS

ANALYSIS SCALES

	OCCURRENCE	EFFECTIVENESS
TEACHER _____	1. Not evident	1. Not effective
OBSERVER _____	2. Slightly evident	2. Slightly effective
CLASS _____	3. Moderately evident	3. Moderately effective
	4. Quite evident	4. Quite effective
DATE _____	N Not applicable	N Not applicable

CATEGORIES (Parts A + B Correspond to Occurrence and Effectiveness in the Analysis Scale)	A. OCCURRENCE	B. EFFECTIVENESS
1. ACCEPTANCE OF FEELINGS: A. Teacher recognizes and accepts students' feelings. B. Teacher responds to students' expression of feelings with sensitivity, possibly empathy.		
2. PRAISE: A. Teacher expresses approval of students' efforts. B. Teacher uses a variety of verbal and nonverbal praise; praise is stated simply and genuinely; accomplishment is specified.		
3. ENCOURAGEMENT: A. Teacher requests students to participate. B. Teacher uses expressions of encouragement to stimulate students to initiate or continue with a task or learning activity.		
4. USE OF IDEAS: A. Teacher acknowledges students' ideas. B. Teacher repeats or paraphrases students' comments; elaborates on students' ideas; refers back to previous ideas of students.		
5. COURTESY: A. Teacher thanks students for help or contributions. B. Teacher uses expressions indicating appreciation for students' assistance, ideas, and efforts; teacher contributes to students' feelings of belonging and having worth and dignity.		

REFLECTIVE CONSIDERATIONS

What evidence is available of the effect of the teacher's supportive behavior on students?

How would you describe the social-emotional climate of the classroom?

ANALYSIS SCALES

TEACHER _____

OBSERVER _____

CLASS _____

DATE _____

OCCURRENCE	EFFECTIVENESS
1. Not evident	1. Not effective
2. Slightly evident	2. Slightly effective
3. Moderately evident	3. Moderately effective
4. Quite evident	4. Quite effective
N Not applicable	N Not applicable

CATEGORIES (Parts A + B Correspond to Occurrence and Effectiveness in the Analysis Scale)	A. OCCURRENCE	B. EFFECTIVENESS
SPONTANEOUS 1. CLARITY: A. Teacher presents information clearly to the students. B. Teacher defines difficult terms and concepts; examples and illustrations are used to aid comprehension.		
2. FEEDBACK: A. Teacher obtains feedback from students during or after information giving. B. Teacher asks students if they have questions, requests they summarize key points, or directly asks review questions.		
MINILECTURE 3. INTRODUCTION: A. Teacher prefaces minilecture with an introduction. B. Teacher communicates to students what content will be covered, why it is important, and how it relates to the lesson/unit being studied.		
4. ORGANIZATION: A. Teacher presents a cohesive body of information/content to the students. B. Teacher's presentation is logically organized; teacher moves from simple to complex ideas, skills, concepts; teaching aids are employed; new content is related to students' current knowledge.		
5. CLOSURE: A. Teacher makes a discrete closure to the minilecture. B. Teacher reviews, or has students review, what was presented; bridge to the next learning activity is made.		

REFLECTIVE CONSIDERATION

How would you describe the students' behaviors during the presentation?

ANALYSIS SCALES

TEACHER _____

OBSERVER _____

CLASS _____

DATE _____

OCCURRENCE	EFFECTIVENESS
1. Not evident	1. Not effective
2. Slightly evident	2. Slightly effective
3. Moderately evident	3. Moderately effective
4. Quite evident	4. Quite effective
N Not applicable	N Not applicable

CATEGORIES (Parts A + B Correspond to Occurrence and Effectiveness in the Analysis Scale)	A. OCCURRENCE	B. EFFECTIVENESS
NONVERBAL 1. EYE CONTACT: A. Teacher maintains eye contact with the students. B. Teacher uses continuous eye contact as the students respond to questions, initiate comments, etc.; eye contact is accompanied with positive facial expressions; teacher does not create discomfort by staring.		
2. FACIAL EXPRESSIONS: A. Teacher facial expression in response to students' comments is evident. B. Teacher shows interest in what the students are saying by smiling, nodding, and changing expressions as appropriate.		
3. BODY POSTURE: A. Teacher "body language" in response to students' comments is evident. B. Teacher uses postures indicating attention and interest; gestures using body, hands, fingers are appropriate and not distracting.		
4. PHYSICAL DISTANCE: A. Teacher moves with apparent purpose regarding student–teacher communication. B. Teacher establishes and maintains close proximity to hear when working with individual students and small discussion groups.		

continued

VERBAL 5. SILENCE: A. Teacher maintains silence as students speak responsibly. B. Teacher uses congruent nonverbal behaviors including eye contact and body posture while listening; does not interrupt except to use brief verbal acknowledgments, paraphrases, or subsummaries.		
6. VERBAL ACKNOWLEDGMENTS: A. Teacher uses verbal acknowledgments while listening to students' extended communications. B. Teacher interjects brief comments communicating interest, concern, and encouragement.		
7. SUBSUMMARIES: A. Teacher responds with mini-summaries during lengthy communications. B. Teacher displays congruent and appropriate nonverbal behaviors while using subsummaries.		

REFLECTIVE CONSIDERATIONS

Describe the general demeanor of the teacher as a listener.

What is the apparent effect of the teacher's listening behavior on students?

■ REFERENCES ■

Allen, D., and Ryan, K. (1969). *Microteaching*. Reading, MA: Addison-Wesley.

Atwood, V., and Wilen, W. (1991). "Wait time and effective social studies instruction: What can research in science education tell us?" *Social Education, 55*(3), 179–181.

Berliner, D. C. (1984). "The half-full glass: A review of research on teaching." In P. L. Hosford (Ed.), *Using What We Know About Teaching*. Alexandria, VA: Association for Supervision and Curriculum Development.

Bloom, B. (Ed.). (1956). *A Taxonomy of Educational Objectives: Handbook I. Cognitive Domain*. New York: McKay.

Brophy, J. (1981). "Teacher praise: A functional analysis." *Review of Educational Research, 51*, 5–32.

Brophy, J., and Good, T. L. (1986). "Teacher behavior and student achievement." In M. Wittrock (Ed.), *Handbook of Research on Teaching* (3rd ed.). New York: Macmillan.

Brophy, J., Rohrkemper, M., Rasid, H., and Goldberger, M. (1983). "Relationships between teachers' presentations of classroom tasks and students' engagement in those tasks." *Journal of Educational Psychology, 75*, 544–552.

Chance, P. (1992). "The rewards of learning." *Phi Delta Kappan, 74*(3), 200–207.

Christenbury, L., and Kelly, P. (1983). *Questioning: A Path to Critical Thinking*. Urbana, IL: ERIC Clearinghouse on Reading and Communication Skills and the National Council for Teachers of English.

Ciardiello, A. (2000). "Student questioning and multidimensional literacy in the 21st century." *Educational Forum, 64*(3), 215–222.

Costa, A., and Lowery, L. (1989). *Techniques for Teaching Thinking*. Pacific Grove, CA: Midwest Publications.

DeCecco, J. P. (1968). *The Psychology of Learning and Instruction: Educational Psychology*. Upper Saddle River, NJ: Prentice Hall.

Dillon, J. T. (1988). *Questioning and Teaching: A Manual of Practice*. New York: Columbia University.

Dillon, J. T. (1990). "Conducting discussions by alternatives to questioning." In W. Wilen (Ed.), *Teaching and Learning Through Discussion*. Springfield, IL: Charles C. Thomas.

Dillon, J. T. (1994). *Using Discussion in Classrooms*. Buckingham, England: Open University Press.

Fisher, C. W., Berliner, D. C., Filby, N. N., Marliave, R. S., Cahen, L. S., and Dishaw, M. M. (1980). "Teaching behaviors, academic learning time and student achievement: An overview." In C. Denham and A. Lieberman (Eds.), *Time to Learn*. Washington, DC: National Institute for Education.

Flanders, N. A. (1970). *Analyzing Teacher Behavior*. Reading, MA: Addison-Wesley.

Gage, N. L., and Berliner, D. C. (1992). *Educational Psychology* (5th ed.). Boston: Houghton Mifflin.

Gallagher, J. J., and Aschner, M. J. (1963). "A preliminary report on analyses of classroom interaction." *Merrill-Palmer Quarterly, 9*, 183–194.

Garrett, S. S., Sadker, M., and Sadker, D. (1990). "Interpersonal communication skills." In J. M. Cooper (Ed.), *Classroom Teaching Skills* (4th ed.). Lexington, MA: Heath.

Good, T., and Brophy, J. (2000). *Looking in Classrooms* (8th ed.). New York: Addison Wesley Longman.

Good, T., and McCaslin, M. (1992). "Teaching effectiveness." In M. Alkin (Ed.), *Encyclopedia of Educational Research* (6th ed.) Vol. 4, pp. 1373–1388). New York: Macmillan.

Guilford, J. P. (1956). "The structure of intellect." *Psychological Bulletin, 53*, 267–293.

Hawes, G. R., and Hawes, L. S. (1982). *The Concise Dictionary of Education*. New York: Van Nostrand Reinhold.

Heath, S. (1983). *Ways with Words: Language, Life, and Work in Communities and Classrooms*. New York: Cambridge University Press.

Hunkins, F. P. (1995). *Teaching Thinking through Effective Questioning* (2nd ed.). Boston: Christopher-Gordon.

Kelly, T. E. (1993). "Calling on nonvolunteers in the classroom: Democratic imperative or misguided invasion?" Paper presented at the annual meeting of the American Research Association, Atlanta, GA.

Latham, A. (1997). "Asking students the right questions." *Educational Leadership, 54*(6), 84–85.

Levin, T., with Long, R. (1981). *Effective Instruction*. Washington, DC: Association for Supervision and Curriculum Development.

Rowe, M. (1987). "Using wait time to stimulate inquiry." In W. W. Wilen (Ed.), *Questions, Questioning Techniques, and Effective Teaching* (95–106). Washington, DC: National Education Association.

Rowe, M. B. (1974). "Wait time and reward as instructional variables, their influence on language, logic and fate control: Part 1. Wait time." *Journal of Research on Science Teaching, 11,* 81–94.

Schuck, R. F. (1985). "An empirical analysis of the power of set induction and systematic questioning as instructional strategies." *Journal of Teacher Education, 36,* 38–43.

Shostak, R. (1990). "Lesson presentation skills." In J. M. Cooper (Ed.), *Classroom Teaching Skills* (4th ed.). Lexington, MA: Heath.

Strother, D. B. (1987). "On listening." *Phi Delta Kappan, 68*(8), 625–628.

Susi, F. D. (1985). "Spatial mapping as a method for observing classroom art instruction." *Studies in Art, 26,* 163–168.

Susi, F. D. (1986). "Physical space and the teaching of art." *Art Education, 39*(2), 6–9.

van Zee, E., Iwasyk, M., Kurose, A., Simpson, S., and Wild, J. (2001). "Student and teacher questioning during conversations about science." *Journal of Research in Science Teaching, 38*(2), 159–190.

Varlas, L. (2002). "Honing the tools of instruction: How research can improve teaching for the 21st century." *ASCD Curriculum Update,* 1–5.

Wang, M., Haertel, G., and Walberg, H. (1994). "What helps students learn?" *Educational Leadership, 51,* 74–79.

Waxman, H. C. (1987–1988). "Effective lesson introductions and preinstructional activities: A review of recent research." *Journal of Classroom Interaction, 23*(1), 5–7.

Wilen, W. (2001). "Exploring myths about teacher questioning in the social studies classroom." *The Social Studies, 92*(1), 26–32.

Wilen, W. W. (1987). "Effective questions and questioning: A classroom application." In W. W. Wilen (Ed.), *Questions, Questioning Techniques, and Effective Teaching.* Washington, DC: National Education Association.

Wilen, W. W. (1991). "Questioning skills, for teachers." In *What Research Says to the Teacher Series* (3rd ed.). Washington, DC: National Education Association.

Wilen, W. W. (1994). "What research says to teachers about classroom questioning." *Social Educator (Australia), 12,* 94–101.

Wilen, W. W., and Clegg, A. A. (1986). "Effective questions and questioning: A research review." *Theory and Research in Social Education, 14,* 153–161.

Wilen, W. W., and White, J. J. (1991). "Interaction and Discourse in Social Studies Classrooms." In J. Shaver (Ed.), *Handbook of Research on Social Studies Teaching and Learning* (pp. 483–495). New York: Macmillan.

Zemelman, S., Daniels, H., and Hyde, A. (1998). *Best Practice: New Standards for Teaching and Learning in America's School* (2nd ed.). Portsmouth, NH: Heinemann.

7

Primary Instructional Methods

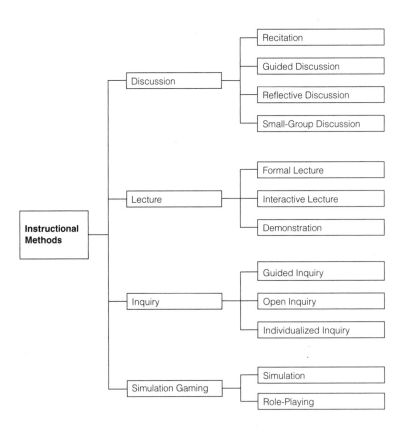

The focus in the previous two chapters has been on planning and teaching skills. In this chapter, we synthesize teaching techniques into instructional methods.

In its most general sense, an instructional method is a pattern of teaching actions designed to achieve student-learning outcomes. Central to this definition is the term *pattern,* which suggests a planned and sequential arrangement of actions. *Actions* refer to the variety of techniques available to teachers as they plan for lessons. Techniques common to all methods are described in Chapter 6. A method can be applied in its essential form to many subject areas and can be used by different teachers recurrently. We are also reminded that there are an indeterminate number of variations of procedure and style as teachers make decisions and plan for the implementation of any one method or for a combination of methods. This within-method variability should be perceived as a strength (Gage and Berliner, 1992).

■ OVERVIEW

The focus of this chapter is on the presentation of four primary instructional methods representing a wide range of subject areas that can be used by teachers at the middle and high school levels. These methods are discussion, lecture, inquiry, and simulation gaming. Several specific forms of each are presented. Each method is designed to achieve a particular kind of learning outcome and is generally flexible enough to be adapted to the range of student abilities and interests. Each form of the four primary methods is described in terms of the instructional techniques essential for successful implementation. Patterns of sequential phases for the four primary methods are presented to assist teachers in using them practically in the classrooms. Experienced teachers accumulate a repertoire of methods and make conscientious decisions regularly about how these methods might be employed effectively to achieve lesson objectives and unit goals. Analysis forms for the discussion, lecture, inquiry, and simulation-gaming methods are included at the end of the chapter to summarize the major features of each method and to aid in your application, observation, and analysis of their use.

SCENARIO

Robert Carl realized that one advantage of getting to school early was that he did not have to wait in line for the copier. This morning he was making a transparency of a map (see Figure 7.1). If all went as well as Mr. Carl had planned, the map would serve as a springboard into a new unit. It was intended to stimulate higher-level thinking in his second-period economics class. Although the students were bright, he thought that they would probably not immediately guess that the countries on the map were shaped and sized unusually because they were drawn to depict the countries' gross national product (GNP) rather than their physical size. As he started back to his room, he smiled at the thought of successfully challenging their critical-thinking abilities.

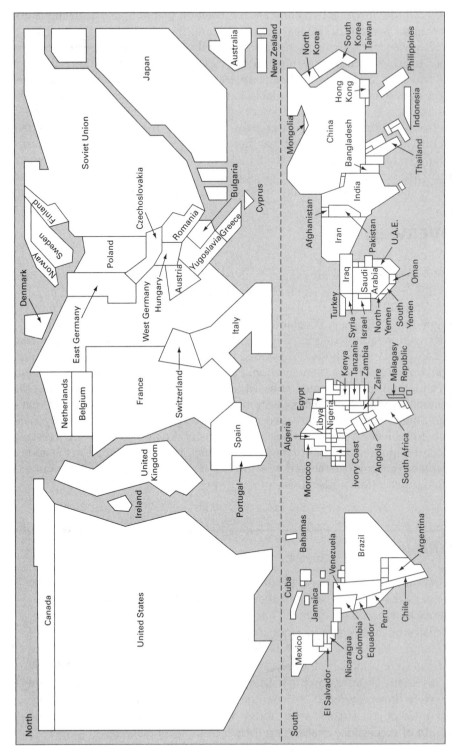

Figure 7.1 From Marta Norman and Richard Tringali. "The World Turned Upside Down—Gross National Product." *Newsweek*, October 26, 1981. Copyright © 1981 Newsweek, Inc. All rights reserved. Reprinted by permission.

"Today we start a new unit, one that will require you to apply what you have learned for the past two months. We have been studying the separate parts of the economy—the roles of consumer, producer, worker, government, corporation, and labor unions—and how each contributes to the big picture. Now we are going to change our focus from microeconomics to macroeconomics and begin a study of the interrelationships among the sectors of the economy and its performance.

"I would like to introduce some new ideas that contain a kind of puzzle for you to try to solve." Mr. Carl noticed two students toward the rear of the room glance up from their desks on the mention of a puzzle. He placed the transparency of a miniature world map on the overhead projector. "What do you see?"

The first response came from Tim, "It's a map of the world with all of the countries. But the countries are shaped differently, with no rounded edges like on a real map."

Joanna jumped in, "China's a lot larger than the United States, but not on this map. It doesn't make any sense."

"The map is divided into Northern and Southern Hemispheres," added Patricia.

At this point, Mr. Carl thought the stage was set to begin the formal inquiry. "The map does make sense if you know the key to the puzzle. I would like you to try to discover it by asking me questions. But there is a hitch. I will answer only 'yes' or 'no' to your questions, so you will have to think carefully as you phrase them."

"Why is the United States the largest country on this map?"

"You will need to rephrase your question so I can answer 'yes' or 'no.' "

"Okay (pause). Could the map measure something other than size?"

"What do you mean by size?"

"Size. How big the United States is physically."

"Yes. The map is measuring something else."

One student pointed out the size of Japan in relation to the other countries. Another wondered why Denmark was almost as large as Australia. Another asked why Australia was part of the Northern Hemisphere and India

a part of the Southern Hemisphere on this map. Still another wanted to know if the map was drawn by a computer. After more discussion, Vanessa offered a hypothesis. "Does the map measure the number of cars in the world?"

"Our first proposed solution to the puzzle. A good idea! Rather than receiving the answer now, what further questions could you ask me to test your guess?"

"What do you mean?" Christopher asked with a puzzled look.

"Remember that when we use inquiry, you have to gather information related to your proposed solutions to a problem. Here we have the same idea, only different in that your questions try to get from me the necessary information to test your hypotheses. Think about the relationships of the countries. How about a 'what if' question?"

(Pause.) "If Mexico doubled its production of cars, would its size on the map double?" asked Anthony.

"No. But its size would increase." Several other students offered hypotheses that also centered on products such as steel, computers, and wheat. Eventually one student hypothesized money as the basis for each country's size, and this quickly led to wealth and GNP. After each hypothesis was tested with more student questions, the solution to the puzzle—the depiction of GNP—was confirmed.

After discussing the clues that led a student to discover that GNP was the answer, Mr. Carl complimented the students on their perseverance and perceptiveness. He then defined *GNP*, gave examples of goods and services included in the computation of GNP, and provided statistics to support the size of some of the countries in both halves on the map. He also explained that the north–south line on the map was not meant to be the equator but rather roughly 30 degrees north latitude.

"We are going to be spending the next several weeks on the concept of GNP because it is one of the most important indicators of economic growth in the United States, or a thermometer of our economic health, in a sense. It is also directly related to our standard of living; in other words, how well we live, what we can buy, and the services available to us.

"Let's take a look at our map again. Why do you suppose the countries roughly south of the 30 degrees north latitude line are smaller than those in the north?"

"They have smaller GNPs."

"Right. But why are so many of the small GNP nations located south of the United States?"

One student suggested it might have something to do with climate because it is hotter in the Southern Hemisphere. He jokingly followed up with a comment about people taking siestas every day. Another thought that the northern countries had more technology. After further discussion, one student commented that some of the most heavily populated countries, such as China and India, were south of the line.

"You have come up with some fine ideas and possible explanations for this problem, and we will have an opportunity to pursue our inquiry further when we learn more about GNP. I have some excellent sources for you to consult and have made arrangements for a guest speaker to visit us on Monday. He is a graduate student from Brazil who is majoring in economics at the university. I think that he will be an excellent source of information and that we will learn a lot about those factors that influence economic growth, particularly in those countries to the south of us."

Noticing that class time was almost over, Mr. Carl reviewed the lesson by asking the students what they had learned about GNP today. He gave Chapter 9 as the reading assignment in the text. "I also want you to watch the news tonight on television or read the paper to find out the latest quarter's GNP figures that are to be reported today. We will use them tomorrow as we begin to formalize some possible explanations and start our search for data. Depending on the number of hypotheses we can come up with, perhaps we can form into small groups for the investigation. So long!"

■ RESEARCH AND THEORETICAL BASE: INSTRUCTIONAL METHODS

Very little research has been conducted on instructional methods, especially that which attempts to determine the effectiveness of various methods in terms of increasing students' learning gains. Most of the research has focused on comparing one method with another. This avenue has not been fruitful because, in general, for most students the use of different teaching methods does not seem to make a difference in learning. Different methods have yielded similar average results when the criterion measured has been achievement. In addition, based on a review of available research, students with varying aptitudes will probably be affected differently by particular methods. This is only one of several factors, including instructional costs, time, and student attitude, that must be considered when choosing among different methods and strategies and making other decisions about instruction (Berliner and Gage, 1976).

Another generalized research finding indicates that using a variety of methods increases the probability that student interest will be maintained and that higher achievement gains will be made. Based on their review of research, Good and Brophy (1987) noted that the "systematic use of a variety of techniques produces better results than heavy reliance on any one technique, even a good one" (p. 342). This finding has been supported in Wise's (1996) meta-analysis of 140 research studies comparing the effects of traditional science teaching strategies with alternative strategies. He found that inquiry-oriented alternative strategies positively influenced students' achievement more than traditional approaches.

Although research suggests that different instructional approaches should be used with low- and high-achieving students, Evertson (1982) found that this does not occur in practice. Her study investigated the differences in instructional methods and activities in higher- and lower-achieving English and mathematics classes at urban junior high schools. Each teacher selected for the study had higher- and lower-ability sections of students. After a year of observation, she noted that the teachers did not vary their activity patterns for the different sections of students. In other words, these teachers did not instruct their high- and low-achieving students differently. Furthermore, she found definite instructional patterns for English and mathematics teachers.

What are teachers' preferences for various teaching methods and strategies? Thompson (1981) used a rating form to get at urban and suburban elementary and secondary teachers' preferences for Joyce and Weil's (1980) teaching models. Their choices indicated that secondary teachers placed more emphasis on strategies stimulating intellectual skills and growth than did elementary teachers, who emphasized the social growth of students.

■ RESEARCH AND THEORETICAL BASE: DISCUSSION METHOD

Along with lecture and recitation, discussion supposedly has been one of the most used instructional methods at all levels. In their review of descriptive studies on interaction patterns, though, Gall and Gall (1976) suggested that discussion is used infrequently. They characterized discussions by "student-to-student interaction and educational objectives related to complex thinking processes and attitude change" (p. 168). In his review, Dillon (1984) indicated that there was a problem because almost all teacher–student interaction sessions were labeled *discussions*, when most should have been labeled *recitations* because of the use of a highly structured interaction pattern to facilitate students' recall of knowledge.

A primary difference between recitation and discussion is the teacher's willingness to encourage students to assume discussion leadership responsibility. Based on their review of research on interaction in social studies classrooms, Wilen and White (1991) concluded that teachers excessively controlled classroom dialogue through the prevalent "teacher question–student response–teacher reaction interaction" pattern. They found that a discussion is characterized more as a group conversation during which there is greater equity and power sharing between the teacher and students. This atmosphere is more appropriate for achieving social studies goals related to citizenship education, particularly those associated with democratic processes and practices.

True discussion, in many ways, is synonymous with the purposes of democracy because it is congruous with such democratic values as a concern for rationality, commitment to fairness, and respect for other people's opinions and feelings (Wilen, 1994). Parker (1992) suggested that teachers give students an opportunity to experience conversation with people of different genders and of different age, ethnic, and ability groups—which is characteristic of democracy—by discussing, for example, common societal issues and problems. In their research on the discussion of controversial issues, Harwood and Hahn (1990) found that students benefited from discussion because their civic feelings and attitudes were positively influenced.

In a review of research on teaching for understanding, Brophy (1992) devised generalized principles and practices for all subject areas, including one on the need for creating discussion environments. He advocates creating classroom learning communities based on interactive discourse designed to encourage the social construction of meaning and to promote conceptual understanding. "Increasingly, research is pointing to thoughtful discussion, and not just teacher or student recitation, as characteristic of the discourse involved in teaching for understanding" (p. 5). Zemelman, Daniels, and Hyde (1998) also included in their standards for "best practice" in social studies the need to increase student participation in interactive and cooperative study by focusing on the open expression of ideas. The standard for discussion can easily apply to other subject areas, such as science, English, and health, that realistically might have analysis of issues and resolution of problems as two of their curricular emphases.

Based on their extensive review of literature on the discussion method, particularly in the area of group dynamics, Gall and Gall (1976) made several recommendations related to the effective use of discussions in the classroom. One recommendation involved using heterogeneous groups for group discussions because of the potential input from a variety of perspectives represented in a diverse group of students. Moderate cohesiveness should be fostered by the teacher so that minority points of view are respected. Another recommendation suggested that teachers consistently model a democratic leadership style rather than an authoritarian one to encourage student thinking and involvement.

Several extensive reviews of research on discussion practices suggest considerable potential for the use of discussion in classroom practice. Gall and Gall (1990) noted that the discussion method is very effective in achieving five types of learning outcomes: (1) subject-matter mastery, (2) problem solving, (3) moral development, (4) attitude change and development, and (5) communication skills. Based on her review of anthropological research on classroom interaction that involved minority students, White (1990) found that teachers could successfully employ a variety of techniques and strategies to encourage culturally different students to participate in discussions.

In his book on classroom discussion, Dillon (1994) described several important characteristics of discussion and suggested guidelines to help operationalize this method for classroom use. In a basic sense, he mentioned that logical conditions needed to be in place for a discussion to take place: People must talk, listen, and respond to one another; and when they talk, they must be offering more than one point of view on the subject. Also, their intention in discussion must be to enhance their knowledge, understanding, or judgment of the subject under discussion. The driving force of a discussion is a question that invites joint inquiry. Teachers need to take care in formulating a key question "which captures the class' present predicament over the subject matter" (p. 61).

One study on discussion examined what teachers envision as discussion and the influences on their use of discussion. Six conceptions of discussion emerged from the data gathered on a group of high school social studies teachers: recitation, teacher-directed conversation, open-ended conversation, a series of challenging questions, guided transfer of knowledge to the world outside and classroom, and practice at verbal interaction. Several major influences on teachers' conceptions of discussion were found: student diversity, lesson objectives, age and maturity of students, sense of community in the classroom, and interest of the students (Larson, 1997). Teachers from other subject areas will undoubtedly also have differentiated views of the role of discussion in their classrooms. Another recent study focused on middle and high school English students' perceptions of their own actions, thoughts, and motives related to text-based discussion. The general finding was the students were aware of the purposes, conditions, and practices of good discussion. Furthermore, teachers can foster a discussion climate by providing frequent opportunities for discussion around topics that engage students, prepare students with group dynamics skills, and guide, but don't dominate, discussion (Alvermann et al., 1996).

Experienced teachers accumulate a repertoire of methods and make conscientious decisions on a regular basis about how these methods might be effectively employed to achieve lesson objectives and unit goals. Passe and Evans (1996), in their current work on examining the use of discussion to teach societal issues, suggested a variety of format styles to conduct discussion including Socratic, council, Quaker, fishbowl, panel, debate, simulation, and role-playing. Each uses large-group and/or small-group discussion approaches and can be used to focus on problematic questions. Parker (2001) presents two other discussion strategies that are particularly appropriate to enhance understanding and decision making in social studies classrooms: The seminar approach is designed to help students understand powerful text material related to issues, and the structured academic controversy approach helps students deal with social problems.

Research indicates that the discussion method is as effective as other approaches in learning subject matter. It may be even more effective than other methods, including the lecture, if achieving higher cognitive-level outcomes is the goal (Gall and Gall, 1976). Parker and Hess (2001) recommend that teachers should teach not only with discussion but also for discussion. Teaching *with* discussion is the strategy of involving students in discussion to help them understand an issue or resolve a problem, for example, whereas teaching *for* discussion is teaching them the method of discussion. Both perspectives, working hand-in-hand, are essential to prepare students for citizenship.

■ APPLICATION TO PRACTICE: DISCUSSION METHOD

In its most basic form, a discussion is an "educative, reflective, and structured group conversation" with and among students (Wilen, 1990, p. 3).

An examination of the concepts included with the general definition of discussion just provided enhances our understanding of its potential use in the classroom. A key word in the definition is *conversation*, which is a form of social intercourse among familiar people, an informal exchange of thoughts and feelings. By intending that the conversation be educative, emphasis is placed on providing purpose and direction through attaining instructional objectives. *Reflective* refers to encouraging students to think critically and creatively at the higher cognitive levels. *Structured* suggests that the conversation is organized and conducted by one or more leaders. A group to most teachers means, of course, a class of 20 to 30 students.

One "quasi discussion" and three types of discussion are used by teachers: recitation, guided discussion, reflective discussion, and small-group discussion. They share a common thread that requires the teacher and students to interact verbally for learning to occur. Each differs in terms of purpose, structure, interaction pattern, and levels of student thinking stimulated.

Recitation (Quasi Discussion)

Recitation has been labeled a quasi discussion primarily because it is not intended to be a group conversation. Whereas it is similar to discussion in that it is structured, involves interaction with students, and is designed to achieve objectives, it is not reflective interaction. Discussions have different purposes and interaction patterns and are used to stimulate higher levels of student thinking (Wilen, 1990). The convention of referring to recitations as quasi discussion was used by Roby (1988) in his research report on discussion models. A teacher uses a recitation primarily to ascertain the extent to which students have memorized pertinent facts. The interaction pattern typically is teacher question, student response, and teacher reaction, a pattern Bellack, Kliebard, Hyman, and Smith (1966) found common in their studies. The pace of the interaction is fairly rapid. Level I low-order convergent questions are the primary ones asked by the teacher to stimulate recall of knowledge. Questions at this level are who, what, when, and where questions. (See Chapter 6 for a review of the four types of questions.) The intent of the teacher using recitation is to engage students in what Hudgins (1971, p. 129) termed *reproductive thinking,* as opposed to *productive thinking,* in which students demonstrate understanding or ability to apply learning. An important questioning technique that teachers need to use consistently during a recitation is directing questions to both volunteering and nonvolunteering students to involve them all and to diagnose the extent of their knowledge.

Recitation is highly structured with the teacher clearly in control and directing the learning. Roby (1988, p. 166) labeled recitation as a "quiz show" because students try to discover the right answers to topic-oriented teacher questions. If, for example, the students have been diligent in reading the chapter from the literature text, observing the history film or physics demonstration, practicing the pronunciations of French vocabulary, and memorizing the spelling words or mathematics formulas, the teacher will be able to cover the content quickly. Recitation is generally efficient in terms of time demands, which is one reason why it is the most widely used form of discussion. Research shows that it is very effective in preparing students for factual tests, including standardized exams. Furthermore, only brief planning or preparation time is required. Teachers can conveniently fit it into practically any part of a lesson. There is a drawback, however, because teachers tend to rely on it too much. Recitation should, ideally, serve as a means to diagnose student progress in learning basic information and their readiness to use that information to develop meaning and deeper understanding.

Guided Discussion

The purpose of guided discussion is to promote understanding of important concepts, generalizations, ideas, values, problems, or issues (Wilen, 1990). The interaction pattern of the guided discussion is similar to recitation in that the teacher generally asks questions, students respond, and the teacher reacts. Differences are apparent, though, because of the emphasis on higher-level thinking. When a teacher asks a question, more than one student may respond, particularly if differences in opinion are expressed. In addition to the possibility of more students responding to each question, some interaction among students may occur. This is certainly not common during recitations, but it is more prevalent during reflective discussions (explained in the next section) and is an absolute necessity during small-group discussions. We should also expect some students to begin to ask questions for the purpose of explanation and clarification.

The cognitive levels of a teacher's questions appropriate to achieve the goals of a guided discussion generally are Level II high-order convergent and Level III low-order divergent. Convergent questions might, for example, request students to make comparisons between country and bluegrass music, explain South Africa's former policy of apartheid, describe how safety is a critical consideration in an industrial arts laboratory, or interpret a political cartoon. Divergent questions might involve students in drawing conclusions to a difficult chemistry laboratory experiment or predicting the future course of U.S. policy in the Middle East. During a guided discussion, a teacher may probe some students' responses because clarification is needed or to extend thinking. Wait time becomes more important because students need time to think of responses to higher-level questions. The teacher will also want to encourage students to begin to ask questions.

A guided discussion is moderately structured in that the teacher still assumes the major role of directing learning. As one might surmise, it is not as structured as a recitation but is more structured than a reflective discussion. The discussion is guided because the teacher wants to lead students to predetermined higher-level understandings. However, students have more freedom to present, explore, and test their ideas. Guided discussions still focus primarily on the cognitive dimension of subject matter in contrast to reflective discussions, which also involve affective learnings.

Reflective Discussion

The reflective discussion is potentially the highest level of discussion in terms of stimulated student thinking and student interaction with others related to the content. It is also the least structured, has the potential to generate the most student–student interaction, and generally requires a greater investment of time than the other modes of discussion. It is probably the most difficult form of discussion to conduct and, in any case, is the discussion format least used by teachers.

The purpose of a reflective discussion is to require students to engage in high-level critical and creative thinking as they synthesize and evaluate information, opinions, and ideas. Students solve problems, clarify values, explore controversial issues, and form and defend positions during reflective discussions (Wilen, 1990). In many ways it is the most exciting of the discussion strategies because of its potential to push students to the highest levels of cognition. For students to respond reflectively to a teacher's questions, they must have a solid understanding of the subject matter that serves as a basis of the discussion. If not, the discussion may turn into what Roby (1988, p. 169) referred to as a "bull session" in which both teachers and students think they have the right answers, freely shared without any supportive data. Reflective thinking requires students to learn the facts and to develop understanding. Without knowledge and understanding, opinions cannot be supported and, therefore, are useless in achieving the goals of a reflective discussion.

The interaction pattern is flexible and can range from a traditional approach that is characteristic of guided discussions to one in which a student or several students have assumed leadership and guide the discussion and inquiry themselves. This is the most open form of a reflective discussion. It permits students considerable freedom for direction and expression. This situation will more likely result if the group is smaller than regular class size and the students are particularly responsible and motivated to learn and participate. The effectiveness of a reflective discussion is also influenced by too much teacher questioning, which may forestall and frustrate student participation, primarily because of the control the teacher may exercise over the discussion (Dillon, 1983). There are several interaction patterns that a teacher must consider when employing discussion. The decision will probably depend on the size of the group and capability of the students.

Levels III and IV low- and high-order divergent questions are the most appropriate to achieve the objectives of a reflective discussion. At Level III, students draw conclusions, make inferences, form generalizations, and analyze information, among other intellectual behaviors. Level IV questions require students to engage in original and evaluative thinking, such as predicting the future in terms of technological advances given current trends and research findings; speculating on how history might have changed if a particular vice president, given his political beliefs, had become president; defining their stands on abortion; or evaluating the impact a famous conductor/composer had on his or her musical era. Discussion is highly appropriate as a means to achieve constructivist principles.

As teachers conduct reflective discussions, they must keep in mind a variety of questioning techniques that will increase the probability that their objectives will be attained. Implementing a recitation requires only basic communication skills, with the most important questioning technique being to involve the widest possible number of students in reviewing factual material. Wide participation is not necessarily important in a reflective discussion because some students may feel uncomfortable sharing their opinions, views, or ideas. The content in reflective discussions often involves students' feelings, attitudes, and values. The questions are on a higher level and therefore are more complex, so question clarity is critical. Teachers will need to use ample wait time with higher-level questions consistently during a reflective discussion to provide students enough time to think of responses. Probing is necessary to encourage students to clarify, expand, and support their responses. Finally, the teacher will need to use a variety of statement forms and to encourage students to formulate questions as alternative, nonquestioning means to stimulate thinking.

The structure of a reflective discussion—that is, the degree of freedom students have to frame an answer—can range from moderate to very low depending on several factors. The most important is the ability and interest level of the students. If students are not stimulated and are not sufficiently mature or capable of assuming responsibility for their own learning, the most open form would be difficult to implement. Reflective discussions focusing on problem solving have similar outcomes to the inquiry method, to be presented later in this chapter. Both require teachers to assume a more dominant role as facilitator than as an instructor in the traditional sense. A facilitator guides, advises, keeps students directed toward the goals established, and often serves as a resource person for the group. As the structure normally provided by the teacher in the discussion decreases and students assume more responsibility, a more democratic atmosphere develops. Students are involved in more decision making as they use the power delegated by the teacher. This characteristic is particularly evident in the inquiry method and also in small groups.

Small-Group Discussion

Dividing the large class into small groups of students to achieve specific objectives permits students to assume more responsibility for their own learning, develop social and leadership skills, use language more, and become involved in an alternative instructional approach. The small-group approach does not have a specific place within the hierarchy of discussion approaches because it is flexible enough to be used to attain the objectives generally associated with guided and reflective discussions, and even with recitation.

Although small groups are most appropriate for promoting problem solving, attitudinal change, and critical and creative thinking that coincides with the purposes of reflective discussions, they can also promote the understanding of subject matter and the learning of facts. To illustrate how reflection about a controversial issue might be stimulated, a government teacher could organize students into groups based on their points of view regarding the need for laws to protect endangered species of animals. The groups might be charged with determining how they would gather evidence to support their points of view, collecting and organizing the evidence, and presenting it to the class in the form of a panel presentation. A variety of critical-thinking skills would be developed as the students reflectively gathered and organized information and supported their points of view. This process is similar to the inquiry method.

To teach students how to understand subject matter, a teacher could have students in a general science class explore the advantages and disadvantages of several forms of energy: gas, solar, nuclear, wind, geothermal, and coal. The class could be divided into small groups—each assigned to investigate one energy source—to gather information in the library, draw conclusions about its effectiveness, and report on it through a multimedia presentation. A teacher interested in teaching basic facts using an alternative instructional approach could arrange the class into small groups of five or six students and challenge them, in a gaming fashion, to use their textbooks and to complete a worksheet of concept definitions accurately in the shortest time possible. Another approach to "teaching" a test or using it as a learning activity is to permit small groups to review their texts or search other sources to correct answers that they missed. In these cases, small groups would be formed only for the limited period of time necessary to complete the task.

The structure that a teacher establishes for small-group instruction depends primarily on the maturity level of the students. If students are to be involved in problem solving, they need freedom to determine direction and make decisions. The teacher monitors group progress and serves as a resource person to assist them in accomplishing their task. More structure may be needed when the objectives center on developing subject-matter understandings and learning facts. Mature students will be able to work without extensive teacher supervision. A problem may occur with less mature students who will need a more structured atmosphere to accomplish a task. These students tend to handle freedom ineptly; thus they probably should not be involved in small-group activities requiring considerable freedom of decision making.

There is a tendency for teachers to refer to small-group discussions as cooperative learning when, in fact, there are major differences particularly in terms of purpose and structure. While the cooperative-learning strategy almost always involves small-group discussion in some form, the small-group-discussion method is generally not used to achieve the purposes of cooperative learning, especially as they might relate to developing positive interdependence and individual accountability. Furthermore, the task structure and specialization, and the reward system, generally, are more defined for the various forms of the cooperative-learning strategy than the typical use of small-group-discussion method. The cooperative-learning strategy is described and illustrated in Chapter 8.

Discussion-Method Phases

Although different kinds of discussions encompass a wide range of purposes, a sequence of phases can be generalized for guided and reflective discussion. They are entry, clarification, investigation, and closure. The intention in providing a sequence of phases is to describe the discussion strategy in action. This provides for a better understanding of its application in the classroom under differing circumstances and presents a flexible step-by-step approach to implementation. Our intent is not to prescribe the only way to conduct discussions. The discussion strategy is probably the most flexible of all the strategies presented in this chapter. Therefore, teachers should feel free to modify the sequence of phases but maintain the integrity of the method to suit their own classroom situations, students, subject matter, and course goals.

Phase I. Entry: Identification of Problem, Issue, or Topic

a. Use a springboard and/or an attention getter.

b. Identify problem, issue, or topic.

c. State objectives and rationale.

As a teacher begins the lesson and introduces the discussion, the entry is important. There are many ways to enter a discussion depending on the nature of the students and their previous learning; the topic, issue, or problem; and the size of the group. The purpose of the entry is to inform students what is to be accomplished and why it is important. The most straightforward way to do this is to inform students of the objective(s) and rationale. This basic approach would be most appropriate for a recitation and could also be used for the other forms of discussion. A more stimulating way to enter a discussion is to use a springboard that serves as an attention getter to arouse student interest. In a guided discussion, for example, an industrial arts teacher could use a brief series of national statistics related to accidents in school labs—what kind and how many—to lead into a discussion on safety. A more dramatic approach would be to show slides of actual industrial lab accidents or to describe graphically an accident that may have occurred in the classroom in the past. Springboards and attention getters are also appropriate for reflective discussions. As an illustration, a life-science teacher could have students ask questions about what the home of the future might be like. The answers that the teacher gives could be based on a recent article, those made up at the moment, or a combination of both. This would serve as an attention-getting lead-in to a reflective discussion on future technology. The entry to a small-group activity could range from the basic introduction that specifies the objective and a rationale to a dramatic entry, depending on the imagination and inclination of the teacher.

Phase II. Clarification

a. Establish procedures.
b. Define terms and concepts related to the problem, issue, or topic.

Informing students of the procedures for a discussion may only be necessary at the beginning of the year or if a particular discussion the teacher has in mind requires specific guidelines. Common rules, of which students may need to be reminded, stipulate that they respect the opinions of others and are not allowed to talk when the teacher or another student is talking. This is particularly appropriate for a reflective discussion. If a controversial issue is to be discussed, the teacher may have other guidelines. A teacher may wish to provide more structure in cases involving less mature students who require more supervision. Small-group discussions may need more structure, especially when first initiated, because students may attempt to take advantage of the social dynamics created by small groups. It is important to keep in mind that too much structure and control will stifle student participation and initiative. This is particularly self-defeating for a reflective discussion in which the emphasis rests on encouraging student freedom. Another factor that influences the extent of rules is the size of the group, which determines whether more structure may be necessary.

Clarification of the problem, issue, or topic may be necessary if the subject to be discussed is particularly complex and difficult for some students to understand. This becomes critical if the text or other material that students have read in preparation for a discussion is ambiguous and confusing. In such a case, definition of terms, clarification of concepts, and elaboration of ideas may be all that are necessary to increase the probability that most of the students will participate and understand. For example, clarification may be necessary at the beginning of a reflective discussion on abortion because of the conflict between legal definitions and the many interpretations by special-interest groups. On the other hand, the teacher may consider clarification of these positions to be an objective of the discussion.

Phase III. Investigation

a. Ask appropriate levels of questions to achieve desired levels of student thinking.

b. Use both questioning and alternative nonquestioning techniques to maintain discussion and to stimulate student involvement and thinking.

c. Encourage student initiative and leadership.

d. Request that students support opinions offered.

e. Ensure sufficient coverage of the problem, issue, or topic.

The investigation is the main body of any discussion because the teacher uses questioning and alternative nonquestioning techniques during this phase to interact with students to achieve the objectives of the discussion. The teacher will ask questions congruent with the levels of student thinking desired: predominantly lower-convergent questions (Level I) during a recitation, predominantly upper-convergent and lower-divergent questions (Levels II and III) during a guided discussion, and lower- and upper-divergent questions (Levels III and IV) during a reflective discussion. The levels of questions specified here are only suggestive because of the need to be flexible. For example, a teacher may want students to compare and contrast the views of citizens representing various economic and social groups regarding the Constitution during the time it was being ratified. If students had not read the assignment, they would not know what the various groups were and how they felt. In this case, after having the students read the chapter section, the teacher will conduct a recitation before having them engage in higher-level thinking involving comparisons and conclusions.

The use of appropriate questioning techniques is critical to conducting effective discussions. Misuse can defeat the purpose of most discussions. This particularly applies to reflective discussions. On the other hand, recitations require a minimal application of questioning techniques. During a recitation a teacher is concerned, for example, with determining what students know about the important facts of a reading assignment. Questions are used to diagnose students' knowledge. For this to be accomplished, all students should ideally be called on several times. This is obviously not the case in the schools because generally less than half of the students are called on to recite and most of them are volunteering students who usually get most of the attention. Also consider that recitation rarely occurs in its pure form with all teacher questions categorized at Level I low convergent. More often teachers incorporate Level II high-convergent questions to encourage students to display some understanding of the facts. In these cases, the recitation has assumed some of the characteristics of the guided discussion.

The guided discussion requires an emphasis on other techniques to achieve its goals. Phrasing, balance, and sequence become more important because the questions are at differing and generally higher cognitive levels. Also, adapting questions to the language and ability levels of the students, particularly in a heterogeneous class, becomes important. Pausing after asking questions and using probing questions to encourage students to complete, clarify, and expand their responses may also be necessary, particularly at the low-divergent level (Level III). Furthermore, student questions can be encouraged.

When the teacher involves students in reflective discussions, all questioning and alternative nonquestioning techniques need to be conscientiously and consistently employed. The emphasis is on developing critical and creative thinking, so it is necessary to probe students' responses to expand their thinking and to provide support for points of view. Another crucial technique is wait time. The majority of questions that are generally asked in reflective discussions are at the low- and high-divergent levels (Levels III and IV), so teachers need to pause at least three seconds after asking questions to give all the students time to think. Pausing several seconds after a student gives a response will also increase the probability that the response will be extended with higher-level thinking involved. Students should be encouraged to ask questions during a reflective discussion. For example, in a discussion dealing with issues related to abortion, a teacher may ask students to pause and come up with some questions that they would ask a convicted abortion-clinic bomber if that person were in class. Also, what responses might this person give to the questions? High-level divergent thinking can be accomplished by having students devise questions.

A note of caution about the use of questions and questioning, particularly in reflective discussions, must be given. As has been previously mentioned, students' participation in discussions can be diminished if teachers misuse questioning techniques. Reflective discussions characterized by too many questions, too rapid a pace, too little attention paid to listening, and too little support for students' contributions will regress to an inappropriate recitation or even a lecture. A sure sign that this is happening is apparent when teachers begin to answer their own questions.

Effective discussions should also involve nonquestion alternatives to stimulate student thinking and participation. In his analysis of several tapes of high school classes, Dillon (1985) found that students spoke more extensively, exhibited more complex thought, and became more personally involved in discussions when the teacher used alternative approaches. Examples of nonquestioning alternatives include a variety of statement forms. For example, a teacher might express a thought that has come to mind in response to what a student has just said ("Well, you know that . . ."), paraphrase or summarize what has been said ("So far, we have been saying that . . ."), express an opinion ("I'm not sure I agree with you . . ."), or refer to what another student has said ("But just a few moments ago, Kim mentioned . . ."). Other alternatives are wait time, student questions and signals that are fillers ("mm-hmm"), verbal encouragers ("go on"), and phatics ("interesting") (Dillon, 1994). Our view is that teachers should attempt to integrate these nonquestioning techniques into their overall questioning approach to provide balance so that a more informal and conversational approach is created that encourages student involvement and thinking.

During the investigation phase of a small-group discussion, the students serve as the principal questioners and respondents as they search for information or attempt to propose solutions to a problem. As a facilitator, the teacher may ask questions in working with individual groups to help guide their inquiry and to keep them on target. The teacher assumes a secondary role as a questioner in most small-group discussions.

Phase IV. Closure: Summary, Integration, Application

a. Summarize in the form of consensus, solutions, insights achieved in relation to topic covered, issue explored, or problem investigated.
b. Integrate lesson with goals and previous learning.
c. Apply discussion outcomes to other situations.

Closure is least important in a recitation and most important in reflective and small-group discussions. In a recitation, closure may center on reviewing those areas in which students displayed the least understanding. Guided discussions involve higher-level thinking, so the teacher needs to use closures to help students summarize important points and integrate understanding with previous learning. Transitions to the lessons following recitations and guided discussions are also appropriate to prepare students for upcoming activities.

Closures are extremely important to reflective discussions because, for many students, this is the point at which ideas, points of view, generalizations, and conclusions are summarized and synthesized and important learning occurs. Syntheses can bring it all together for students who may have been confused at some point during the discussion. Application and transition are also appropriate within the closure because it is often at this point that decisions students reached in connection with a course of action, for example, might be further examined and evaluated in the real world. Suppose that after reflective discussion students reached the decision to support actively a welfare-reform bill being considered in Congress. Near the end of the lesson, the teacher could suggest some of the problems that students will face as they become actively involved, focusing on cost in terms of time and money or opposition from fellow students, parents, and so on. This would be an ideal problem for further investigation that could be the focus of the next day's class. More than likely, the teacher has the inquiry method in mind as a means to involve students in dealing with this reality.

The closure of a small-group discussion is the point at which students generally present what they have found as a result of their investigations. If the students were guided by higher-level thinking questions and activities, each group might report, for example, the benefits and disadvantages of the energy source it investigated or support for its position on a balanced-budget amendment. At the end of the lesson, we would expect the teacher to follow with a summary and integration of the various points of view and, perhaps, a consensus if it were the objective. In the case where the teacher "taught the test" using small groups of students to search out the answers to the objective test items, the closure could simply be a review of the test with the right answers based on students' findings. The closure is important because it provides the teacher with a final opportunity at the end of a lesson to ensure that objectives have been achieved, that learning has occurred, and that students will be prepared for the next lesson.

Scenario Analysis

In the introductory scenario, Mr. Carl engaged in considerable interaction with the students, but the students did most of the questioning. He was using a form of guided inquiry (presented later in this chapter). After the students discovered the solution to the "puzzle," Mr. Carl engaged them in another form of the inquiry method that required him to conduct a minidiscussion to get students to hypothesize reasons why countries of the world generally to the south of the United States have lower GNPs. At two other points, Mr. Carl had "discussions," but they were, in essence, simply short episodes of reflective interaction facilitating inquiry. The lesson could have been easily conducted as a guided discussion. Instead of having the students question him, Mr. Carl could have used Levels II and III high-convergent and low-divergent questions to stimulate thinking about what the map depicted—for example, "What do you think is the reason why the countries are shaped the way they are?" (key entry-level question); "How do the sizes of the United States and India compare on a real map?"; "Why is the United States the largest country on this map?"; "If GNP increases by 10 percent this year, what will that do to the size of the United States on this map?"; "How can we summarize what this map is trying to show us?"; and "Why is GNP important?" (key closing question). A recitation would have been appropriate if the objective were for students to recall the countries with the largest GNPs and other characteristics that distinguish them from one another. As a natural follow-up to the inquiry lesson, Mr. Carl could have as his objective for a reflective discussion that the students evaluate U.S. foreign policy toward several developing nations in terms of the approaches we are using to help these countries raise their standard of living.

Hints for the Beginning Teacher

Leading a successful discussion with a classroom of students is definitely not as easy as some experienced teachers make it seem. See if you can incorporate some of the specific suggestions in this chapter that can increase student participation or elevate the level of thinking in your next class discussion.

APPLICATION for DIVERSE CLASSROOMS

The methods of discussion, inquiry, and simulation gaming are appropriate for teaching at-risk students if structured carefully and include supportive teacher feedback. Teaching at-risk students calls for similar effective teaching practices as one would use with all other students, but with increased structure and support as well as challenge. However, the lecture method should be used sparingly because interactive teaching is essential with active involvement in learning experiences. At-risk students will need ample opportunity to practice and receive feedback on their learning of content and skills. It is important to provide them with success experiences as they learn (Kauchak and Eggen, 1998). Teachers need to have high expectations for at-risk students as they do for all other students, or they may internalize that the teacher expects less from them and that they are capable of only limited understanding and achievement.

■ SUMMARY POINT ■

Discussion is one of the most useful instructional methods because of its potential to stimulate students' application of knowledge and active involvement in learning at a variety of levels of thinking. Three types of discussion and one quasi discussion have been presented. The recitation has as its purpose the diagnosis of student knowledge of basic facts. The guided discussion aims to promote student understanding through processing information. The goal of the reflective discussion is to stimulate students' critical thinking about issues and problems. Finally, use of small-group discussions is an alternative to large-group discussion. It encourages students to assume more responsibility for their own learning. The decision about which form of discussion to use when planning will depend on the level of student understanding and thinking desired, and this, of course, will be reflected in the teachers' objectives for the lesson.

A discussion-method analysis form is included at the end of the chapter to aid in the observation and analysis of your and others' teaching.

■ RESEARCH AND THEORETICAL BASE: LECTURE METHOD

The instructional method most associated with higher education is the lecture, and it is within this setting that most of the research on it has been conducted (McLeish, 1976). In their review of the research literature on lecturing across all levels, Gage and Berliner (1992) concluded that it is as effective as other methods. Furthermore, they suggested that the lecture was superior to other methods when "(a) the basic purpose is to disseminate information; (b) the material is not available elsewhere; (c) the material must be organized and presented in a particular way for a specific group; (d) it is necessary to arouse interest in the subject; (e) the material needs be remembered for only a short time; and (f) it is necessary to provide an introduction to an area or directions for learning tasks to be pursued through some other teaching method" (p. 457).

Three studies conducted at the university level found that the traditional didactic lecture was ineffective compared to approaches that involved students in the lectures in some way. In one study involving large classes of psychology students, active-learning exercises were infused into lectures requiring students to write "minute papers" on general questions about lecture content and to share their responses in small groups. The researchers found that students responded positively, attendance improved, and learning was slightly enhanced (Butler, Phillmann, and Smart, 2001). Another approach is to have students work in small groups after a lecture in order for each student to produce a complete set of lecture notes. Following this, students then write one question each, based on their notes, which is then to be discussed in their small groups (Toole, 2000). In another study, students were more successful at solving chemistry problems after participating in an interactive lecture treatment during which students answered and asked questions (Robinson and Niaz, 1991). In a study involving three groups of university remedial-reading and study-skills students, the group that generated and answered questions and the group that wrote original summaries based on the lecture performed better than the group that took and studied notes in the traditional fashion (King, 1992). It appears that lectures can be more effective if students are more actively participating with the subject matter in various ways.

The findings of several other research studies have implications for the use of the lecture method in secondary classrooms. Based on their review of the literature, Good and Brophy (2000) advocate the use of advance organizers, first proposed and investigated by Ausubel (1968), to help students organize and structure their thoughts in preparation for receiving information through a lecture. In addition to using advance organizers, lecturers need to capture and hold attention. Research has shown that expressiveness, as demonstrated through verbal and nonverbal behaviors, affects students' ratings of lecturers and may enhance learning (Cooper and Galvin, 1984; Michael and Weaver, 1984). Another study examined sixth- and seventh-grade students with mild to moderate learning disabilities (LD) and their performances on tests following two instructional treatments involving lecture. Students performed better on tests when the lecture was broken into segments, each one followed by teacher-guided practice with reinforcement (Hudson, 1997). Very recently, researchers at Mid-continent Research for Education and Learning identified teachers' use of advance organizers as one of the nine instructional techniques most likely to improve student achievement across all content areas and grade levels (Varlas, 2002).

■ APPLICATION TO PRACTICE: LECTURE METHOD

The lecture method is essentially a teacher-centered, one-way presentation of information and ideas. This method, like the discussion method, consists of a generalized sequence of phases that is easily adaptable to several varieties of lecture that are commonly used by teachers in secondary level classrooms. Information giving, a technique presented in Chapter 6, was described as a minilecture, or a shortened and informal form of the lecture. These primarily spontaneous introductions, explanations, and demonstrations can last from less than a minute when the teacher is responding to a student's question to 5 to 10 minutes that a teacher might devote to introducing a guest speaker or simulation game. The lecture method is generally reserved for more formal presentations of subject matter and demonstrations lasting for as long as a full class period. It is appropriate for more extensive and complex one-way communication.

The research has indicated the lecture method is as effective as other methods in achieving its intended goals. Compared to other methods, lecturing is particularly effective when the purpose is presenting information that is not readily available elsewhere. It is also effective when information presentation needs to be tailored to a particular group and there is an intended follow-up using other methods. Furthermore, it is useful when long-term retention of the information presented is not the major consideration (Gage and Berliner, 1992). A lecture has its strengths and limitations that are consistent with the objectives for which it is intended.

Although all teachers need to be able to give information effectively in the classroom, not all teachers can lecture effectively, nor should they be expected to. Critical to the success of presenting a lecture is the effective application of communication skills. Another related factor is the personality of the presenter. The ideal lecturer is dynamic and presents material in a well-organized and convincing manner. To be effective, teachers need to make a thoughtful selection of those skills that help hold students' interest and attention and that stimulate their mental involvement. Particular attention needs to be paid to those motivating behaviors and skills presented in the previous chapter: physical movement, nonverbal behaviors, voice, lesson pace, and instructional variation. Each contributes to the creation of an enthusiastic teaching image. The application of these qualities is desirable whenever a teacher is instructing. They seem most pertinent and necessary, however, when a teacher is presenting information over extended periods of time. When communication is two way, such as during discussions, students' attention is not directly focused on the teacher every minute. The teacher's ability to induce motivation seems to be more critical during one-way communication.

The most important quality of a good lecturer is the ability to present material in an organized manner so that it is well understood by the listeners. A teacher delivering a lecture will obviously need to be well prepared on the topic. The most dramatic and flamboyant lecturers will be ineffective if they do not deal with matters of substance! Some lecturers rely on planned notes to deliver a talk. The well-planned teacher will incorporate visual aids to assist in the presentation of the content. They may range from a single transparency of a lecture outline to an elaborate demonstration involving numerous materials and artifacts. Another, more technologically oriented, approach is to present notes and accompanying graphics via PowerPoint or through a multimedia presentation. Styles of lecturers will vary as widely as their personalities and mannerisms; the effectiveness of a presentation is better measured in terms of outcomes rather than delivery style.

Three of the most common forms of the lecture method are discussed here: formal lecture, interactive lecture, and demonstration. They have in common the primary emphasis on one-way communication over an extended period of time (more than 10 minutes), and they differ with respect to the degree of student interactive involvement.

Formal Lecture

The formal lecture at the secondary school level is the least used form of the lecture method. It is the most common strategy at the university level. An average student's attention span at the secondary school level is not extensive. After approximately 20 minutes, students' minds wander, even at the high school level. Younger students have even shorter attention spans. The exception is noticed in advanced-placement and honors classes in which coverage of content is emphasized and many teachers feel obligated to prepare their students for teaching and learning in the typical university classroom.

The formal lecture is sometimes noticed in schools that have flexible scheduling and emphasize other instructional approaches that complement lectures. Scheduled small-group classes are arranged to discuss the material presented in large-group sessions, and independent-study projects fulfill the needs of the more capable and motivated students who want to pursue topics, problems, and issues in depth. In these cases, large-group lectures are sometimes presented by guest speakers who have a particular field of expertise, such as a local historian, the president of the chamber of commerce, a labor union official, or a politician. The large-group lecture, in which students are, for the most part, passively involved, would not be effective if it were not supported by a variety of other instructional approaches to encourage and stimulate students' active involvement in learning.

Interactive Lecture

This is the most common form of the lecture method in secondary schools. When teachers describe themselves as lecturers, they usually mean that they teach using interactive lectures. Teachers realize that students' attention spans are not long. Therefore, they attempt to involve students through the use of questioning by encouraging them to ask questions at various points during the presentation. Although some may wait until the presentation is completed before entertaining questions and comments, most lecturers encourage their students to contribute their thoughts and questions during the lecture.

The objectives teachers have for the interactive lecture will primarily determine the level of questions they will ask during or after the presentation. It is common to hear all four levels of questions asked during an interactive lecture. For example, a world history teacher in an interactive lecture on the Protestant secession might pause to review key facts and to ask students the names of the six popes who ignored calls for reform during the Renaissance and brought the papacy into disrepute (Level I). At another point, the teacher might ask students to compare the reigns of Leo X and Clement VII in terms of acts that inadvertently helped pave the way for the secession (Level II). To stimulate some higher-level thinking near the end of the lecture, the teacher might ask students for some principles that future popes might have learned from the six decades of papal misrule (Level III). At the end of the lecture, time permitting, a final high-divergent question might be asked: Which pope do you think could have had the greatest influence and opportunity to avert the Protestant secession? Questions judiciously interspersed throughout a lecture can successfully stimulate students' active involvement and increase the probability of longer-term learning.

Demonstration

Demonstrations, as typically used by teachers at the middle, junior, and high school levels, are basically formal or interactive lectures depending on the extent that student involvement is encouraged. Although many demonstrations are brief, not extending beyond 10 minutes, others are complex and attempt to provide students with more information. Demonstrations provide teachers with an opportunity to show students a procedure or illustration from which they will be able to learn. For example, a physics teacher performs a demonstration using the Van de Graaff generator to show the effects of static electricity to the students. In an art class, the teacher demonstrates the technique of the Pointillists by creating a painting in their once-popular style. The teacher's intention in this case is not for the students to learn the technique but to appreciate and understand more about this school of painters, especially Georges Seurat and his devotees. The demonstration has the potential to contribute substance and immediacy to a lecture, to breathe life into it!

Teachers more commonly use demonstrations to model particular skills that students are expected to learn. Often, specific levels of performance are demonstrated. Examples include a basketball layup shot in a physical education class, computation of compound interest within a consumer mathematics unit, turning wood on a lathe in a technology class, or several ways to back up a disk in a computer class. If students are expected to practice and perform the skill the teacher has demonstrated, the teacher is training students using the demonstration as a model.

Lecture-Method Phases

Phase I. Entry: Preparation for Learning

a. State objectives and rationale.

b. Provide a context for the new material to be presented.

c. Focus attention on a key concept, generalization, or principle that encompasses the lecture (advance organizer).

The purpose of the entry to a lecture or a demonstration is to inform students of what the teacher intends to accomplish and why it is important and to prepare students to understand what will be presented. The objectives could be verbally stated generally or more formally in specific terms. They might even be listed on a handout or a transparency. In this way, the students will know what the teacher expects them to learn as a result of the presentation.

A rationale provides students with a purpose for the presentation and how it fits into the unit being studied. This generally satisfies students' urge to know why they are studying something. Teachers often overlook this component of a lesson because they assume that it should be obvious to students. Following a rationale could be a brief summary of what has been covered to a certain point to provide a learning context for students. Another approach to providing a learning context is to preview or give an overview of what will be covered in the presentation. The order of lecture-entry components is flexible and depends on the level of structure of the presentation.

Preparation for students to assimilate information to be presented in a lecture would not be complete without an organizer. The purpose of the organizer is to focus students' attention on and help them understand the "big idea" of the lecture. In many respects, the organizer is the common thread weaving through all the information presented (Ausubel, 1968).

The key to the effective use of organizers is to identify a central concept, generalization, term, or principle that encompasses the material to be presented and then to relate it to what students already know or have experienced. Research confirms that organizers can increase students' comprehension of new learning material. It is logical that the more difficult the learning material, the more useful and necessary an organizer. To prepare students for a formal lecture on the Romantic period of poetry, a teacher might use the organizer "love" to help students understand the works of Keats, Shelley, and Byron. The teacher could start off with formally defining it from the dictionary and including some other diverse definitions from several other sources, including some teenagers' definitions. This would help relate the concept to students' lives. If using an interactive-lecture approach, the teacher might ask students what love means to them. Going a step further might involve comparing and contrasting the love students have for parents, pets, friends, and the nation. The interactive approach significantly increases the chance that students will understand the concept and, therefore, the subsequent information on the Romantic period.

Another illustration of an organizer applies in a middle-school science class. A science teacher wants to use an interactive lecture to demonstrate the principle of air pressure. An organizer can be used to ensure that students understand the concept of *pressure.* The teacher might explain the concept and use examples of pressure within the realm of students' experiences, such as tires on a bicycle, a shaken can of soda, or blood pressure. Once the teacher is sure that the students understand what pressure is, several planned demonstrations may proceed.

Phase II. Presentation

a. Sequence content from simpler to complex understandings.
b. Enhance presentation with visual aids.
c. Stimulate attention with verbal and nonverbal behaviors.

During the presentation phase, the main body of the lecture is presented or the demonstration occurs. Comprehension will be enhanced if the learning material is sequenced from simple to complex understandings and visual aids are used to illustrate key or difficult concepts, processes, or other content. For example, in a formal or interactive lecture on the Constitutional Convention's "Great Compromise," a U.S. history teacher might use as an organizer the principle that a compromise results when one gives up something to acquire something else. The teacher could easily relate it to students' lives by describing a conflict between a brother and a sister over watching television at a particular time. An even more effective and appropriate question for an interactive lecture would be to ask students about their conflicts with brothers and sisters and how they were resolved. After presentation of the organizer, the teacher would need to present logically the differing views on a plan of government of the large and the small states. The Virginia and New Jersey plans could be compared by analyzing their strengths and weaknesses from the perceptions of the delegates to the convention and, perhaps, by consideration of current political scientists' views on that episode in history. Finally, the formation, presentation, and acceptance of the Connecticut Plan, or "Great Compromise," would need to be explained and the process of compromise analyzed.

In this illustration, the teacher progressed from the presentation of basic facts and information related to the Virginia and New Jersey plans to the more complex analysis of the role of compromise in resolving the conflict. The ability of the students to comprehend the lecture is increased because of the logical development and presentation of content. We can also imagine the teacher using several Power-Point slides detailing the provisions of each of the two plans, another of the Connecticut Plan that was finally accepted, and one on the process of compromise.

Phase III. Closure: Review of Learning

a. Integrate with students' knowledge and experiences.
b. Transition to next lesson or activity.

A teacher has the opportunity during the closure of a formal lecture to reinforce what has been presented with a review of key points, concepts, and ideas. Students should also be able to raise questions and make comments, all of which will help teachers determine how effective they were in presenting the lecture. In the case of the interactive-lecture illustration, the teacher might use questions to have the students examine the process of compromise that they have used with friends and parents to get what they want and compare it with the one that led to the formation of our legislative branch of government. In this way, the teacher can diagnose the students' understanding of the content in the lecture by having them apply it to their own lives. This is a powerful approach to integration. The same approach could be applied to the closure of a demonstration.

The last component of the lecture, whether it is formal, interactive, or a demonstration, is the transition during which the teacher bridges the gap to the next lesson. The lecture is primarily one-way communication; thus, students' higher levels of thinking are generally not being stimulated directly through questions. This, of course, is a major advantage that the interactive lecture has over the formal lecture. In the case of a formal lecture or an interactive lecture in which little high-level thinking has been encouraged, the transition is the ideal time to challenge students with a problem or assignment that will serve as the basis for the next lesson. This follow-up should be aimed at engaging students in divergent thinking (Levels III and IV). For example, the U.S. history teacher might have students attempt to locate in the newspaper at least one instance of a compromise that was reached at any level of government over any issue and evaluate the decision reached based on their perceptions of the criteria for a compromise. Several goals are accomplished through such transition. The bridge to the next lesson is made, students are applying what they have learned in the lecture, and students' higher-level divergent thinking is involved. The closure provides teachers with an opportunity to evaluate directly students' understanding of the information presented and to encourage their application of what has been learned. Student performance during the closure and during the next class session is, indirectly, an evaluation of the teacher's effectiveness in applying the lecture method.

Scenario Analysis

Mr. Carl used the inquiry method that incorporated guided discussion in the hypothetical teaching situation. After the students had discovered the solution to the map "puzzle," he provided some background information on the concept of GNP definition, examples of goods and services, and some statistics comparing the GNP of different countries. His instructional approach could be classified as information giving rather than lecture, primarily because of the brevity of the explanation.

The lesson could have been a formal or interactive lecture. The entry might have focused on the organizer "standard of living," with Mr. Carl giving illustrations of families who have different living standards. He then could have related it to students' lives by asking them to examine their own and family members' needs now and in the future. The lecture would naturally be on several aspects of GNP intended to be covered, supplemented perhaps with transparencies that illustrate some of the more complex concepts and processes: circular flow of money and products, categories of spending, and leading economic indicators. During the presentation, Mr. Carl could use the transparency of the map depicting countries, each with a different-size GNP. Another possibility would be to use it in the closure for the purpose of summarizing and reviewing.

■ SUMMARY POINT ■

The lecture method is the most straightforward instructional approach. It is the most effective way to convey large amounts of information that are not readily available to students. It also presents an opportunity for teachers to lay the groundwork for higher-level thinking during follow-up class sessions.

Three closely related forms of the lecture method have been presented: formal lecture, interactive lecture, and demonstration. They all have as their primary purpose the presentation of content using a one-way communications approach. The interactive lecture is the most familiar. This requires that teachers purposely incorporate questions at several levels to stimulate student involvement and thinking during the lecture. The formal lecture is the noninteractive form of the lecture method. Demonstration is essentially an interactive lecture, featuring display or performance and explanation. Teacher decision making in relation to the lecture during the planning stage involves selecting which form to use to achieve the lesson's objectives. Selection of the form will depend primarily on the amount of content to be covered, the ability level of the students, and the extent of interaction desired.

A lecture-method analysis form is included at the end of the chapter to aid in the observation and analysis of your and others' teaching.

■ RESEARCH AND THEORETICAL BASE: INQUIRY METHOD

Inquiry is a generic term that applies to methods with which teachers engage students' critical-thinking skills to analyze and solve problems in a systematic fashion. Whereas lecture and recitation are used extensively by teachers, inquiry is used sparingly. Most of the research literature on inquiry centers on comparing it with other methods. One dissertation surveyed studies comparing discovery and expository approaches from 1908 to 1975 and could not conclude that one was superior to the other (Weimer, 1974). Ponder and Davis (1982) found a tendency in students who were taught by methods requiring students' use of critical-thinking skills, such as inquiry, to perform as well as students who were taught by methods of factual learning. Two other studies conducted since then favored inquiry over expository approaches (Andrews, 1984; Selim and Shrigley, 1983).

As has been previously mentioned, there is a growing movement toward viewing teaching and learning from a constructivist vantage point. Theorists believe that students should no longer be relegated to the role of passively receiving information but, rather, that teachers should encourage them to mediate it actively by relating it to what they know and developing and applying it in meaningful ways. Inquiry, or problem solving, is being advocated by educators as one approach to help students achieve the goal of subject-matter understanding. Several of the components of Good and Brophy's (2000) model that describes good subject-matter teaching relate directly to the need for learning activities that call for students to engage in critical thinking, problem solving, and decision making. Zemelman, Daniels, and Hyde (1998) likewise strongly advocate the use of the inquiry or problem-solving approach as best-practice instruction in the subject areas of science, mathematics, and social studies. Palincsar, Cutter, and Magnusson (2002) concluded on their review of the research, "virtually all contemporary educational reform efforts call for the teaching of science to be inquiry-based" (p. 88).

Martin-Hansen (2002) provided an analysis of the essential features of science classroom inquiry. In her conceptualization, learner self-direction is increased as the learner:

1. Poses and engages in scientific-oriented questions
2. Prioritizes evidence in responding to the questions
3. Formulates explanations from the evidence

4. Connects explanations to scientific knowledge

5. Communicates and supports explanations

In order for learner self-direction to increase, the extent of teacher direction needs to decrease. Kovalainen and her colleagues (2002) examined the role of the teacher during class inquiry discussions and synthesized several key modes of teacher participation:

1. *Evocative*—Stimulating student questioning and opinions

2. *Facilitative*—Collecting students' ideas and modeling inquiry processes

3. *Collective*—Encouraging and orchestrating participation

4. *Appreciative*—Supporting and valuing students' contributions to the community of inquiry

■ APPLICATION TO PRACTICE: INQUIRY METHOD

Inquiry is an extremely versatile instructional method because it can be used to teach content, problem solving, critical-thinking skills, and decision making. Many consider inquiry to be synonymous with discovery, inductive teaching, reflective teaching, and problem solving. Writers vary somewhat in their interpretation of what it is and, in fact, the term is often used by teachers for much of what they do (Martin-Hansen, 2002). In its most general form, inquiry is the analysis of a problem in a systematic fashion. Several key words help us to understand more about inquiry. A problem is central to inquiry and can take many forms. It could be academic problem solving, such as mathematics students attempting to discover the process by which an answer was obtained. The problem could occur in social studies, such as what the students of a government class can do to help get a particular candidate they support to be elected to the city council. The problem could be personal, such as a student's attempt to decide what to do to help a friend in a personal crisis. The word *analysis* suggests that the problem will be dissected into parts and studied; *systematic* means that the problem will be methodically worked on using a step-by-step procedure. Inquiry is a process that students can learn and experience as they work to solve problems through reflective thinking.

Although the steps of inquiry vary depending on the specific objectives the teacher intends to achieve, there is general agreement on a basic form. That form is Dewey's model of reflective thinking (1910). An adaptation is presented here:

1. Identify and clarify the problem.

2. Form hypotheses.

3. Collect data.

4. Analyze and interpret the data to test hypotheses.

5. Draw conclusions.

The problem is created out of a discrepancy in perceptions of data. The more puzzlement involved and the more personal attachment the students have toward the problem, the better the potential for inquiry. Hypotheses are the students' proposed solutions to the problem based on experiences and information that they have related to the problem. Data collection requires consulting resources for information that is related to the hypotheses. Once data have been collected, they need to be analyzed and interpreted to reduce the number of hypotheses. As a result of this process, a conclusion will be drawn that reflects an acceptance, rejection, or modification of the hypotheses. Depending on the problem, the conclusion could be a solution, a generalization, or an explanation.

With the inquiry method, both content and process are taught at the same time. Whether content or process is more important and therefore emphasized will depend on the objectives for the lesson and the teacher's judgment. Research confirms that inquiry is as effective as other methods in teaching content and may be better than most in teaching other learnings, especially the process of inquiry.

Teaching the process of inquiry is an opportunity for students to learn and practice skills associated with critical thinking. Helping students develop the ability to think is receiving increased emphasis because of the realization that students will benefit from being independent and reflective thinkers in the real social world (Paul, 1984). Byer (1984) proposed a series of critical-thinking skills and several practical approaches to teaching these skills sequentially within a K–12 curriculum. The skills include: "(1) distinguishing between verifiable facts and value claims; (2) determining the reliability of a claim or source; (3) determining the accuracy of a statement; (4) distinguishing between warranted or unwarranted claims; (5) distinguishing between relevant and irrelevant information, claims, or reasons; (6) detecting bias; (7) identifying stated and unstated assumptions; (8) identifying ambiguous or equivocal claims or arguments; (9) recognizing logical inconsistencies in a line of reasoning; and (10) determining the strength of an argument" (p. 557). Most of these skills can be taught and practiced as students engage in inquiry in connection with analyzing social issues and problems and investigating phenomena in the physical world. In this case, the process taught would be inquiry, with the content being information related to a current social issue such as updating immigration laws, corruption in law enforcement, increase in teenage suicides, violence in movies, or the growing influence of political action committees. Specific critical-thinking skills could also be thought of as the content that is to be taught.

When we think about preparing students to deal with personal problems, the skills associated with decision making come to mind. It should be apparent that there is considerable similarity between the processes of inquiry and decision making. To a great extent, both are appropriate in solving social and personal problems. However, personal attitudes and values generally play a greater role in decision making. Personal values need to be considered along with information gathered from sources. Solutions can then be proposed for which the consequences of each need to be considered. Finally, a decision is reached, implemented, and eventually evaluated to determine its appropriateness (Armstrong, 1980).

Three forms of the inquiry method are presented: guided inquiry, open inquiry, and the individualized inquiry investigation. All three are primarily subject-matter oriented and have as their structure the process of inquiry. These forms differ in the extent of guidance provided by the teacher and, in the case of the individualized form, the number of students involved.

Guided Inquiry

The extent of the teacher's involvement during the implementation of inquiry is the primary difference between the guided and open forms. As the teacher becomes more involved, more structure is provided, and this results in less freedom for students to take initiative and direction for their own learning experiences. The teacher assumes these responsibilities. During guided inquiry, the teacher provides the data and the students are questioned to help them inductively arrive at an answer, a conclusion, a generalization, or a solution. The teacher generally has the "right" answer or a narrow range of acceptable answers in mind, so the students are led to the conclusion (Shulman and Tamir, 1973). In this case the teacher, being actively involved, is more a director of students' learning and thinking than a facilitator. The guided inquiry form of the method is especially appropriate as a way to introduce the inquiry process to students. The structure serves as security as they venture into a new area involving different kinds of thinking.

The necessity of providing guidance makes the teacher's questioning behavior important in the guided-inquiry process. Although the questions asked by the teacher cover the full range of thinking levels, the most effective questions to stimulate inductive thinking are those classified at Levels II, III, and IV—high-convergent, and low- and high-divergent thinking. As a result of the direct involvement of the teacher in questioning students, the effective use of a full range of questioning skills becomes critical.

One illustration of guided inquiry takes place in an eighth-grade science classroom. The teacher shows the students three test tubes, all half-filled with clear liquid. A few drops from the first test tube are poured into the second, and the liquid turns bright purple. Some of the clear liquid from the third tube is poured into the second, and the purple liquid becomes completely clear again. As the students stare in amazement, the teacher asks them, "What happened?" to start the inquiry with a review of the facts. Once the problem has been clarified, hypotheses are generated as tentative explanations for the unusual event. The most difficult part is using questions to lead them to test their ideas, such as "What is this liquid?" "Suppose we poured the liquid from the first tube into the third?" and "What would happen if . . . ?" The teacher needs to probe students' responses to focus, clarify, extend, and expand their thinking as they are guided to discover that the first tube contained a base (ammonia), the second contained a small amount of phenolphthalein in water, and the third was an acid (white vinegar). Phenolphthalein is an indicator of a base, and the acid serves as a neutralizer. As the result of being guided by the teachers' questions, the students are able to discover inductively the explanation for the puzzling event.

Open Inquiry

Students' freedom to initiate and think is expanded in open inquiry. In essence, they assume more responsibility for their own learning and, as a result, lessen their dependence on the teacher. The inquiry process remains the same with the focus on inductive thinking as students propose solutions, gather data, and draw conclusions. A primary difference lies in the data-collection phase. During guided inquiry, the teacher provides the data to help students draw conclusions; during open inquiry, the students gather the data (Shulman and Tamir, 1973). Student questioning becomes more important during open inquiry, because students ask questions and search for the answers. The teacher's role is to facilitate by assisting students within the phases of the process. As part of this role, the teacher also serves as a resource person, suggesting sources students might consult, such as those in the library or on the Internet, and helping arrange other out-of-school sources, such as people in the community. Although the teacher usually commences open inquiry with a problem related to what is being studied and assists students in hypothesis formation, the students assume responsibility for data collection and generalizing. This is an essential component in open inquiry.

An illustration for an open-inquiry lesson centers on a class of U.S. government students who are interested in establishing a recycling center in their community. Assume that the class has been studying environmental issues with a particular emphasis on what they perceive as their community's problems. Inquiry was initiated when students decided to focus on ascertaining the extent of community support for a recycling center. Naturally, they were hopeful that this would lead to the development of a center. The teacher guided them as they proposed ideas about how residents could obtain support. Some of their brainstormed approaches were to interview city officials for their suggestions and their perceptions of problems and issues associated with building a center, to conduct a survey of citizens, to attend a city council meeting to propose the center, to contact a nearby community that has a center to find out how residents built support, and to write to the state and federal governments to see what guidelines might exist. Clarification was achieved as their purpose was more sharply defined, and the list of ideas was reduced to four. The data-gathering phase was initiated when it was decided that the class could be divided into small groups, each assuming responsibility for investigating one of the proposed approaches. For example, one group planned to present formally the idea of a recycling center to the city council to find out if it had been considered in the past, if the council might give tentative support to the idea now, or if council members had suggestions for building more support or for proceeding to get the idea approved.

The data gathering could take several weeks, most of it being conducted by the groups outside of the regular class sessions. After the information is gathered and analyzed by the groups, a class session will need to be set aside for the presentation of the group findings. The culminating activity of the inquiry process is drawing a conclusion and, in this case, finding out the extent to which the community supports the construction of a recycling center. In the open form of the inquiry method, the students are more involved in determining the direction of the learning process as they start with a problem of concern to them, propose solutions, gather and analyze the data, and draw conclusions.

Individualized Inquiry Investigation

The individualized-inquiry-investigation method (Wilen and McKenrick, 1989) involves identifying able and interested students who will benefit from engaging in independent study. This interpretation of the inquiry method most closely approximates the format of the open-inquiry form because of the freedom given to students. The issue or problem devised should naturally relate to the unit currently under study and, most importantly, have personal meaning for the student. Examples are an American literature student who, after reading several of Ernest Hemingway's novels and short stories for a class assignment, wants to find out more about how his work has influenced other writers, or an algebra student who is interested in constructing a computer program to solve a problem, or a U.S. history student who wants to find out more about how the Japanese treated U.S. prisoners during World War II because his great uncle survived the infamous Bataan "death march." Once a willing student has been identified and preliminary research has yielded a general issue or problem area, a contract should be drawn up to specify the conditions of the inquiry investigation. The contract could be formal or informal, written or verbal, depending on the needs of the teacher and the student. Important questions must be answered directly: How much time should the student devote to the investigation? Under what conditions should the student be excused from class sessions to pursue the inquiry? Should that student take the tests with other students? What is to be the method of reporting the investigation? How will the student's effort be evaluated? How will this grade influence the marking-period grade? The contract must be designed to clarify mutual expectations.

Once the contract has been agreed on, the investigation should continue with a formal statement of the problem in question form. This will help ensure specific direction. The teacher then should assist the student to reflect on tentative explanations or solutions to the problem to guide the inquiry. It is important for the teacher to be supportive and nonjudgmental to encourage intellectual freedom. After assistance from the teacher and perhaps the librarian or media specialist in identifying key sources, the student should be left alone to pursue the inquiry. The role of the teacher is to encourage and facilitate, offering assistance when necessary. The method of reporting the project could take many different forms including a paper (the traditional approach), a display, an oral report, a computer multimedia presentation, a videotape, or a bulletin board. The individualization of inquiry investigations provides teachers with an opportunity to encourage responsible students to pursue their own interests within an agreed-upon structure.

Inquiry-Method Phases

The phases of the inquiry method basically have their roots in the steps of reflective thinking as conceived by Dewey (1910) and reported in many other current references. Although there is flexibility, the sequence of phases is considered more important than in the other methods presented in this chapter because inquiry is designed to teach an investigative process as well as content.

Phase I. Entry: Presentation and Clarification of a Problem, Issue, or Query

a. State objectives; provide rationale.
b. Identify a problem, issue, or query.
c. Relate to students' experiences and lives.
d. Clarify the problem.

The nature of the problem or issue selected as the basis for the inquiry investigation is important for motivational purposes. Although it probably will be at least indirectly related to the unit currently under study, students' attachment to the problem can be greatly enhanced if it in some way relates to their lives. Another motivational approach is to select a problem that causes a discrepancy between what students expect to happen and what actually does happen. Regarding disequilibrium, "Students are challenged by phenomena that cause them to question ideas and beliefs they previously held" (Skolnik, 1995). A way to accomplish this is to present statistics that can be interpreted differently. The diverse interpretations can serve as a springboard to an inquiry problem. Statistics related to drug usage and abuse might stimulate inquiry in a health class, for example.

The objectives and rationale can be presented before or after the problem is presented, depending on a teacher's preference for an entry format. A problem may evolve naturally out of lesson content and be suggested by a student or a small group. Student initiation is a powerful motivator, particularly if a majority of students express an interest. The teacher generally plans for the investigation. Although a teacher-selected problem can be presented conveniently during the rationale, it should be presented in an interesting way to grab students' attention. For example, a description of the final days of the Heaven's Gate tragedy in 1997 would be an interesting way to lead sociology students into investigating why and how people can be brainwashed into committing themselves so completely, and sometimes tragically, to "religious" cults.

How the problem, issue, or query is presented in the entry is equally important to all forms of the inquiry method. The opportunity for students to explore problems with which they feel close attachment probably occurs more often with the individualized approach because the student has a choice and therefore would not be engaging in inquiry without interest. Open inquiry should also be a stimulus to some extent because of the freedom students have in gathering data. In the case of the guided-inquiry approach, teachers tend to control students' involvement more directly because it is more structured.

Phase II. Formation of Hypotheses

a. Encourage the formation of tentative explanations or solutions.

b. Clarify hypotheses.

A hypothesis is a plausible but tentative explanation for a discrepancy in information or student beliefs or a proposed solution to the problem. They are considered tentative until they have been tested by data that will be gathered in the next phase. The teacher initially wants to encourage as many solutions as possible. In some cases, few solutions may be offered because students are unfamiliar with the inquiry process, so the teacher will have to encourage them. Creativity may even be one of the teacher's objectives during this phase, and the students are therefore expected to brainstorm solutions. In this case, quantity is the primary emphasis, with the quality of proposed solutions being the focus later as the hypotheses are clarified.

The teacher can encourage hypotheses to be generated in the large-group situation or in small groups or, in the case of the individualized approach, in a one-to-one meeting. Using small groups to form hypotheses may take somewhat more time than in the large group, but students may not feel as inhibited and may therefore contribute more. Once the students have generated hypotheses in their small groups, they need to be reconvened in the large group to share solutions and devise a list reflecting their collective thinking. While the hypotheses are being discussed for inclusion on the final list, terms are defined and assumptions clarified. The result should be a list of tentative solutions clearly understood by the students.

Phase III. Collection of Data

a. Facilitate the identification of sources for evidence.

b. Assist in the evaluation of the evidence.

The purpose of the data-collection phase is to provide information leading to the acceptance or rejection of each hypothesis. By this stage, the students have shared some information about the problem by virtue of the fact that the problem was clarified and tentative solutions were formed. Sharing common knowledge and experiences is important in the initial phases of inquiry, but at some point information needs to be gathered from a greater diversity of sources and from more authoritative sources outside the classroom. Sources may range from references in the school library or on the Internet to interviewing experts in the field in the community or via e-mail. Students may also wish to create the data themselves, as in the case of a survey form to be administered to peers in school, parents, or a sample of community members. In other cases, students may need to generate data through observation and experimentation in a science laboratory. The quality of generalizations students reach at the end of an inquiry investigation can often be directly related to the quantity and quality of sources consulted during this phase.

The teacher's role is to assist students in their identification of sources for evidence and to facilitate the collection and evaluation of the data. This interpretation of the teacher's role applies primarily to the open-inquiry form of the strategy. Thoughts about sources might be shared immediately after the hypotheses are clarified. Of course, the range of sources will be limited by the problem under investigation. The teacher will have to take a more active role in acquainting students with possibilities for sources, particularly if they are neophytes to the inquiry process. The rich possibility of finding evidence to support hypotheses from nonprint sources such as videotapes, records and audiotapes, and computer databases is often forgotten. The teacher's responsibility during this phase is to serve as a resource person who continually encourages students to keep an open mind as they consult and explore a variety of sources.

The teacher also needs to help students evaluate the quality of the sources from which they are gathering information. All sources consulted should not be given equal weight when deciding their influence on validating students' hypotheses. Students will need to know the differences between primary and secondary sources, how a writer's frame of reference influences the work, and how to detect a writer's biases and prejudices, for example. Standards for judging sources should apply to all sources, including nonwritten ones.

A major difference between the three forms of the inquiry method is noticed in the data-gathering phase. In guided inquiry, the teacher provides the data and structures how students will use it to support or refute their hypotheses. In the case of the open and individualized forms, the students gather the data with the assistance of the teacher, whose role is to facilitate rather than direct. As an illustration, in Suchman's (1962) interpretation of the inquiry method, the teacher provides a science-related discrepant event and the students inductively proceed through the stages by asking questions to which the teacher responds "yes" or "no." During the hypothesis formation and data-gathering phases, the teacher structures the inquiry so that students' questions are focused on the variables and conditions of the event. This knowledge is used to hypothesize and test relationships within the data. The formation of causal relationships leads to an explanation for the event. In essence, the students first hypothesize and then collect and analyze the data through their questions, as guided by the high structure provided by the teacher. Suchman's (1962) inquiry-training form of the method is essentially guided inquiry. It becomes more open as students gather data themselves as, for example, in the case when they literally test their hypotheses by performing experiments in a laboratory situation.

Phase IV. Testing Hypotheses

a. Assist in organizing the data.

b. Assist in analysis and evaluation of the data.

The purpose of this phase is to examine the evidence that has been gathered to determine the extent to which it validates or invalidates the hypotheses. In essence, the students are testing the hypotheses. As the information is gathered and recorded, students will need to be concerned with how to handle the quantity of data, some of which might be incomplete and conflicting. Organization and presentation of the data are particularly important for the beginner in the inquiry process. Armstrong (1980) suggested that the data be recorded and categorized in chart form so that students might analyze and evaluate them more easily. For example, each proposed solution or explanation might be placed on a separate large piece of paper or transparency. Three columns might be set up, labeled *Evidence Supporting, Evidence Not Supporting,* and *Evidence Neutral.* Students can then categorize the evidence they have found based on its worth in supporting or refuting each hypothesis. This structure will make it easier for students to evaluate the data.

This phase is similar for the guided, open, and individualized forms of the inquiry method. The structure that the teacher provides for the process will depend on the capacity of the students to pursue inquiry. This is another reason for selecting a particularly capable and responsible student for individualized inquiry investigations. Once students have analyzed and evaluated the evidence, they are ready to draw a conclusion.

Phase V. Closure: Drawing Conclusions

a. Develop a generalization, explanation, or solution.

b. Integrate into the unit of study.

The final stage of inquiry is the acceptance, the rejection, or the modification of the hypotheses. Drawing a conclusion is the natural follow-up to analyzing and evaluating the data that have been gathered. In fact, these phases often run together, depending on the nature of the problem being investigated and how the teacher structures the hypothesis testing. Although the data may strongly suggest that a particular hypothesis be accepted over others, the teacher should encourage students to support their view by reexamining the evidence. Questions that may need consideration are: Have enough data been gathered to arrive at a conclusion? Does the evidence support only one conclusion, or could others be considered? How final is the conclusion? The conclusion reached, whether a generalization drawn from a collection of data, an explanation of a phenomenon or observations, or a solution to a problem, should be considered tentative. Students may tend to accept a conclusion, particularly to a major investigation, that involves the opinions of experts as the final answer or the truth. Reality suggests that any conclusions drawn should be considered tentative because all the evidence related to any issue, topic, or problem can never be available at one time. Students and teacher may have missed several key and influential sources. Furthermore, a conclusion reached may have to be rejected completely if new evidence is reported that refutes it.

The final stage of the inquiry method is basically the same for the three forms discussed in this section. In the case of the individualized approach, the teacher may meet with the student doing the investigation to review the conclusions drawn before writing the paper, if this is to be the means for reporting findings from the inquiry. The review made and the questions raised during this final phase will increase the chances that the student will arrive at a conclusion consistent with the evidence gathered.

■ WEBSITE RESOURCE ■

The Mathematics and Science Education Center is sponsored by the Northwest Regional Educational Laboratory and is designed to provide K–12 teachers with "resources and services to support challenging, effective mathematics and science curriculum, instruction, and assessment for all students" at

www.nwrel.org/msec/index.html.

Two particularly good inquiry-oriented links are the Science Inquiry Model and the Mathematics Problem Solving Model with many ideas for teaching strategies and resources, including links to other websites.

Scenario Analysis

Mr. Carl used guided and open inquiry to achieve his objectives. The first part of the lesson centered on applying an adaptation of Suchman's (1962) inquiry-training approach to stimulate students to explain the discrepant event as represented by the puzzling world map. Clarification was achieved as the students responded to "What do you see?" The inquiry was formally begun after Mr. Carl explained the procedure of student questioning as the means to gather data from the teacher. The second phase began after a series of student questions related to specifics about the map were asked and a tentative solution was offered. At that point, Mr. Carl asked the student to test his hypothesis by gathering more evidence with more questions. He wanted the student to begin to form causal relationships ("Think about the relationships of the countries. How about a 'what if' question?").

After several other student questions yielded other hypotheses and more data, one student eventually came up with the correct explanation that the map depicted countries' GNPs. Mr. Carl rounded out this part of the lesson with a brief discussion on the clues, or pieces of evidence, that led to the discovery of the explanation. Guided inquiry was used effectively by the teacher to grab students' attention initially through the use of a discrepant event. Student questioning was structured to stimulate inductive thinking that eventually led to the explanation for the event.

After providing some information on GNP, Mr. Carl initiated the final phase of the lesson with a shift to open inquiry. He referred students back to the map and asked why there was a tendency for the smaller GNP countries to be located south of approximately 30 degrees north latitude. Students responded with several tentative explanations, and then he suggested that inquiry would be pursued in the next class period. We can envision him beginning the next class period with a review and clarification of the hypotheses offered so far. One indication of a data source was a guest speaker from one of the lower GNP countries to the south. The suggestion was also made that small groups might be formed for the investigation based, perhaps, on the hypotheses formed. If Mr. Carl continues with open inquiry, we can expect the students will assume the major responsibility for gathering the data. Although time-consuming, open inquiry provides students with the opportunity to examine significant issues and problems in-depth, using a process practiced by both physical and social scientists.

■ WEBSITE RESOURCE ■

Webquest is designed to serve as a resource to teachers who want to identify inquiry-oriented lesson plans. The website is located at

http://webquest.sdsu.edu/webquest.html.

Go to Examples to get a matrix of illustrative lesson plans according to groupings of grade levels and subject areas: art and music, business, English/language arts, foreign language, health/PE, life skills/careers, math, social studies, science, professional skills, and technology. The plans are detailed and contain supplementary materials needed to teach the lessons.

You can even search for specific information and lessons by clicking on Search.

■ SUMMARY POINT ■

Inquiry is a versatile instructional method used to involve students in a process to analyze a problem or issue in a logical and systematic way. Inquiry is exceptionally appropriate as a means to apply constructivist ideals because of its emphasis on higher-order thinking to investigate and solve problems. The problem is defined generally and can be identified within subject-matter content, societal issues, or personal situations. The process of inquiry begins with the problem, issue, or query for which an explanation or solution is desired. Students propose hypotheses, gather data, analyze and evaluate the data, test hypotheses, and draw conclusions. A key consideration that teachers need to take into account when deciding whether the inquiry method is appropriate is the extent to which inductive thinking and learning the inquiry process itself are among the objectives. The inquiry method teaches content, but its unique strength lies in its ability to teach an investigative process that has applications to life.

Three forms of the inquiry method have been presented with their commonality being the process itself. Their differences lie in the extent to which the teacher structures the students' inquiry by directing or facilitating the collection of data. With the guided and open forms, whole classes of students are generally involved, and in the case of the individualized approach, one or more responsible students are usually encouraged.

An inquiry-method analysis form is included at the end of this chapter to aid in the observation and analysis of your and others' teaching.

■ RESEARCH AND THEORETICAL BASE: SIMULATION-GAMING METHOD

Teachers would probably agree that the instructional method most associated with active student interest and involvement is simulation gaming in either of its two primary forms: simulation and role-playing. Although discussion and inquiry as methods can stimulate high levels of participation and excitement, depending on the issue being discussed or the problem being investigated, simulation gaming generally exceeds them in inducing motivation because of its emphasis on role-playing and decision making to achieve goals. When we think of peak experiences in our schooling, a simulation is often recalled. Some of those powerful roles may have been a married couple trying to raise a child on a limited budget in a sociology class, an environmentalist trying to avert a community ecological disaster in a science class, a foreman trying to solve a building-construction problem in an industrial arts class, or an investor trying to make the most money in the stock market in an economics class. The dynamics of these peak experiences are remembered long after the regular content taught in traditional ways has been forgotten. This is one reason why simulation is a potentially powerful method to apply constructivist principles.

Some definitions are needed before pursuing a review of research. The following terms associated with this method are often used synonymously: simulation, game, role-playing, simulation game, instructional game, and gaming simulation. A simulation is a dynamic model that illustrates a physical (nonhuman) or social (human) system that is abstracted from reality and simplified for study purposes (Greenblat, 1982; Gilliom, 1977). It may or may not involve competition and winners and losers as the key ingredients of a game. This definition also applies to a wide variety of computer simulations that serve the same purpose. Role-playing is acting out or dramatizing hypothetical or real-life characters, often in problem situations (Clegg, 1991; Gilliom, 1977). Role-playing is an important component of all human simulations, but it is not synonymous with them. The simulation-game instructional method, then, is a hybrid form involving a simulated situation during which roles are played that may or may not involve gamelike activity (Greenblat, 1982). For the purposes of this discussion, the terms *game* and *simulation* will be used interchangeably, as they are generally found in the literature.

Three major comprehensive reviews of research on simulation gaming provides us with a realistic picture of the potential for the application of this method in classrooms (Clegg, 1991; Greenblat, 1982; Randel, Morris, Wetzel, and Whitehill, 1992). The vast majority of the literature on simulations are anecdotal accounts, game descriptions, handbooks of guidelines for playing, and books on the general theme of simulations. Comparatively little research has been conducted and the findings from these, for the most part, have been mixed (Clegg, 1991).

Evaluation of simulations has been difficult because of their diversity. Research generally shows that cognitive learning takes place during simulations, but it is not greater when simulations are compared to traditional techniques (Greenblat, 1982). In their review of research, Randel and colleagues (1992) found that students reported more interest in simulations compared with traditional methods. They concluded that "subject matter areas where very specific content can be targeted are more likely to show beneficial effects for gaming" (p. 261). Greenblat (1982) concluded that limited evidence seems to support the claims that gaming helps to develop general and interpersonal relations skills and problem-solving abilities.

In his review of the literature on simulations, Patterson (1996) concluded that simulations have the potential to be powerful emotional and educational experiences for students. This finding was supported in his investigation of the well-known Model United Nations simulation because he found that the students he sampled were deeply impacted by their involvement during their class participation and after graduation. Patterson found that most of the participants' attitudes changed; they acquired a sense of political efficacy and engaged in low-level acts of civic activity, and for some, participation led to life-altering experiences.

Computer simulations are on the rise with the increasing incorporation of this technology in the schools, but as a result of its relative newness, little research has been conducted. Two current perspectives provide a frame of reference for classroom application. Harper, McDougall, and Squires (2000) have taken advantage of the new multimedia technology and advocate developing simulations informed by constructivist principles, the key element of which is experiential involvement of the learners. They have found that it is most important to prepare students for the simulations and provide guidance while they are engaged in it. In their analysis of when teachers should use simulations, Hargrave and Kenston (2000) strongly support using simulations prior to formalized instruction in the content. They have found that students arrive at instruction with a more personalized understanding of the content. Thus, they are ready for more "cognitively active" roles in making sense of the content.

■ APPLICATION TO PRACTICE: SIMULATION-GAMING METHOD

As a method, simulation gaming has potential in helping to facilitate the goals associated with constructivist theory. Constructivism, as has been previously asserted, emphasizes encouraging students to make connections between new information and their existing networks of prior knowledge and experiences. This is accomplished, in part, by providing opportunities for students to process and apply new learning in authentic task and problematic situations. The more the application situations are social, involving interaction with other students about the content being taught, the better because students learn from each other (Brooks and Brooks, 2001; Good and Brophy, 2000). A primary purpose of simulation gaming is for students to become actively and thoughtfully involved in problematic situations that represent in-depth extensions and applications of the content being taught. In addition, most simulations involve students in highly interactive team situations as they make decisions and work to solve problems. Simulation gaming seems to be an ideal method to operationalize the constructivist-oriented principles and practices of good subject-matter teaching that Brophy (1992) offered based on his review of research. An instructional strategy that also meets this constructivist criteria is cooperative learning, which is presented in Chapter 8.

Simulation

Simulations are designed to help students study and analyze a real-world social situation or process while being active participants within it. As students are involved in simulations, they role-play by acting out characters and interacting with each other. They also make decisions and experience the consequences of their decisions. Many simulations have been commercially prepared as simulation games and therefore include the element of competition. But competition, producing winners and losers, is not a means or an end in a simulation unless the simulation focuses on analyzing the processes and forces of the competition to understand better the real social situation being portrayed. The teacher's role is to structure and facilitate the simulation and to conduct the debriefing discussion.

Simulations help prepare students to make the transition from the classroom to the real world. Traditionally, the emphasis of most subject areas has been on the transmission of information to passive students with little regard for the understanding and application of what has been "learned." Students saw little relevance in what was taught because it did not relate to their present or future lives. In the area of social studies, for example, for which many of the simulations have been developed, the goal is to develop students' critical-thinking skills as they engage in inquiry, decision making, and social action. The ideal end product is citizens equipped with the necessary skills and dispositions to reflect critically on societal issues and problems and participate actively in their resolution. Ideally, simulations encourage students to see relevance in what they are being taught and to encourage them to become actively involved in their own preparation to make political, economic, social, and personal decisions as young adults.

The range of simulations available to teachers at all grade levels in all subject areas is impressive. Simulations have been used in classrooms from kindergarten through adult levels. A list of 88 simulations for elementary social studies classrooms was compiled for *Social Education* by Muir (1980). Catalogs of simulations by the company Simile II are intended for universities and colleges and can be used for businesses and the military as well. Some familiar names are Plea Bargaining, Starpower, Access, and Crisis. Simulations can be free, as many published teacher-made simulations are, or quite expensive, especially if they involve multimedia packages. The journal *Simulation and Gaming* publishes at least one simulation each month for a wide audience of readers (for the cost of a subscription or free at many libraries). Two recent political science and cross-cultural psychology games are Balance of Power (Chapin, 1998) and Dynamic Circles (Kacen, 1998). At the other end of the price continuum are technologically oriented simulations published by Tom Snyder Productions (1998), for example, that involve Macintosh and Windows software, and video and CD-ROM applications. One of the most expensive is the complete series of the Decisions, Decisions computer simulations costing more than $1,500. Whereas most simulations are designed to be completed in one or two class periods, some are quite long. Dig 2 for grades 9 through 12 (Interact, 1998) takes 15 to 21 hours, whereas Congress in the Classroom (Schlemmer and Hill, 1977) was designed for high school government courses to be completed in as few as six weeks but could easily be run for a full semester.

A brief description of one popular simulation will give you a sense of the potential this method has for classrooms studying units related to values, ethics, or futuristics. In Humanus (Simile II), students role-play survivors of a worldwide catastrophe. They are linked to the outside world through their survival computer, Humanus. Humanus monitors and controls them through a "voice print-out" recorded on audiotape and requires the survivors to make a variety of decisions: What 10 items do you want the computer to provide beyond basic life-support needs? How can the members of the cell create an environment in which each person's viewpoint is valued? Should a potentially contaminated survivor be allowed to enter the cell?

The debriefing phase involves the different groups of students in guided and reflective discussions sharing the decisions they have made and the reasons for their decisions. Students analyze the emotional aspects of their decisions and the cultural, philosophical, and experiential backgrounds contributing to their views. This simulation can be played over two class periods with a regular-size class of students and requires minimal preparation time and no consumable forms. Only a tape recorder is necessary.

Role-Playing

Role-playing is a critical component in all of the simulations mentioned because most simulations are socially oriented and interaction between participants is necessary. Although there are some simple role-playing situations, particularly at the elementary level, in which a student might dress up in the character of a famous political, social, or military leader and read an important speech, most role-playing used in secondary classrooms involves problematic situations. While all social simulations involve role-playing, not all role-playing involves socially simulated situations. Shaftel and Shaftel (1967) commented on the parallels between simulation, gaming, and role-playing. They have a mutual concern in: "1. conflict of interests, personal or interpersonal or intergroup, in which players 2. face alternatives from which to choose, and 3. must make individual decisions" (p. 12).

Role-playing is designed to help students understand the perspectives and feelings of other people regarding a wide range of personal and social issues. This is accomplished by having several students act out, or dramatize, situations in which people are in conflict or faced with a dilemma of some sort. Role-playing provides an opportunity for students to step into the shoes and get into the minds of others confronted with problematic situations. Shaftel and Shaftel (1967, p. 8) referred to this process as helping students become "inner-directed" so that they might learn to live in groups and develop intelligent concern for others. The majority of the class not directly involved in the role-playing will be indirectly involved by observing and analyzing the words and actions of the role-players. Their roles are equally as important because they function as a source of feedback. Just as in a simulation, the teacher's role is to structure and facilitate the role-playing and conduct the critical follow-up debriefing discussion.

A brief description of a role-playing episode will help clarify the procedure and suggest the potential this method has for many classrooms. The subject is U.S. history and the topic for the role-play is women and the Constitution. The objective is for students to role-play a conversation between Abigail Adams, Mercy Otis Warren, and John Adams, reflecting accurately the values of the players and the period. In preparation for assuming their roles, the students have read a variety of primary and secondary sources. Role cards for the three roles are distributed and the scene created: Abigail has just read John's negative response to her letters pleading that women not be omitted from the Constitution. She and her friend, Mercy, a strong feminist of the time, are discussing the letters and the issues over tea. Partway through the discussion, John enters and joins them.

The ensuing conversation is intended to depict the ideas and feelings of the participants. The observers are to focus on the values being held by the participants as reflected in what they say and how they behave. The enactment might last for 5 to 10 minutes, followed by the debriefing. The discussion is comprised of reviewing the events, values, positions, realism, and accuracy of the role-play. A reenactment may be necessary if the teacher and students feel that other values need to be portrayed or emphasized. The final discussion centers on comparing colonial and contemporary women and, most importantly, generalizing the role women play and do not play in society today and the inherent problems of inequality. An essay in which students individually and privately reveal their points of view might follow (Shelly and Wilen, 1988).

The previous example is an illustration of one of several reasons that a teacher might want to use role-play—depicting historical or contemporary problems. Other types of role-playing center on dealing with immediate human-relations problems. Joyce, Weil, and Calhoun (2000) elaborated on several types in this category. Interpersonal conflicts involve conflicts between people, and role-playing can be used to discover approaches to overcome them. Intergroup relations might become problematic when ethnic and racial stereotyping develops, for example. Another reason is authoritarian beliefs. Role-playing can help uncover negative attitudes and prejudices. Individual dilemmas occur when a person is caught between two contrasting values or when one person's values contrast with another person's. Role-playing might help clarify and suggest solutions for these potentially difficult and sensitive situations.

Simulation-Gaming Phases

The phases of simulation gaming have been generalized for simulation and role-playing and have been adapted from the work of Joyce, Weil, and Calhoun (2000). Our intention is not to prescribe a format for conducting all simulations and role-playing but to provide a general structure that teachers can modify to suit their own classroom situations. Suggesting phases will help operationalize simulation gaming by providing a mind's-eye view of how this method might unfold in the classroom.

Phase I. Orientation

a. Explain simulation/role-playing.
b. Develop an overview of simulated/problem situation.
c. State objectives to be achieved.

Students need to be oriented to simulation and role-playing, particularly if they have not previously encountered these methods. The general purpose of using simulation or role-playing over other methods and the general goals that you hope this method will achieve should be mentioned and discussed to help students understand why you are taking this different approach.

The most important component of this introductory phase is presenting the problem situation in role-playing or the overview of the simulation. Students need to understand the problem fully to step into the shoes of a character in the case of role-playing. Another consideration is that emotions may be quite high if the problem to be dealt with is based on an interpersonal classroom conflict. In this case, a particularly positive and supportive classroom environment needs to be created for the role-playing to be effective. In both role-playing and simulations, the teacher should inform students of the objectives he or she wants to achieve through the play or game to provide a sense of direction and tie in to the content being taught.

Phase II. Participant Preparation

a. Set up and interpret scenario/problem.
b. Establish procedures.
c. Organize teams/select participants.

The specific roles participants assume in the simulation or the role-playing may call for more specific interpretation, and this should be encouraged to increase the probability that goals will be met. For both simulations and role-playing, setting the stage and establishing lines of action are necessary so that roles can be understood. In role-playing, those students who are not directly participating need to be prepared as observers. Perhaps a list of questions that different groups observing the action are to answer as they view the enactment and reflect on it may help structure their involvement. This will depend on the characteristics of the students involved.

Procedures need to be established and understood; this includes classroom-management standards. One of the major advantages of simulations and role-playing is that students assume considerable freedom in determining the direction of their learning. Those students who are immature and irresponsible may decide to abuse this freedom so different behavioral standards may need to be established.

Phase III. Simulation/Enactment Operations

a. Commence simulation/role-play.

b. Facilitate operations.

c. Close simulation/role-play.

This phase is the main body of the method—the actual simulation or enactment. It is during this phase that all the efforts made previously come together to provide the learning experience. Students are to assume their roles, and the teacher's primary responsibility is to facilitate the enactment or simulation. One role of the teacher is to serve as a resource person to help provide the materials and sources necessary or to suggest where they may be found to keep the operation moving. Facilitating is an important role because, on one hand, you want to allow students enough freedom to analyze situations, solve problems, and make decisions without intervening too much. Students may sense they are doing things (displaying the "right" attitudes and values in a role-play, for example, or arriving at the "right" decisions or solutions in a simulation) for the teacher rather than themselves if intervention is too heavy handed. On the other hand, the teacher needs to provide structure and direction when necessary, particularly to keep students on-task. The teacher will also need to determine when to terminate the role-play or the simulation and begin the debriefing or to prepare for reenactment in the case of a complex role-playing situation.

Phase IV. Debriefing Discussion

a. Review action, perceptions, and problems.

b. Relate simulation/enactment to real world.

c. Connect to previous learnings and future goals.

The role-play and the simulation are learning experiences, but learning really can't be determined until the debriefing discussion. This phase cannot be emphasized too heavily. Often, students are so wrapped up in the role-play or the simulation that they need to step back and reflect on their actions and intentions and make connections to the real world outside the classroom. In her research on debriefing, Lederman (1992) stated, "The debriefing sessions, like the experiential activity, is learner-based: it is discovery learning in which participants are provided with incentives to examine and analyze their inner thoughts and reflections" (p. 154). The experiences the students have undergone essentially become the raw data for learning, and the process of debriefing makes connections possible.

Stadsklev (1980) proposed the following structure for debriefing: (1) experience, (2) identify, (3) analyze, and (4) generalize (EIAG). The experience part is the actual simulation. Identify means to describe the experience in terms of decisions made or data gathered, for example, and the reasons for engaging in specific behaviors. In a role-play, feelings need to be described and consequences identified. During the analyze phase, higher-level reflection is required to look back on the role-play or the simulation for deeper meanings and understandings. Cause-and-effect relationships should be explored, alternative approaches and decisions should be considered, and the impact of problem solutions should be reasoned. The final phase is to generalize. At this point, students should be ready to express what they have learned in terms of the simulation or role-play. Further, because the simulation was an abstraction of reality, they should be able to make connections to the real world. Students also need to see the connection of the simulation or the role-play to content previously taught and content to be taught. Teachers also need to ensure that the original objectives guiding the method be reviewed.

The teacher's role during the debriefing is more active and directive than during the role-play or the simulation because of the discussion responsibilities involved. A major responsibility is guiding students to discover what has been learned, whether positive or negative, rather than being didactic. It would be entirely appropriate to implement either the guided or reflective discussion depending on the nature of the simulation or the role-play and the interest and ability level of the students.

One other possibility is to incorporate journal writing as a final phase. Petranek, Corey, and Black (1992) contended that learning from simulations occurs on three levels: participating in the game, debriefing in discussions, and writing in a journal. "Journal writing is . . . a means to validate knowledge, to organize material, to understand ideas, and to substantiate the experience" (p. 183). Students can write about their personal experiences, problems, and growth resulting from the simulation. Further, they can write more specifically about the integration of their experiences with real life.

Scenario Analysis

Mr. Carl did not use role-playing or simulation in the introductory economics-class scenario. One simulation he might consider implementing during the GNP unit is *Development*, which is available from Science Research Associates, Inc., and is presented in Gordon (1972). *Development* explores the relations between the major world powers and the developing nations of the world. The two major powers are labeled *East* and *West,* and they compete for the loyalty of the developing countries. The competition partly centers on the distribution of foreign aid. The goal for the developing countries is to improve their standard of living by accepting foreign aid without giving up political independence and freedom of action on the world stage.

■ WEBSITE RESOURCE ■

Interact and Tom Snyder

Interact is a company devoted to producing classroom simulations and other learning activities (thematic units, cross-curricular activities, and pull-out programs) that encourage students to interact with their teacher and with each other. The simulations are for teachers in all subject areas and at all levels at

www.interact-simulations.com.

You can browse their catalogs on the main webpage or search by key word for simulations. Descriptions of the simulations are provided along with the process to order them. Click on Free Activities to download almost 150 learning activities that have been adapted from their units.

In addition, Tom Snyder Productions includes an extensive computer software catalog for teachers in primarily social studies, science, math, and language arts at all levels:

www.teachtsp.com.

Click on Quick Jump to get you to the catalog and main services or the Pick a Product pull-down menu to get to specific software titles. The Free Stuff pull-down menu allows you to select a software product and search to see whether any free materials are associated with it.

■ SUMMARY POINT ■

The method of simulation gaming is experiential and, therefore, a different alternative to the other methods presented. Here lies its strength and appeal to students because they get an opportunity to assume a more active role as they "do" science, health, history, or sociology. The appeal to teachers who are oriented toward constructivism is that, through an authentic learning experience such as a simulation or a role-play, students learn by making connections between their own knowledge and experiences and the real world. This method encourages students to go deeper into an issue or problem as they engage in social interactions with their peers. The result is a higher probability that meaning will be constructed and understanding of more complex ideas will result.

A simulation-gaming analysis form is located at the end of the chapter.

■ SUMMARY POINT ■

1. Many factors need to be considered in choosing a particular strategy or method.
2. No one method can be totally relied on.

3. If a method is to be used effectively, the teacher needs to become proficient in its use.

4. The most effective teachers potentially are those who effectively use several modes.

5. The teacher's choice of methods has been less often a rational decision than defaulting to a comfortable pattern.

6. Making instructional choices based on instructional purposes is a promising approach to improving instructional effectiveness.

7. Specific methods are effective for particular sorts of learning outcomes; compatibility is the key factor.

Instruction is the means for "turning knowledge into learning" (Jones, Bagford, and Wallen, 1979, p. 1). Without a knowledge of and practical experience with a variety of instructional techniques and methods, Mr. Carl would not have been able to accomplish what he had intended in his lesson. The implementation of a planned sequence of instructional approaches brought the concept of GNP to life. The probability is high that the knowledge the students gained from reading was turned into learning by the teacher as a result of decisions he or she made while planning the lesson. Effective decision making is basic to effective teaching.

> *The most effective teachers, in terms of enhancing students' learning, use a variety of instructional methods rather than depending on any one method.*

■ QUESTIONS FOR REFLECTION ■

1. Mr. Carl, in the scenario introducing the chapter, used a discrepant event to stimulate guided inquiry. The discrepancy created a clever puzzle that students were to solve through their questioning. What is one discrepant event you can devise in your subject area that might have the same impact on students' curiosity?

2. Research shows that teachers generally do not teach their high- and low-ability students differently. What are some of the disadvantages of not individualizing instruction more for these groups of students?

3. Why is there a persistence of teachers' use of recitation even though the literature is much more supportive of discussion as the primary method to teach for understanding?

4. What would you recommend to your cooperating teacher as to how he or she might promote more equity and power sharing with students during a large-group discussion?

5. What can you learn as a teacher from watching a talk-show host effectively conduct a discussion with guests and live and call-in audiences?

6. Considering that reflective discussion is the most difficult form of discussion, what might you do in your classroom to make it easier to conduct a reflective discussion?

7. What are some entries you might devise to commence a guided or reflective discussion in your subject area?

8. Do you think it is appropriate to offer your personal opinion or position on an issue during a discussion? Provide evidence to support your view.

9. What are some approaches that you might use to encourage students to generate questions during a discussion to encourage their participation and thinking?

10. What do you think are some of the assumptions teachers have about how students learn when they use lectures in one form or another as the primary instructional method?

11. Some theorists suggest that the lecture is the most difficult instructional method to use in the classroom, whereas others suggest it is the easiest. What support could you provide to support both points of view?

12. Think of a complex topic in your subject area that you might be teaching. What advance organizer might you use to help students understand your topic better?

13. What have you read that would help to distinguish the terms generally used synonymously with inquiry: *discovery, reflective teaching, inductive teaching,* and *problem solving*? Based on your readings, what definitions would you apply?

14. Think of a topic or theme that you are or will be teaching. What are some problematic situations you could devise for which the inquiry method might be appropriate?

15. Who is one of the students you are, or will be, teaching that you would classify as above average in terms of ability and motivation? Would you encourage this student to engage in an individualized inquiry investigation? If so, how might you go about it?

16. Observe a videotape of a teacher using one of the forms of discussion, lecture, or inquiry. What would you suggest to the teacher as to how the performance might be improved based on the information presented in the chapter? Use the appropriate analysis form as a structure to observe the lesson.

17. Supposedly, simulations and role-playing situations are peak experiences that people readily recall as being exciting and memorable learning activities long after being out of school. Can you recall such a simulation or role-playing situation from your schooling? Why do you think it had such an impact?

18. If you had the time and opportunity to design a simulation for a topic, event, issue, or problem that you teach or will be teaching, what would it look like?

19. Think of a human relations problem that a small group of students in one of your classes is having, or possibly could have. How might role-playing be a useful method to help clarify or solve the problem?

ANALYSIS SCALES

TEACHER _____

OBSERVER _____

CLASS _____

DATE _____

OCCURRENCE	EFFECTIVENESS
1. Not evident	1. Not effective
2. Slightly evident	2. Slightly effective
3. Moderately evident	3. Moderately effective
4. Quite evident	4. Quite effective
N Not applicable	N Not applicable

CATEGORIES	A. OCCURRENCE	B. EFFECTIVENESS
PHASE I: ENTRY: IDENTIFICATION OF PROBLEM, ISSUE, OR TOPIC A. Use a springboard and/or attention getter.		
B. Identify problem, issue, or topic.		
C. State objectives and rationale.		
PHASE II: CLARIFICATION A. Establish procedures.		
B. Define terms and concepts related to the problem, issue, or topic.		
PHASE III: INVESTIGATION A. Ask appropriate levels of questions to achieve desired levels of student thinking.		
B. Use questioning techniques such as probing, wait time, and redirection to maintain discussion, and to stimulate student involvement and thinking.		
C. Use alternative nonquestioning techniques such as various statement forms to maintain discussion and to encourage student involvement.		
D. Encourage student initiative and leadership.		
E. Request that students support opinions offered.		
F. Ensure sufficient coverage of problem, issue, or topic.		

continued

PHASE IV: CLOSURE: SUMMARY, INTEGRATION, APPLICATION A. Summary in the form of consensus, solutions, insights achieved in relation to topic covered, issue explored, or problem investigated.		
B. Integrate lesson with goals and previous learning.		
C. Apply discussion outcomes to other situations.		

REFLECTIVE CONSIDERATIONS

How would you describe the interaction pattern of the discussion?

To what extent was student discussion leadership evident?

Based on the nature of your students and content to be taught, why did you decide on the discussion method to achieve objectives?

To what extent did you achieve your purpose?

How do you know?

		ANALYSIS SCALES	
ANALYSIS FORM			*LECTURE METHOD*

ANALYSIS FORM *LECTURE METHOD*

ANALYSIS SCALES

TEACHER _____

OBSERVER _____

CLASS _____

DATE _____

OCCURRENCE
1. Not evident
2. Slightly evident
3. Moderately evident
4. Quite evident
N Not applicable

EFFECTIVENESS
1. Not effective
2. Slightly effective
3. Moderately effective
4. Quite effective
N Not applicable

CATEGORIES	A. OCCURRENCE	B. EFFECTIVENESS
PHASE I: ENTRY: PREPARATION FOR LEARNING A. State objectives and rationale.		
B. Provide a context for the new material to be presented.		
C. Focus attention on a key concept, generalization, or principle that encompasses the lecture (advance organizer).		
PHASE II: PRESENTATION A. Sequence content from simpler to complex understandings.		
B. Enhance presentation with visual aids.		
C. Stimulate attention with verbal and nonverbal behaviors.		
PHASE III: CLOSURE: REVIEW OF LEARNING A. Integrate with students' knowledge and experiences.		
B. Transition to next lesson or activity.		

REFLECTIVE CONSIDERATIONS

Why did you decide using the lecture method was the best approach to teach the content?

What verbal and nonverbal behaviors did students display to indicate they understood the content of your lecture?

To what extent did you achieve your objectives?

ANALYSIS SCALES

TEACHER _____

OBSERVER _____

CLASS _____

DATE _____

OCCURRENCE	EFFECTIVENESS
1. Not evident	1. Not effective
2. Slightly evident	2. Slightly effective
3. Moderately evident	3. Moderately effectiv
4. Quite evident	4. Quite effective
N Not applicable	N Not applicable

CATEGORIES	A. OCCURRENCE	B. EFFECTIVENESS
PHASE I: ENTRY: PRESENTATION AND CLARIFICATION OF A PROBLEM, ISSUE, OR QUERY A. State objectives; provide rationale.		
B. Identify a problem, issue, or query.		
C. Relate to students' experiences and lives.		
D. Clarify the problem.		
PHASE II: FORMATION OF HYPOTHESES A. Encourage the formation of tentative explanations or solutions.		
B. Clarify hypotheses.		
PHASE III: COLLECTION OF DATA A. Facilitate the identification of sources for evidence.		
B. Assist in the evaluation of the evidence.		
PHASE IV: TEST HYPOTHESES A. Assist in organizing the data.		
B. Assist in analysis and evaluation of the data.		
PHASE V: CLOSURE: DRAWING CONCLUSIONS A. Develop a generalization, explanation, or solution.		
B. Integrate into the unit of study.		

REFLECTIVE CONSIDERATIONS

What variation in the inquiry process did you use to achieve your goals?

How did students respond and react to your guidance as they were led through the inquiry process?

To what extent did students assume a leadership role as they engaged in inquiry?

What evidence do you have that the students were engaged in critical and creative thinking?

TEACHER _____

OBSERVER _____

CLASS _____

DATE _____

ANALYSIS SCALES

OCCURRENCE	EFFECTIVENESS
1. Not evident	1. Not effective
2. Slightly evident	2. Slightly effective
3. Moderately evident	3. Moderately effective
4. Quite evident	4. Quite effective
N Not applicable	N Not applicable

CATEGORIES	A. OCCURRENCE	B. EFFECTIVENESS
PHASE I: ORIENTATION A. Explain simulation/role playing.		
B. Develop an overview of simulated/problem situation.		
C. State objectives to be achieved.		
PHASE II: PARTICIPANT PREPARATION A. Set up and interpret scenario/problem.		
B. Establish procedures.		
C. Organize teams/select participants.		
PHASE III: SIMULATION/ENACTMENT OPERATIONS A. Commence simulation/role-play.		
B. Facilitate operations.		
C. Close simulation/role-play.		
PHASE IV: DEBRIEFING DISCUSSION A. Review action, perceptions, and problems.		
B. Relate simulation/enactment to real world.		
C. Connect to previous learnings and future goals.		

REFLECTIVE CONSIDERATIONS

What was there about the simulated (simulation) or problem (role-playing) situation that was motivating to the students?

What criteria were used to select students for the teams (simulation) or enactments (role-playing)?

Was your amount of involvement during the simulation or enactment correct? Why or why not?

What were some of the direct and indirect clues that you picked up from the students during the debriefing that indicated they learned about the real world?

■ REFERENCES ■

Alvermann, D., Young, J., Weaver, D., Hinchamn, K., Moore, D., Phelps, S., Thrash, E., and Zalewski, P. (1996). "Middle and high school students' perceptions of how they experience text-based discussions: A multicultural case study." *Reading Research Quarterly, 31*(3), 244–267.

Andrews, J. (1984). "Discovery and expository learning compared: Their effects on independent and dependent students." *Journal of Educational Research, 28,* 80–89.

Armstrong, D. (1980). *Social Studies in Secondary Education.* New York: Macmillan.

Ausubel, D. (1968). *Educational Psychology: A Cognitive View.* New York: Holt, Rinehart & Winston.

Bellack, A., Kliebard, H., Hyman, R., and Smith, F. (1966). *The Language of the Classroom.* New York: Columbia University Press.

Berliner, D., and Gage, N. (1976). "The psychology of teaching methods." In N. Gage (Ed.), *The Psychology of Teaching Methods: 75th Yearbook of NSSE.* Chicago: University of Chicago Press.

Brooks, J., and Brooks, M. (2001). *The Case for Constructivist Classrooms.* Upper Saddle River, N.J.: Merrill/Prentice Hall.

Brophy, J. (1992). "Probing the subtleties of subject-matter teaching." *Educational Leadership, 49*(7), 4–8.

Butler, A., Phillmann, K., and Smart, L. (2001). "Active learning within a lecture: Assessing the impact of short, in-class writing exercises." *Teaching of Psychology, 28*(4), 257–259.

Byer, B. (1984, April). "Improving thinking skills." *Phi Delta Kappan, 65*(8), 556–560.

Chapin, W. (1998). "Balance of power game." *Simulation and Gaming, 29*(1), 105–112.

Clegg, A. (1991). "Games and simulations in social studies education." In J. Shavers (Ed.), *Handbook of Research on Social Studies Teaching and Learning.* New York: Macmillan.

Cooper, P., and Galvin, K. (1984). "What do we know about research in teacher training in instructional strategies?" Paper presented at the Annual Meeting of the Central State Speech Association, ERIC, Chicago.

Dewey, J. (1910). *How We Think.* Lexington, MA: Heath.

Dillon, J. (1983). *Teaching and the Art of Questioning.* Bloomington, IN: Phi Delta Kappa.

Dillon, J. (1984). "Research on questioning and discussion." *Educational Leadership, 42*(3), 50–60.

Dillon, J. (1985). "Using questions to foil discussion." *Teaching and Teacher Education, 1,* 109–121.

Dillon, J. (1994). *Using Discussion in Classrooms.* Buckingham, England: Open University Press.

Evertson, C. (1982). "Differences in instructional activities in higher and lower achieving junior high English and math classes." *Elementary School Journal, 82,* 329–350.

Gage, N., and Berliner, D. (1992). *Educational Psychology* (5th ed.). Boston: Houghton Mifflin.

Gall, J., and Gall, M. (1990). "Outcomes of the discussion method." In W. Wilen (Ed.), *Teaching and Learning through Discussion* (pp. 25–44). Springfield, IL: Charles C. Thomas.

Gall, M., and Gall, J. (1976). "The discussion method." In N. L. Gage (Ed.), *The Psychology of Teaching Methods: 75th Yearbook of the NSSE.* Chicago: University of Chicago Press.

Gilliom, M. (1977). "Simulations." In E. Gilliom (Ed.), *Practical Methods for the Social Studies.* Belmont, CA: Wadsworth.

Good, T., and Brophy, J. (2000). *Looking in Classrooms* (8th ed.). New York: Addison Wesley Longman.

Gordon, A. (1972). *Games for Growth.* Chicago: Science Research Associates.

Greenblat, C. (1982). "Games and simulations." In H. Mitzel (Ed.), *Encyclopedia of Educational Research* (Vol. 2). New York: Macmillan.

Hargrave, C., and Kenston, J. (2000). "Preinstructional simulations: Implications for science classroom teaching." *Journal of Computers in Mathematics and Science Teaching, 19*(1), 47–58.

Harper, B., McDougall, A., and Squires, D. (2000). "Constructivist simulations: A new design paradigm." *Journal of Educational Multimedia and Hypermedia, 9*(2), 115–130.

Harwood, A., and Hahn, C. (1990). *Controversial Issues in the Classroom: ERIC Digest.* Bloomington, IN: Clearinghouse for Social Studies/Social Science Education.

Hudgins, B. (1971). *The Instructional Process.* Chicago: Rand McNally.

Hudson, P. (1997). "Using teacher-guided practice to help students with learning disabilities acquire and retain social studies content." *Learning Disability Quarterly, 20*(1), 23–32.

Interact (1998). *Catalog*. El Cajon, CA.

Jones, A., Bagford, L., and Wallen, E. (1979). *Strategies for Teaching*. Metuchen, NJ: Scarecrow Press.

Joyce, B., and Weil, M. (1980). *Models of Teaching* (2nd ed.) Upper Sadle River, NJ: Prentice Hall.

Joyce, B., Weil, M., with Calhoun, E. (2000). *Models of Teaching* (6th ed.). Boston: Allyn & Bacon.

Kacen, L. (1998). "Dynamic circular exercise: Intergroup bridging." *Simulation and Gaming, 29*(1), 101–104.

Kauchak, D., and Eggen, P. (1998). *Learning and Teaching* (3rd ed.). Boston: Allyn & Bacon.

King, A. (1992). "Comparison of self-questioning, summarizing, and notetaking-review as strategies for learning from lectures." *American Educational Research Journal, 29*(2), 303–323.

Kovalainen, M., Kumpulainen, K., and Vasama, S. (2002). "Orchestrating classroom interaction in a community of inquiry: Modes of teacher participation." *Journal of Classroom Interaction, 37*(2), 17–28.

Larson, B. (1997). "Social studies teachers' conceptions of discussion: A grounded theory study." *Theory and Research in Social Education, 25*(2), 113–136.

Lederman, L. (1992). "Debriefing: Toward a systematic assessment of theory and practice." *Simulation and Gaming, 23*(2), 145–160.

Martin-Hansen, L. (2002). "Defining inquiry." *The Science Teacher, 69*(2), 34–37.

McLeish, J. (1976). "The lecture method." In N. Gage (Ed.), *The Psychology of Teaching Methods: 75th Yearbook of the NSSE*. Chicago: University of Chicago Press.

Michael, T., and Weaver, R. (1984). "Lecturing: Means for improvement." *Clearing House, 57*, 389–391.

Muir, S. (1980). "Simulation games for elementary social studies." *Social Education*, 35–39.

National Council for the Social Studies (1994). *Curriculum Standards for Social Studies*. Washington, DC: Author.

Neves, J., and Sanyal, R. (1992). "Upside down: A cross-cultural simulation." *Simulation and Gaming, 23*(3), 370–375.

Palincsar, A., Cutter, J., and Magnusson, S. (2002). "Supporting guided-inquiry instruction." *Teaching Exceptional Children, 34*(3), 88–91.

Parker, W. (2001, November). "Teaching teachers to lead discussions: Democratic education in content and method." Paper presented at the annual meeting of the College and University Faculty Assembly of the National Council for the Social Studies, Washington, DC.

Parker, W. (1992, November). "The possibilities of discussion." Paper presented at the annual meeting of the College and University Faculty Assembly of the National Council for the Social Studies, Detroit, MI.

Parker, W., and Hess, D. (2001). "Teaching with and for discussion." *Teaching and Teacher Education, 17*, 273–289.

Passe, J., and Evans, R. (1996). "Discussion methods in an issue-centered curriculum." In R. Evans and D. Saxe (Eds.), *Handbook on Teaching Social Issues* (pp. 81–88). Bulletin #93. Washington, DC: National Council for the Social Studies.

Patterson, J. (1996). "Model United Nations Simulations: An Inquiry into Active Learning, Role Playing, and Role Identification as They Impact Participants' Sense of Political Efficacy." Unpublished doctoral dissertation, Kent State University.

Paul, R. (1984). "Critical thinking: Fundamental to education for a free society." *Educational Leadership*, 4–14.

Peterson, P. (1979). *Aptitude-Treatment Interaction Effects of Three Teaching Approaches: Lecture-Recitation, Inquiry, and Public Issues Discussion* (ERIC Document Reproduction Service No. ED 186427). Madison, WI: Research and Development Center for Individualized Schooling.

Petranek, C., Corey, S., and Black, R. (1992). "Three levels of learning in simulations: Participating, Debriefing, and Writing." *Simulation and Gaming, 23*(2), 174–185.

Ponder, G., and Davis, O. (1982). "Social studies education." In H. Mitzel (Ed.), *Encyclopedia of Educational Research*. New York: Free Press.

Powers, R. (1993). "Visit to an alien planet." *Simulation and Gaming, 24*(4), 509–518.

Randel, J., Morris, B., Wetzel, C., and Whitehill, B. (1992). "The effectiveness of games for educational purposes: A review of recent research." *Simulation and Gaming, 23*(3), 261–276.

Robinson, W., and Niaz, M. (1991). "Performance based on instruction by lecture or by interaction and its relationship to cognitive variables." *International Journal of Science Education, 13*(2), 203–215.

Roby, T. (1988). "Commonplaces, questions and modes of discussion." In J. Dillon (Ed.), *Classroom Questions and Discussion*. Norwood, NJ: Ablex.

Schlemmer, D., and Hill, R. (1977). *Congress in the Classroom*. Washington, DC: Congressional Quarterly.

Selim, M., and Shrigley, R. (1983). "Group dynamics approach: A sociopsychological approach for testing the effect of discovery and expository teaching on the science achievement and attitude of young Egyptian students." *Journal of Research in Science Teaching, 20,* 213–224.

Shaftel, F., and Shaftel, G. (1967). *Role Playing for Social Values: Decision-Making in the Social Studies.* Upper Saddle River, NJ: Prentice Hall.

Shelly, A., and Wilen, W. (1988). "Sex equity and critical thinking." *Social Education,* 52(3), 168–172.

Simile II. *Catalog.* Del Mar, CA: Author.

Shulman, L., and Tamir, P. (1973). "Research on teaching in the natural sciences." In R. Travers, (Ed.), *Second Handbook of Research on Teaching.* Chicago: Rand McNally.

Skolnik, S. (1995). "Launching interest in chemistry." *Educational Leadership,* 53(1), 34–36.

Stadsklev, R. (1980). *Handbook of Simulation Gaming in Social Education.* University, AL: Institute of Higher Education Research & Services.

Suchman, J. (1962). *The Elementary School Training Program in Scientific Inquiry: NDEA Project 216.* Urbana, IL: University of Illinois.

Thompson, B. (1981). "Teachers' preferences for various teaching methods." *NASSP Bulletin,* 65, 96–100.

Tom Snyder Productions (1998). *Catalog.* Watertown, MA: Author.

Toole, R. (2000). "An additional step in the guided lecture procedure." *Journal of Adolescent and Adult Literacy,* 44(2), 166–188.

Weimer, R. (1974). "A critical analysis of the discovery versus expository research studies investigating retention or transfer within the areas of science, mathematics, vocational education, language, and geography from 1908 to the present." (Doctoral dissertation, University of Illinois, 1975). Dissertation Abstracts International, 35.

White, J. (1990). "Involving different social and cultural groups in discussion." In W. Wilen (Ed.), *Teaching and Learning Through Discussion.* Springfield, IL: Charles C. Thomas.

Wilen, W. (1990). "Forms and phases of discussion." In W. Wilen (Ed.), *Teaching and Learning Through Discussion.* Springfield, IL: Charles C. Thomas.

Wilen, W. (1994, June). "Democracy and reflective discussion in social studies classrooms." Paper presented at the International Social Studies Conference, Nairobi, Kenya.

Wilen, W., and McKenrick, P. (1989). "Individualized inquiry: Encouraging able students to investigate." *Social Studies,* 80, 36–39.

Wilen, W., and White, J. (1991). "Interaction and discourse in social studies classrooms." In J. Shaver (Ed.), *Handbook of Research on Social Studies Teaching and Learning.* New York: Macmillan.

Wise, K. (1996). "Strategies for teaching science: What works?" *Clearing House,* 69(6), 337–338.

Zemelman, S., Daniels, H., and Hyde, A. (1998). *Best Practice: New Standards for Teaching and Learning in America's Schools* (2nd ed.). Portsmouth, NH: Heinemann.

8

Teaching Strategies for Promoting Learning and Achievement

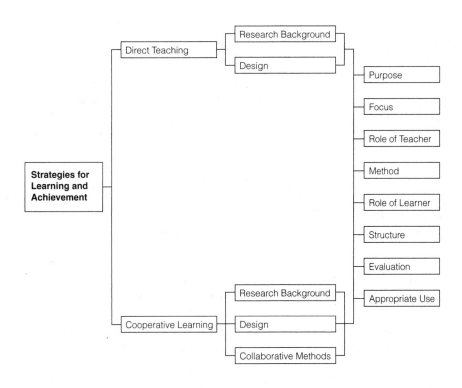

There is not one single teaching strategy that is the best approach, but certain strategies, used in certain contexts, have been documented by researchers as improving achievement.

The preceding chapters have discussed teaching techniques verified by effective-teaching research, supported by learning theory, tested by teachers, and essential to every teacher's practice. This chapter examines strategies that have been identified as promoting achievement and student learning. A strategy for the purpose of this chapter subsumes a variety of methods such as were described in the previous chapter. A strategy serves as an organizer and a focus for the delivery of instruction by guiding decision making about the teacher's role, the students' role, the selection of methods, and instructional materials. A strategy helps the teacher make optimal use of methods and resources in achieving particular goals. This chapter examines strategies that have been identified in the research as promoting achievement on standardized tests.

The strategies presented in this chapter emerged from the effective-teaching research (Good and Brophy, 1986; Teddlie, Kirby, and Stringfield, 1989; Cruickshank, 1990) but are very much a part of the present educational reform initiatives. The Alliance for Curriculum Reform, an organization of 30 major professional subject-matter organizations, identified two strategies along with a number of other generic practices as having the research base that attests to their improving student achievement (Cawelti, 1995, p. 3). Direct teaching is widely used in secondary classrooms because it increases time-on-task and focuses on achieving learning objectives. Cooperative learning is the strategy widely identified as a viable approach for the heterogeneous classroom with its inclusion of multicultural, multiethnic, multilingual, at-risk, disabled, and multitalented students in which "diversity is celebrated within a cooperative content" (Putnam, 1993, p. 6). Cooperative learning also fits comfortably into the constructivist classroom.

Joyce and Weil pointed out in their influential work, *Models of Teaching* (2000), in which they described more than 20 models of teaching, that no single teaching strategy is the best approach. Teachers need a variety of approaches to address their many instructional purposes and students' varied learning styles and needs. Teachers will have more impact on student learning if they employ a variety of strategies and methods. Strategies provide teachers with an organizational pattern or plan with which to structure the curriculum, determine curriculum materials, and guide teacher behaviors with students. Strategies are the pedagogical arsenal to accommodate a wide range of instructional maneuvers. However, keep in mind that classroom research has not identified certain instructional behaviors that work well for all types of students and situations. Research-based information can only inform teachers about alternatives; it can't make those decisions for them (Good and Brophy, 2000).

APPLICATION for DIVERSE CLASSROOMS

To improve student achievement, teachers must be sensitive and responsive to students' cultural backgrounds; learning styles; languages; and positive relationships with teachers, parents, and peers. Communication styles must be understood and capitalized on to increase learning, not to build barriers (Dilworth and Brown, 2001).

■ OVERVIEW

This chapter describes two general strategies of teaching in sufficient detail to enable teachers to recognize their potential and consider their use. The direct-teaching strategy emphasizes structure, high teacher visibility, focused objectives, and effectiveness in promoting on-task student behavior. The cooperative-learning strategy takes advantage of students' natural inclination to sociability. After learning the skills of communication, group process, and leadership, students become an effective source of instruction for each other as they work together in small groups.

SCENARIO

Millie Blaine, a second-year high school English teacher, was reviewing her plans for her next unit on Past and Future Heroes and Heroines with the fifth-period class. She thought about the difficulties she had encountered in her first try at cooperative learning that year and what she was going to change in the second try as a result.

Millie felt that a cooperative-learning approach for this new unit on literature, writing, and self-reflection was the strategy to use because of the diverse makeup of her classes that continued to present difficulties for her in terms of management and achievement of learning outcomes. Having come from a small midwestern town, she has been continually challenged by the mix of students in her classes that includes diverse cultural, racial, and socioeconomic groups, as well as special-needs students.

With such diverse needs and strengths in that section, Millie felt that another cooperative group project would be appropriate. She would make changes in her practices based on what she had learned and what the students had learned from the first attempt. She would start the unit tomorrow with a discussion on the final self-evaluation reports the class had submitted at the conclusion of the initial cooperative-learning unit. She would solicit suggestions from them as to how

to make this attempt successful for everyone. She would encourage much reflective discussion about how they built (or were not able to build) group interdependence.

Building interdependence had been a problem. She recalled the written self-evaluation from Junko:

> I really do not prefer working in groups because I fear that others in my group may not work as hard as I do to do my best, and I would end up having to do the group's project. However, I was satisfied to find that all but one in my group did their part and contributed to the group project. I am not sure if I could have done as well by myself because I do not have the artistic ability two people in my group had. But, I still like to depend only on myself.

Millie was not sure how much she should try to change attitudes about cooperative learning similar to Junko's. However, this time she thought that she would structure the groups even more carefully to ensure a heterogeneous balance of cultures, races, and special needs, as well as distribution of students with leadership abilities now that she knew her students better. She would start her class the next day with a think-pair-share activity in which partners within the groups would think about their past cooperative experiences and how to improve them and then form ideas together to share with another group and then with the whole class.

Fortunately, Millie had her own team partner down the hall—Miguel Fernandez—who had been her mentor her first year. Now they both were using the cooperative-learning approach and sharing ideas on meeting the challenges of teaching diverse student populations.

Upstairs in the science lab, Rose Fortunato, using the direct-teaching approach, was ready to move from the presentation phase of the lesson, in which she had conducted a model demonstration on chemical bonding, into the group-practice stage. During the group practice, she would review the concept using transparencies and models and ask the students a number of questions to check on their understanding of the principle before they did their small-group practice in the laboratory.

Rose Fortunato felt comfortable with the use of the six instructional functions of direct teaching to structure her chemistry lessons because they facilitated her lesson planning on key principles and helped her maintain much student involvement through comprehension checks and group practice. She was pleased with the achievement level of the class.

These teachers were encouraged by their principal to examine and extend their instructional practices to accommodate strategies that were reported in educational research as increasing students' achievement. They had received information and an orientation to these strategies in a series of in-service meetings held in the district. Small summer stipends had been made available for curricular planning to implement the strategies. The school district was committed to focusing on the improvement of instruction to increase achievement levels and student learning.

■ RESEARCH AND THEORETICAL BASE

The first achievement-raising strategy to be examined is direct teaching. Direct teaching is in the group of teacher-centered instructional strategies that include the lecture, recitation, and demonstration teaching. These strategies focus on the teacher providing the information or forming the questions to stimulate thinking and interaction among the students. Direct teaching, as defined in this text, refers to the teacher presentation, interaction, and practice format that is highly effective in helping students learn specific knowledge and skills. Direct teaching is the instructional approach emerging from the works of Berliner, Bloom, Harnischfiger, and Wiley (in Peterson and Walberg, 1979) on the impact of time and content covered on student success. It is also based on the system of direct instruction developed by Good, Grouws, and Ebmeier (1983) for the teaching of mathematics following a structured approach that became identified as lesson functions. The teaching functions considered part of the direct-teaching strategy reflect the information from researchers, working independently, who arrived at similar findings on the systematic approach to instruction being used by teachers whose students had higher rankings on achievement tests (Rosenshine and Stevens, 1986). Although most of the research on direct teaching comes from studies of elementary school classrooms, the strategy is widely employed by secondary teachers. Direct teaching refers to academically focused, teacher-directed classrooms using sequenced and structured materials. It also refers to teaching activities in which goals are clear to students, sufficient time is allowed for instruction, coverage of content is extensive, performance of students is monitored, and feedback is academically oriented (Rosenshine, 1979).

In a report on direct teaching, Rosenshine and Stevens (1986) indicated that across a number of studies the more effective teachers (in terms of promoting student achievement) were those who maintained a strong academic focus and spent less time in nonacademic activities. Studies by Soar (1973), Stallings and Kaskowitz (1974), and Solomon and Kendall (1979) showed that teachers who most successfully stimulated gains in achievement played the role of a strong leader. Rosenshine (1979) described the direct teacher as the more successful instructor in teaching content measured by achievement tests. Direct teaching emphasizes meeting specific objectives keyed to learning outcomes and is particularly effective for the acquisition of basic skills. The report from the Alliance for Curriculum Reform stated that "more than fifty studies showed that careful sequencing, monitoring, and control of the learning process raises the learning rate" (Cawelti, 1995, p. 16).

In the past, the picture of the direct teacher was that of a grim, didactic authority figure who instructed the class as a whole and dominated the class time with much teacher talk. This teacher made the instructional decisions and taught through lecture and drill for a high percentage of correct rote-memory responses. This picture caused many educators to question the negative side effects that this approach could produce. However, researchers confirmed to the contrary that direct teachers in more structured, formal classrooms with higher achievement results are warm, concerned, and flexible and allow more freedom of movement (Rosenshine and Stevens 1986). These studies and others reported that direct teaching is effective in teaching skill subjects such as reading and mathematics and does not produce a negative classroom climate (Wang, Haertel, and Walberg, 1993). Other strategies may be more appropriate for achieving creative and expressive goals because there is no single strategy for effective instruction, just as there is no single list of teaching behaviors that will guarantee achievement. These strategies and teaching behaviors need to be part of a teacher's information so that they can be employed to accomplish certain goals, such as teaching basic skills or key concepts to students who may learn best through more teacher direction.

Cooperative or collaborative learning strategies are student-centered strategies that focus on the student's working with ideas, projects, and experiences to gain knowledge by "doing" rather than by being told the information by the teacher. Student-centered learning includes such strategies as discussion, discovery learning, inquiry, simulations and games, mastery learning, and independent study. Among these, cooperative learning has been most heavily researched and identified as the strategy that helps promote student achievement and more positive attitudes toward learning.

Cooperative learning uses peer tutoring and team cooperation to encourage student learning. It emphasizes motivation and, like the other model, can be implemented by teachers in both elementary and secondary school classrooms using the instructional materials of that system. The key components of the strategy are peer interaction, cooperation, and communications.

Historically, social interaction has been a major theme in the work of Vygotsky, the late Russian psychologist, which has had considerable impact on early childhood education. He theorized that a child learns first by social interaction and then internalizes this knowledge to the psychological-cognitive level. Today, despite the pressure of high-stakes testing and stress on achievement, teachers are using collaborative methods recognizing that students can learn through interaction and are reassured by the research that shows social interaction can enhance academic learning (Slavin, 1995).

In their review of the research on cooperative learning, Stallings and Stipek (1986) found that this learning strategy has been used to accomplish at least four purposes: (1) to raise students' perception of the value of academic achievement among students and to encourage students to help each other learn; (2) to use cooperation and peer instruction to benefit both high- and low-ability students; (3) to provide an alternative cooperative model to the competitive model most used in schools; and (4) to improve human relations among races and ethnic groups in a school.

Recent surveys of several hundred teachers and principals from around the country revealed that educators across all subject areas see cooperative learning as the possible premier instructional strategy. Principals and teachers agreed on the academic and social benefits but were uncertain of the well-known different structures of cooperative learning and how they were employed in the classroom (Tomlinson, Moon, and Callahan, 1997).

Of the many cooperative-learning methods that have been researched and evaluated, five seem to be particularly appropriate and effective for teaching and learning at the middle school through high school levels. The Student Teams–Achievement Division (STAD) and Teams-Game-Tournament (TGT) forms of cooperative learning were developed at Johns Hopkins University by Slavin and his associates (1990) and are among the oldest and most heavily researched. Jigsaw was developed by Aronson, Blaney, Stephan, Sikes, and Snapp (1978), with a variation devised by Slavin (1995). Johnson and Johnson and their associates (1999) developed the Learning Together model, which is also widely used, and Sharon and Sharon (1976) developed the Group Investigation approach. All of these approaches emphasize cooperation rather than competition, with students helping and encouraging each other in groups to learn.

Cooperative learning is one of the most heavily researched instructional methods, with close to 200 studies conducted (Slavin, 1990). In a review of research, Slavin (1991) concluded that cooperative-learning approaches enhance student achievement when they incorporate group goals and individual accountability. Achievement effects of cooperative learning were found to be consistently positive in 37 of 44 experimental/control comparisons of at least four weeks' duration. Further achievement effects were found to be equally positive for students at all grade levels (2–12), in all major subject areas, in all types of schools (urban, rural, and suburban), and for high, average, and low achievers. Finally, cooperative learning has also consistently and positively influenced a variety of other outcomes including students' self-esteem, intergroup relations, acceptance of academically handicapped students, and attitudes toward school (Slavin, 1991). The amount of empirical research data on cooperative learning as an effective teaching strategy is very impressive (Ellis and Fouts, 1993).

The effectiveness of cooperative-learning strategies with students with disabilities is important to note for today's inclusive classrooms (Tateyamo-Sniezek, 1990). In studies involving the mildly handicapped (those with learning disabilities, mental retardation, or sensory and physical impairments), the reviews by Johnson and Johnson (1981, 1989) and Slavin (1990) showed increased achievement and social acceptance for the disabled students.

Cooperative-learning investigations with moderately and severely disabled students have been conducted in both elementary and secondary schools with varied activities such as science projects, art, cooking, music, academic and preacademic tasks, and group recreation activities. Putnam (1993) reports that cooperative learning in these studies is found to produce certain positive social and verbal interactions, greater interpersonal attraction, and academic gains comparable to those in competitive and individualistic situations (Putnam, 1993). Kagan (1992) cited a significant finding from the research that showed the lowest-achieving students and minority students benefiting the most academically from this approach.

Because an essential dimension of cooperative learning is training in social skills that encourages students to interact with each other and to learn how people can work together, it has been cited as an effective approach to accommodate needs of students from many different backgrounds (Kagan, Zahn, Widaman, Schwarz-wald, and Tyrrell, 1985). In the multicultural classroom and in classrooms with students with limited English proficiency, research findings cite cooperative-learning strategies as encouraging confidence, self-esteem, and social skills in learners (Parrenas and Parrenas, 1993). At-risk students can benefit from cooperative-learning experiences as well (Slavin, 1989). Sudzina and Douvre (1993), in their review of the research on use of cooperative learning with at-risk students, concluded that "cooperative learning can enable teachers to concentrate on the risk factors that can be influenced"—learned helplessness, limited student strategies for handling learning tasks, and student avoidance of literacy tasks. The teacher must realize, however, that the use of cooperative learning for students rejected by their peers, for students who do not want to cooperate, or for those not capable of completing the group task could result in strengthening the group's negative feelings toward those students (Harris, Milich, and McAninch, 1998). This means that the teacher must design a group task, or at least a part of the group task, in which all can succeed but not be bored because the task is too simple.

There is a general consensus that cooperative-learning methods enhance student achievement and learning, but the vast majority of studies, which were strongly supportive, were conducted in grades 2 through 9. Only a few studies support effectiveness in grades 10 through 12. Another concern is the appropriateness of cooperative-learning approaches for developing higher-order conceptual learning. Most of the studies have focused on the basic skill areas of mathematics, language arts, and reading, but relatively few studies have been conducted in other areas. Several, however, have found strong effects of higher-order understanding in creative writing, reading, and social studies (Slavin, 1990). Although the research evidence is quite strong in favor of cooperative learning as an instructional strategy, teachers' use of a variety of instructional strategies is still recommended when considering all the dynamics of classroom teaching and learning. Also, one must keep in mind that this strategy requires training, motivation, and determination to keep trying it if students are to reap the benefits.

■ APPLICATION TO PRACTICE

Each of these achievement-improvement strategies—direct teaching and cooperative learning—is examined in this chapter regarding how it fulfills the following aspects of its instructional design:

Purpose	Structure
Focus	Evaluation
Role of teacher	Appropriate subjects and types of learners
Method	Application for diverse classrooms
Role of learner	

Direct Teaching

Direct-teaching strategy does not fit the constructivist approach to teaching because it separates the curriculum into smaller pieces of knowledge with emphasis on teacher-identified skills and content acquisition. Constructivist classrooms approach curriculum by working with larger concepts and encouraging students to identify the skills and additional content that they will need to build the larger cognitive structure. However, if direct teaching moves away from emphasis on the "correct answer" toward building on the present understandings and needs of students, then it can be more student centered.

In direct instruction, teachers are actively involved by introducing content, demonstrating skills, directing large-group experiences with the content, checking students' understanding and monitoring individual or small-group work, as well as providing review. The focus is on teacher interaction with students rather than students interacting mainly with materials after a brief explanation by the teacher.

Direct instruction is examined here as a key strategy because it emphasizes meeting specific objectives keyed to learning outcomes and is particularly effective for acquisition of basic skills. This approach continues to be widely used today because it helps increase on-task learning time (Gettinger, 1986) that contributes to student achievement when learning key concepts and basic skills.

This strategy also may be called systematic teaching or active teaching. The information about this strategy was obtained mainly from the following authors: Rosenshine (1979), Barnes (1981), Good (1982), Rosenshine and Stevens (1986), and Stallings and Stipek (1986). For more detail on this instructional approach, readers are urged to examine these key sources, as well as the work of Hunter (1994) and Good and Brophy (2000).

Purpose   The purpose of direct teaching is to increase achievement by the teacher's attention to specific, analytical, academic objectives, by coverage of objectives to be tested, and by active engagement of the student in academic tasks. Attention is to be given to promoting student success through a variety of means, such as those described in Chapter 2. The teacher takes charge of the classroom to provide a climate for learning that is student involved and task oriented.

Focus   The focus of the strategy is academic and teacher centered, with a structured curriculum useful for teaching skills and acquiring new information. Within this focus the teacher conveys that the business of the classroom is learning.

Role of Teacher   This is a teacher-directed strategy, which means that the teacher carefully sequences the lessons and the activities and controls the time spent on the phases of the lesson. The strategy requires the teacher to be a good motivator keeping students on task, to be very clear in explaining the information, and to be task oriented for students learning the concept or process. There is much interaction of the teacher with the students in all phases of the lesson. The teacher's immediate corrective feedback is important for student learning. When teachers are not involved in the presentation or in leading group practice, they are monitoring students' progress by moving around the room, keeping students on task, giving feedback, and working with individuals.

Method   A teacher planning to use direct teaching needs to divide the curriculum into small segments or steps through such curriculum techniques as skill analysis and conceptual mapping. First, skills, processes, and concepts are identified and arranged in a meaningful order. Then they can be presented in small steps, after which students are provided with classroom time for practice and feedback.

The structuring of the lesson is important in this model. Rosenshine (1983) and Rosenshine and Stevens (1986, p. 379) produced from a number of research sources a list of six instructional functions that are essential to the structure of direct teaching. These functions include daily review, structuring and presentation, guided practice, feedback and correctives, independent student practice, and weekly and monthly reviews. These functions do not have to be in every lesson. Teachers must decide which functions are necessarily dependent on the complexity of the material and students' needs. Details of the functions as described by Rosenshine and Stevens (1986) are as follows:

1. *Daily Review*

   Check homework (routines for students to check each other's papers).

   Reteach when necessary.

   Review relevant past learning (may include questioning).

   Review prerequisite skills (if applicable).

2. *Structuring and Presentation*

   Provide short statement of objectives.

   Provide overview and structuring. (Show how new information is related to previous student knowledge.)

   Proceed in small steps but at a rapid pace.

   Intersperse questions within the demonstration to check for understanding.

   Highlight main points. (Teacher could provide outline of new material.)

   Provide sufficient illustrations and concrete examples.

   Provide demonstrations and models.

   When necessary, give detailed and redundant instructions and examples.

3. *Guided Practice*

   Initial student practice takes place with teacher guidance.

   Teacher asks many questions and encourages student questions as they practice together.

   Teacher checks for understanding (CFU) by evaluating student responses.

   During CFU, teacher gives additional explanation, processes feedback, or repeats explanation where necessary.

   All students have a chance to respond and receive feedback; teacher ensures that all students participate.

Prompts are provided during guided practice (where appropriate).

Initial student practice is sufficient so that students can work independently.

Guided practice continues until students are firm.

Guided practice is continued (usually) until a success rate of 80 percent is achieved.

4. *Feedback and Correctives*

Quick, correct responses can be followed by another question or a short acknowledgment of correctness (e.g., "That's right").

Hesitant correct answers might be followed by process feedback (e.g., "Yes, Linda, that's right because . . .").

Student errors indicate a need for more practice.

Monitor students for systematic errors.

Try to obtain a substantive response to each question. (Use probing questions—"Yes, now what does that mean?" "What is the next step?")

Corrections can include sustaining feedback (i.e., simplifying the question, giving clues), explaining or reviewing steps, giving process feedback, or reteaching the last steps.

Try to elicit an improved response when the first one is incorrect (e.g., "No, let's go back and look at that again. What does it say under the diagram on page 81? Now, how would you use that information to answer the question?").

Guided practice and corrections continue until the teacher feels that the group can meet the objectives of the lesson.

Praise should be used in moderation; specific praise is more effective than general praise.

5. *Independent Practice (Seat Work)*

Provide sufficient practice (even to the point of overlearning).

Practice is directly relevant to skills/content taught.

Practice to overlearning.

Practice until responses are firm, quick, and automatic.

Ninety-five percent correct rate during independent practice.

Students alerted that seat work will be checked.

Students held accountable for seat work.

Actively supervise students, when possible.

6. *Weekly and Monthly Reviews*

Systematic review of previously learned material.

Include review in homework.

Frequent tests.

Reteaching of material missed in tests.

All the instructional functions need not be present in every lesson, nor do they limit instructional methods to the lecture mode. Within the function phases a variety of methodologies may be used. Direct teaching does not mean lecturing.

The following are some examples of direct teaching using a variety of approaches in various subject areas. These lessons might be conducted over several days.

Science or the Arts

Presentation stage—Modeling or demonstration.

Guided practice—Students try demonstration in groups as teacher circulates and gives feedback.

Independent practice—Students individually write their reports on the demonstration.

Mathematics

Presentation stage—Lecture on process and meaning of a mathematical procedure, such as solving polynomials. Teacher makes up a story to fit the formula presented and goes over each step to show how the story fits the process.

Guided practice—Teacher puts problems on the board and has class explain how to complete each step to solve the problems.

Independent practice—Students do problems on their own and make up their own stories to fit the formula.

Social Studies

Presentation stage—Teacher role-plays situation that could lead to a revolution. Teacher explains the concept of revolution, identifies its critical characteristics, and then examines the Revolutionary War for how it fits those characteristics.

Guided practice—Teacher holds a guided discussion about revolutions, examining whether the Industrial Revolution fits the characteristics of a revolution.

Independent practice—Small groups examine the similarities and differences of the computer age and the sexual revolution with the concept of a revolution and share their findings with the class. Students could write their own papers on a revolution of their choosing.

Language Arts and English

Presentation stage—Teacher reads several examples of several different types of poetry and then briefly explains using a PowerPoint presentation on the elements of poetry. Teacher then selects one or two of the elements to focus on for the lesson.

Guided practice—Class in small groups analyzes several poems as to how those elements are present. Teacher monitors; class shares their analyses.

Independent practice—In pairs or singularly, students write their own poems including the elements. Students present poems to the class.

To summarize, the methodology of direct teaching must be varied and should include many methods with a systematic approach to instruction to teach basic concepts, principles, and skills.

Hints for the Beginning Teacher

The teacher needs to keep in mind that 10 to 20 minutes for adolescents is the length of time that memory can keep on a subject before the short-term memory decides to discard it or store it (Sousa, 1995). That means secondary teachers should present information in the first 10 to 15 minutes of the class period and follow up with activities or discussion to reinforce the information.

Role of Learner   Within this academically focused classroom, the role of the learner is to follow, stay on-task, and perform. If this structure appears to be stifling the creativity of the learner, the teacher can provide opportunities for the learner to use divergent and creative thinking in some of the learning experiences planned for the independent and review functions. For example, if one of the skills being taught were problem solving, the student could demonstrate knowledge of the problem-solving process by describing a situation and the different steps groups of people might use to solve a problem (e.g., solving the problem of dealing with a class bully in an eighth-grade gym class).

Evaluation   The direct-teaching strategy includes both formative (during instruction) and summative (conclusion of instruction) evaluation. The teacher giving corrective feedback during guided practice and independent practice is a key to students' achievement. Frequent tests are given during the weekly and monthly reviews so that reteaching of key material can take place as needed.

Appropriate Subjects and Content   This direct-instruction strategy is reported to work best with teaching-skill subjects such as reading, writing, mathematics, grammar, computer literacy (Gelder and Maggs, 1983), factual parts of science and history, and introducing new concepts (Rosenshine and Stevens, 1986). Those bodies of knowledge that are hierarchical in structure with step-by-step progression can best be taught with the direct-instruction model. This strategy has been widely adapted by those teaching basics and special education (Condon and Maggs, 1986).

Direct instruction is useful when textbook material, or a concept or skill, is difficult to understand and needs to be subdivided into smaller parts in order to be explained more clearly. When helping students master essential facts, principles, and skills that are necessary for further learning in an area, direct instruction is the strategy to use. Students will need more time in guided practice to achieve mastery. This approach continues to be widely used today because it emphasizes meeting specific objectives that require more on-task learning time.

APPLICATION for DIVERSE CLASSROOMS

As to which types of learners benefit most from this systematic approach, research tells us that it is helpful for young children, slower learners, and students of all ages and abilities during the first stages of learning informative material or material that is difficult to learn (Berliner, 1982). Opportunities are provided for students to have considerable feedback and practice. Teachers can make adaptations in the model by shortening the time spent on guided practice and independent practice for more mature learners and increasing the presentation time for new material. Care must be taken to assure that lessons are not too advanced for those who comprehend more slowly or too repetitive for those who grasp concepts quickly. Contextual cues and integration of facts and tasks with the larger concepts or skills are important when using direct instruction with second language learners (Ortiz and Wilkinson, 1989).

Here is a sample lesson plan detailing all the steps to use in planning and teaching a lesson using direct instruction.

Standard: Student is able to use the tools of punctuation accurately in order to communicate clearly in writing.

Objective: Student will be able to demonstrate four of the seven uses of a semicolon in the next reflection paper or assigned composition.

Instructional Approach

1. *Daily Review*

   Students check each other's returned compositions and circle all semicolons used.

   Teacher checks on student knowledge of semicolon by asking students to give examples of how they are used.

   Motivation—Teacher takes a paragraph with no semicolons, asks students to read it aloud to each other, and then discusses the problem they may have encountered in understanding the paragraph.

2. *Structuring and Presentation*

   Teacher explains today's objective and rationale.

   Teacher explains the relation of this lesson to the writing skills being developed.

Teacher presents and explains each of the seven uses of the semicolon and provides examples.

Teacher questions students as to why semicolon was used in each example.

Students look at their own compositions with the circled semicolons or no semicolons. They are to identify the use of the semicolons by the specific punctuation rule on the board or in their grammar books. If they used no semicolons, they are to determine where semicolons should go and insert them into their compositions.

Teacher hears student reports and questions on their use of the semicolon in their compositions.

Teacher goes over the rules and gives more examples as needed.

3. *Guided Practice*

Teacher provides worksheets with paragraphs taken from the current short stories or novels they are reading. Teacher has removed semicolons. Teacher and students do some of the worksheet together, identifying where and why semicolons should be placed.

Teacher identifies those students who need more practice on semicolons. Those students become a small group that the teacher works with while the rest of the class goes on to independent practice.

4. *Feedback and Correctives*

Throughout the guided practice, students are reinforced if responses are correct or guided to the rules if they become confused.

5. *Independent Practice*

Students write their reflective logs for the day on the novel they are reading for class or on their past week's learning experiences—in or out of class—using all seven of the semicolon constructions. The papers are to be turned in the next day.

Teacher circulates around the room monitoring their work and answering their questions.

6. *Evaluation*

Students are to write a poem about the semicolon or a letter to the semicolon including references to its function in punctuation.

7. *Weekly and Monthly Reviews*

Teacher expects semicolons to be used in student writing. Grading of papers will include correct use of punctuation.

If students do not retain information, semicolon worksheets will be available for further drill and practice.

Teacher will ask students to bring in examples of semicolon use from newspapers and magazines. These will be put up on the Punctuation Tool Bulletin Board, along with class-selected poems, letters, and pictures about the semicolon.

Another Model Using Direct Teaching   Madeline Hunter's Instructional Theory into Practice (ITIP) contains many of the features of the direct-teaching strategy and has been implemented via in-service workshops in many parts of the country. The program includes identifying clear instructional objectives, teaching at the correct level of difficulty, structuring instruction with lesson functions almost identical to those named by Rosenshine and Stevens (1986, p. 377), and emphasizing the importance of comprehension checks and use of the principles of learning, such as motivation and reinforcement theories. It is a teacher decision-making model based on learning theory applied to practice.

During the 1980s, many school administrators adopted the ITIP model as the effective way to teach. Teachers were evaluated as to their ability to follow the ITIP principles. At its peak, the Hunter program was being used in districts in all 50 states (Ellis and Fouts, 1993).

The ITIP model was the subject of a thorough longitudinal study done from 1981 to 1985 in two schools in Napa Valley, California (Stallings, 1987). The findings were that achievement did improve in the target schools over four years but took a considerable drop in the fourth year. The study raised many questions about the model's effectiveness in improving student achievement. The ITIP model was based on psychological research in the area of learning, but the model had no research base concerning its effectiveness in raising student achievement (Ellis and Fouts, 1993).

From the Hunter movement, educators have learned that effective teaching that raises achievement develops students' thinking skills and problem-solving abilities and uses a variety of teaching methods and strategies rather than a single method such as direct instruction, which is geared more appropriately for basic-skill teaching.

APPLICATION for DIVERSE CLASSROOMS

To help students for whom English is their second language, be aware of their home language. Use instructional strategies that encourage student language use such as cooperative learning, discussions, and peer tutoring (Fitzgerald, 1995).

Cooperative Learning

For the second achievement strategy, the reader may recall Mrs. Blaine's classroom in the scenario in which she was planning to implement a cooperative-learning approach for her next unit. She had carefully considered the heterogeneous makeup of the class and decided that this cooperative strategy could benefit her students. She anticipated increases in both achievement and positive attitudes for her students caused by their working together.

SCENARIO

We return to Millie Blaine to examine more of her thinking about cooperative learning.

As Mrs. Blaine was considering her next attempt at teaching a unit through cooperative learning, she thought fondly of Mrs. Duea, her methods teacher at the state university, who had stressed cooperative-learning strategies as one approach to help meet the diverse needs of students. Now that this class had completed one experience with cooperative learning with mixed success— three groups functioned well, two groups floundered but did produce a group project, and one group fell apart—she was eager to try again with the fifth-period class, knowing that a teacher needs much experience and knowledge about cooperative learning to use it successfully.

She chose the fifth-period class because it had the most diverse needs, with the following mix of students:

1. Seven academically weak students who had reading skills at the fourth-grade level and lacked motivation to turn in assignments

2. Several students with excellent writing skills

3. Four students who were social isolates, ignored by the rest of the class (two of these were low-achieving students, and one was from Mexico and had minimal skills in reading and speaking English)

4. Class of mixed races and cultures including African Americans, Latinos, European Americans, and Asian Americans

5. Two students with learning disabilities, one who also had motor-skills impairment

Millie thought about the positive self-report she had received from Jeffrey, who had resource-room support for his learning disability and had failed English once before. He was an isolate in her class last year, preferring to be uninvolved. In the first group experience this year, he became a helper to Carmen, the student with minimal English skills. In a think-pair-share task, he helped her understand, and they began to work together frequently. He also was taking seriously his role of keeping the group on-task. Millie learned from that experience the importance of selecting at least one student who might be a potential friend for an at-risk student and to limit one or two at-risk students to a group.

Millie's concerns resurfaced as she recalled group four, which never did accomplish a group project. The group broke into two pairs, each pair of good friends working separately, while the fifth member chose to work on his own. The projects were satisfactory, but the objectives of developing intergroup cooperation, communications, and interpersonal skills were not met.

> She knew that she would have to work with the groups this time on build-ing cooperative group skills and interdependence. She would identify a role for each individual while citing the analogy of the football team. The quarterback is dependent on the line to block the defensive team while he throws the ball to the receiver, who is also looking for blocking protection. No touchdown re-sults unless everyone does his job. She hoped the girls would provide a sports analogy of their own.
>
> The objective Millie would emphasize as a result of the class's first coopera-tive attempt would be building cooperative skills, such as practicing active lis-tening, paraphrasing what others say, providing positive feedback to each other, and examining different points of view without criticizing each other. To em-phasize the learner approach, the first piece they would read would be an Up-dike short story about a former football player. Thereafter, the groups would choose the stories and novels to read and films to watch in pursuit of the heroes and heroines. She would provide them with a list to guide their choices, but they might add others. The group project would be a report on the heroes/heroines, as developed from their review of the literature, and individual papers on them-selves as heroes or heroines. All writing would be edited by the group.

Millie Blaine, like most of secondary teachers in the 1990s and in the 2000s, has chosen to use at some period in her instruction a form of cooperative learning. The decision is a sound one based on the knowledge we have concerning how students learn. The Association of Supervision and Curriculum Development (1999) re-ported in its 1999 yearbook that the process of learning has passed from simple self-organization to collaborative, interpersonal, social problem-solving activity dependent on conversation, practical and meaningful involvement, and real-world experience and application. Collaboration in learning is an essential feature in to-day's classroom. The following explanation of Johnson and Johnson's (1999) ap-proach to cooperative learning is an important guide to structuring meaningful collaboration for learning.

Purpose   The purpose of the cooperative-learning strategy is (1) to increase achievement through group collaboration that enables students to learn from each other; (2) to provide an alternative to the competitive structure of most classrooms today that discourages the poorer student; and (3) to improve human relations in the classroom by promoting interdependent activities that teach collaborative skills.

Focus   The focus of cooperative learning is both academic and affective, with emphasis on achievement of shared goals through cooperative efforts. To accom-plish this focus, five basic elements must be included (Johnson and Johnson, 1999). The elaboration of the five basic elements is adapted from Baloche (1998):

1. *Establishment of positive interdependence*—Each in the group has an important role necessary to the success of the group. The most frequently used approach

to establish interdependence is through *resource interdependence.* Each member is given one part of the materials needed to do the task or each member is to provide different pieces of information that will be brought together to accomplish the group task. Another approach to establishing interdependence is through *assigned roles.* The roles are designed to help students get their tasks done, and each role is important to either accomplishing the task or building practice relationships within the group. Groups can be given a group grade for *evaluation interdependence.*

2. *Establishment of face-to-face promotive instruction*—The teacher encourages students to help others in the group learn and succeed. If cooperative learning is progressing, the support and feedback should come from within the group. They should be encouraged to reinforce each other by giving positive feedback, commending each other for work done well and on time, sharing with the group their dissatisfaction if work is not progressing, and providing suggestions for how group or individuals may move forward. Each group member should be concerned about the success of everyone in the group.

3. *Individual accountability*—Students need to be assured individually as to their mastery of the content and skills. They need to receive individual grades as well as a group grade. Each member could be held responsible by the group to contribute or complete a specific part of the task or project.

4. *Promotion of interpersonal and small-group skills and communication*—Some of the essential skills needed for cooperative groups to work include skills that help students get into groups; skills that help students work together and get the tasks done; skills that help students learn how to use the group to increase their own learning; and skills of reflection and self-evaluation. Students also must learn how to listen to others in the group, show appreciation for others, assume responsibility to the group, encourage others in the group to participate, take turns speaking, handle conflicts, and compromise.

5. *Ensurance that groups process their achievement and maintenance of effective working relationships*—Use reflective logs for students to write about how they practiced their cooperative-learning skills and how they want to improve them. Teachers need to provide many opportunities for students to practice their skills of cooperative learning. Teacher and students can develop a rubric on an effective cooperative group, and that rubric can be used as a progress check for groups from time to time.

Role of Teacher   The teacher role differs considerably in this strategy from traditional approaches to instruction. In cooperative learning, teachers relinquish some of their control; that can be a challenge for some teachers who prefer a more authoritarian style. Teachers act as facilitators in cooperative learning by establishing groups whose members work together on shared goals. However, the teacher may teach basic concepts and skills. As facilitator, the teacher must monitor the functioning of the groups, intervene whenever necessary to teach small-group skills, provide assistance when needed, and evaluate students and groups as to how well members work together (Johnson, Johnson, and Smith, 1991). Essential to the teacher's role is his or her interpretation along with student input of what is happening in the classroom in terms of students' thinking and understanding and the changes that need to be made as a result of that information. In the planning stage, the teacher's responsibilities include: (1) structuring the curriculum into units with objectives that can be achieved cooperatively and (2) establishing groups to work together on reaching shared objectives. These objectives must be clearly specified with both cognitive objectives and collaborative skill objectives.

In the preparation stage, the teacher must work with the students to help them learn how to perform each of the roles in the group (see Structure section, Phase II, number 6). Also, students need to be introduced to the learning skills such as pacing, giving specific feedback, and the research skills that they will be using. Students, in addition, need to become aware of the social skills that they will be expected to employ, such as using active listening, communicating feelings, praising, giving constructive criticism, and providing support (Goor and Schween, 1993).

In the instructional stage, the teacher's role involves the following (Johnson, Johnson, Holubec, and Roy, 1984/1990): (1) clearly explaining the task, goal structure, lesson objective, and learning activity to the students; (2) monitoring the effectiveness of the cooperative-learning groups, providing assistance as needed, and giving feedback on students' work with content and group skills; (3) monitoring students' academic and social progress carefully to assure that certain students do not dominate and break down the interdependence; and (4) evaluating students' achievement and encouraging their self-evaluation. Teachers will need to develop strategies for listening to and interviewing students as well as observing their progress toward meeting identified goals (McCaslin and Good, 1992).

Method   The major methodology used is the small-group approach. Within that approach, discussion, inquiry, and modeling methods may be used by the teacher. Certainly the strategy of cooperative learning would not be used exclusively for all class work. Students need to experience independent work and some competitive experiences as well. At times, the teacher will teach the whole class, using a range of instructional methods. However, the methodology utilized most frequently will include methods that accommodate group-process skills and cooperative-learning skills.

Five common formats used for cooperative-learning activities are the following:

1. *Student Teams–Achievement Divisions (STAD)*—Teacher presents the content or skill. Students complete common work assignments in groups of four or five and then are tested individually. A team score is calculated by noting results of individual students' improvement over past performance (Lewis and Doorlag, 1991). (More detail is on page 298 of this text.)

2. *Think-pair-share*—Students first try to answer a question or to learn material by themselves, then discuss their thoughts and understandings with partners, and finally share with their whole group or the class (Kagan, 1992).

3. *Jigsaw*—Each group member in a home group is given one piece of information and then meets with members from other groups who hold the same

piece, to learn that information together and to decide how to teach it to their home groups. Then all return to their home groups to teach that piece of information. In Jigsaw II, students obtain their own information and share it with the group. Students then are tested individually (Kagan, 1992). (More detail is on pages 299 and 300 of this text.)

4. *Team accelerated instruction*—This approach involves individualized instruction because students are assigned materials at their own achievement level and are assisted by their group members in learning the material. Group points are obtained through improvement on individual tests (Olson and Platt, 1992).

5. *Group investigation*—A constructivist approach to challenge groups at a higher level in which students take responsibility for their own learning. The group decides what to investigate, what contribution each will make, and how each will communicate what he or she has learned (Lewis and Doorlag, 1991). Another variation is cooperative problem solving—groups of three students who study and solve a problem. Each group working on the same problem meets with two other groups to share solutions and form a merged group consensus. Solutions from merged groups are shared with the class. Class determines which solutions would work best and why (Johnson, Johnson, and Holubec, 1990).

The teacher may set up a base group—a long-term, heterogeneous cooperative-learning group with stable membership whose main responsibilities are to provide support, encouragement, and assistance in completing assignments and striving to learn (Johnson, Johnson, and Smith, 1991). These base groups act as support groups to monitor and look out for each other, and to care about each other's growth and welfare throughout the year.

Formal cooperative-learning groups are set up to accomplish a task or handle a unit of content from a few days to a few weeks long with such approaches as those previously described. Informal cooperative-learning groups are short-term, random groups used to provide opportunities for peer discussions or to offer variety within a lesson. Think-pair-share is an example of an informal cooperative-learning group (see page 290).

■ WEBSITE RESOURCE ■

 Roger and David Johnson have established the Cooperative Learning Center at the University of Minnesota, and their website,

www.clcrc.com/index.html,

offers information, research findings, essays, and a new question-and-answer link on hot topics related to implementing cooperative learning in classrooms.

Some of the more specialized topics related to cooperative learning are: the cooperative school, decision controversy, conflict resolution, peacemaking, social interdependence theory, culturally diverse classrooms, and promoting safe educational and community environments.

Role of Learner   This strategy gives students much control within the group structure. They become both teachers and learners as they practice communication and group-process skills, as well as leadership skills. Each student is expected to utilize these skills to promote group success. Students are to give and receive assistance, feedback, reinforcement, and support to each other. Students are to be in a positive interdependent role in which one cannot succeed without all succeeding. Positive interdependence encourages students to see how their work benefits others and their group members' work benefits them. They are responsible for each member's learning. The reward structure promotes group importance and interdependence. In most cooperative-learning models, the students work in small groups of four or five and receive an individual grade for their work with the group.

The students are held responsible for determining whether cooperative skills are practiced within the group. They are encouraged to analyze the progress of the group in light of each member's role. Peer feedback and self-evaluation are solicited. Therefore, the student's role involves responsibility to the group as well as to oneself for academic progress.

APPLICATION for DIVERSE CLASSROOMS

Find a task that the low-status student is good at and able to teach others. Help the student to be as well prepared as the teacher. Prepare the class to understand why this information or skill being taught by the student is important. Another approach is to design a situation so that the low-status student is in control of and understanding the initial materials needed for the group task. Giving the student an opportunity to talk early in the experience may help the student be more influential in the group (Cohen, 1994).

Structure   As one can observe in the scenario describing Mrs. Blaine's planning for a unit, cooperative learning is structured around a curriculum designed to be learned through cooperative groups of students who have individual responsibilities for accomplishing their group's goals. Specific lesson objectives are established within a group task. Much time must be spent in planning how to implement the curriculum and to prepare students for this cooperative approach to instruction.

The following steps for implementing cooperative learning are from Johnson and colleagues (1984/1990), *Circles of Learning,* as well as Johnson, Johnson, and Smith (1991), and provide an outline of the procedure to use in structuring this model. Note the number of steps in the planning and preparation phases.

Phase I: Planning

1. Specification of instructional objectives—both academic objectives and collaborative-skills objectives.

2. Decisions on the size of the group—range from two to four or five.

3. Assignment of students to groups—heterogeneity recommended.

4. Arrangement of room to accommodate working groups.

5. Arrangement of instructional materials to promote interdependence—all given same materials or each given different resources.

Phase II: Preparing Students

6. Assignment of roles to ensure interdependence—each member given a responsibility, such as reader, taskmaster, recorder, calculator, checker, reporter, materials handler, reflector, encourager of participation, praiser, checker for understanding (Johnson, Johnson, and Smith, 1991).

7. Explanation of the academic task.

8. Communication of group's interdependency—reward structure explained, mutual goals established, materials shared, roles assigned.

9. Communication of individual's accountability—each individual, as well as the group, will be assessed by such measures as quizzes and student work assessed by group.

10. Promotion of intergroup cooperation—encouragement of groups working together through giving rewards or praise.

11. Explanation of criteria for success.

12. Specification of desired behaviors, such as contributing, helping, listening to others, encouraging others to participate, asking for help or clarification, using self-monitoring skills, using quiet voices (Johnson et al., 1991).

13. Teaching collaborative skills—active listening, paraphrasing what others say, giving compliments, resolving controversy without criticism, summarizing, checking for understanding.

Phase III: Monitoring and Intervening

14. Encouraging face-to-face interaction with oral summarizing, giving and receiving explanations, and elaborating.

15. Monitoring students' behavior—giving feedback, reinforcement, and praise.

16. Assistance provided, where needed.

17. Intervention to teach collaborative skills.

Phase IV: Evaluation and Processing

18. Evaluation of quality and quantity of students' learning.

19. Assessment of how well group functioned—groups can list things they did well in working together and things they need to improve.

20. Providing closure to the groups and individual learners—both teacher and students can summarize, share groups' work, review.

Evaluation   Formative evaluations of individual and group progress, as well as self-monitoring, are important throughout. Formative evaluations of groups can take place each week, with the group analyzing strengths and weaknesses in accomplishing group goals. Summative evaluation includes group and individual assessment measures. A criterion-referenced approach may be used to assess that the specified objectives within the assigned concepts and skills were accomplished. Students may receive both a group grade and an individual grade. Their grade may be contingent on a group project or the average of each student's progress toward meeting group objectives. Having to share the same grade encourages students to provide support for those members who are having trouble reaching goals, be they academic goals or the performance of cooperative learning skills. However, individual accountability should be maintained to meet specified objectives. Students may also receive a grade as to their individual ability to function within the group. Teachers may require a work log to be kept by each group that includes what each student was to have contributed, what they did contribute, and how the group evaluated the effort.

Johnson, Johnson, and Smith (1991) describe the individual test followed by a group-test approach in which an examination is given to each individual for a grade. The teacher scores the answers and then gives the test again to the cooperative groups. In the group examination, the students confer on the answers to each question. The task is to answer each question correctly. The cooperative goal is for all group members to understand the material. The group is to agree on one answer and identify how it arrived at that answer. Each group is responsible for ensuring that all students understand the material they missed on the individual test. Bonus points can be given if all members of the group score 90 percent or better on the group test. These bonus points are added to students' individual scores to determine their individual grades for the test.

The preceding is an example of an approach to grading in a cooperative group. The decision as to how grades will be arrived at depends on the type of interdependence the teacher wants to establish among the students. Johnson, Johnson, and Smith (1991) provide the following suggestions:

1. Individual score plus bonus points based on all members reaching the criterion (see preceding example).

2. Individual score plus bonus points based on lowest score.

3. Link individual score to group average.

4. Individual score plus bonus based on improvement scores over past tests.

5. Total members' individual scores; all members receive the total.

6. Average members' individual scores.

7. Group score based on a single product produced by group.

8. Randomly select one member's paper to score and to decide the group grade. All papers in the group have been certified as correct and acceptable.

9. Randomly select one member's exam to score and all group members receive that score.

10. All members receive lowest member score. Group members have prepared each other for the exam.

11. Average academic scores plus collaborated skills performance score.

12. Give dual academic and nonacademic award, such as a pass on homework. Members receive an individual grade and a group reward if group meets the group goal.

Here is a sample lesson plan following the Johnson, Johnson, and Smith (1991) procedure to use in structuring the cooperative-learning unit or lesson. The unit includes consideration of multiple intelligences and has a multicultural, international focus.

Fairy Tale Unit for Middle School Students

Language Arts Standard: The students will be able to analyze various forms of literature as to their literary elements or characteristics.

Phase I: Planning

1. *Objectives*

   Knowledge: Students will identify the core elements and common themes of tales from different cultures.

   Skills: Students will demonstrate the skills of analysis and synthesis and of working in cooperative groups.

   Dispositions: The students will develop appreciation for similarities and differences of fairy tales or folktales from different countries and cultures, and the interest and color obtained from different cultural perspectives.

   Multiple intelligences: Students will use a variety of intelligences in creating and presenting their own fairy tales. They are to choose a particular country from which the tale might have come.

2. *Size of Groups:* Three in a group.

3. *Assignment of students to groups:* Teacher makes the assignment using heterogeneous groups. Multicultural and special-needs students are dispersed among the groups.

4. *Room arrangement:* Chairs and desks in groups of three facing each other.

5. *Arrangement of materials:* Each group is given two fairy tales to examine—each from a different country or culture—and a worksheet with questions to use in examining the task. Example:

   What is the theme of the story?

   What common elements do you see in both stories?

   What cultural elements did you notice?

   Is a fairy tale different from a folktale?

Phase II: Preparing Students

6. *Assignment of roles:* One person is reader; one is note taker to record group responses to questions; one is research person to gather more data on a country. All are responsible for final project.

7. *Explanation of academic task:* Teacher explains task by reviewing "Little Red Riding Hood" and some of the core elements in it. He or she explains the final project as to length of time to do project and explains multiple intelligences' approaches and how any or multiples of these could be used in their project.

8. *Communication of group's interdependence:* Teacher explains that each group will receive a group grade on the worksheet and the final project. A rubric will be developed by teacher and students to access final projects.

9. *Communication of individual's accountability:* Individual grades will be given on quizzes and on individual's ability to work with the group. A rubric will be put together for assessing individual's work within the group.

10. *Promotion of intergroup cooperation:* Teacher provides feedback and encouragement to groups while monitoring their progress. The teacher sends notes to groups with feedback on teacher's perception of how each group is demonstrating cooperative-learning skills. Students encouraged to provide positive feedback to each other as they progress with their work.

11. *Explanation of criteria for success:* Rubrics will be developed by the class and the teacher for assessing final project and individual work within the group. All students will know the criteria for successful completion of the project and for assessment of their work within the group.

12. *Specification of desired behaviors:* Teacher encourages groups to help each other, ask questions of each other as well as of the teacher, demonstrate group process skills, use analysis and synthesis skills.

13. *Teaching collaborative skills:* Teacher teaches active-listening skills and summarizing skills, as well as conflict-resolution skills or other group-processing skills, to the entire class or to certain groups, as needed.

Phase III: Monitoring and Intervening

14. *Encouraging face-to-face interaction:* Teacher checks that students are able to analyze core elements, are able to see cultural differences and similarities in the tales, and share these with each other. Students report to whole class their analyses of common elements.

15. *Monitoring students' behavior:* Teacher monitors group behavior and gives feedback and reinforcement. Students evaluate the progress of their group as well as self-evaluate using the cooperative-learning rubric developed by the class and the teacher.

16. *Assistance provided:* Teacher provides assistance on knowledge and skill objectives when needed.

17. *Intervention:* Teacher works with individual groups on collaborative skills as needed in the areas of following directions, respecting each other's contribu-

tions, managing group time, understanding individual responsibility, speaking one at a time, giving and accepting ideas, compromising, and so on.

Phase IV: Evaluation and Processing

18. *Evaluation of student learning:* Evaluation methods include quizzes, self-evaluations, student logs, and evaluation of final project using rubrics developed by the class and the teacher.

19. *Assessment of how well group functioned:* Students assess group progress regularly, as well as at the conclusion, as to what worked well and what needed to be improved.

20. *Providing closure:* Students present their own fairy tales in any of a variety of forms—written, acted out, danced, painted, performed with puppets, presented on video, and so on. Students are to explain the core elements they used and the cultures in which they placed the tales.

Appropriate Subjects   The cooperative-learning approach can be used with most learning tasks, especially concept attainment, problem solving, categorizing tasks, skill attainment, and judging tasks. Any lesson can be structured into a group-learning situation that promotes collaborative skills. However, any small group activity is not cooperative learning. Cooperative-learning activities are carefully structured, as described in this chapter, and emphasize interdependence as well as individual responsibility.

Cooperative learning has been used in such diverse subject areas as business classes and computer training (Johnson et al., 1984/1990). Recent studies support the academic benefits of using cooperative learning in secondary mathematics classrooms (Whicker and Bol, 1997). The approach has been used with kindergarten students up through adults in college. In *Circles of Learning* (Johnson et al., 1984/1990), a list of schools and teachers around the country that use cooperative learning was printed. This listing included teachers in all grade levels, as well as in higher- and continuing-education classes. The authors of this text use cooperative learning in both their undergraduate and graduate classes.

APPLICATION for DIVERSE CLASSROOMS

It appears that low-achieving students can benefit considerably by cooperative learning because they are coached and helped to achieve objectives through group support. The effect on their self-image and motivation can be very positive. High achievers can benefit also because they are working toward group success rather than their individual achievement and hence feel less isolated. They also can find challenges in the opportunity to learn decision making, leadership roles, and conflict management skills. Putnam (1993) maintains that cooperative learning is a major strategy for the inclusion classroom because it enables teachers to meet the needs of diverse learners by the tasks assigned to students and the group's responsibility to team learning. She says that children with varying cognitive abilities, developmental and learning disabilities, sensory impairments,

(continued)

and different cultural, linguistic, and socioeconomic backgrounds will benefit both academically and socially in cooperative-learning classrooms. Although student achievement is improved because students help each other, it is in the area of human relations that the strength of this strategy appears to lie. Students develop interpersonal and group skills that encourage them to work well with others and accept each other's differences.

Cooperative-Learning Methods in Action: Student Teams–Achievement Divisions   One of the most versatile forms of cooperative learning is Student Teams–Achievement Divisions (STAD). As Slavin (1990, 1991) explained, STAD has been used in many subject areas including mathematics, social studies, science, and language arts, where the focus is on teaching specific objectives that emphasize the learning of factual knowledge with single, right answers. Students who represent a range of ability levels, gender, and ethnicity are assigned to four-member teams. The teacher presents a lesson, and then the students work within their teams to learn the content or master the skill. They work cooperatively to ensure that all team members know the material. The students then individually take quizzes in the traditional way, without helping one another.

The following is an actual illustration of STAD that has been applied in a seventh-grade mathematics class based on a chapter on percentage (Wilen, 1991). Prior to involving students in a cooperative-learning unit, the teacher prepared her students by informing them of the purposes, the procedures, and the expected outcomes. She also identified important small-group social and communication skills and had her students describe appropriate verbal and nonverbal behaviors characteristic of these skills. Students were told that evaluation was based on their quiz and team-improvement scores. Quizzes were administered once each week. Individual improvement scores were computed after every quiz and were based on how well students were doing compared to their base scores. An important goal for students was to work toward maintaining or increasing their base scores. Team improvement scores were based on the averages of the team members' individual improvement scores, and they became 20 percent of the final grade for each student.

Four-member teams were formed, representing a cross section of each of the classes in terms of academic performance and gender. The classes contained only one minority student. Academic performance was based on students' base scores, which were computed from previous test averages. Each team contained one high- and one low-achieving student and two average-achieving students. The students were informed of the formula for team composition and accepted the arrangement with minimal concerns.

The daily procedure provided the structure for this application of STAD. At the beginning of each period, while the class was studying percentage, students met with their teams to check and discuss their assignment related to percentage problems that they had completed individually prior to class. A good deal of the time was spent answering questions that different team members had about the assignment. This phase lasted about 10 minutes. The teacher then presented a short lesson of about 10 to 15 minutes about percent of increase and percent of decrease, for example, and gave a homework assignment based on it. The students then returned to their teams to help each other start the homework. Once a week, a quiz was given that each student took individually. Team improvement scores were computed once per week, and students were informed of their status. During the orientation period, the students were told that there were three major sources for help, the most important of which was the students themselves. The other sources to be consulted by the students were the textbook and the teacher, in that order. The emphasis was on decreasing student dependency on the teacher and increasing it on team effort. The teacher spent class time circulating among the teams, listening to students' interactions. Interventions were often necessary and served as opportunities for the teacher to model appropriate cooperative-learning behaviors, such as asking questions and giving responses. Classroom management was accomplished by keeping students on task, maintaining close proximity, and encouraging students' efforts.

Cooperative-Learning Methods in Action: Jigsaw   The original Jigsaw was developed by Aronson and his colleagues (1978), and a version was produced by Slavin (1990), which he called Jigsaw II. Jigsaw is appropriate for every subject area that has academic material that can be broken down into sections. English, science, and social studies are particularly appropriate subjects because they deal with written material that is generally in narrative form. In Jigsaw, according to Slavin (1990, 1991), students are assigned to four- to six-member heterogeneous teams with the task of working on content material that has been divided into different sections. Students are responsible for their own section that contains specific and unique information. After reading the material, one student from each team who has the same material meets with others as an "expert" group to discuss the material, to help each other to learn it, and then to design ways to teach it to others unfamiliar with it. Students return to their teams to teach their pieces of the puzzle to team members who, in turn, also teach their puzzle pieces. An evaluation exercise can follow, such as a test or a report, that requires all the students to know all parts of the material.

The following is an eleventh-grade U.S. history lesson that uses the original Jigsaw method as the primary instructional approach (Vocke and Capps, 1990). According to the objective, the students will "write a description of the changes in Mary Chestnut's personal views and attitudes toward the South's chances for success during the Civil War" (p. 8). The focus of this lesson is on learning from a primary source, which in this case is the diaries of Mary Chestnut (1823–1886), who was married to Brigadier General James Chestnut, an aide to Jefferson Davis, and had lived in several southern states during the war. Four "expert" groups of students were formed, each group having a different diary entry: July 24, 1861; June 29, 1862; August 19, 1864; and March 30, 1865. Their task was to identify the main event about the war Mary was describing in each entry, her reaction to the event, and other ideas and attitudes from the diary entry. After the "expert" students return to their teams to teach their parts of the puzzle, a culminating activity such as a quiz could be used to test key facts, or an essay assignment could be used to synthesize information from the parts of the diary.

Another approach appropriate for U.S. history classes using Jigsaw is to have students read quotations and excerpts from various people and sources related to the use of the atomic bomb at the end of World War II. Four "expert" groups could be formed to investigate the arguments for using the atomic bomb, arguments for not using the bomb, impact of the bomb on Hiroshima and its people, and reactions to the bombing of Japan. After the four sections of material are taught to team members, a culminating activity could center on having students assume the role of President Truman, with the benefit of hindsight, and make a reasoned decision as to whether the bomb should have been used to end World War II (Vocke and Capps, 1990).

Jigsaw II   This adaptation of Jigsaw by Slavin (1990) is similar to the original except that students read a common narrative instead of different sections. In Jigsaw II, no students possess unique knowledge; instead, students teach each other common knowledge such as that found in a short story in an English literature class, a chapter from a science text, or a journal article in a government class. Students work in heterogeneous teams as in STAD with "expert" teams formed to learn and teach sections or topics of the narrative. Students in their expert groups answer and discuss questions from worksheets designed by the teacher for the purpose of having students recall important information and relate the content to broader themes. For example, if the students had been reading a chapter of *The Adventures of Huckleberry Finn,* several questions might relate to specific facts associated with Huck's deciding not to turn Jim in to the authorities. Other questions might deal with the broader themes of friendship or slavery that cut across several chapters. Students then return to their original teams to teach what they have learned about their topics. Next they take a quiz that covers all of the topics, and team scores are computed as in STAD. Students' individual-improvement scores are the basis of the team scores, and the high-scoring teams earn the rewards, also as in STAD. As Slavin (1990) summarized, "The key to Jigsaw is interdependence: every student depends on his or her teammates to provide the information he or she needs to do well on the quizzes" (p. 104).

Other Collaborative Methods and Social Dynamics   Present research on collaborative learning, such as that of Howe and colleagues (2000), alerts the teacher to consider the context—social, intellectual, cultural, and historical—within which collaborative methods are placed. Students' values, gender, peer group, and cultural and racial background influences will affect their responses to the cooperative tasks. Their own identities are being renegotiated with the new group structure (Howe, Duchak-Tanner, and Tolmie, 2000). What this means to the teacher is that one should not focus solely on the cognitive skills of cooperative learning but also consider affective influences and the learning environment acting within and on the students.

One simple cooperative-learning strategy that helps students and the teacher get to know each other better (essential when setting up a group) is the scavenger hunt (Golub, 2000). The teacher compiles a list of approximately 30 descriptive items. Each person, including the teacher, takes a copy of the items and moves around the room, talking with classmates to see who fits one of the descriptions.

When a person is identified with an item, that person signs his or her name by that item on the person's sheet. Players must get only one signature beside each item. One person can sign no more than two items on a sheet. At the close of time allotted for the scavenger hunt, students share information stories learned about classmates during the hunt.

The scavenger hunt can include such descriptive items as the following:

1. has never had a cavity
2. has lived in a foreign country
3. subscribes to at least two magazines
4. has gone bungee jumping
5. has an e-mail account
6. is an only child
7. received a traffic ticket
8. has won a contest
9. has an unusual pet (not a cat, dog, bird, or fish)
10. knows the principal's first name

A number of other strategies using group learning activities that build a sense of community can be found in *Making Learning Happen* (Golub, 2000).

Grouping Practices   Although group work enhances many students' learning, not all learning should be relegated to groups. Teachers must analyze content and learning goals carefully to decide when collaborative work is best suited to the learning outcomes. Students respond to variety in instruction and opportunities to work in less competitive situations. Here are additional group structures that can be used for collaborative-learning experiences (Mallery, 2000, pp. 20–21).

Grouping Configurations

Computer Groups	Keyboard operator, observer, and editor work together on the completion of a product.
Review Buddies	Working in pairs, students review each other on a list of student-generated questions about key concepts in the unit.
Editing Partners	One student reads a composition. A small group of classmates listen and make suggestions for revision.
Group Reports	Students choose a topic related to a theme or concept being studied. Students brainstorm questions on the topic, research answers to their questions, and design a reporting format.
Dyads	Working in pairs, students read several pages of text together orally or silently. The recaller paraphrases the text, and the classifier listens and edits the information.

Focus Trios	Working in threes, students summarize what they already know about the content and develop questions to answer during their reading. After reading, students discuss the answers to their questions, clarify content, and summarize their answers.
Problem Solving	Students work collaboratively in small groups on a research project of their choice. They identify a major problem to resolve, sources of information to examine, and format of the final product.
Test Coaches	Small groups of students each review a chapter of a text, identify the major ideas, order the concepts on a graphic organizer, develop three broad questions linking the concepts, share the graphic organizer with the class, and ask the focus questions.
Strategy Teachers and Concept Clarifiers	Working in teams, students practice metacognitive strategies of prediction, drawing inferences, and generating rationales for their opinions.

Peer Tutoring   In cooperative learning, students are arranged to help each other reach certain outcomes identified by the teacher or the group. Peer tutoring does occur as part of the cooperative-learning experience or may be arranged in the classroom following constructivist principles that emphasize student-to-student interaction. Peer tutoring may be thought of as an instructional approach in which learners help one another and learn by teaching (Goodlad and Hirst, 1989).

Selected studies on peer tutoring and teaching show that both the tutor and the tutee benefit from the experience. Waggoner (1971, p. 98) summarized a series of studies that identified the following advantages of peer teaching:

1. Peer teaching can reduce anxiety caused by differences in age, status, and background between students and teachers. A peer tutor may communicate more easily with other students as well.
2. More individualized instruction is possible.
3. The tutor may increase his or her own understanding as well as self-esteem and self-confidence.
4. Peer tutors may be more patient with a slower learner.
5. Peer teaching reinforces learning, may reorganize knowledge more effectively, and increases understanding.

As Pierce (1982) reported, evidence suggests that the tutoring experience can sharpen the understanding and abilities of the tutor, as well as increase a student's self-esteem and positive attitude toward school.

The important point here is that students should realize that we learn from one another and that we all are teachers and learners at different times. Good and Brophy (1994) recommend that teachers model this understanding by pointing out to their students what they—the teachers—have learned from the class. We need to remind students that the goal is their learning, not the comparison of their progress to others in the class.

Good and Brophy (1994, pp. 307–308) provided some guidelines for arranging peer tutoring as follows:

1. The teacher provides guidance to the tutor with suggestions on how to approach the content for that student being tutored and the materials to use.

2. The teacher switches tutoring assignments every couple of weeks.

3. The teacher arranges for all students to be tutors at times so that they feel that everyone can help each other learn.

4. A tutor or tutors may work with a small group. A mixture of students with various talents who use their skills to accomplish a learning objective help students appreciate different approaches and each other's talents. One student may be able to develop metaphors or creative examples while another one can depict information with a diagram.

5. The teacher needs to monitor the tutoring to see when he or she needs to provide some assistance, such as modeling appropriate instructional behaviors for a pair or for the class.

6. Careful planning of pairings is necessary. Best friends may not be able to stay on-task or may become too critical of each other.

7. Tutors are not to test their fellow students to establish a grade for their learning. This responsibility needs to remain with the teacher.

8. Communication to the parents and to the principal is important. Let them know that you are using peer tutoring, what your purpose is, and what you hope the outcomes will be.

APPLICATION for DIVERSE CLASSROOMS

A systematic approach to peer tutoring called Class Wide Peer Tutoring appears to benefit low achievers and students with mild disabilities as an effective instruction intervention to encourage achievement, especially in the areas of reading and mathematics (Greenwood and Delquadri, 1995; Enright and Axelrod, 1995; Fuchs et al., 1997). Class Wide Peer Tutoring involves the entire class in working in tutor–tutee pairs; each pair is part of one of two learning teams. The teacher uses 20 minutes or so a day for tutoring time instead of class time for homework or seatwork. As students are tested on materials and are successful, they win points for their team (Greenwood and Delquadri, 1995).

Another helpful approach for diverse learners is to use reciprocal tutoring to help new immigrant students entering high school. Each new student can be paired with another student who is trained in tutoring and mentoring. The tutors not only work with their tutees on academics but also serve as personal guides and interpreters of the school system and culture (Gartner and Riessman, 1994).

Hints for the Beginning Teacher

Ask a fellow teacher into your classroom to record observations about student involvement in a lesson. For an episode of direct teaching, ask the observer to record interactions between you and the students, your checks for understanding, or students' off-task behaviors. For a cooperative-learning lesson, ask the observer to record instances of positive interdependence.

■ SUMMARY POINT ■

This chapter has focused on two strategies—direct teaching and cooperative learning—whose positive effects on achievement have been studied and documented. These approaches were developed from compensatory education programs in the late 1960s and early 1970s for urban elementary school children but have since been used throughout the country in all school settings and with students of all ages.

Direct teaching is a structured approach that requires sequenced curriculum materials. Direct instruction moves the class along as a group but allows for individual differences in learning through individual practice activities and group work. Cooperative learning, an indirect student-centered strategy, emphasizes improved achievement through collaborative learning with positive group identity.

In the preceding strategies, the cooperative-learning approach is the one most compatible to the climate of the constructivist classroom. By challenging groups to construct their own understandings of concepts and principles through shared group experiences, learning takes on personal meaning. With its solid research base, it has become the most widely used instructional innovation (Clark, Wideman, and Eadie, 1990). Direct instruction, if it creates a dependent role, de-emphasizes student independent thinking by the teacher giving too much explanation and guidance.

Neither of these strategies should be used as the sole approach to instruction. There is no single model for effective instruction. Each has much to offer in presenting strategies for accomplishing particular learning objectives. Teachers' decision making enters in when determining which parts of the curriculum can be accomplished most effectively by using a particular strategy. Beginning teachers need opportunities to instruct various units of the curriculum using these strategies and others to develop a varied teaching repertoire. The more techniques, methods, and strategies the teacher is able to use, the better decisions the teacher can make in choosing appropriate instruction to help each learner understand the curriculum content. Remember, however, that learning takes place only within the learner; the teacher cannot ensure student learning with the best of lesson plans and instructional strategies. The key to student learning is to have students actively involved in meaningful experiences that help them form connections with the knowledge and skills they need to make decisions and build their understanding of the world.

As you choose the instructional strategies for your lessons, you must consider your students and their developmental level, cultural background, academic abilities, special talents, and socioeconomic background. Also, the curriculum content must be considered—the major concepts and skills and their interrelation to other knowledge students are learning. With all these considerations, teachers are continually challenged by the complex decisions they must make concerning instruction.

■ QUESTIONS FOR REFLECTION ■

1. Do you think that the strategies presented in this chapter have a link to student achievement? Why?

2. Considering some of the different approaches to assessing students in cooperative learning, which do you feel is the one you would use in your preferred grade level or subject area?

3. In the cooperative-learning strategy, the teacher has the least control over the class. Would this bother you as a teacher? How would you deal with giving so much control to your students?

4. What advice would you give Millie Blaine about the way she is structuring her next cooperative-learning venture? Is she over-

looking any important step in the preparation process?

5. The direct-teaching approach is widely used in today's classrooms. Is it incompatible with constructivist thinking about instruction? How so?

6. What must the teacher keep in mind as factors to consider when planning instruction? Explain how they may influence the teacher's decision about methods or strategies to use.

7. Which of the instructional strategies in this chapter would you be most comfortable using in your classroom? Explain why. What does this decision tell you about your comfort zone in teaching? What are the advantages and disadvantages?

	ANALYSIS SCALES	
	OCCURRENCE	EFFECTIVENESS

TEACHER _____

OBSERVER _____

CLASS _____

DATE _____

OCCURRENCE	EFFECTIVENESS
1. Not evident	1. Not effective
2. Slightly evident	2. Slightly effective
3. Moderately evident	3. Moderately effective
4. Quite evident	4. Quite effective
N Not applicable	N Not applicable

CATEGORIES	A. OCCURRENCE	B. EFFECTIVENESS
1. Is this a teacher-directed classroom in which the teacher makes decisions about activities and materials and controls students' time in the classroom?		
2. Does the instruction have a stated academic purpose?		
3. Is there considerable interaction between the teacher and students?		
4. Is the amount of off-task time for students kept to a minimum?		
5. Does the teacher have the curriculum divided into small units with skills, process, and concepts identified?		
6. Has the teacher prepared the students for the lesson with review and overview?		
7. Do the students know the objective of the lesson and how it fits in with the unit being studied?		
8. Does the teacher use a variety of approaches to presenting lessons including a. presenting material in small steps? b. presenting outlines when material is complex?		

continued

9. Does the teacher provide time for guided practice with teacher and students working together as a group?		
10. Is there a high frequency of questions and overt student practice?		
11. Does the teacher conduct comprehension checks while involved in the presentation and group practice phase?		
12. Does the teacher give immediate corrective feedback?		
13. Does the teacher reteach when necessary?		
14. Does the teacher provide time for individual practice with evaluation and feedback?		
15. Does the teacher monitor the class during the group practice and independent practice phases?		
16. Does the teacher plan weekly and monthly reviews?		

ANALYSIS SCALES

TEACHER _____

OBSERVER _____

CLASS _____

DATE _____

OCCURRENCE	EFFECTIVENESS
1. Not evident	1. Not effective
2. Slightly evident	2. Slightly effective
3. Moderately evident	3. Moderately effective
4. Quite evident	4. Quite effective
N Not applicable	N Not applicable

CATEGORIES	A. OCCURRENCE	B. EFFECTIVENESS
1. Has the teacher structured the curriculum into units with objectives that can be achieved cooperatively?		
2. Is group collaboration evident in the classroom?		
3. Are students encouraged to learn from one another?		
4. Is there an emphasis in the room on the use of communication and group-process skills?		
5. Is it evident from observing the groups that the following elements have been addressed: a. positive interdependence? b. cooperative learning skills? c. individual accountability for completing tasks? d. promotion of face-to-face interaction?		
6. Does the teacher give feedback on students' progress with group skills as well as progress with academic objectives?		
7. Are students encouraged to self-evaluate their academic and group success?		

■ REFERENCES ■

Aronson, E., Blaney, C., Stephan, C., Sikes, J., and Snapp, M. (1978). *The Jigsaw Classroom.* Beverly Hills, CA: Sage.

Association for Supervision and Curriculum Development. (1999). *ASCD Yearbook.* Alexandria, VA: Author.

Baloche, L. (1998). *The Cooperative Classroom: Empowering Learning.* Upper Saddle River, NJ: Prentice Hall.

Barnes, S. (1981). *Synthesis of Selected Research on Teaching Findings.* Austin, TX: Research and Development Center for Teacher Education, University of Texas.

Berliner, D. (1982). "Should teachers be expected to learn and use direct instruction?" *ASCD Update, 24,* 5.

Cawelti, G. (Ed.). (1995). *Handbook of Research on Improving Student Achievement.* Arlington, VA: Educational Research Service.

Clark, J., Wideman, R., and Eadie, S. (1990). *Together We Learn.* Toronto: Prentice Hall.

Cohen, E. (1994). *Designing Group Work* (2nd ed.). New York: Teachers College Press.

Condon, D., and Maggs, A. (1986). "Direct instruction research: An international focus." *International Journal of Special Education, 1,* 35–47.

Costa, A. (Ed.) (1991). *Developing Minds: A Resource Book for Teaching Thinking.* Alexandria, VA: Association for Supervision and Curriculum Development.

Cruickshank, D. (1990). *Research that Informs Teachers and Teacher Educators.* Bloomington, IN: Phi Delta Kappa Educational Foundation.

Davidson, N., and Worsham, T. (1992). *Enhancing Thinking through Cooperative Learning.* New York: Teachers College Press.

Dilworth, M., and Brown, C. (2001). "Consider the difference: Teaching and learning in culturally rich schools." In V. Richardson (Ed.), *Handbook of Research on Teaching* (4th ed.). Washington, DC: American Educational Research Association.

Ellis, A., and Fouts, J. (1993). *Research and Educational Innovations.* Princeton Junction, NJ: Eye on Education.

Enright, S., and Axelrod, S. (1995). "Peer-tutoring: Applied behavior analysis working in the classroom." *School Psychology Quarterly, 10*(1), 29–40.

Fitzgerald, J. (1995). "English-as-a-second-language-learners' cognitive reading processes: A review in the United States." *Review of Educational Research, 65*(2), 145–190.

Fitzpatrick, K. (1982). "The effect of a secondary classroom management training program on teacher and student behavior." Paper presented at the annual meeting of the American Educational Research Association, New York.

Fuchs, D., Fuchs, S., Mathes, P., and Simmons, D. (1997). "Peer-assisted learning strategies: Making classrooms more responsive to diversity." *American Educational Research Journal, 34*(1), 174–206.

Gartner, A., and Riessman, F. (1994). "Tutoring helps those who give, those who receive." *Educational Leadership, 52*(3), 58–60.

Gelder, A., and Maggs, A. (1983). "Direct instruction microcomputing in primary schools: Manipulation of critical instructional variables." *Research in Science and Technology Education, 1,* 221–238.

Gettinger, M. (1986). "Issues and trends in academic engaged time of students." *Special Services in the School, 2,* 1–17.

Golub, J. (2000). *Making Learning Happen.* Portsmouth, NH: Boynton/ Cook.

Good, T. (1982). *Classroom Research: What We Know and What We Need to Know.* Austin, TX: Research and Development Center for Teacher Education, University of Texas.

Good, T., and Brophy, J. (1986). "School effects." In M. Wittrock (Ed.), *Handbook of Research on Teaching* (3rd ed.). New York: Macmillan.

Good, T., and Brophy, J. (1994). *Looking in Classrooms.* (6th ed.). New York: HarperCollins.

Good, T., and Brophy, J. (2000). *Looking in Classrooms* (8th ed.). New York: Addison Wesley Longman.

Good, T., Grouws, D., and Ebmeier, H. (1983). *Active Mathematics Teaching.* White Plains, NY: Longman.

Goodlad, S., and Hirst, B. (1989). *Peer Tutoring.* London: Kogan/Page.

Goor, M., and Schwenn, J. (1993). "Accommodating diversity and disability with cooperative learning." *Intervention in School and Clinic, 29*(1), 6–16.

Greenwood, C., and Delquadri, J. (1995). "Class wide Peer Tutoring and the prevention of school failure." *Journal of Applied Behavior Analysis, 39*(4), 21–25.

Harris, M., Milich, R., and McAninch, C. (1998). "Expectancy effects and peer rejection." In J. Brophy (Ed.), *Advances in Research on Teaching.* Greenwich, CT: JAI Press.

Howe, C., Duchak-Tanner, V., and Tolmie, A. (2000). "Co-ordinating support for conceptual and procedural learning in science." In R. Joiner, K. Littleton, D. Faulkner, and D. Miell (Eds.), *Rethinking Collaborative Learning*. London, New York: Free Association Books.

Hunter, M. (1994). *Enhancing Teaching*. New York: Macmillan.

Hunter, M., and Russell, D. (1981). "Planning for effective instruction: Lesson design." In *Increasing Your Teaching Effectiveness*. Palo Alto, CA: Learning Institute.

Johnson, D., and Johnson, R. (1999). *Learning Together and Alone: Cooperative, Competitive, and Individualistic Learning*. (5th ed.) Boston: Allyn & Bacon.

Johnson, D., Johnson, R., and Holubec, E. (1990). *Circles of Learning: Cooperation in the Classroom*. Edina, MN: Interaction.

Johnson, D., Johnson, R., Holubec, E., and Roy, P. (1984/1990). *Circles of Learning: Cooperation in the Classroom*. Alexandria, VA: Association for Supervision and Curriculum Development.

Johnson, D., Johnson, R., and Smith, K. (1991). *Active Learning: Cooperation in the College Classroom*. Edina, MN: Interaction.

Johnson, R., and Johnson, D. (1981). "Building friendships between handicapped and nonhandicapped students: Effects of cooperative and individualistic instruction." *American Educational Research Journal, 18*(4), 415–423.

Johnson, R., and Johnson, D. (1989). *Cooperation and Competition: Theory and Research*. Edina, MN: Interaction.

Joyce, B., and Weil, M., with Calhoun, E. (2000). *Models of Teaching* (6th ed.). Boston: Allyn & Bacon.

Kagan, S. (1992). *Cooperative Learning*. San Juan Capistrano, CA: Resources for Teachers.

Kagan, S., Zahn, G., Widaman, K., Schwarzwald, J., and Tyrrell, G. (1985). "Classroom structural bias: Impact of cooperative and competitive individuals and groups." In R. Slavin, S. Sharan, S. Kagan, R. Hertz-Lazarowitz, C. Webb, and R. Schmuch (Eds.), *Learning to Cooperate*. New York: Plenum.

Lewis, R., and Doorlag, D. (1991). *Teaching Special Students in the Mainstream*. New York: Merrill/Macmillan.

Mallery, A. (2000). *Creating a Catalyst for Thinking*. Boston: Allyn & Bacon.

McCaslin, M., and Good, T. (1992). "Compliant Cognition: The misalliance of management and instruction goals in current school reform." *Educational Researcher, 21*, 4–17.

Olson, J., and Platt, J. (1992). *Teaching Children and Adolescents with Special Needs*. Columbus, OH: Merrill/Macmillan.

Ortiz, A., and Wilkinson, C. (1989). "Adapting IEPs for limited English proficient students." *Academic Therapy, 24*, 555–568.

Parrenas, C., and Parrenas, F. (1993). "Cooperative learning, multicultural functioning, and student achievement." In L. Malave (Ed.), *Annual Conference Journal of the National Association for Bilingual Education Conferences*. National Association for Bilingual Education. (ERIC Document Reproduction Service No. ED 360 877).

Peterson, P., and Walberg, H. (Eds.). (1979). *Research on Teaching: Concepts, Findings and Implications*. Berkeley, CA: McCutchan.

Pierce, M. (1982, April 13). "Partner learning: Concept and rationale." Paper presented at 60th CEC Conference, Houston, TX.

Putnam, J. (Ed.). (1993). *Cooperative Learning and Strategies for Inclusion*. Baltimore: Paul H. Brookes.

Rosenshine, B. (1979). "Content, time, and direct instruction." In P. Peterson and H. Walberg (Eds.), *Research on Teaching: Concepts, Findings, and Implications*. Berkeley, CA: McCutchan.

Rosenshine, B. (1983). "Teaching functions in instructional programs." *Elementary School Journal, 83*(4), 335–351.

Rosenshine, B., and Stevens, R. (1986). "Teaching functions." In M. Wittrock (Ed.), *Handbook of Research on Teaching* (3rd ed.). New York: Macmillan.

Sharon, S., and Sharon, Y. (1976). *Small-Group Teaching*. Englewood Cliffs, NJ: Educational Technology Publications.

Slavin, R. (1989). "Students at risk of school failure: The problem and its dimensions." In R. Slavin, N. Karweit, and N. Madden (Eds.), *Effective Programs for Students at Risk*. Boston: Allyn & Bacon.

Slavin, R. (1990a). *Cooperative Learning* (2nd ed.). Boston: Allyn & Bacon.

Slavin, R. (1990b). "Achievement effects of ability grouping in secondary schools: A best evidence synthesis." *Review of Educational Research, 60*, 471–499.

Slavin, R. E. (1991). "Synthesis of research on cooperative learning." *Educational Leadership, 48*, 71–82.

Slavin, R. E. (1995). *Cooperative Learning: Theory, Research, and Practice* (2nd ed.). Boston: Allyn & Bacon.

Soar, R. (1973). *Follow through Classroom Process Measurement and Pupil Growth*. Gainesville, FL: University of Florida, Institute for Development of Human Resources.

Solomon, D., and Kendall, A. (1979). *Children in Classrooms: An Investigation of Person–Environment Interaction.* New York: Praeger.

Sousa, D. (1995). *How the Brain Learns.* Reston, VA: National Association of Secondary Principals.

Stallings, J. (1987). "For whom and how long is the Hunter-based model appropriate? Response to Robbins and Wolfe." *Educational Leadership, 44,* 62–63.

Stallings, J., and Kaskowitz, D. (1974). "Follow through classroom observation evaluation, 1972–1973" (SRI Project URU\M7370, Stanford, CA: Stanford Research Institution). In M. Wittrock (Ed.), (1986), *Handbook of Research on Teaching* (3rd ed.). New York: Macmillan.

Stallings, J., and Stipek, D. (1986). "Research on early childhood and elementary school teaching programs." In M. Wittrock (Ed.), *Handbook of Research on Teaching* (3rd ed.). New York: Macmillan.

Sudzina, M., and Douvre, S. (1993). "Using cooperative learning to teach 'at risk' students." Paper presented at the annual meeting of the Association of Teacher Educators, Los Angeles, CA. (ERIC Document Reproduction Service No. ED 355 221).

Tateyamo-Sniezek, K. (1990). "Cooperative learning: Does it improve the academic achievement of students with handicaps?" *Exceptional Children, 56,* 426–437.

Teddlie, C., Kirby, P., and Stringfield, S. (1989). "Effective versus ineffective schools: Observable differences in the classroom." *American Journal of Education, 97,* 221–236.

Tomlinson, C., Moon, T., and Callahan, C. (1997). "Use of cooperative learning at the middle school level: Insights from a national survey." *Research in Middle Level Education, 20*(4), 37–55.

Vocke, D. E., and Capps, K. (1990, November). "Cooperative learning: Why and where in the American history curriculum." Paper presented at the Annual Conference of the National Council for the Social Studies, Anaheim, CA.

Waggoner, K. (1971). "Higher math in lower school." *Yale Alumni Magazine, 34*(9), 24–25.

Wang, M., Haertel, G., and Walberg, H. (1993). "What helps students learn?" *Educational Leadership, 51*(4), 74–79.

Whicker, K., and Bol, L. (1997). "Cooperative learning in the secondary mathematics classroom." *Journal of Educational Research, 91*(1), 42–48.

Wilen, W. (1991, February). Interview with Kathryn L. Wilen, mathematics teacher, Davey Junior High School, Kent, Ohio.

9

Differentiated Instruction: Meeting Special Needs of Students

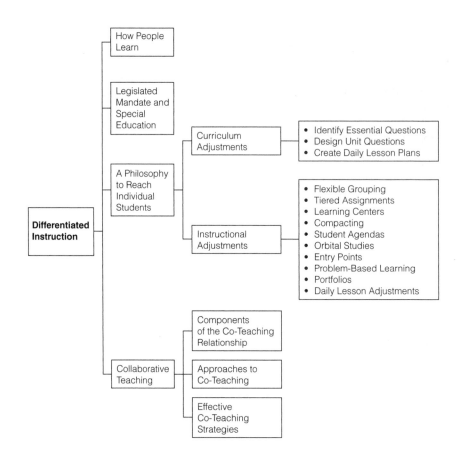

In a comic strip peek into a typical American living room, a young boy comforts his agitated father who is staring at a report card. "Don't worry about my being at the bottom of the class, Dad," says the boy. "They teach the same at both ends." This one-size-fits-all treatment of students characterizes far too many classrooms and schools in our country. Students are different from one another; they differ in size, age, interests, ability, background, and experience. Yet, as Gregory and Chapman (2002) put it:

> . . . *for years we have planned "The Lesson" and taught it to all, knowing that we were boring some and losing others because they were not ready for that learning. Still we expect students to adjust to the learning when the learning should really be adjusted to the learner. (p. x)*

Over one hundred years ago, the one-room schoolhouse was the teacher's domain. Some students came from homes with no books while others came already reading. These same children of all ages working in one room came with different reasons for learning. Each student had his or her own interests, motivations, background, parental support, and so forth. Except for the broad age differences, today's teacher finds the same challenges. We believe that the past century has provided us with approaches for addressing these individual differences and needs. We now know enough about modifications in the curriculum, in instruction, and in evaluation, that today's teacher should be prepared to meet the needs of individual learners in a classroom with the same spectrum of talent, strengths, interests, and weaknesses present in the one-room schoolhouse over one hundred years ago.

■ OVERVIEW

One decision that many new teachers find especially challenging has to do with differentiated instruction. When questions like "How can I challenge this obviously gifted student?" and "What can I do with these two students on IEPs in my regular education classroom?" are asked without a solid understanding of how to modify the curriculum and adapt instruction, the teacher may resort to "teaching the same at both ends." Unless the teacher is aware of the many resources available to help in differentiating instruction, decisions about *what* to teach and *how* to do it may become nagging doubts until, finally, he or she may give in to the "one-size-fits-all" mentality of many classrooms.

The ideas and suggestions found in previous chapters certainly provide a solid basis for teaching in the secondary classroom. The aim of this chapter is to help new and experienced teachers construct a framework for decision making about differentiated instruction. Background information about laws regulating how schools must serve students with special needs will be provided. Current theory and research about differentiated instruction will be reviewed. Finally, the chapter will address both ends of the continuum of student needs, from the student with specific academic weaknesses to the gifted student. Practical suggestions for modifying and adapting the curriculum, instruction, and evaluation will be provided as well.

SCENARIO

Bill Anders, a high school English teacher, was entering his second year of teaching. In the previous year, his schedule of classes included two ninth-grade general (i.e., low-track) and three eleventh-grade college-prep English classes. He had seen definite academic and behavioral differences between the two groups of students. The freshmen were, well, freshmen. On any given day, they demonstrated the capacity to behave like children and, in the same class period, like young adults. Because this general-level course tended to attract lower-tracked students, the majority of the students shared similar reading and writing abilities. In one of Bill's two ninth-grade classes, two students definitely stood out. They not only had strong reading comprehension skills, but also wrote at higher levels. Their paragraphs were developed with very few errors in mechanics. Bill could always count on these two students to set the standard for an A in each assignment. He enjoyed their interest in the class novels and felt neglectful when he had to spend much of their class time going over plot, setting, character development, and the like with the rest of his struggling readers. On some days, Bill let these two "bright stars" go to the library during book discussions so they could use the computers or read other material. At the end of the year, Bill recommended to the students and their parents that they enroll in college-prep English classes during their sophomore year.

Bill's eleventh-grade course was another story altogether. In one of the three classes, he had four students on IEPs (individual education plans) and in another class he had three students on IEPs. Bill had learned about IEPs in his teaching-preparation courses so he knew to consult with the school support staff (counselors, psychologists, and special education teachers). For five of the

seven students, Bill felt confident that the assignments he sent to the Learning Disorder (LD) tutor helped meet the goals in these students' IEPs. Each of these five students met daily with a tutor for an entire class period. Once a week, the tutor would meet with Bill during his planning period to go over each student's progress and to put together a tutorial folder of review work and remedial activities. Bill also made sure the tutor had copies of the class literature anthology, the grammar book, the vocabulary workbook, and all the novels his students were required to read.

Bill did not feel so secure about the support he provided to the other two juniors on IEPs. They did not work with a tutor and Bill often felt frustrated in trying to meet their academic needs. Both students struggled with reading rate and comprehension; their writing was poor in both mechanics and content. Bill and the two students tried to meet at various times throughout the year, at lunch and before and after school, but quite often the meetings never took place. Either the students would have other commitments such as athletic practices or jobs, or Bill had meetings to attend. By the end of the school year, each of the students barely passed the course. Bill knew full well that, too often, he had failed to meet their needs.

This new school year would, hopefully, be different for Bill and his next group of students. Bill's course load had changed slightly. This year he would have one general ninth-grade, two college-prep tenth-grade, and two college-prep eleventh-grade English classes. Two significant changes that had occurred gave Bill hope about meeting the needs of all his students, regardless of abilities. First, the high school Special Education Department had created collaborative-teaching roles for inclusive classrooms. Instead of relying solely on tutoring, students on IEPs could work with special education teachers within the regular education classroom. Bill felt that the addition of daily support would also help the students who were not on IEPs. The other change this year was that, over the summer, Bill had attended a workshop on differentiated instruction at a local university. That one-week workshop had been well worth the time and the money because Bill learned about being an effective team-teaching member. A panel of co-teachers—that is, special education and regular education teachers who had worked together in the same classrooms—came in one morning of the workshop and offered practical suggestions about inclusion. For example, Bill learned five different ways that he and his co-teacher could present a lesson, depending on the content and the students. Bill also learned some ways to modify the language arts curriculum to meet the needs of his special education students.

A pleasant surprise in the workshop was the information on enriching the learning of gifted students in the regular classroom. Before the workshop, Bill had assumed that gifted students would be found only in the advanced-track of classes. Once he learned that students can be gifted in many different ways, Bill reflected on the students he had met in his student teaching and in his first year on the job who were, in fact, gifted and talented and, unfortunately, bored and unchallenged in his classroom. The workshop provided Bill with some practical strategies for challenging gifted students and enriching their learning. Bill spent part of the summer after the workshop designing independent study projects to be used in three of the units in his ninth-grade class and four of the units in his eleventh-grade class. He also created some learning contract forms that he would later tailor to individual students in all of his classes. Bill was particularly excited about something called "curriculum compacting," which involved pretesting fundamental skills and designing enriching alternative activities.

Bill knows that he has much to learn about differentiated instruction. He also knows that, because he is discovering new resources and supports, the one size he had used before to plan, to teach, and to evaluate, would expand some-day into a more individualized, custom-made fit.

■ RESEARCH AND THEORETICAL BASE

At the very beginning of this book, *pedagogy* was defined in Chapter 1 as a "rational approach to teaching" that should undergird a teacher's decision making. This rational approach to teaching rests on a foundation of scholarly research that informs educators as they go about the work of teaching. We know, for example, in-depth details about how people learn. The contributions of educational psychologists and cognitive psychologists abound. Much of this research has led to the current emphasis on constructivist beliefs and practices. Let us briefly examine some key findings:

- Learners construct their own meaning from the inside rather than processing it and internalizing it as it is presented to them by teachers (Dewey, 1938; Piaget, 1952; and Vygotsky, 1962).
- Learning styles in students consist of differences in cognitive styles, receptive styles, affective styles, attention styles, and physiological styles (Keefe, 1987).
- Understanding is multifaceted. To reduce understanding of a concept, a skill, and the like, renders learning to an incomplete and immature state (Wiggins and McTighe, 1998).
- Human learning is a social activity involving cooperation, feedback, and input (Dewey, 1938; Vygotsky, 1962).
- Lesson components (e.g., lecture content, activities, assignments, etc.) that are too difficult for a student lead to frustration and limit the amount and the level of learning that takes place (Howard, 1994; Vygotsky, 1962, in Tomlinson, 2001).
- Failure to learn is directly linked to giving students the wrong work to do (Schlechty, 2001).
- Learning is positively impacted by climate. An enriched learning climate is not created "only by materials but also by the complexity and variety of tasks and challenges and feedback" (Caine and Caine, 1997; Jensen, 1998, in Gregory and Chapman, 2002, p. 15).
- Intelligence is not a single thing; it is multifaceted (Sternberg, Thorndike, and Gardner in Tomlinson, 1999).

- Varied and vigorous learning changes the physiology of the brain (Caine and Caine, 1997; Sylvester, 1995, in Tomlinson, 1999).

- The human brain resists meaninglessness and seeks meaningful patterns. Meaning is highlighted by teachers who connect old learning to new learning and who design lessons with high interest and relevance (Tomlinson, 1999).

- Moderate challenges stimulate the human brain while simple tasks suppress thinking and problem solving (Howard, 1994; Vygotsky, 1962).

To a degree, the classroom teacher can choose how to respond to this research about how humans learn. Unfortunately, many teachers have responded by ignoring these findings and, instead, opt to plow ahead with the one-size-fits-all approach to teaching. The classroom teacher does *not* have complete freedom of choice, however, when it comes to teaching students with special needs. According to Dwyer (in Telzrow and Tankersley, 2000), currently in our public schools, "Approximately 6 million children in the United States receive special education and related services each year. Their entitlement to a free appropriate public education (FAPE) was the result of parent efforts and court decisions that moved Congress to action and in 1975 culminated in P.L. 94-142, subsequently renamed the Individuals with Disabilities Education Act (IDEA)" (p. xi). Since 1975, this legislation has been amended and expanded a number of times. One outcome of this legislation that affects nearly all teachers has to do with a process called *inclusive education.* IDEA requires that children with identified special education and related-services needs "be placed in the general educational environment unless the school or institution can demonstrate that the education of the individual student with a disability cannot" be satisfactorily achieved (Fisher, Sax, and Pumpian, 1999, p. 10). This principle is known as the "least restrictive environment" (LRE) for special education students. The implications for the regular (or general) education teacher vary according to student needs. Students who will benefit from learning in a regular education classroom tend to receive services either through an *inclusive classroom model* or through a collaboration between the regular education teacher and special education providers such as a special education teacher, a tutor, a speech therapist, and a work/study coordinator.

Collaborative teaching in an inclusive classroom requires instructional approaches that many new teachers have never learned or experienced. Lombardo (2000) contends that inclusive classrooms often "shock teachers who historically have worked solo, keeping tabs on their own students and controlling the flow of the lessons without any outside help" (p. 1). Some teachers may find themselves working in an *inclusive school setting* in which co-teaching with a special education teacher is not used as much as are curriculum and instructional adaptations. These adaptations include approaches such as modifying length of assignments, prioritizing lesson objectives, and offering assistance on tests. Other adaptations will be described in detail in the following section, Application to Practice. Practical suggestions for making collaborative teaching work in an inclusive classroom will also be covered.

Reaching and teaching all learners, as stated earlier, is both an option and a legislated mandate. Classroom teachers are compelled by federal law to meet the needs of students with specifically identified special needs. But what about those other millions of students who do not have IEPs? What about the student who struggles with his reading? What about the learner who is bored in her biology class because she has already read much of the material on her own? No laws compel the teacher to alter instruction or modify the curriculum in most of these cases. What does force us to change how and what we teach is a sense of professional responsibility to teach each of our students. The term in use today that applies to teachers' attempts at meeting the diverse needs of their students is *differentiated instruction.*

According to Gregory and Chapman (2002), differentiated instruction "is a philosophy that enables teachers to plan strategically in order to reach the needs of the diverse learners in classrooms today" (p. x). Heacox (2002) claims that differentiated instruction is "not a new trend. It is based on best practices in education. It puts students at the center of teaching and learning. It lets their learning needs direct your instructional planning" (p. 1). The reader should be reminded of the discussion in Chapter 4 about constructivism or teaching for understanding or active learning. Differentiated instruction is a constructivist approach put to use with diverse learners.

This idea of putting students "at the center of teaching and learning" is echoed in Tomlinson's (2001) research. "At its most basic level," she writes, "differentiating instruction means 'shaking up' what goes on in the classroom so that students have multiple options for taking in information, making sense of ideas, and expressing what they learn" (p. 1). Most classroom teachers (as well as students and their parents) have experienced undifferentiated instruction throughout their school years. For this reason, Tomlinson begins her treatment on differentiated instruction by clearing up some misconceptions about what happens when teachers try to solve the problems of one-size-fits-all teaching. Differentiated instruction is *not* the "individualized instruction" of the 1970s nor does it occur in a chaotic, out-of-control classroom environment. Tomlinson continues clearing up some misperceptions about differentiated instruction by claiming that it is *not* "just another way to provide homogeneous grouping." Finally differentiated instruction is *not* just "tailoring the same suit of clothes." Superficial modifications such as grading on effort or letting students choose which questions they will answer on a test are simply not enough (pp. 2–3).

In contrast to these mistaken notions of what differentiated instruction is, Tomlinson (2001) describes this new way of thinking about teaching and learning:

- Differentiated instruction is *proactive.*

  Instead of planning a single approach for all students and then "reactively trying to adjust the plans when it becomes apparent that the lesson is not working for some of the learners for whom it was intended," the teacher plans a variety of approaches. (pp. 3–4)

- Differentiated instruction is more *qualitative* than quantitative.

  Varying the amount of work given to students (e.g., one book instead of two; a seven-page report instead of ten pages) is a way to meet some students' needs.

But merely "adjusting the *quantity* of an assignment will generally be less effective than adjusting the *nature* of the assignment." (p. 4)

- Differentiated instruction is *rooted in assessment*.

  In a differentiated classroom, assessment is not an end-of-the-unit event. Rather, assessment is an ongoing process to determine individual students' needs throughout the unit of instruction. The teacher uses multiple methods of assessment to monitor and adjust instruction including strategies such as anecdotal record keeping, journal entries, observations, and individual conferences. (p. 4)

- Differentiated instruction provides *multiple approaches* to content, process, and product.

  Teachers in differentiated classrooms offer different approaches "to *what* students learn, *how* they learn it, and how they *demonstrate what they've learned*. All these different approaches have the common goal of enhancing student learning. (pp. 4–5)

- Differentiated instruction is *student centered*.

  At the secondary level, it is very tempting to equate teaching with telling. Lecturing to a large group of learners, even with sophisticated technology, is still lecturing and, except for a handful of students, not very engaging. In a differentiated classroom, the teacher strives for active, meaningful engagement for all students. (p. 5)

- Differentiated instruction is *a blend* of whole-class, group, and individual instruction.

  All teaching is highly contextual; there are times when whole-class instruction is more effective than small-group or individual instruction. In a differentiated classroom, student grouping is a fluid matter and depends on such factors as content, student ability, and time. (p. 5)

The following section, Application to Practice, covers specific differentiated instructional strategies. What is important to remember in this review is that differentiated instruction is a way of meeting the needs of all students, particularly those at either end of the ability continuum. Much of this discussion about legal mandates and pedagogical approaches has focused on the needs of students who struggle in our classrooms. At the other end of the ability continuum are those students who have mastered or nearly mastered the unit and/or lesson objectives the teacher has planned. Many times, these students come into their classes having already learned the material. They may have taken an early interest in the subject, or perhaps they had been in a previous class in which the material was taught. These students deserve to be engaged and challenged. Differentiated instruction is an effective way to meet their needs.

One special population of learners with high abilities is the gifted and talented students. Too often, these students become bored in class and either tune out or become noticeably frustrated. Teachers do not always know how to challenge these learners; often, teachers do not even know how to identify them. Identification of gifted students is complicated by the erroneous assumption that all high-achieving students are gifted and/or that all gifted students are high achievers. According to Heacox (2002),

> To appropriately differentiate instruction for gifted learners, it's important to understand this distinction. Giftedness reflects innate, advanced aptitudes that may or may not emerge as exceptional academic talent over time. In other words, you can be gifted but not talented. High-achieving students know what it takes to be successful in school and are willing to put in the time and effort. Those students who are gifted underachievers may be unable to achieve academic goals because of learning differences or difficulties. They may also be unwilling to commit the time and effort necessary for school success. (p. 135)

Many of the strategies identified in the next section have been developed by experts such as Susan Winebrenner (1992), whose work in curriculum compacting and learning contracts is highly regarded in the area of gifted education. It is important to note that these strategies may be effectively used with gifted learners as well as with many high achievers. The focus is on the student regardless of his or her label. In a student-centered environment, the teacher's responsibility "is not to teach the *content*. A teacher's responsibility is to teach the *students*, and to make sure that all students learn new content every day" (Winebrenner, 1992, p. 1).

■ APPLICATION TO PRACTICE

Curriculum Adjustments

What we teach in a unit of instruction can be adjusted to meet the needs of the struggling student. Curriculum adjustment does *not* mean that the teacher "waters down" the content or leaves gaps in the sequence of learning objectives. A critical characteristic of differentiated instruction is that it is relevant—that is, "it focuses on essential learning: those curricular objectives that are fundamental, significant, and most important for students to grasp" (Heacox, 2002, p. 53). After a few years in the classroom, teachers often develop favorite units, projects, and activities. But unless the objectives in these lessons are directly aligned with the district's curricular goals, the teacher needs to put these favorites aside.

The first task in adjusting curriculum is for the teacher to "identify the essential concepts and principles" of the curriculum or subject (Heacox, 2002, p. 53). Asking essential questions helps to "frame" a course and, consequently, enables the teacher to "sort the crucial content from the fluff—the learning activities that take the focus away from what is most important for students to know, understand, and do" (p. 53). Wiggins and McTighe's (1998) work, *Understanding by Design,* is an excellent source for teachers who want to learn more about "uncovering the important ideas at the heart of each subject" (p. 28). Essential questions, according to Wiggins and McTighe, are characterized by what they do:

- Go to the heart of a discipline.
- Recur naturally throughout one's learning and in the history of a field.
- Raise other important questions.

- Have no obvious "right" answers.
- Are deliberately framed to provoke and sustain student interest. (pp. 29–30)

Examples of essential questions are:

- History: "Is U.S. history a history of progress?"
- Life Science: "How does an organism's structure enable it to survive in its environment?"
- Health: "What is healthy eating?"
- Literature: "What makes a 'great' book?"
- Art: "How does art reflect the time and the society it springs from?"
- Foreign Language: "What distinguishes a fluent foreigner from a native speaker?"
- Mathematics: "When is the 'correct' answer not the best solution?"
- Writing: "How can writing lead to self-discovery?"

Once the teacher creates the essential questions for the subject (usually four or five essential questions suffice), unit questions are designed. Heacox (2002) claims that the purpose of unit questions is to "provide specific content and facts about essential questions. They add depth and specificity" (p. 55). The distinction between essential questions and unit questions is that essential questions are larger concepts that the teacher returns to throughout the year and throughout different topics. Unit questions are "subsets of essential questions that address specific content and skills" (p. 55). Not every essential question has to be addressed in each unit; not every essential question will have only one unit question (p. 56). Some examples of essential questions with their related unit questions follow.

From Life Science (Heacox, 2002, p. 55)

Essential Questions:

1. What are living organisms?
2. What are some characteristics of living organisms?
3. How are living organisms classified in science?
4. What are common laws or principles of living organisms?
5. What are common cycles or patterns of living organisms?

UNIT: AMPHIBIANS

Unit Questions:

1. What are the characteristics of amphibians?
2. What animals are included in the class *Amphibia*?
3. Which laws or principles of living organisms govern the life cycle of amphibians?
4. Which cycles or patterns of living organisms do amphibians follow?

From Literature (Wiggins and McTighe, 1998, p. 31)

Essential Question:

Must a story have a moral, heroes, and villains?

UNIT: *HUCKLEBERRY FINN*

Unit Questions:

1. What is the moral of the story of Huck Finn?
2. Is Huck Finn a hero?
3. Who are the villains in the story of Huck Finn? Why are they considered villains?

From Mathematics (Heacox, 2002, p. 60)

Essential Questions:

1. What ways of thinking are used in mathematics?
2. How are mathematical thinkers problem solvers and problem posers?
3. What are essential tools for mathematics?
4. How is mathematical knowledge useful in everyday life?

UNIT: INTRODUCTION TO GEOMETRY

Unit Questions:

1. What is geometric thinking?
2. What is geometric problem solving?
3. How are algorithms used to describe shapes?
4. How do Escher-like figures represent geometric concepts?
5. How is geometry represented in shadow and light?

Creating essential questions and unit questions takes place in the planning phase of teaching. As you recall from Chapter 5, once unit goals are developed, the teacher next creates objectives for daily lesson plans. This linear process of deciding *what* to teach, framed within the guidelines of state and local standards, should help the teacher eliminate the "nice-to-knows" from the "need-to-knows." The essential and unit questions should then be used to differentiate instruction.

Let's revisit the essential and unit questions from the *Huckleberry Finn* unit in a literature class. As the teacher begins to make decisions about lesson activities, assignments, projects, and so on, he or she will keep the two sets of questions foremost in mind. At the end of the course (i.e., at the end of the semester or the end of the year), *all* the students should be able to argue if a story must have a moral. *How* the students may learn this will depend on their individual needs, backgrounds, interests, and skills. Similarly, at the end of the unit, *all* the students should be able to explain the moral of the story of Huck Finn. Again, *how* the students demonstrate this understanding will be highly individualized. Some students who struggle with language arts, particularly reading comprehension and writing, may demonstrate their understanding of the novel's moral in a conference with the teacher. Other students with highly developed language arts skills may demonstrate this same understanding in a debate, an allegory, or a comparison/contrast of Twain's major works.

Adjusting the curriculum is the process of identifying "the essential concepts and principles of your curriculum or subject" (Heacox, 2002, p. 53). Once you are certain about what all students should know, you can then begin the process of differentiating your instruction.

■ WEBSITE RESOURCE ■

The Association for Supervision and Curriculum Development (ASCD) offers tutorials in its professional development section on a variety of topics including differentiated instruction. Text and videos are presented including application of differentiated instruction in high school and elementary classrooms at

www.ascd.org/pdi/demo/dikffinstr/ differentiated1.html.

Included are comments from teachers, references, and other resources readily available to explore more in-depth.

Instructional Adjustments

Some of the most creative work teachers can do is designing instruction. Making decisions about *how* students will learn content is part of the art of teaching. The range of colors on the teacher-artist's palette is substantially enlarged when a differentiated instructional approach is used. For instance, a high school health teacher may have students in his tenth-grade class with reading levels ranging from fourth grade to post–high school. The teacher uses mixed-ability grouping to conduct research on different mental illnesses by gathering information from materials at each individual student's own reading level. Using a Jigsaw cooperative-learning method (see Chapter 8), the groups split up into mental illness "expert" groups. The original groups reconvene with every member teaching the other group members about each mental illness. Lower-ability students teach higher-ability students. Each student finds and reads research material at his or her own level. Students hold each other accountable for content mastery and learning pace.

This scenario demonstrates only two ways a teacher can differentiate instruction—mixed-ability grouping and variety of reading texts. Classroom teachers have various options to differentiate instruction in their classrooms.

1. *Flexible instructional grouping*—Students' learning needs direct the size and makeup of each group. These groups are not used in every lesson, and each

group's activity time "varies according to the complexity of the task" (Heacox, 2002, p. 85). Students meet in small groups with the teacher for "additional instruction or extended learning experiences" (p. 85). In a high school English class, for example, during a research paper unit, the teacher may spend part of the class period working with a more advanced group on evaluating electronic data sources and then work with a lower-level group on proper paraphrasing.

2. *Tiered assignments*—Students' learning needs help the teacher decide which learning tasks should be demonstrated by which students. According to Heacox (2002), teachers can tier assignments based on:
   - challenge level (using Bloom's taxonomy)
   - complexity (from least complex to most complex presentation of learning)
   - resources (using materials at various reading levels and complexity of content)
   - process (e.g., all students write a report but some use basic reference materials while others use more advanced research skills like interviewing)
   - product (students demonstrate their mastery of learning goals through differentiated products such as skits, visual displays, speeches, etc.)

3. *Learning centers or stations*—At the secondary level, stations or "challenge centers" can be used to differentiate instruction by setting up various areas in the classroom where different groups or individuals work on different tasks at the same time (Tomlinson, 1999). Gregory and Chapman (2002) describe a high school history teacher's use of "choice centers." The goal for each group was to collect information about different civilizations from a variety of sources and to present their discoveries to the rest of the class. The teacher planned detailed directions and rubrics for this unit and then set up ancient civilization learning centers that included the students' choice of China, Japan, Africa, the Middle East, Southeast Asia, and the Pacific (pp. 107–108).

4. *Compacting*—Compacting is the process of selecting learning objectives at the correct level of difficulty. Lesson objectives can be turned into pre-assessment questions, and those students who have already mastered the objectives do not have to continue working on what they already know. By documenting competencies, students, in essence, "buy time" to work on more challenging activities like a project or special investigation (Tomlinson, 1999; Winebrenner, 1992).

5. *Student agendas*—A student's agenda is "a personalized list of tasks that a particular student must complete in a specified time" (Tomlinson, 1999, p. 66). In secondary blocked classrooms, teachers usually select the first part of the block for students to work on their agenda items. In other classes, agendas can be used once a week or "as anchored activities when students complete other assigned work" (p. 66). For example, in an English class, agenda items could include vocabulary work, essay interpretations, paraphrasing exercises, and sustained silent reading. During the time that students work on their agendas, teachers can work with individuals or small groups who need instruction or monitoring.

6. *Orbital studies*—Orbital studies are independent investigations that revolve or "orbit" around some facet of the curriculum (Tomlinson, 1999, pp. 71–74). Students choose their own topics for investigation and work with the teacher who guides and coaches their work. Orbital studies generally last from three to six weeks and require documentation of time spent on the study, resources used, and skills gained.

7. *Entry Points*—Gardner's (1983) work on multiple intelligences has led to a deeper understanding of the varied ways students take in information, solve problems, and express their learning. The Entry Points strategy allows students to explore a topic through as many as five avenues or Entry Points: Narrational Entry Point (presenting a story), Logical-Quantitative Entry Point (using numbers or deduction), Foundational Entry Point (examining philosophy and vocabulary), Aesthetic Entry Point (focusing on sensory features), and Experiential Entry Point (hands-on).

8. *Problem-Based Learning*—Medical students have substantial experience with this instructional approach when, presented with a patient's symptoms, they assume an active role in problem solving. The teacher in a secondary classroom can use Problem-Based Learning by presenting students "with an unclear, complex problem" (Tomlinson, 1999, p. 92). The students are expected to "seek additional information, define the problem, locate and appropriately use valid resources, make decisions about solutions, pose a solution, communicate that solution to others, and assess the solution's effectiveness" (p. 92). The flexible grouping and teacher coaching that can be a part of Problem-Based Learning provide support to struggling students and challenge to higher-level students.

9. *Portfolios*—Not only do these collections of student work allow for alternative assessment, they also provide differentiation in classroom instruction. Students are encouraged to choose work samples representative of their development over time that will go into their portfolios. Students are also encouraged to establish appropriate learning goals and to evaluate their own work. Portfolios are considered a viable part of differentiated instruction because they are put together, over time, from student interests, skills, learning styles, and personal goals (Tomlinson, 1999).

10. *Daily lesson adaptations*—On a given day as the lesson progresses, the teacher can always consider adapting assignments. For instance, a student who

has difficulty with test taking	could be given extra time for testing or be allowed to take the test orally or have essay length shortened
has poor reading skills	could be given an outline of important points from the reading material or be given a tape of the material or be read to by a tutor or a peer

has poor listening skills	could be given a copy of presentation notes
	or be allowed to tape record lectures, discussions, and so on
	or be taught how to outline, take notes, and the like
has difficulty completing assignments independently	could be given a list of all steps necessary to complete each assignment
	or have the assignment reduced into manageable sections with specific due dates

These kinds of lesson adaptations are interactive decisions made by the teacher during the course of instruction. These are only *some* of the many adjustments a teacher can make with a diverse group of learners. The lesson adaptations may not be revolutionary or time-consuming, but they are meaningful ways to differentiate instruction because they help fulfill the teacher's primary responsibility, which is "not to teach the *content*" but "to teach the *students,* and to make sure that all students learn new content every day" (Winebrenner, 1992, p. 1).

■ WEBSITE RESOURCE ■

Leon County Schools in Tallahassee, Florida, has a website on differentiated instruction that includes links to many sources of information. Most valuable are the sample lesson plans from teachers experiment- ing with differentiated learning in their K–12 classrooms at

http://tst1160–35.k12.fsu.edu/ mainpage.html.

Hints for the Beginning Teacher

Adapting the instruction in your classroom can be facilitated by careful documentation of student learning. As students progress through a unit near the beginning of the year, keep a running record of their progress, strengths, weaknesses, and so forth. A simple way to do this is to keep a three-ring notebook with a "progress page" on each student. As you observe how each student is mastering lesson and unit objectives, make abbreviated notes on his or her page. When it is time for the next unit of instruction, you can begin to make adaptations based on these observations.

Collaborative Teaching

A common method of meeting the needs of special education students in our schools has been through collaborative teaching. This service delivery system, a direct result of special education legislation, is a part of what could go on in an "inclusive school," a school where the general education program is "rich and flexible enough to accommodate the unique needs of each learner" (Fisher, Sax, and Pumpian, 1999, p. 10). Collaborative teaching, also known as co-teaching or team teaching, is a partnership between special education teachers and regular education teachers. Teacher collaboration does not just happen. Rather, effective team teaching occurs when the teachers involved know the components of the co-teaching relationship, the different approaches of co-teaching, and effective co-teaching strategies.

Components of the Co-Teaching Relationship Imagine beginning your first year of teaching and finding out that in your fifth- and sixth-period classes, you will be working each day with a teacher from the special education department. You not only will be responsible for planning lessons, assessing learning, and selecting materials, but also you will be expected to work with another adult to plan, assess, and select for a handful of students in your classes. How will you work with this person? Who makes the decisions about teaching the class? What else could crop up in this unforeseen relationship?

Like any relationship, co-teaching is a developmental process, one that requires some getting used to and a great deal of practice. According to Gately and Gately (2000), co-teaching relationships tend to go through three stages—the beginning stage, the compromise stage, and the collaborative stage (p. 40). Gately and Gately have also identified eight components to the co-teaching relationship: interpersonal communication, physical arrangement, familiarity with the curriculum, curriculum goals and modifications, instructional planning, instructional presentation, classroom management, and assessment. An awareness of how these eight components develop throughout the teaching relationship may help enhance the teaching relationship. What follows is a summary of Gately and Gately's (2001) examination of the co-teaching relationship:

Stages	Beginning	Compromise	Collaborative
Interpersonal Communication	Reserved; guarded	Genuine, sophisticated dialogue about students	Verbal and nonverbal before, during, and after lesson
Physical Arrangement	Students with more disabilities may sit apart from rest of the students	More movement and shared space	Classroom is jointly owned
Familiarity with Curriculum	Lack of confidence in each other's subject/skill areas	Increased competence and confidence	Modifications in curriculum made jointly

(continued)

Stages	Beginning	Compromise	Collaborative
Curriculum Goals and Modifications	Textbook-driven planning with accommodations restricted to IEP mandates	Essential questions asked about what *all* students should be learning	Modifications of content, activities, and assessment for *all* students
Instructional Planning	Two separate events for two sets of students	Shared	Mutual activity before and during lesson
Instructional Presentation	Two separate lessons with one teacher "leading" and the other "helping"	Shared responsibility	Equal engagement with all students
Classroom Management	Special educator acts as "behavior manager"	Mutual development of rules and routines	Mutual responsibility often accompanied by individual behavior plans
Assessment	Two separate grading systems	Mutually agreed upon assessment strategies	Variety of assessment options mutually designed to meet the needs of *all* students

To help ensure success in co-teaching, the regular educator and the special educator must be willing to discuss these relationship components. Before the school term even begins, the teachers should talk about their expectations for all the students in the classroom, planning responsibilities, discipline procedures in the classroom, student assessment, physical arrangement of the classroom, and curriculum issues. This conversation will need to be continued and refined throughout the school year. Bringing in other support staff such as administrators and counselors will enhance the co-teaching relationship as it becomes more and more collaborative.

Different Approaches of Co-Teaching   There is not a singular model for co-teaching. Lombardo (2000) identifies five co-teaching approaches that have been successfully used in classrooms:

One teaches, one supports. While one teacher leads the lesson, the other teacher moves around the room, assisting students and gathering data.

Parallel teaching. The two teachers divide the class into two heterogeneous groups and teach them simultaneously. Learning can be enhanced if the teachers vary their content so that, once the group is reconvened, students can share what they learned.

Station teaching. Content and students are divided, with one teacher who is more knowledgeable about the subject teaching new content to one group, while the other teacher reviews previous lessons or teaches learning strategies such as note taking, outlining, or speed reading. Students rotate through each group.

Alternative teaching. One teacher facilitates enrichment or alternative activities while the other teacher reviews important concepts. Students are pulled out of the larger group for review, tutoring, and so on based on specific learning needs.

Team teaching. The two teachers share in the delivery of the lesson. For example, one teacher can lecture while the other teacher writes material on the board or uses the overhead projector.

Effective Co-Teaching Strategies Becoming comfortable with co-teaching takes time and concerted effort. Some suggestions for making collaborative teaching successful come from Lombardo (2000) and Fisher, Sax, and Pumpian (1999):

- Co-teaching should be a mutual decision made by both teachers and not a top-down mandate handed down by district or building administrators.
- The goal of co-teaching should be improved student learning.
- Both teachers should be given time to work together before the school year begins and throughout the school year.
- The regular educator should be as committed to learning about differentiating instruction as the special educator is to learning the subject area of the class.
- Collaborative teaching is a relationship in process, which time and patience help improve.
- Co-teachers should learn how to make the most of planning time with tailored agendas. These meeting times must be productive and not just complaint sessions.
- Co-teaching can be strengthened by consistent and ongoing feedback from the teacher partners, from students, from parents, and from administrators.
- Staff development on inclusion should be consistent and ongoing.
- The same instructional resources that enhance regular education teaching can enhance co-teaching. Co-teachers should be open to using technology, outside speakers, field trips, distance learning, and so on.

Secondary teachers who are serious about meeting the needs of all their students have exciting opportunities ahead of them in the area of co-teaching. Pairing the special educator's methods expertise with the general educator's content expertise is a major step in school reform. The time and energy that must be invested in this professional relationship are well spent when the effects on student learning are considered.

■ SUMMARY POINT ■

The one-room schoolhouse is no longer the norm in public education. The one-size-fits-all mentality of many current classrooms should be and can be a relic of the past as well. Differentiated instruction, as explained in this chapter, can be seen as both an ethical decision and a legal mandate for teachers. The research, theory, and practical suggestions presented in this chapter should help new teachers construct a framework for making decisions about meeting the needs of all the students in their classrooms.

■ QUESTIONS FOR REFLECTION ■

1. Describe some of your own experiences as a student when your needs were not met. Consider a time in school when the instruction was too fast paced or the content was too difficult. Also, consider a time when the instructional pace moved too slowly and the content was too easy for you.

   In both circumstances, how did you feel about the class, about the instructor, and about yourself?

   What adjustments could the instructors have made to meet your needs?

2. What aspects of constructivism do you find in this chapter's description of differentiated instruction?

3. Identify three or four essential questions from a subject you plan on teaching. Then consider a unit of instruction that you might teach in this subject. (For example, a unit could be based on a novel or a textbook chapter or a period in history.) List three or four unit questions.

4. Of the ten instructional adjustments suggested in this chapter, which two do you see yourself using early in your teaching career? Why? Which two do you think might not be a part of your early teaching repertoire? Why?

5. At some point in your teaching, you may work with a special education teacher in a co-teaching relationship. What concerns do you have at this time about that kind of relationship? How might you address or solve some of these concerns?

■ REFERENCES ■

Caine, R., and Caine, G. (1997). *Unleashing the Power of Perceptual Change: The Potential of Brain-based Teaching.* Alexandria, VA: Association for Supervision and Curriculum Development.

Danielson, C. (1996). *Enhancing Professional Practice: A Framework for Teaching.* Alexandria, VA: Association for Supervision and Curriculum Development.

Dewey, J. (1938). *Experience and Education.* New York: Macmillan.

Fisher, D., Sax, C., and Pumpian, I. (1999). *Inclusive High Schools: Learning from Contemporary Classrooms.* Baltimore, MD: Paul H. Brookes.

Gardner, H. (1983). *Frames of Mind: The Theory of Multiple Intelligences.* New York: Basic Books.

Gately, S. E., and Gately, F. J. Jr. (2001). "Understanding coteaching components." *Teaching Exceptional Children,* 33(4), 40–47.

Gregory, G. H., and Chapman, C. (2002). *Differential Instructional Strategies: One Size Doesn't Fit All.* Thousand Oaks, CA: Corwin Press.

Heacox, D. (2002). *Differentiating Instruction in the Regular Classroom.* Minneapolis, MN: Free Spirit.

Howard, P. (1994). *The Owner's Manual for the Brain.* Austin, TX: Leornian Press.

Keefe, J. W. (1987). *Learning Style: Theory and Practice.* Reston, VA: National Association of Secondary School Principals.

Lombardo, L. (2000). *Collaborative Teaching: Making It Work in Your Inclusive Classroom.* Horsham, PA: LRP Publications.

Piaget, J. (1952). *The Origins of Intelligence in Children.* NY: International University Press.

Schlechty, P. C. (2001). *Shaking Up the School House: How to Support and Sustain Educational Innovation.* San Francisco: Jossey-Bass.

Telzrow, C. F., and Tankersley, M. (2000). *IDEA Amendments of 1997: Practice Guidelines for School-Based Teams.* Bethesda, MD: NASP Publications.

Tomlinson, C. A. (1999). *The Differentiated Classroom: Responding to the Needs of All Learners.* Alexandria, VA: Association for Supervision and Curriculum Development.

Tomlinson, C. A. (2001). *How to Differentiate Instruction in Mixed-Ability Classrooms* (2nd ed.). Alexandria, VA: Association for Supervision and Curriculum Development.

Vygotsky, L. (1962). *Thought and Language.* Cambridge, MA: MIT Press.

Wiggins, G., and McTighe, J. (1998). *Understanding by Design.* Alexandria, VA: Association for Supervision and Curriculum Development.

Winebrenner, S. (1992). *Teaching Gifted Kids in the Regular Classroom.* Minneapolis, MN: Free Spirit.

10

Evaluation of Classroom Performance

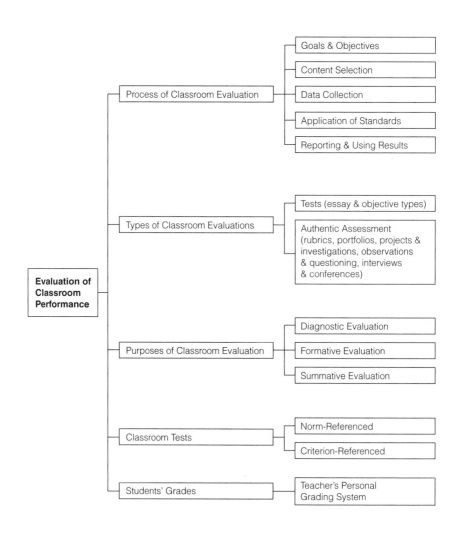

```
                                                    ┌─ Goals & Objectives
                                                    ├─ Content Selection
                    ┌─ Process of Classroom ────────┼─ Data Collection
                    │  Evaluation                    ├─ Application of Standards
                    │                                └─ Reporting & Using Results
                    │
                    │                                ┌─ Tests (essay & objective types)
                    │  Types of Classroom ──────────┤
                    │  Evaluations                   └─ Authentic Assessment
                    │                                   (rubrics, portfolios, projects &
 Evaluation of      │                                   investigations, observations
 Classroom ─────────┤                                   & questioning, interviews
 Performance        │                                   & conferences)
                    │
                    │                                ┌─ Diagnostic Evaluation
                    │  Purposes of Classroom ───────┼─ Formative Evaluation
                    │  Evaluation                    └─ Summative Evaluation
                    │
                    │                                ┌─ Norm-Referenced
                    │  Classroom Tests ─────────────┤
                    │                                └─ Criterion-Referenced
                    │
                    └─ Students' Grades ──────────────── Teacher's Personal
                                                         Grading System
```

Evaluation is one of the three major components of teaching, along with planning and instruction. Yet in the informal view of teachers, evaluation is often perceived as the stepchild of teaching. Writing tests, grading them—especially essay tests—and reporting students' grades are grudgingly executed as onerous chores of teaching. Very few teachers are attracted to teaching by this aspect of the job. It is not surprising, then, that evaluation is probably the major aspect of teaching that receives the least professional attention from teachers, and so is an area in which many teachers can substantially improve. This chapter is designed to initiate thinking toward the development of a sound concept and effective practices of evaluation.

Although evaluation has been described here as one component of teaching, it is not mutually exclusive from the other parts. Evaluation occurs in planning in the selection of particular topics and strategies. As objectives are being written, it is intended that they will become the basis for subsequent evaluation. Teachers need to plan daily for collecting data on student progress, and during instruction, evaluation occurs as teachers observe student behaviors, consider student responses, provide feedback and correction to students, and judge the extent to which instruction has been effective. At the completion of a unit of work, written tests, projects, exhibitions, and other demonstrations of achievement typically occur. The many aspects of evaluation deserve thoughtful consideration by teachers if evaluation principles and practices are to contribute optimally to the effectiveness of teaching.

In a fundamental sense, evaluation means placing a value on some entity, thus expressing an indication of its worth. As such, a key responsibility for the teacher is to determine what he or she deems most valuable in a unit of instruction. Implied within the process is a standard, usually in the form of a criterion or a comparison, and a decision. Evaluation as decision making should conform to the principles of decision making described in Chapter 1. Evaluation should be made on the basis of the best information or evidence available and should be, as much as possible, a rational process.

■ OVERVIEW

This chapter describes the role and process of teacher classroom evaluation. This broad perspective will serve as a framework for the teacher's continuing development of an informed comprehensive approach to this component of the teacher role. Brief commentary on three major components of teacher classroom evaluation is also presented: grading, test writing, and using alternative and authentic forms of assessment.

This limited treatment of the topic is intended to help the reader understand evaluation as a pervasive and integral part of teaching. It does not make a pretense at being comprehensive. Many fine textbooks devoted entirely to assessment and evaluation are readily available to provide in-depth information and methodology.

SCENARIO

The end of the second six-week grading period at Jefferson County Local High School was approaching. John Sykes, the school's art teacher, remembered clearly the end of the first grading period. As a teacher with several years' experience, he had proceeded to assign the first six weeks' grades in his Art I class much the same as in the past years. Art was not considered to be one of the difficult courses in the school, but this particular class had less apparent ability than any John remembered. He had assigned quite a few C grades as well as two Ds and an F.

John's approach to assigning grades had always been rather casual. He examined the artwork each student turned in and made an overall judgment of its quality. He prided himself on his connoisseurship approach, including the critique he wrote on every project, but he also tempered his evaluation with compassion when he thought students deserved it. In the academic aspect of the course dealing with art principles and art history, he examined the numerical scores, looked for natural breaks throughout the range of scores, and assigned letter grades by inspection.

After grades had gone out, John got calls or visits from four of his students' parents from that class, in his experience a surprisingly large number. The parents did not understand why their children had received grades as much as two letters below expectation. He explained the basis for the grade as best he could and tried to enlist parents' cooperation in urging students to take their artwork seriously and conscientiously. Mrs. DeTano, a parent and herself a teacher in another district, was one of the parents to visit. Her daughter, Lynn, had been assigned a D, and Mrs. DeTano was not satisfied with John's explanation of how he determined the grade. She pointedly referred to the explanation as "unconvincing" and asked John to produce explicit standards, a term John had not heard before in this context. Her Lynn, she said, had been unable to produce a copy of any such standards or to inform her of any that had ever been communicated to the class.

John spent an uncomfortable half hour with Mrs. DeTano. She was obviously knowledgeable but rather self-righteous, he thought. He was shaken and had therefore responded defensively in the conference, but in later reflection he was willing to grant that she might have a point. He felt that she was being condescending when she insisted on sending him a copy of the rubric she used to assign grades, but nevertheless he examined it when it arrived. He also talked with several fellow teachers whose judgment he respected. Then he set about rethinking his approach to evaluation.

Art, he reasoned, is not only for artists. But as he examined the grade distribution for the first six weeks, he realized that the students who had a knack for art had been rewarded with the high grades. He intended to encourage these students, but he wondered if it had been at the expense of some of the others. What, in fact, is important in a beginning art course? Is it the same for everyone? Can individual differences be accommodated without abandoning reasonable standards? His implicit answers to these questions were reflected in the new grading criteria he established after a week of thoughtful consideration. Four categories for evaluation were included:

Artistic rendition
  Technical skill
  Creativity
Attitude and effort
  Attendance and punctuality
  Work habits
  Preparation and initiative
Self-assessment
  Goal identification
  Progress reports
Academic achievement
  Quality of participation
  Test scores

John Sykes was especially pleased with the final touch to his system. The categories were weighted 2–1–1–1, but students would individually select which category was to be given the 2 weight. This would be considerably more fair to students with only moderate talent. When he initiated the new system, including his first attempt at developing a rubric, he spent a whole period describing it to the class and inviting their comments. He was encouraged by their enthusiasm.

The following day, after making minor modifications based on the students' feedback, he provided a copy of the system to each student. He asked them to share it with their parents and to decide which weighting alternative they each preferred. He also set up a system whereby he would keep anecdotal notes on each student that would be useful for evaluating attitude and effort. It would be more work, he realized, but if nearly 50 percent of some of the students' grades was to be determined by this sort of information, he would need credible documentation; enough, he thought, to satisfy Mrs. DeTano.

As John talked with his colleagues prior to setting up his own new system, one of them impressed him with the idea that evaluation should be an integral part of instruction and that students needed thoughtful feedback and correction to contribute to the learning process. "I certainly do this as they are doing their projects," John thought, "but not while we are focusing on principles and history." He decided, therefore, to use quizzes in class occasionally that would include several objective items and a short essay item. In most cases, John did not collect the quizzes. The correct answers to the objective items were given immediately; then the papers were passed on to another student to critique the essay. Following this phase, they were passed on once more, and both the essay and the first critiquer's comments were critiqued. When the papers were returned to the writer, John solicited questions about the essay and the critiques. On the several occasions he had done this over the past five weeks, animated discussions that featured thoughtful insights occurred. Using these "teaching quizzes," both he and the students had the opportunity to engage in feedback and correction. At first, he thought the students might object to their peers reading their papers, but they actually enjoyed this approach. When John Sykes did plan to collect quizzes and grade them himself, he announced it a day ahead.

Now, as grades were about to be assigned for the second six weeks, John felt reasonably comfortable with this new, more accountable approach. But one student, Bree, still concerned him. Bree had missed school sporadically throughout the term due to complications following a summer bout with mononucleosis. Bree was an average student but a wholly undistinguished artist. Now she had fallen behind considerably in all aspects of her work. Her grade for this period, based on the established criteria, was clearly an F.

Mr. Sykes called Bree in and informed her of the situation. Almost in tears, Bree nodded her understanding. "But, Bree," said Mr. Sykes, "suppose I assign you a C grade because I'm sure you could have made it if your health had been up to par. However, it would be conditional. I will ask you to sign a contract specifying what you'll need to make up from these past several weeks in addition to the regular work for the next grading period. And we will need to see improvement over your work so far. By the way, how is your health now? Are you up to it?"

Bree's eyes had lit up. "Oh, yeah. You bet, Mr. Sykes. I sure appreciate the chance. I just can't afford to get any Fs in high school. I won't disappoint you—or myself."

As a delighted Bree retreated down the hall, John thought, "So what's a grade for after all? I feel better about grades this grading period than I ever have before." Then he smiled as he uttered half aloud to himself, "Thank you, Mrs. DeTano."

■ RESEARCH AND THEORETICAL BASE

Although research has accumulated at a rapid rate in education as a total enterprise throughout this century, the attention has been uneven from area to area. One of the areas about which the available research is limited is teachers' classroom-evaluation practices (Lazar-Morris, Polin, May, and Burry, 1980; Stiggins, Bridgeford, and Conklin, 1986). The relative effects of various evaluation approaches and the effect of particular student testing and grading practices are not well documented in the literature. On the other hand, the treatment of the principles of evaluation and measurement is extensive.

Teachers tend to feel comfortable in the testing aspect of evaluation (Gullickson, 1984). They generally feel confident with and rely heavily on their own judgment (Lazar-Morris et al., 1984). On the other hand, grading is a painful responsibility (Gage and Berliner, 1991). This apparent paradox is at least partly explained by the findings that teachers are often not well prepared to conduct classroom evaluation and that their formal training is minimal and narrow in scope (Rudman, Kelly, Wanous, Mehrens, Clark, and Porter, 1980; Stiggins et al., 1986). Furthermore, teachers learn their evaluation techniques primarily from their colleagues, as well as from personal experience (Stiggins, 1985). As the findings indicate, teachers tend to employ intuitive and expedient practices in evaluation. They express little concern about the mechanical aspects of test writing and grading. Yet, they do not, as a rule, have a well-developed, pedagogically defensible system of evaluation that they trust. Dealing with the affective implications of evaluation is thus often emotionally stressful.

Much of the literature on evaluation in recent years has been on authentic assessment, also termed alternative, naturalistic, or performance assessment (Perrone, 1991; Herman, Aschbacher, and Winters, 1992; Marzano, Pickering, and McTighe, 1993; Madaus and Kellaghan, 1993; Zemelman, Daniels, and Hyde, 1998; Wiggins, 1993). These authors recognize the shortcomings of assessment as it has traditionally been conducted using paper-and-pencil tests primarily to ascertain students' acquisition of factual knowledge. Recently recommended practice targets students' ability to acquire personal meaning and to use knowledge in realistic tasks. Wiggins (1993) maintains that "we are not preparing students for real, 'messy' uses of knowledge in context—the 'doing' of the subject" (p. 202). Also, broader sampling of students' achievements over time is encouraged, with the use of portfolios to collect and preserve appropriate evidence (Graves and Sunstein, 1992; Grady, 1992). In a review of the research on the use of portfolios Herman and Winters (1994) reported that relatively few studies were available on the effectiveness of portfolios. They did comment that most educators were positively disposed in principle to the use of portfolios but that portfolios posed a demanding evaluation task to the teacher, a characteristic that limits their potential.

Evaluation is a complex—perhaps deceptively complex—aspect of teaching. In addressing this concern, Stiggins and colleagues (1986) stated, "We begin to comprehend the complexity of classroom assessment as we explore the range and frequency of teachers' decisions and the plethora of student characteristics they must consider in making those decisions" (p. 10). They go on to report that a review of several studies produced 66 student characteristics used by the sample teachers in evaluation-related decision making. One may conclude from this report that evaluation can no more be a totally rational process than can instruction. Teachers' sensitivity and values are inevitable factors in the effectiveness of their evaluation.

Teacher-made tests are a staple in most teachers' approaches to assessment of student progress. Rudman and associates (1980) found that teachers prefer norm-referenced tests (i.e., graded on an in-class comparative basis) over criterion-referenced tests (i.e., graded on the basis of a predetermined absolute standard). However, Lazar-Morris and colleagues (1980) reported that norm-referenced tests are considered by most experts to be characterized by narrowness of focus, bias, and unreliability. The preferred alternative is the criterion-referenced test because of its diagnostic, placement, and remediation uses, and its ease of interpretation. Except in those instances in which ranking of students' performance is necessary, criterion-based measures are recommended.

Tests work to teachers' and, in a sense, to students' advantage because by their very nature they are an incentive to students. Halpin and Halpin (1982) reported that students increase their study efforts when they know a test is imminent. Every experienced teacher knows this, for teachers commonly exhort students with the reminder that certain material will be on a test. In some cases, it is virtually posed as a threat. Nungester and Duchastel (1982) found that students' retention of learned material was enhanced if they were tested on it. Tests, therefore, are useful in serving both instructional and evaluative purposes.

A clear similarity is apparent between teachers' verbal questioning and the items they write for classroom tests: both tend to emphasize factual recall. Fleming and Chambers (1983) indicated that teachers preferred matching questions and used few essay questions. Carter (1984) reported both from her own study and a review of the literature that teachers had a limited repertoire of test-writing skills and found it difficult to write items for testing higher-order thinking skills, in particular, inference and prediction. One may conclude that, to a large extent, teacher-made tests are superficial. If teachers are, in fact, concerned about students' higher-order thinking skills, it is not always apparent from their tests.

The grading system affects the curriculum in the view of teachers (Agnew, 1983). They feel that it trivializes learning because it establishes a predisposition for readily assessed low cognitive-level learning; the curriculum is "covered" rather than "uncovered." Furthermore, from the students' viewpoint, grades as the measure of achievement replace achievement itself as the prized outcome of classroom learning activities. Grades become the hidden—but not very well hidden—curriculum.

Part of the complexity of evaluation has to do with the nature of decisions placed on the teacher. Traditional forms of evaluation and, therefore, grading are designed to answer questions of a quantitative nature; for example, according to Hebert (1998), standardized tests help answer the question, "Which student knows more?" and teacher-made tests tend to answer the question, "How much did the students learn?" As new conceptions of learning have emerged, that is, as constructivist beliefs and practices have found their way into the classroom, alternative forms of evaluation are being developed to answer such questions as "How are the students going to use this knowledge?" and, in the case of portfolios, "What does this student know?" One question is not better than the others; posing each of these questions can offer a more comprehensive perspective of a student's work in school (Hebert, 1998, p. 585).

Evaluation, then, is not a clear-cut issue, nor does it have a singular purpose. Haney (1991) expressed concern about the tendency in schools to use a single means of evaluation, that is, testing, to serve multiple purposes including program placement, college admission, hiring, and curriculum evaluation. "In short," wrote Haney, "trying to use one test for such a range of purposes is rather like trying to use one tool—say a screwdriver or a hammer—for jobs ranging from brain surgery to pile driving" (p. 144).

In an effort to more closely match evaluation purposes with evaluation tools, various forms of alternative assessment have been developed and utilized. A number of terms are used to describe alternative forms of evaluation—authentic assessment, direct assessment, and performance assessment. According to Worthen (1993), the movement to supplement standardized and teacher-made tests with alternative forms of evaluation is a response to public demands for accountability, inappropriate uses of high-stakes testing (e.g., as determinants for promotion and graduation), negative consequences of high-stakes testing (e.g., teaching-to-the-test), and increased criticisms of standardized tests. Guskey (1996) points to advances in technology that offer new opportunities to evaluate and report student progress. Guskey also maintains that "no one method of grading and reporting serves all purposes well" (p. 16). For instance, multiple forms of evaluation allow teachers to:

- (C)ommunicate the achievement status of students to parents and others.
- (P)rovide information that students can use for self-evaluation.
- (S)elect, identify, or group students for certain educational paths or programs.
- (P)rovide incentives to learn.
- (E)valuate the effectiveness of instructional programs. (p. 17)

Teachers must make decisions about evaluating student learning. A sophisticated understanding of evaluation takes into account the multiple layers of this aspect of teaching. The question "Why evaluate?" can be answered in many ways. To settle for the simplistic answer "For a grade" is to reduce what teachers do to a mere dispensing of information. It is time that we begin to link instruction with evaluation (Herman et al., 1992). Earl and LeMahieu (1997) agree that when educators view assessment as learning, the question for one approach to evaluation is replaced by a "more differentiated view of assessment purposes and approaches" (p. 150).

From the research on classroom evaluation, we discern that the problems affecting evaluation practices in the classroom tend to involve human complexity and diversity more than mechanical or technical issues. The philosophical and emotional aspects of assessment are more difficult to deal with than matters of form or measurement. We realize that we search in vain for final solutions

Evaluation can no more be a totally rational process than can instruction. Teachers' sensitivity and values are inevitable factors in the effectiveness of their evaluations.

to the most vexing problems of evaluation. In the final analysis, ongoing judicious decision making based on a sound understanding of the principles of evaluation holds the greatest promise. In this aspect of teaching, as in planning, instruction, and discipline, there is simply no substitute for informed teacher decision making.

■ APPLICATION TO PRACTICE

The Role of Evaluation in the Classroom

Why evaluate? A good question. The simplest answer a teacher might give is "Because I am required to assign grades to students." That answer expresses an unassailable fact of teaching. But there is much more to it. Would teachers evaluate if it were not for the necessity of assigning a grade? Certainly, teachers committed to excellent instruction would use evaluation in several ways: to diagnose students' readiness, to individualize learning, to ascertain the interim progress of students, to decide when tutoring or reteaching is advisable, and to assess the effectiveness and the outcomes of instruction.

Evaluation is sometimes considered to be an add-on to the instructional process, or something that occurs only after a unit of study to assign a grade to a student. This is a decidedly myopic view. As is implied in the opening section of this chapter and the subsequent comments, evaluation is an integral part of the teaching process. Evaluation is an important aspect of planning as content is selected, objectives are written, and remediation and enrichment are considered. During a unit of study, evaluation provides continuing feedback to the teacher and students and is an important source for making adjustments.

At the completion of a unit of study, evaluation focuses on assessing the level of learning students have attained, assigning grades, and obtaining evidence of instructional effectiveness. In one sense, some of these aspects of evaluation tacitly occur regardless of teacher intentions. It is important to note that purposeful attention to evaluation enhances the several kinds of contributions that evaluation potentially makes to classroom outcomes.

The Process of Classroom Evaluation

Goals and Objectives Written goals and objectives serve nominally as the beginning of the evaluation process. However, because evaluation is cyclical (i.e., the evaluation from one unit of study may affect planning for the next), there may be no absolute starting point. Care must be taken during the writing of objectives, especially at the unit and specific-outcomes levels, that they lend themselves to evaluation. Improperly or vaguely written objectives seriously impede evaluation of learning. John Sykes, in his art course, may have had as a program goal:

- Students will understand the contribution of color to the intent of an artwork.

Obviously, there is no way Mr. Sykes could see inside the students' minds to assess the level of understanding of this concept. Therefore, he would need to have at least one—and probably more—specific objectives, which, when fulfilled, he would accept as evidence of probable understanding. Such specific objectives might be:

- Students will match a list of color tones to a set of possible intents.
- Students will explain Klee's use of color to emphasize the graphic dimension of his art.
- Students will produce a colored-pencil sketch in which they use color tone to express a feeling level.

If teachers are to evaluate learning at the various levels of thinking (six levels were presented in the planning chapter), then objectives must be written at the respective levels. The various levels of objectives, if used as guides to direct instruction, result in developing learning activities conceived at those levels. However, evaluation would have to occur in terms of these objectives at those levels to determine the actual learning outcomes.

Goals and objectives are also used as the basis for building tests with a table of specifications. In its simplest form, each goal that the test covers is listed and assigned a percentage weighting. Within each goal, each objective is assigned a percent. In writing or selecting items to be included on the test, the appropriate number of items may then be included for each objective and goal to ensure a sampling of subject matter. Table 10.1 is a general example.

Alternative forms of evaluation will also use unit goals and objectives as the bases for developing scoring criteria (rubrics for written inquiries, projects, or presentations), designating content (portfolios), or identifying appropriate questions (conferences or interviews).

Content Selection   The selection of content and the development of learning objectives occur more or less simultaneously, each complementing the other. From the curricular point of view, courses are essentially a body of content; from an instructional point of view, courses are a sequence of learning activities.

John Sykes probably views his art course both in terms of knowledge to be learned and activities to engage in and each becomes very much a part of the other.

TABLE 10.1   GENERALIZED TABLE OF SPECIFICATIONS

GOAL 1 60%

Objective 1.1	30%
Objective 1.2	15%
Objective 1.3	15%

GOAL 2 40%

Objective 2.1	25%
Objective 2.2	15%

For this group of students, basic information about art will have to be presented, including principles of form, balance, perspective, and medium. He will also want students to be aware of the role of art in our cultural setting and the contribution of art in the practical and aesthetic dimensions. Finally, of course, he will want students to create works of art at whatever level they are capable.

A variety of levels of learning and several types of learning outcomes are implied by the content this teacher intends to teach. He must make two kinds of decisions: What content in what sequence is most pertinent for this group of students, and what learning activities are most appropriate to achieve the objectives related to that content? By knowing his content well, making reference to the course syllabus, and becoming increasingly familiar with his students, Mr. Sykes will correlate content and activities. However, continuing evaluation of achievement and instructional effectiveness will be used to redirect and fine-tune teaching as necessary.

Data Collection   Evaluation has two components: information on achievement or performance and a standard that provides a base for measuring. Information on achievement is obtained in a variety of ways. Informally, teachers make evaluations continuously as they observe students. Students' willingness to attend class, ability to respond, and demonstration of interest and initiative provide the teacher with a sense of how things are going and what adjustments are expedient. Teachers also notice patterns of behavior in individual students and begin to determine where extra help may need to be given, where enrichment is possible, and where additional monitoring is required. In the scenario, John Sykes noticed that Bree had a unique problem, and he devised a unique approach in the form of a conditional grade and a contract to accommodate him.

More formally, teachers use instruments to collect data useful for evaluation. They may be in the form of checklists and various kinds of tests. Also, data collection may involve such assignments as homework papers, journals and notebooks, reports, and creative projects. Anecdotal record keeping is another way to collect data on student learning. The classroom teacher records observations about an individual student's work habits, reading selections, progress, concerns, and so forth on specially designed record-keeping sheets. Some teachers use a chart to record notes; other teachers have individual pages for each student in a "class observation notebook." During the course of a unit, evaluation based on these sources, often through the use of student-developed portfolios, should be used to assess students' progress, diagnose students' problems, and provide continuous feedback to students. Teachers should make sure that students are well informed about their progress through the systematic use of feedback and correction procedures and that no student's learning and achievement problems go unattended for long.

We observe John Sykes using "teaching quizzes" as a means of providing useful interim evaluation to students and the opportunity for immediate correction. In this regard, the most important consideration was student learning, not assigning grades.

Establishing a standard against which data are compared is the second aspect of evaluation. Teachers' astute judgment is required for this task. In some cases, teachers allow their standards to remain implicit, as John Sykes initially did. This may lead to difficulty, as is illustrated in the scenario. Standards must be clearly stated to be as useful as possible, and they must be communicated to the students, often in the form of a rubric. Students are thus provided with a benchmark that clarifies levels of achievement and performance.

Applying Standards Teachers sometimes think of their grading scales as standards, such as 65 percent or a D mark as passing. These are only a part of the standards. It still leaves open the questions, 65 percent of what, a D based on what? A teacher's well-written course and program goals provide the basis for establishing the "what" part of the standard. However, the teacher must still determine how the level of compliance with the standard is to be measured and the appropriate scale to express the level of compliance.

In the case of John Sykes, a program objective is: "Students will understand the contribution of color to the intent of the artwork." He may establish, according to the specific objective related to this goal, that (1) students must match with at least 70 percent accuracy color tone with possible intent; (2) students must show in a brief paragraph that they are aware of the concept of *graphic dimension* and how color may contribute to it; (3) students will render a sketch that in his practiced view expresses (marginally at least) feeling through the use of color tone. This is about as explicit as standards for performance can be for this type of learning. Students who do not achieve the minimums stated will have to be retaught until they do. If Mr. Sykes is using the ABCDF scale, then the correct number of matching items, the extent of students' understanding of Klee's use of color tone, and the quality of the sketch will all have to be translated into grade symbols. He will have to depend on his judgment to do this. Experience will be helpful in making these judgments. Consequently, new teachers will find this to be one of the more difficult aspects of teaching.

Solomon (1998) has identified important decisions to make to help the teacher get started on assessment procedures. Some of her points follow:

- Decide on your content standards (what your students need to know and be able to do).
- Describe the end result level that will indicate your students have accomplished each content standard and objective. These will become your performance standards.
- Make a list of the audiences who will be interested in how your students achieved their results (e.g., students themselves, parents, administrators, teachers).
- Decide where you will place more formal systematic assessments and in what form they might be.
- Plan to include some assessments in each activity.

Reporting and Using the Results of Evaluation The foregoing commentary implies that evaluation is useful only if it is communicated to concerned parties. Teachers, of course, immediately use the results of evaluation for making decisions about appropriate strategies, pacing, individualizing, and assessing instructional effectiveness. Students need to know the results of evaluation to guide them in their ongoing work and possibly to provide incentive for their continued efforts. Others who are indirectly involved with classroom learning—counselors, administrators, and parents—also have the need to be informed at least periodically about students' classroom achievement.

The results of evaluation procedures are reported to students both informally and formally. Casual comments by the teacher in class in response to students' answers or during a supervised study period constitute a useful kind of feedback. Marks and comments on homework papers provide a somewhat more structured means for assessment reporting. Conferences with students to attend to individual situations are useful, as was John Sykes's conference with Bree. Quizzes administered in class, the results of which may or may not be recorded as a grade in the gradebook, constitute an even more structured form of evaluation. Formal evaluations usually occur in the form of weekly or unit tests, or assessments of some type of performance such as timed events or the quality of a creative effort. In Chapter 2, a section is devoted to describing effective feedback and corrective practices that the teacher uses as a component of instruction.

All the separate evaluations that occur during a grading period, usually six to nine weeks in duration, are accumulated, processed according to the teacher's predetermined plan, and entered on a report form as the official grade assigned to the student. These grading-period grades are averaged again at the end of the semester and at the end of the year so that ultimately all the student's academic achievement in a course is reported as a single mark.

When grades are viewed in this perspective, their possible shortcomings are apparent. Are they reliable? Are they valid? Do they really convey meaning? Generally speaking, they are, in fact, as reliable as any other predictor of future academic achievement. They are also useful in that they have become the basis of a convention of communication that is widely understood among the many parties who ultimately make use of them. Finally, no alternative assessment or evaluation method has become widely enough accepted that one can predict that in the foreseeable future standard letter grades will be deemphasized, let alone replaced.

Types of Classroom Evaluations

Tests In the course of comprehensive classroom evaluation, both formal and informal data will be obtained in several ways. Observation of students provides a continuing series of impressions. Anecdotal records, checklists, and rating scales are used to collect and record more substantive information, but, on the whole, paper-and-pencil tests are the source of most of the formal evaluation-related information that teachers obtain.

Paper-and-pencil tests are made up of essay and objective items. The essay items may be short-answer questions that require a sentence or two, or they may be extended to involve several paragraphs. The most common types of objective items are true–false, completion, matching, and multiple choice.

Essay Items. Essays are especially useful for measuring higher-order thinking, including analysis, synthesis, and evaluation. However, they take a relatively long time to answer compared with objective items, so only a limited sample of learning can be measured with essay items. Factual information and basic comprehension are much more efficiently measured with objective test items.

Essay tests take much less time to write than multiple choice tests primarily because far fewer items are included. However, a thoughtfully written essay item may require a considerable expenditure of time to get it just right. Care must be taken to write the items clearly and specify precisely what the response should address. An essay item can cover only a relatively limited range of information; thus, items should be judiciously selected, based on a priority of objectives. In other words, sampling is a prime concern. In John Sykes's class, we can imagine as a test item: "What is the contribution of art to our culture?" Obviously, entire books have been written on the topic and whole courses are devoted to investigating certain aspects of it. Although he may want students to begin to appreciate the contribution of art in his course, we can imagine students' frustration in attempting to respond to such a broad question. We also wonder how a teacher would grade their responses.

A more limited question in this class might be: "What was Paul Klee's contribution to the art of the first half of this century?" Here again, however, we recognize some problems. Did Paul Klee make only one contribution? Should the students simply name the contribution in a brief phrase or sentence, or should they provide a context, some description, and the impact? How much should the student write? The item does not meet the criteria of clearness and preciseness.

Consider one more example: "In a one-page essay (approximately 150 words) describe what you consider to be the single most identifiable characteristic of Paul Klee's painting in the 1920s and 1930s, and give an example of how his work influenced other artists of his time." In this item, three things are made clear to the students: the length of the essay, the expectation that they will describe the single most identifiable characteristic of Klee's painting, and the criterion that they must produce evidence supporting the assertion that Klee had professional influence. Although writing essay items may be done more quickly than writing most objective items, much care must still be taken to write selectively and precisely. The time spent writing such items will pay off when teachers grade them. It is so much easier when teachers know exactly what to look for!

Grading essays that students write both in response to test questions and as general term-paper assignments is laborious, mentally fatiguing work. Reading dozens of papers all addressing the same topic challenges the teacher's mind to remain alert and discriminating, but it is unlikely that there will ever be an electronic device to do it for you, so be prepared. Many teachers avoid this unsavory task by simply not using essay items or assignments. This self-serving practice is unacceptable in any class in which constructivist teaching and students' higher-order learning (meaning making) are involved.

The following suggestions are helpful in grading essays fairly, quickly, effectively, and with a minimum of mental fatigue.

1. Write the essay question or the statement of the essay assignment incisively, as described previously.
2. Inform the students clearly about the expectations you have for their essays; a rubric for this purpose is recommended.

3. Determine what components will be assessed and the weighing to be used: for example, comprehensiveness—60 percent, expressive quality—20 percent, insight and creativity—20 percent. Points may be used rather than percent if one chooses.

4. Make a list of points that the essay should address to ensure focus and consistency in your marking.

5. Read several selected papers before marking to get a feel for the manner in which students have responded.

6. Respond to students' papers with praise where deserved and with constructive corrective feedback that will be helpful. Keep in mind that essays (and all tests) are most useful as instruments for students' learning when accompanied by such feedback.

The art course that has been used as a setting for the previous examples is not a language arts course, which presents another concern. To what extent do students' word-comprehension skills related to reading and interpreting an item and their expressive skills related to responding to an item become factors in the evaluation of a student response? In other words, teachers may find themselves grading students' language skills as much as their acquisition of understanding in the art course. This is a dilemma without an immediate solution. At the very least, students should be made aware of the extent to which expression will count as a factor in grading—if it counts at all. Also, every effort should be made to use clear, basic language in writing test items. Finally, students who are known to have limited comprehension and expressive skills should be given whatever consideration is helpful and fair. Within the context of these considerations, the goal should be informed teacher decision making that focuses on the students' best interest.

Objective Items. Most tests are made up primarily or entirely of objective items. They have the advantage of covering a lot of material efficiently, of being easy to score, and of being easy to translate into students' grades. On the other hand, they are most commonly used to test at the lower thinking levels, primarily recall and comprehension, although it is possible to have objective items at all levels of thinking. Teachers tend to use objective items because of these advantages, but there is a danger of trivializing the evaluation of learning outcomes. Objective means of measuring learning are necessary but not sufficient as a comprehensive approach to evaluation.

Matching, completion, and true–false items are the usual means of assessing students' recall. To the extent that some information is very important to students' understanding and becomes the "raw material" for subsequent information processing, these types of assessments are useful. However, it is clear from the research that these items are used with disproportionate frequency, or at the very least they are not supplemented by a sufficient number of items that test at the higher levels of thinking.

Although these three kinds of objective test items are straightforward in form, they nevertheless must be carefully written. True–false items, for example, deal in absolutes. However, absolutes that are also not self-evident are rather difficult to find. Students become testwise and realize that an absolute or specific determiner such as *always* or *never* usually signifies a false answer. Ambiguity is a problem as well. For example, a true–false statement might be: "Michelangelo was a sixteenth-century artist." A knowledgeable student would realize that Michelangelo produced one of his greatest sculptures, the *Pieta,* in the last years of the fifteenth century, so in the absolute sense the statement is false. Yet the teacher would probably intend this as a true statement. In writing any objective test item, a teacher must constantly keep in mind the concern for avoiding ambiguity.

The multiple-choice form is the most difficult to write but is the most useful objective test item. It involves producing a stem that describes the substance of the item and from three to five possible answers from which to select. This type of item can potentially assess all the levels of thinking, but it is most useful for measuring recall and comprehension. In some cases, it may also measure application and analysis.

The best approach to writing a multiple-choice item is to write a stem and correct response that deals with a pertinent and important aspect of the unit of study and is directly related to a unit goal. Then write at least two, but preferably three or four, so-called distractors, or possible responses that would be attractive to a person who was insufficiently informed. This latter task is the most difficult, and the effectiveness of the item is especially dependent on the finesse with which the distractors are written. But plausible distractors are difficult to write, so most multiple-choice items include four instead of five possible responses from which the student picks one. In some cases, only three possible responses are included, but the chances of guessing right considerably reduces the discriminating power.

Some examples of multiple-choice questions provide a basis for examining their qualities.

1. Michelangelo is associated most closely with which Italian city?

   a. Bologna

   b. Rome

   c. Milan

   d. Florence

This is a straightforward example of a recall-level item. Of course, one might have used a true–false item to test for the same knowledge. One might also have embedded this bit of information in a format that requires matching artists with locales.

2. Michelangelo's greatest artwork is

   a. *David.*

   b. *Mona Lisa.*

   c. *Pieta.*

   d. Sistine chapel ceiling.

This item has at least two flaws. First, one will probably encounter more argument than agreement about which was the greatest work of art. There is clearly no best response, and ambiguity results. Second, *Mona Lisa* is a ringer in this list, because another artist painted it. Students might very likely form unintended impressions if *Mona Lisa* is included as a distractor. In a more general sense, *Mona Lisa* lies outside the range from which appropriate distractors should be selected; it is of a different genre.

3. The "power" in Michelangelo's art lies primarily in his ability to
    a. give embodiment to a transcendent level of human experience.
    b. create a perfect mirror image of reality in both sculpture and painting.
    c. use line and perspective to produce unusual spatial relationships.
    d. represent common and familiar objects in unique, emotionally charged images.

This analysis level item may be appropriate for a college-level course in art history or art appreciation. However, if this were a question asked in Mr. Sykes's ninth-grade class or in any level of high school class, students could probably not handle the language level. It would be as much a test of reading comprehension or specialized vocabulary as of art knowledge.

4. Michelangelo can appropriately be formally considered a "Renaissance man" primarily because
    a. he lived in the fifteenth and sixteenth centuries.
    b. he was a master of several forms of art.
    c. he was a friend of powerful people in his time.
    d. his art was not limited to the traditions of his time.

This example of an analysis level item meets the criteria presented later for writing effective multiple-choice items.

Writing multiple-choice test items, according to Gage and Berliner (1991), is "a kind of art form" (p. 645). This should not discourage teachers from writing them; rather, it advises teachers not to take the skill for granted and to work at developing it. The previous examples begin to give a sense of the intellectual task involved in producing these items. A set of suggestions will help to guide the writing of such items. Practice in developing a feel for them will contribute to improving the skill.

1. Keep the language at the students' level; use good grammatical form.
2. Write the stem and correct response first; then add three or four plausible distractors.
3. Express as much of the substance of the item as possible in the stem.
4. Avoid ambiguity; be certain that one response is clearly the best response.
5. Keep the responses in an item consistent in type and length.
6. Avoid specific determiner words and absolutes such as *every, none, always,* and *never.*
7. Avoid the use of negative words *no* and *not* in the stem if possible; always avoid a double negative or a word used both in the stem and in the response.
8. Do not use *all of the above* as a distractor.

Authentic Assessment   Until the mid-1980s, the literature on classroom assessment dealt almost exclusively with the traditional sorts of topics that are described in the other sections of this chapter. Previous editions of this book have included the statement that the last major change in assessment practices was adoption of the letter grade (ABCDF) scale based on research conducted by Starch (1913, 1918). That assertion is no longer accurate. A new perspective based on practices that are termed *authentic* (or *alternative, performance,* or *naturalistic*) *assessment* has been given an increasingly prominent place in the literature, and we can predict with a fair degree of confidence that the several practices of authentic assessment will continue to gain in prominence. One major reason is that teachers are becoming increasingly convinced that traditional practices are insufficient to fulfill all the functions evaluation should serve in the classrooms, although they will continue to be used for the purposes they serve well. A second major reason is that teachers are increasingly approaching their teaching and their students' learning in constructivist terms, as has been described throughout this book. This places the emphasis on students doing more than simply knowing. Zemelman, Daniels, and Hyde (1998) said it this way:

> *Today, teachers are no longer satisfied to assess students' growth solely on the basis of classroom quizzes and standardized achievement tests, which tend to treat the curriculum as a pyramid of atomized subskills, and which often miss what kids can really do with coordinated, higher-order activities like writing, researching, experimenting, or problem solving. Instead, innovative teachers are increasingly using kidwatching, observational notes, interview questionnaires, checklists, student artifacts and work samples, performance assessment, student self-evaluation, evaluation conferences, portfolios, and other tools to get a better understanding of kids' learning and more clearly explain their progress. (p. 185)*

Zessoules and Gardner (1991) investigated classroom environments that supported what they termed an assessment culture as opposed to a testing culture. Four critical conditions for an assessment culture were identified: "nurturing complex understandings, developing reflective habits of mind, documenting students' evolving understandings, and making use of assessment as a moment of understanding" (p. 51). These conditions exist minimally, if at all, in classrooms in which virtually all evaluation occurs as tests administered following instruction, and in which students view learning as the means to "earn" a grade. Authentic assessment requires that learning be recognized as an evolving event, that its occurrence (or nonoccurrence) is evident in a variety of ways to the alert and concerned teacher, and that it should, where feasible, be evaluated as students' demonstrated ability to use knowledge or skill to accomplish meaningful tasks.

In the discussion on constructivism in Chapter 4, Harvard's Teaching for Understanding Project (Perkins and Blythe, 1994) was described as an example of ways educators can teach for understanding. The program illustrates four aspects of teaching for understanding—the use of generative topics, the shared understanding of unit goals, the design of performances that support unit goals, and the conducting of ongoing assessment.

As teachers move from a traditional stance to a more constructivist stance in their approaches to teaching, a commensurate shift in approaches to evaluation is obviously necessary. If we strive to "teach for student understanding," we must at the same time attempt to assess that understanding in multiple ways.

In some learning settings, authentic learning is a virtual aspect of the activity. In art, music, technology education, and physical education classes, for example, the respective outcomes are usually performances or artifacts that reflect the level of learning that has been achieved. No contrived and noncontextual "test" is necessary. Teachers in other content areas that do not lend themselves by their essential nature to authentic assessment have been generally complacent in their efforts to employ authentic assessment practices, although in fairness we must acknowledge that many informed and conscientious teachers have used creative and realistic methods of evaluation. The following several examples provide a sense of what teachers may do.

- In mathematics classes, teachers use realistic word problems that require students to use problem-solving skills. Also, teachers challenge students to write their own realistic problems that they own as a class.
- In economics class, the teacher conducts a stock-market competition between student groups in the class. Each group is allowed a $10,000 credit at the beginning to invest, and each group vies to make the greatest profit on their investment. Working in groups and having to discuss and agree on investment decisions is a further benefit of this activity.
- In biology class, the students accept the task of identifying the plant life along the metropolitan park nature trails and producing plaques with pertinent information for the benefit of nature enthusiasts.

The authentic activities described above and the many more that you undoubtedly can think of once you are on a roll appear to be learning activities more so than assessment practices—and that is just the point! Authentic assessment is, as much as possible, integral to the learning itself. The question then arises, "What about a grade?" It is a fair question, even though a glib first response might be, "So who needs a grade?" But until schools have evolved considerably from their current posture, teachers will be required to grade students on the ABCDF scale.

Rubrics.   One means of translating authentic assessment into letter grades is through use of a rubric. A *rubric* is a set of descriptions of behaviors, outcomes, or criteria identified with each grading symbol. "The current interest in rubrics comes as educators throughout the United States try to define learning outcomes, set standards for student achievement, and expand the use of performance assessments to evaluate what students know and can do" (O'Neil, 1994). Developing rubrics is acknowledged to be difficult, but they do make explicit the standards that may otherwise be vague to both the teacher and students.

The first step in developing rubrics (Glatthorn, 1998) is to identify the criteria to use. Four to seven criteria are recommended and identified by asking, "What do I look for when I evaluate this paper or performance?" The second step is to decide how many levels of performance to describe. Three to six levels are the most commonly used. Starting by identifying the highest level and the weakest level seems to be the best approach to take in forming a rubric.

Here is a rubric developed for scoring the presentation of a group project (adapted from Glatthorn, 1998, p. 56).

Criteria Levels	Superior	Very Good	Satisfactory	Minimally Satisfactory	Unsatisfactory
Group Work	Makes several valuable contributions; provides leadership	Makes several useful contributions; helps group work well	Makes several contributions without disruption	Makes one or two contributions, disrupts group occasionally	Does not contribute to group; often disrupts
Use of Historic Knowledge	Able to tie in several points showing relationship of historic data	Able to mention at least three points from historic data	Makes two contributions with historic data	Makes one mention of relevant historic data	Does not contribute any historic knowledge
Reasoning Ability	Demonstrates use of higher-order thinking and problem solving	Demonstrates use of higher-order thinking skills	Presents in logical form but is on knowledge and comprehension	Presents in confused form but uses knowledge and comprehension levels	Talks but does not show reasoning ability
Communication Skills	Able to communicate clearly main ideas of project with energy; uses visuals; listeners can recall three points made	Able to communicate main ideas with clarity and articulateness; uses visuals; listeners can recall two points	Able to communicate clearly; uses one visual; listeners can recall main idea	Able to communicate main idea; no visuals	Not well prepared; presentation confused; no visuals

Illustrations of rubrics appropriate for use in different content areas include the following:

Math: Accuracy of Written Problem Solving

5—Accurate work throughout solution. All calculations are correct, carried out to the required degree of precision/measurement error, and labeled correctly.

4—The work throughout the solution is mostly accurate and complete. All relevant calculations are correct and carried out to the required degree of precision. The few errors in the solution are related to minor calculations. The student's work can be understood because of proper labels and clear demonstration of thought.

3—The work is accurate with most relevant calculations done correctly. Some relevant calculations are incorrect. The student's work can be difficult to read due to unclear thinking or untidy work.

2—The work has inaccuracies throughout the solution. The student's solution is difficult to follow due to inaccurate calculations, unclear thinking, and/or untidy work.

1—The work has several inaccuracies and is very difficult to follow.

Social Studies: Group-Performance Task

17–20 points—Almost all students enthusiastically participate. Responsibility for task is shared. Students reflect awareness of others' views and opinions and include references to other opinions or alternatives in presentation and answer. Questions and answers illustrate forethought and preparation.

13–16 points—Students show adeptness in interacting. At least three-fourths of the students actively participate. Lively discussion centers on the task.

9–12 points—Some ability to interact. At least half of the students confer or present ideas. Attentive reading of documents and listening. Some evidence of discussion of alternatives.

5–8 points—Strong reliance on spokespersons. Only one or two persons actively participate. Sporadic interaction. Conversation not entirely centered on topic.

1–4 points—Exclusive reliance on one spokesperson. Little interaction. Very brief conversations. Some students are disinterested or distracted (adapted from California Assessment Program, 1990; in Herman, Aschbacher, and Winters, 1992, p. 46).

■ WEBSITE RESOURCE ■

This site is a collection of links to websites that contain rubrics found on the Web:

http://dante.udallas.edu/edu5352/rubrics.htm.

Some of the specific categories include subject-specific and general rubrics, student web page rubrics, and educator skill rubrics. Most of the links, though, are included under the miscellaneous list.

Portfolios. Portfolios have achieved prominence among teachers as an alternative assessment approach. Originally, the term was associated with artists' collections of their works. The portfolio expedited the examination, evaluation, and possible sale of their products. This idea of a collection of artifacts has been extended into the classroom, and it takes myriad forms as teachers and students in a range of classrooms assemble and organize materials representing students' progress and achievement over time.

A *portfolio*, originally a folder or large envelope containing artwork, has been appropriated by educators to incorporate any collection of classroom-produced artifacts. It may take the form of a folder, notebook, box, or drawer—whatever is a convenient organizing device. The concept of an organized collection is the key to portfolio development.

Portfolios have two characteristics that make them valuable as an assessment approach. First, they provide an ongoing means of monitoring students' progress. They include the actual products—an evolving contextual record—rather than only isolated grades in the teacher's gradebook. Second, they may be controlled to a significant degree by the students—that is, the students decide what to include in the portfolio that best represents their ability, interests, and achievement. Grady (1992) described it this way:

> Students have a vested interest in the creation of their portfolios, certainly more than they have for a file of test scores in the main office. The portfolio represents a range of efforts and tangible achievement; it presents a learning history. In a well-designed portfolio system, the students select the pieces of work to be included in the portfolio. The student has the chance to revise it, perfect it, evaluate it, and explain it. It is different from work completed just to fulfill an assignment or written for the teacher's eyes; a piece created for the portfolio bears a piece of the student's identity. Whether the work is a self-generated word problem in math or a persuasive essay, the student claims ownership. It represents the student in a concrete and authentic way that a stanine score cannot do. . . . With portfolios, assessment is an important part of the learning cycle, rather than being merely a result. (pp. 12–13)

The following steps can serve as a guide for using portfolios as part of the assessment process:

1. Identify your purpose for the portfolio and share that purpose with your students. Borich (2000, p. 459) identifies several purposes that portfolios can accomplish:
   - Monitoring student progress
   - Communicating what has been learned to parents and to the students themselves
   - Evaluating how well something has been taught
   - Showing off what has been accomplished
   - Using for part of a course or project grade

2. Identify the specific knowledge, skills, and dispositions that students are to demonstrate through the pieces they place in their portfolios. Share these knowledge, skills, and dispositions with your students and address them in the assessment rubrics. Borich (2000) explains that students can show knowledge acquisition or knowledge organization through the work in their portfolios; can use higher-order thinking processes including analysis, synthesis, evaluation, planning, organizing, and research; procedural skills such as clear communication, editing, and drawing; metacognition through use of self-monitoring and self reflection; dispositions such as acceptance of criticism, persistence, collaboration, desire for meaning, and learning.

3. Decide on which products to put into the portfolio and the number of samples to be included. The products should represent the knowledge, skills, and dispositions.

4. Build the portfolio rubric, preferably with your students. Decide on what will be considered excellent, satisfactory, and poor in each category. For the knowledge objectives, use the key outcomes expected. Do the same for skills and dispositions.

Some general suggestions for portfolio entries include:

- Excerpts from a class journal
- Lists of books read
- Annotated bibliographies of books read
- Lists of journal articles read
- Annotated bibliographies of journal articles read
- A subject-area autobiography
- Computer disc of various work
- Videotaped recording of readings, presentations, demonstrations, and so on
- Audiotaped recording of readings, presentations, reports, and so on
- An applied use of the subareas/topics in another discipline
- Artwork
- Photographs
- A written description of an individual project or investigation
- An example of classroom note taking
- Personal goals sheet
- Student's contributions to a group project
- Responses to open-ended questions
- Inquiries generated by the student
- Parent reflections on portfolio
- Student explanation of each item in the portfolio
- Table of contents

As mentioned in the case of authentic assessment, the grading of portfolios needs special consideration. It is especially appropriate that the teacher and students cooperatively decide on the expectations that pertain and develop a rubric for students' self-evaluation as well as the teacher's evaluation. Decisions have to be made about the extent to which various factors will be weighted, such as the amount and quality of content; the effort expended; the students' explanation, insight, and evaluation; and neatness and organization. With standards clearly in place and owned by students, focus is provided for their learning, and motivation is enhanced as well.

The following is an example of a social studies senior high portfolio unit rubric. The ideas for the performance tasks mentioned in the rubric are from Burz and Marshall (1998).

Social Studies Standards-Based Portfolio Rubric

Content Categories

Knowledge Concept in Standards—Global connections and conflicts affect everyone.

Skills

Higher-level thinking—analysis, synthesis, problem solving

Logical thinking—organization, arguments

Communication skills—presenting, use of visuals, spelling, and sentence structure

Dispositions—Increased interest in community, world news

RATINGS

Knowledge

4. Shows excellent insight in documentation about the knowledge concept; able to identify a number of global connections, conflicts, and effects that existed in the past and in the present and able to show their impact on various people today.

3. Shows good insight into knowledge concepts by identifying two global connections—one from past and one from present—and their impact on one or more countries or people.

2. Able to show one global connection and conflict or effect on the United States today.

1. Not able in the documentation to address the knowledge concept in enough detail to establish that concept is understood.

Skills—Higher-Level Thinking Skills

4. Able to compile information using a variety of sources; analyze and provide a graphic depiction of relationships found among several local businesses and other countries; report results in a creative form with predictions of trends.

3. Able to compile information using at least two sources; analyze and provide graphic depiction of relationships found among two local businesses with other countries; report results with predictions of trends.

2. Able to compile information with one source; analyze and report on relationship found among one local business and one or more other countries and report effects.

1. Able to report on one company and its ties with another country. Does not show impact or predict trends.

Skills—Communication Skills

4. Able to document clearly, explain the concept, and include graphics; no spelling or grammatical errors; citation of references included.

3. Able to document and explain clearly the concept and include graphics; has a few spelling and/or grammatical errors; references are cited.

2. Explains concept with limited documentation; uses only one graphic; has a number of spelling and/or grammatical errors; not all references are cited.

1. Explains concept with confusion; no graphics are used; a number of spelling and grammatical errors occur; no references are cited.

Dispositions

4. Shows in documentation additional research and reading beyond the task requirements; shares information with local community group or groups; or becomes involved in a community service project.

3. Shows in documentation additional research and reading in this area; makes plans to share information with local groups.

2. Shows additional research and reading in this area.

1. Does not show in documentation any further exploration of this concept.

Reflections—(turn in with a self-evaluation of portfolio using the above rubric)

1. What was the most important learning experience for you in this unit? Explain its importance.

2. What did you learn about the community that you did not know before?

3. How would you change your approach to the performance task if you do a similar project in the future?

4. What would you change about the unit and the performance tasks?

In addition to students' self-evaluating with the portfolio rubric, they should be encouraged to write a reflection on their portfolio using some of the following questions:

Why did you select this particular material or paper for the portfolio?

How well does the material you chose demonstrate the completion of the required task or the addressing of a particular objective?

What do you consider your best work in the portfolio? Why do you consider it your best work?

What work would you like to improve in the portfolio? Why?

What are the five most important things you have learned about (subject) _____ in this project?

■ WEBSITE RESOURCE ■

A website about electronic portfolios for students, teachers, and "lifelong learners" can be found here:

www.eduscapes.com/tap/topic82.htm

Links to portfolio articles and websites are provided. Many links to sample electronic portfolios are included from K–12 teachers and students, professors, doctoral students, and student teachers.

Projects and Investigations.   While classroom projects have long served as valuable instructional activities, the move toward more authentic forms of assessment has shifted these activities into a dual role—as learning tools and as assessment tools. Hart (1994) views projects as long-term, extended tasks with multiple goals. A student's grasp of key concepts within a unit of instruction can be assessed throughout the instructional unit or at the end of a course of study with projects. Hart gives examples of projects in secondary schools, all characterized by a high level of "inquiry and expression" (Wiggins, 1989; in Hart). At the Walden III High School in Racine, Wisconsin, seniors must complete a number of "rite of passage" activities to receive their diplomas. One of the required activities is a research project on a topic of the student's choice in American history. The student presents the paper to a committee of staff, students, and an outside adult and is orally questioned on his or her research. A list of real projects offered in *Alternative Assessment in the Mathematics Classroom* (1993) suggests that students investigate the connections of math to food and fitness, cars, space, and sports. These projects have the potential to "involve students in open-ended situations that may have a variety of acceptable results" and they are "embedded in problem-solving context (that) can be used by students to explore, study, think about, and pursue ideas that develop their understanding in all the important content areas of the mathematics curriculum" (p. 18).

Steinberg (1998) has identified six critical attributes of project-based learning that can help the classroom teacher design rich experiences for students and, at the same time, provide a detailed look at individual student development. Steinberg calls these attributes the Six A's of Designing Projects:

Authenticity

- Does the project emanate from a problem or question that has meaning to the student?
- Is it a problem or question that might actually be tackled by an adult at work or in the community?
- Do students create or produce something that has personal and/or social value beyond the school setting?

Academic rigor

- Does the project lead students to acquire and apply knowledge central to one or more discipline or content areas?
- Does it challenge students to use methods of inquiry central to one or more disciplines (e.g., to think like a scientist)?
- Do students develop higher-order thinking skills and habits of mind (e.g., searching for evidence, taking different perspectives)?

Applied learning

- Does the learning take place in the context of a semistructured problem that is grounded in life and work in the world beyond school?
- Does the project lead students to acquire and use competencies expected in high-performance work organizations (e.g., teamwork, appropriate use of technology, problem solving, communication)?
- Does the work require students to develop organizational and self-management skills?

Active learning

- Do students spend significant amounts of time doing field-based work?
- Does the project require students to engage in real investigation, using a variety of methods, media, and sources?
- Are students expected to communicate what they are learning through presentations and/or performances?

Adult relationships

- Do students meet and observe adults with relevant expertise and experience?
- Do students have opportunity to work closely with at least one adult?
- Do adults collaborate on the design and assessment of student work?

Assessment practices

- Do students reflect regularly on their learning, using clear project criteria that they have helped to set?
- Do adults from outside the classroom help students develop a sense of the real-world standards for this type of work?
- Will there be opportunities for regular assessment of student work through a range of methods, including exhibitions and portfolios? (pp. 24–25)

Observations and Questioning. Observing students and asking them questions are common teacher behaviors. As new practices that fall under the broad umbrella of constructivism emerge, the techniques of observations and questioning become ways of assessing students' understanding of concepts at levels beyond knowledge and comprehension; for example, in a mathematics class, the "best types of questions to ask students to assess their knowledge of the process standards are open-ended questions. Such questions do not have a single answer. They allow students an opportunity to think for themselves and to demonstrate their understanding of a problem or other situations" (*Alternative Assessment in the Mathematics Classroom*, 1993, p. 8). Examples of such questions include, "Would you explain the problem in your own words?" "What are two different strategies you could use to solve this problem?" and "Explain why the solution to the equation is incorrect."

As students become comfortable answering these kinds of questions, the teacher can begin using observation as another form of assessment. Observing students' critical-thinking skills can be accomplished "by listening to students explain their reasons for their work, that is, by observing their minds at work through the use of language" (*Alternative Assessment in the Mathematics Classroom*, 1993, p. 9). Observing can be used to assess performance in these areas:

- thinking processes
- problem-solving approaches
- persistence
- working in small groups
- communication skills
- creativity

Interviews and Conferences. In attempting to answer the question, "What does this student know?" the classroom teacher who engages in authentic forms of assessment may consider using interviews and conferences as ways to meet with individual students to discuss their learning. According to *Alternative Assessment in the Mathematics Classroom* (1993), an interview can be structured around questions that relate to a specific topic. In a literature class, the teacher might pose specific questions about the student's interpretation of a poem by Wordsworth. The student describes his or her interpretation of the poem and explains the thinking behind the interpretation. Student responses are recorded in an abbreviated format on an interview sheet. A conference is not as focused as an interview; instead, it is an informal discussion involving the teacher and the student. The teacher looks for student thinking and for student self-assessment. As in an interview, conference notes are made to record examples of student thinking, student learning goals, and student requests for needed resources to reach these goals. Some teachers keep interview and/or conference notes in binders with pages for each student in the class. Individual student development over time becomes obvious through this detailed record keeping.

Formative Evaluation This aspect of evaluation asks the question, "How am I doing?" It is not particularly different in form from the other tests, although it may be somewhat informal. These

> *In order to evaluate student learning, the classroom teacher must decide what is of value in a unit of instruction. If recall of specific facts is essential, then objective-type quizzes can quickly assess this type of learning outcome. If application or synthesis of a concept is of value, then student projects or investigations can be used. If evaluation is critical, then student portfolios might work. Knowing what is to be assessed and why will aid in making decisions about classroom evaluation.*

are tests or other approaches to evaluation that are administered at opportune times to provide feedback to the teacher and students regarding achievement. They serve a diagnostic function within a course of study. They serve as a basis for the teacher in ascertaining instructional effectiveness, making midunit curricular decisions, determining the impact of instructional innovations, and deciding whether reteaching should occur. They serve as a means for the student to gauge progress at any point and identify gaps or weaknesses in the mastery of the unit goals. Grades from formative evaluation tests may be recorded and counted as part of the student's achievement for the grading period, but this is not their major purpose.

For example, during a unit of painting in John Sykes's art course, a particular student may have been found to be quite adept in sketching the outlines of an intended painting. This student would be introduced to the next phase involving mixing colors while other students continued to improve their sketches. In the scenario, another sort of formative evaluation occurred as John Sykes used "teaching quizzes." These not only gave the students information on the extent to which they were meeting the teacher's expectations but also were an incentive to increase study efforts.

Summative Evaluation   When most people—especially nonteachers—think of evaluation, summative evaluation is what they have in mind. Summative evaluation occurs at the completion of a unit of study, and its primary purpose is to determine the extent to which each student has achieved the unit goals/objectives. Summative evaluation can occur in a variety of forms (including timed performances, written reports, or presentations to the group) but usually occurs as a written test. The scores derived from summative evaluation exercises are usually a primary source for determining students' grades.

If evaluation is considered to be a cyclical process, summative evaluation may also serve a diagnostic function. The end-of-the unit test indicates to the teacher the extent to which students have benefited from a unit of instruction. Some students in an algebra class, for example, simply may not be ready to proceed to second-order equations if they have not mastered simple linear equations. Remediation may be prescribed based on diagnosis from the summative evaluation outcome.

Classroom Tests

Teacher-made tests are a traditional and indispensable part of evaluation. They serve several functions, including, of course, measuring achievement. The items on a test provide the teacher with the opportunity to select for the student those aspects of the unit of study that are most important and thus reinforce learning of the material one last time during the study of the unit. Furthermore, students' attention is entirely devoted to the test for the duration of the time, resulting in some of the most intense learning that occurs in a classroom. This is a strong rationale for writing powerful tests.

A test score has no meaning until it is compared to a referent. Three types of referents are presented in this chapter. The teacher's purposeful choice of the appropriate referent is an important evaluation-related decision.

Norm-Referenced Tests   The referent for norm-referenced tests is the average of the students' scores on that particular test. It is an attractive approach to teachers because it lets them off the hook regarding making prior decisions about levels of achievement. Either by eyeballing a set of scores after the fact and assigning letter grades using break points in the range, or even by using a more sophisticated approach involving normal curve statistics, teachers establish norm-referenced student grades. It has the effect of neutralizing the teacher's possible shortcomings as an instructor because the highest score made is the highest score possible.

Many standardized tests are norm-referenced, using what Gage and Berliner (1991) referred to as the "distant peer group." Teachers or administrators often wish to know how their students compare with their cohort group districtwide, statewide, or nationwide. Teachers may make curriculum decisions or revise expectation levels based on the results of such tests. State proficiency tests are norm-referenced to give schools feedback about how their students are doing in comparison with statewide test norms.

Also, students may wish to know their standing within a certain population. The Student Achievement Test (SAT) and American College Test (ACT) are examples of norm-referenced standardized tests that provide college-bound students with important information about their current levels of achievement, which in turn are predictors of future academic achievement.

The use of norm referencing is widely criticized in the literature. In their evaluation-related decisions, teachers tend to default to norm referencing even when it is not the pedagogically recommended approach. However, norm referencing is a useful—in fact, indispensable—means of addressing the evaluation purposes for which it is intended.

In cases in which it is useful to rank students in the class, to cite achievement in terms of percentiles, or to employ a competitive approach usefully, norm-referenced grading is appropriate. However, it does allow the teacher to get by with unclear objectives and expectations and with marginally effective instruction. In general, teachers should think carefully before using norm-referenced tests in the classroom.

Criterion-Referenced Tests   As the term implies, students are required to meet a predetermined level of performance to be assigned a particular grade. Establishing the appropriate level, or criterion, may be a difficult task for the teacher, especially an inexperienced teacher. A criterion set too low results in unreasonably high grades and little grade dispersal. At the other extreme, a criterion set too high dooms a disproportionate number of students to low grades. This results in disappointed students and a grim teacher who is shaken by the specter of personal failure. Setting appropriate criteria is an important but risky part of evaluation.

Although the major disadvantage of criterion-referenced testing is the difficulty of establishing appropriate standards, the advantages far outweigh this disadvantage. The criterion-referenced approach allows teachers to establish, in their judgment, reasonable targets for student performance. If a target is not met, the teacher may need to analyze the possible causes and perhaps revise expectations, but it is not a reason to abandon the use of the approach. Criterion-referenced testing also allows the teacher to set a level of mastery that determines when reteaching should occur. Each student's level of competence is clearly represented because this approach is based on an absolute referent.

The objectives within a unit of study may, in fact, be written in terms of criteria. In an art class, the teacher may set as an expectation: "Students will mix three shades of each of the secondary colors within the ranges displayed on the classroom chart." This statement clearly established what students are to accomplish and further specifies the criterion against which it is to be compared. Other objectives in Chapter 5 on planning are examples of the relationship of objectives to criterion-referenced approaches to evaluation.

Students' Grades

Grades (the term *marks* is also used) have been called the coin of the students' realm. They usually are the object of the students' ardent desire. Receiving high marks is a satisfying experience for students; receiving low marks may be devastating. School marks are an important factor in students' determination of their self-images.

In the most basic sense, school marks are symbols with which the teacher communicates to students and other interested parties an estimate of each student's academic performance. From an academic point of view, grades convey pertinent and useful information. But grades are so emotionally charged that the academic uses of grades are frequently overshadowed.

The academic functions of grades are straightforward. Wrinkle (1947) and Adams and Torgerson (1964) identified four functions: (1) administrative, for determining such things as promotion, transfer, class standing, and eligibility for honors; (2) guidance, for identifying characteristics of strength and weakness, advising on enrollment in particular programs, and planning for careers; (3) informing, for communicating the results of evaluation to interested parties, primarily students and parents; and (4) motivation, for providing an incentive for students when innate interest in learning is minimal.

Although there is general agreement that grades are necessary (some might say a necessary evil), an informed and sensitive approach to evaluation can attenuate some of the negative outcomes of grading. A teacher who takes an arbitrary, self-righteous approach to grading will almost certainly hurt some students unnecessarily. On the other hand, a teacher who uses a positive, developmental approach to determining grades, as Mr. Sykes did in the case of Bree, can take advantage of the contribution that grades can make to promoting classroom achievement while minimizing contingent negative effects.

As you develop your personal approach to assessing students' work and assigning marks, establish clearly for yourself those principles and beliefs that reflect your philosophy of teaching. In the author's view, democratic values, including respect for the worth and dignity of every student and acceptance of individual differences, are fundamental propositions for teachers in American classrooms. What values emerge, then, in your approach to classroom evaluation? Following are some suggestions for your consideration:

1. Assessment practices should be consistent with modern methodology as presented in the professional knowledge base of teaching.

2. The primary purpose of classroom evaluation is to contribute to the learning process.

3. Assessment practices should demonstrably be in the best interest of the students.

4. Any classroom marking practice or individual mark that induces discouragement, disillusionment, resignation, or defeat is suspect. Further, a failing mark given to a student is in some measure a failure of the teacher as well.

5. A system of classroom evaluation should include opportunities for self-evaluation and, where feasible, cooperative evaluation.

APPLICATION for DIVERSE CLASSROOMS

Working with students who receive low grades and give up easily when they become frustrated with the assignment requires a teacher to adapt a planned evaluation approach with them. Findings from the Classroom Strategies Study (Brophy, 1996) showed that teachers who were rated more effective used a combination of support, encouragement, and task assistance to encourage gradual improvement. Teachers assured students they would give them work they could do, monitor their progress, provide assistance as needed, give much feedback, and provide them opportunities to share their accomplishments with others.

Mastery-learning strategy may be effective for these students who accept failure as their approach to schooling. The content would need to be broken into small parts and tasks to accomplish, tutoring should be available, and contracts for a certain level of performance could be helpful (Good and Brophy, 2000).

The Teacher's Personal Grading System The system the teacher uses to compute a student's grade is, by and large, a personal invention. Although the teacher must operate within the school's grading policy, which at the very least specifies what is marked (e.g., achievement, effort, citizenship, attitude), what scale and symbols are used, and the length of grading periods, the teacher generally has a wide range of freedom in selecting or devising personal marking practices. No one system is recognized as the best.

One factor in determining a grading system is the nature of a particular course. In a case in which grades are accumulated from a series of periodically administered, objectively scored tests, straightforward averaging is sufficient. If a variety of sources of evaluation is involved, matters of accumulating and weighting add complexity to grading. Three general criteria apply for any system: It should be functional fair, and clear.

Informing the students early and clearly regarding the teacher's approach to grading is more important than what approach is used. The students deserve to know what factors are taken into consideration, what relative weight is assigned to each factor, and the minimum expectations for achieving each grade. Describing this information in writing and delivering it to students with explicit directions on the sheet that it is to be shared with parents is the best approach; no student or parent can claim not to have been informed insofar as the teacher is culpable.

Hints for the Beginning Teacher

Set up your own website or get some help from the technology consultant in your school to get you started. The website can contain much information that will be valuable for your students and their parents. Here are some suggestions of items to include:

Course syllabus	Homework assignments
Materials needed	Lesson outline or notes
Project descriptions	Grading scale
Portfolio requirements	Rubrics
References	Book lists
Links to helpful websites	Extra-credit possibilities
Information on class members	Information on teacher
Photos	E-mail link to you

■ SUMMARY POINT ■

Classroom evaluation is an inevitable component of teaching. However, it is underused as a contributor to teaching effectiveness. Potential will be realized through a comprehensive understanding of the several dimensions of classroom evaluation and the discerning and imaginative application of its pertinent principles. This potential includes greater scope in planning, more informed decision making during instruction, and an increased base of information for assessing achievement.

■ QUESTIONS FOR REFLECTION ■

1. At the close of the scenario, John Sykes asked the rhetorical question, "So what's a grade for after all?" Your own philosophical approach to grading can be brought to the level of explicit awareness by writing a paragraph in response to John's question.

2. Given a typical unit of study in your subject area, what evaluative data will you obtain, and how will you obtain it, to accomplish the formative and summative functions of evaluation?

3. In developing a grading system for your classroom that is functional, fair, and clear, what will be the major features you will incorporate?

4. How do the principles of constructivist teaching contribute to a fuller understanding of the concept of authentic assessment?

5. How would you deal with the evaluation implications of the following situations?

   a. A student has been placed in your class who is clearly unable to achieve at what you consider to be a minimally acceptable (mastery) level of accomplishment. (The principle of inclusion is especially pertinent here.)

   b. Both knowledge and performance (or creative) outcomes are included in the course, yet you are limited to assigning only one final mark.

   c. A student is found to have cheated on an important unit test.

   d. A student has a poor attendance record, has completed only about half the homework assignments, was often late turning in work, but scored well on the unit test.

6. Describe a student project in your subject area that would meet the Six A's of quality school projects; that is, authenticity, academic rigor, applied learning, active learning, adult relationships, and assessment practices.

■ REFERENCES ■

Adams, G., and Torgerson, T. (1964). *Measurement and Evaluation in Education, Pschology, and Guidance.* New York: Holt, Rinehart & Winston.

Agnew, E. (1983). "A study of the letter grade system and its effect on the curriculum." Paper presented at the annual meeting of the AERA, Montreal. (ERIC Document Reproduction Service No. ED 238 143).

Alternative Assessment in the Mathematics Classroom. (1993). Westerville, OH: Glencoe Division of Macmillan/McGraw-Hill.

Brophy, J. (1996). *Teaching Problem Students.* New York: Guilford.

Borich, G. (2000). *Effective Teaching Methods* (4th ed.). Upper Saddle River, NJ: Merrill Prentice Hall.

Burz, H., and Marshall, K. (1998). *Performance-Based Curriculum for Social Studies.* Thousand Oaks, CA: Corwin Press.

Carter, K. (1984). "Do teachers understand the principles for writing tests?" *Journal of Teacher Education, 35*(6), 57–60.

Earl, L. M., and LeMahieu, P. G. (1997). "Rethinking assessment and accountability." In A. Hargreaves (Ed.), *Rethinking Educational Change with Heart and Mind.* Alexandria, VA; Association of Supervision and Curriculum Development.

Fleming, M., and Chambers, B. (1983). "Teacher-made tests: Windows on the classroom." In W. E. Hathaway (Ed.), *Testing in the Schools: New Directions for Testing and Measurement.* San Francisco: Jossey-Bass.

Gage, N., and Berliner, D. (1991). *Educational Psychology* (5th ed.). Boston: Houghton Mifflin.

Glatthorn, A. (1998). *Performance Assessment and Standards-Based Curricula: The Achievement Cycle.* Larchmont, NY: Eye on Education.

Good, T., and Brophy, J. (2000). *Looking in Classrooms* (8th ed.). New York: Addison Wesley Longman.

Grady, E. (1992). *The Portfolio Approach to Assessment* (Fastback series). Bloomington, IN: Phi Delta Kappa Educational Foundation.

Graves, D., and Sunstein, B. (1992). *Portfolio Portraits.* Portsmouth, NH: Heinemann.

Gullickson, A. B. (1984). "Teacher perspectives of their instructional use of tests." *Journal of Educational Research, 77*(4), 244–248.

Guskey, T. R. (1996). "Reporting on student learning: Lessons from the past prescriptions for the future." In T. R. Guskey (Ed.), *ASCD Yearbook: Communicating Student Learning.* Alexandria, VA: Association for Supervision and Curriculum Development.

Halpin, G., and Halpin, G. (1982). "Experimental investigations of the effects of study and testing on student learning." *Journal of Educational Psychology, 72*, 32–38.

Haney, W. (1991). "We must take care: Fitting assessments to functions." In V. Perrone (Ed.), *Expanding*

Student Assessment. Alexandria, VA: Association for Supervision and Curriculum Development.

Hart, D. (1994). *Authentic Assessment: A Handbook for Educators.* Menlo Park, CA: Addison-Wesley.

Hebert, E. A. (1998). "Lessons learned about student portfolios." *Phi Delta Kappan, 79*(8), 583–585.

Herman, J., Aschbacher, P., and Winters, L. (1992). *A Practical Guide to Alternative Assessment.* Alexandria, VA: Association for Supervision and Curriculum Development.

Herman, J., and Winters, L. (1994). "Portfolio research: A slim collection." *Educational Leadership, 52*(7), 48–55.

Kellaghan, T., Madaus, G., and Airasian, P. (1982). *The Effects of Standardized Testing.* Boston: Kluwer-Nijhoff.

Lazar-Morris, C., Polin, L., May, R., and Burry, J. (1980). *A Review of the Literature in Test Use* (Rep. No. 144). Center for the Study of Evaluation, Los Angeles, CA: University of California.

Madaus, G., and Kellaghan, T. (1993). "The British experience with authentic testing." *Phi Delta Kappan, 74*(5), 458–469.

Marzano, R., Pickering, D., and McTighe, J. (1993). *Assessing Student Outcomes.* Alexandria, VA: Association for Supervision and Curriculum Development.

Nungester, R. J., and Duchaster, P. C. (1982). "Testing versus review: Effects on retention." *Journal of Educational Psychology, 74*, 18–22.

O'Neil, J. (1994). "Making assessment meaningful." *Association for Supervision and Curriculum Update, 36*(6), 1, 4–5.

Pedulla, J. J., Airasian, P. W., and Madaus, G. F. (1980). "Do teacher ratings and standardized test results of students yield the same information?" *American Education Research Journal, 17*(3), 303–307.

Perkins, D., and Blythe, T. (1994). "Putting understanding up front." *Educational Leadership, 51*(5), 4–7.

Perrone, V. (1991). *Expanding Student Assessment.* Alexandria, VA: Association for Supervision and Curriculum Development.

Rudman, H., Kelly, J., Wanous, D., Mehrens, W., Clark, C., and Porter, A. (1980). *Integrating Assessment with Instruction* (Research Series No. 75). Lansing, MI: Institute for Research on Teaching, Michigan State University.

Solomon, P. (1998). *The Curriculum Bridge.* Thousand Oaks, CA: Corwin Press.

Starch, D. (1913, October). "Reliability and distribution of grades." *Science, 38*, 630–636.

Starch, D. (1918). *Educational Measurements.* New York: Macmillan.

Steinberg, A. (1998). *Real Life, Real Work: School-to-Work as High School Reform.* New York: Routledge.

Stiggins, R. J. (1985). "Improving assessment where it means the most: In the classroom." *Educational Leadership, 43*(2), 69–74.

Stiggins, R., Bridgeford, N., and Conklin, N. (1986). "Classroom Assessment: A Key to Effective Education." *Educational Measurement, 5*(2), 5–17.

Wiggins, G. (1993). *Assessing Student Performance.* San Francisco: Jossey-Bass.

Worthen, B. R. (1993). "Critical issues that will determine the future of alternative assessment." *Phi Delta Kappan, 74*(6), 444–454.

Wrinkle, W. (1947). *Improving Marking and Reporting Practices in Secondary Schools.* New York: Rinehart.

Zemelman, S., Daniels, H., and Hyde, A. (1998). *Best Practice: New Standards for Teaching and Learning in America's Schools* (2nd ed.). Portsmouth, NH: Heineman.

Zessoules, R., and Gardner, H. (1991). "Authentic assessment: Beyond the buzzword and into the classroom." In V. Perrone (Ed.), *Expanding Student Assessment.* Alexandria, VA: Association for Supervision and Curriculum.

11

Toward Effective Teaching

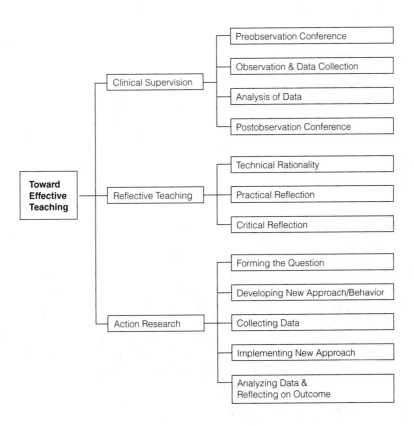

This book has presented dozens of ideas about teaching and especially about instruction. No reader could or should remember them all separately. What the reader should have acquired as a synthesis of the book's contents is a sense of what a mature and professional teacher is, the respect this teacher has for the science of teaching, the approach this teacher takes to decision making; the model this teacher provides for students as a scholar and a leader; the skill with which this teacher employs a range of teaching methods; and the tolerance this teacher has for conditions that cannot be directly controlled.

The challenge to the novice teacher, as is perhaps now clear, is not to emulate precisely some expert model but rather to be an effective decision maker. Training is most useful in highly predictable and repetitious situations. Teaching is not like that. At any moment, the situation in the classroom is shaped by the interplay of numerous dynamic variables. Conditions change quickly within a classroom and vary markedly from class to class. The task of the teacher is to control as many variables as possible and be able to react with assurance to those that are not directly controllable. Teachers, therefore, depend much more on knowledge and judgment than on training to be effective decision makers. The fact that the answers are not "out there" to be found is at first difficult to accept. The fact is that the answers— or at least the decisions—come from within. This sometimes makes teaching a lonely job, and not a job for the faint-hearted or the insecure.

The effective teacher is not a single, readily described entity. Effective teachers share some common general traits, but in practice those traits are exhibited in unique and personal ways. In a real sense, aspiring teachers must reinvent the effective teacher based on their knowledge, beliefs, perceptions, personality, and interaction with students in various contexts. Assistance with this task is available from this book, from teacher educators, and from practicing teachers. However, the ultimate responsibility for acquiring identity in the teacher role and integrity as a professional educator lies with each prospective teacher.

We presume that by now the reader has considered the many ideas in this book and the image of the effective teacher has begun to take shape. The next likely step is to develop one's teaching skills through extensive teaching. This phase usually occurs as student teaching or the internship. This book was designed for teacher-education students, student teachers, and first-year teachers to provide direction in applying instructional skills. Activities were devised to aid beginning teachers and supervisors in obtaining data to help measure the effectiveness of these skills on students and, in turn, influence instructional decisions. The data-collection instruments included in many chapters are intended for this purpose. We suggest, therefore, that this book's contribution, more than one of informing per se, has the potential to contribute to one's actual entry into teaching.

■ STUDENT TEACHING AND INTERNSHIP

Student teaching or an internship is the usual culmination of the teacher-education program. In the view of student teachers or interns, it is the most important phase because they finally encounter the real demands of the teacher role. It is typically approached with some anxiety and perceived to be a trial-by-fire or a sink-or-swim proposition. Realistically the possibility of this exists, but students who have been reasonably successful in preparation experiences prior to student teaching have little rational basis for fear. It is essentially a very special time for learning in ways that have been previously unavailable because preparation prior to this phase has taken place primarily in college classrooms and has focused on the knowledge base. Now as the preparation responsibility for the development of preservice teachers is carried over into the first years of in-service teaching, more personalized and practical assistance is available to the beginner through and beyond student teaching. The profession is acknowledging that an optimally effective teacher develops only after a substantial period of study and practice. The support increasingly provided to novice teachers is the sign of a maturing profession.

As student teachers or interns adjust to their first intensive periods of teaching, their focus shifts from the cognitive, or intellectual, preparation to experiential engagement. This shift presents a new set of demands to the student teachers or interns about which they will feel some measure of stress. This stress can cause a beginning teacher to abandon newly acquired, pedagogically endorsed ideas and revert to more comfortable intuitive ones. This is a time for tough-minded decision making on the part of the student teacher or intern. Student teaching and the internship will be more valuable experiences if deliberate efforts are made to employ approaches and practices as they are described in this book. Resisting the temptation to practice without consideration of effective-teaching techniques will diminish the extent of necessary relearning later to function as an optimally effective teacher. Those who initially played golf using a flawed swing and then needed to relearn a proper swing will appreciate the logic of this suggestion.

Student teaching and the internship enlist the services of a successful practicing teacher, variously referred to as the cooperating or mentor teacher, to supervise the beginner. The function of the cooperating teacher is far more than simply making a classroom available to the student teacher. An important contribution made by this person is in observing the student teacher's or beginning teacher's performance to provide descriptive and evaluative feedback. Receiving impressions and advice from a perceptive observer is valuable. To the extent that the data provided are focused, systematically obtained, carefully analyzed, and thoughtfully interpreted, it is especially valuable. The entire process that is referred to as "clinical supervision" in the literature is facilitated by the instruments provided in this book. Further, the process of action research contributes meaningfully to teachers' efforts to improve their teaching.

SCENARIO

Denton Coleman had been student teaching in a Spanish III class for six weeks. He had gotten by the initial jitters and uncertainty and was beginning to establish his own teaching style. He realized that he tended not to be as structured in his approach as his cooperating teacher, Kay Obrock; however, she did not insist on more structure. She was willing to let Denton experiment and find his own most comfortable and effective way. Denton had felt a sense of relief after the first three weeks when he realized he was able to manage acceptably well as a teacher. With the relief came a surge of confidence and exhilaration about teaching. Now, however, at the six-week point, he experienced some self-doubt and a decided letdown. The students in his Spanish III class seemed complacent. They had not been well prepared for class, nor had they been as enthusiastic in their participation as he remembered they were for Ms. Obrock.

When he shared his concern with his cooperating teacher, she responded, "I've noticed it, Denton. Part of it, I guess, is that the honeymoon is over. When you are a new face and a different personality, the kids are naturally curious and interested. Every teacher experiences that, and it usually works to your advantage at first. When you don't have that going for you any more, you have to look more carefully at what is happening." They talked for a few more minutes, but he still felt uneasy and didn't have any clear notion of what to do about it. Then something Kay Obrock had said came to mind: "Look more carefully at what is happening." He remembered the text he had used in his principles and methods course that included a series of instruments for analyzing instruction.

Denton took the book from the bookshelf when he got home and began to look through it. As he revisited the familiar pages, he thought it just might be what he needed. The next day, in their first-period conference, Denton showed the book to Kay—especially the analysis instruments. "We

didn't have anything like this when I was in college," she said, "but it looks interesting." She spent some time during the day looking through the book. When they met again after school for their daily wrap-up, each had some ideas. Denton said, "The problem seems to be motivation. They aren't working very hard, and they are fooling around in class more and more. Isn't there something in the book about motivation?"

"Yes," Kay replied. "But motivation is a big topic. A lot of things contribute to motivation. As I see it, that is one of the advantages of the book, that it helps make you aware of the parts and gives you a way to examine them." After some discussion, Kay went on to say, "Look, there is an instrument in Chapter 6 called 'Motivating Behaviors.' It includes six different aspects of motivation. Why don't I use this in class tomorrow, and it will help us focus more specifically on something we can handle. The book suggests making a videotape so that you can do some analysis, too. Maybe I can get the video camera away from the football coach for a day or two, and maybe we can use this 'problem' you're having and these analysis tools to conduct an action research project."

Denton Coleman liked the idea of using *his own questions* about *his own teaching* as the basis of a research project. He also liked the idea because he was learning about the process of action research in his student teaching seminar back on campus. The structure of action research gave him a framework for posing further questions about his problem, for gathering data, for reading related literature, and for analyzing the situation. So, the next day, Denton taught while Kay Obrock observed with the instrument before her. Then they both viewed the videotape later. Their analysis, done independently and then compared, revealed a similar pattern. Denton used his voice well enough, changed the instructional mode frequently, and controlled the pace appropriately. He did less well in displaying enthusiasm. However, moving about the classroom and using purposeful nonverbal behaviors were identified as the motivation areas of most need in both of their analyses.

They discussed the results of their initial analyses at some length. Then Kay said, "Denton, you can't change everything at once. Let's take one thing at a time. Suppose we create a brief list of questions related to this issue of motivation."

Denton and Kay brainstormed and came up with two specific questions all stemming from the primary question, "What can I do to increase my students' motivation to learn?": Will the students be more motivated if move around the classroom more, and will the students be more motivated if I use a variety of nonverbal behaviors to create a presence?

Then Denton and Kay discussed what kind of data they would collect to answer these questions. "Because we're going to begin by looking at your movements around the room," Kay suggested, "why don't I make a diagram of the room and chart your movements during that class for the next two weeks? I can also identify situations that should be monitored and see if you respond by moving there."

"Sounds good to me," Denton agreed enthusiastically. "Now maybe I should give some thought to just how I can move effectively. I have an article about teacher movements from class that I can read. That should be a good start."

■ APPLICATION TO PRACTICE

Clinical Supervision

Clinical supervision is the highly structured and intensive means with which the cooperating teacher contributes to the process of systematic analysis. Goldhammer (1969) and Cogan (1972) originally described clinical supervision, and numerous authors have written more recently on the topic (Acheson and Gall, 1997; Daresh and Playco, 1995; Glickman, 2002; Guskey, 2000; Danielson and McGreal, 2000).

In a regular in-service setting, clinical supervision tends to be somewhat unwieldy because of the extensive amount of time required of the supervisor unless it is part of an assistance program for beginning and marginal teachers. With a designated mentor or support teacher to give the beginning teacher feedback on teacher behaviors and their effect on student behaviors, the clinical supervision model can be a valuable tool to promote informed decision making for the beginning teacher. Clinical supervision is ideally suited for the internship and the student-teaching phases because the student teacher and cooperating teacher or support teacher necessarily work in a close relationship over a considerable period of time. The time the cooperating teacher or support teacher spends observing the beginning teacher will be used to maximum advantage if clinical supervision is implemented.

Clinical supervision varies in its number of steps from author to author, but in essence the process is the same. The following four steps describe the process in its simplest form using the student teacher–cooperating teacher titles, but the process is the same for intern–support teacher and beginning teacher–supervisor:

Step 1—Preobservation Conference. The student teacher and cooperating teacher decide together what aspect of the student teacher's performance will be targeted. This idea is then behaviorally defined in terms of its discrete components. An instrument comprised of a series of components such as those in this book provides such a definition. Next, a criterion or goal stated in measurable terms is established. Finally, if an instrument is not already available for collecting pertinent data, one will have to be devised.

Step 2—Observation and Data Collection. The cooperating teacher may actually use the instrument to collect data during the student-teaching episode. However, the cooperating teacher might more usefully operate a video camera to ensure that the episode is expertly taped. The tape can then be used later for obtaining data. Ideally, both the student teacher and the cooperating teacher will tabulate and analyze data independently for later comparison, discussion, and evaluation.

Step 3—Analysis of Data. Whatever the situation is regarding data collection, it is essential that the cooperating teacher use the data-collection instrument. Examination of the data, either independently or cooperatively, should reveal patterns that in turn suggest underlying meanings. The cooperating teacher needs to be certain that thorough analysis does occur and the implications are translated into appropriate teaching strategies.

Step 4—Postobservation Conference. The cooperating teacher and the student teacher compare their respective analyses and implications. Considerable attention should be given to probing underlying meanings together and discussing promising strategies. A new target or goal should be agreed on and the student teacher should be made responsible for developing a plan to reach it. This initiates a new cycle of clinical supervision, and the cycle continues as long as it is productive in any area of teaching improvement.

■ SUMMARY POINT ■

Effective teacher decision making about instructional improvement or any other aspect of teaching requires an informed belief system. Although a popular aphorism postulates experience as the best teacher, teaching experience alone provides no guarantee of instructional improvement over time. However, decisions made in the interest of improving instruction that are based on systematically obtained data are virtually certain to produce targeted goals.

> *A key decision that the classroom teacher can (and should) make that is supported by the process of clinical supervision has to do with what is focused on in the classroom. If student learning is the focus, then data can be collected from tests, homework, and so on. If the teaching itself is the focus, then the teacher must decide how best to answer these two questions: "What did I do to help the students learn?" "What could I do differently to help the students learn more?"*

■ WEBSITE RESOURCE ■

The North Central Regional Educational Laboratory (NCREL) provides research-based knowledge particularly related to science, mathematics, literacy, and technology that is useful and usable to teachers at all levels. There is a major emphasis on professional development and school improvement at

www.ncrel.org.

Beginning teachers will find Voices of Teachers on Teaching especially useful and friendly. Written and oral commentary from teachers about all aspects of teaching can be found at

www.ncrel.org/he/tot.

■ WEBSITE RESOURCE ■

Suggestions from first-year teachers on working with veteran teachers, parents, principals, and university education professors can be found at this site. There's

also an information source of websites, most of which are free, at

www.ed.gov/pubs/survivalguide/index.html.

■ WEBSITE RESOURCE ■

Scholastic has a website on Starting Your Teaching Career consisting of resources for new and future teachers. Topics include journals and organizations, tools and resources, and finding a job. Getting started topics include important beginning for beginners, routines and procedures, procedures checklist, classroom organization, paperwork, planning, general conduct, and time management at

http://teacher.scholastic.com/ professional/futureteachers/index.htm.

Also included is a discussion group where you can get teaching tips and share your experiences with other new teachers.

Reflective Teaching

The term *reflective teaching* is used rather loosely in the literature to refer to teachers' scrutiny of and decision making about their teaching practices. Ginsberg and Clift (1990) defined *reflection* as "the systematic and concerted synthesis of theory and practice—praxis" (p. 454). Kennedy (1990), in synthesizing references from the literature, concluded that "reflection is an ongoing process that enables teachers to continually learn from their own experiences by considering alternative interpretations of situations, generating and evaluating goals, and examining experiences in light of alternative goals and hypotheses" (p. 817).

We hope that teachers have always reflected in the ways described, and certainly it has occurred in varying degrees. However, relatively little study was made of teachers' reflectivity. Dewey's treatise on the topic, *How We Think* (1933), was widely applauded, but had little impact on teaching generally. In the mid-1980s, educators rediscovered the book and have made wide reference to it in the literature. In it, Dewey asserted that problem solving is a matter of systematic inquiry to determine a preferable course of action, but that any course of action is subject to continuing review and revision.

Since 1990, much literature has been published that integrates the process of reflective teaching with the professional development of teachers. Lieberman (1995) summarized this integration when she wrote:

> *What everyone appears to want for students—a wide array of learning opportunities that engage students in experiencing, creating, and solving real problems, using their own experiences, and working with others—is for some reason denied to teachers when they are the learners. In the traditional view of staff development, workshops and conferences conducted outside the school count, but authentic opportunities to learn from and with colleagues* inside *the school do not. (p. 591)*

> *The ways teachers learn may be more like the ways students learn than we have previously recognized. Learning theorists and organizational theorists are teaching us that people learn best through active involvement and through thinking about and becoming articulate about what they have learned. (p. 592)*

Darling-Hammond and McLaughlin (1995) reiterate this message about reflective teaching and professional development:

> *The vision of practice that underlies the nation's reform agenda requires most teachers to rethink their own practice, to construct new classroom roles and expectations about student outcomes, and to teach in ways they have never taught before and probably never experienced as students. (p. 597)*
>
> *Teachers learn by doing, reading, and reflecting (just as students do); by collaborating with other teachers; by looking closely at students and their work; and by sharing what they see. This kind of learning enables teachers to make the leap from theory to accomplished practice. In addition to a powerful base of theoretical knowledge, such learning requires settings that support teacher inquiry and collaboration and strategies grounded in teachers' questions and concerns. To understand deeply, teachers must learn about, see, and experience successful learning-centered and learner-centered teaching practices. (p. 598)*

The Process of Reflective Teaching

Over the last decade, we find that the term *reflective teaching* has been used in a more expansive way. Originally used to describe teacher thinking, teacher reflection is currently used in the literature as a viable option for professional development. Danielson and McGreal (2000) state, "Few activities are more powerful for professional learning than reflection on practice" (p. 24). Reflective teaching is also a critical component in what Lambert (1998) calls "building leadership capacity in schools." As schools design opportunities for teacher reflection (e.g., study groups, peer coaching, critical friends, etc.), new roles and responsibilities for teacher leadership will emerge (Lambert, Collay, Dietz, Kent, and Richert, 1996).

Feiman-Nemser (1990) considered reflective teaching to be a generic professional disposition. This is true in the sense in which it has already been described. On the other hand, it has also been referred to as a process. It is not a single specific process that is once and for all written in stone, but it is a general process that incorporates the spirit of inquiry. Van Manen (in Zeichner and Liston, 1987) postulated three levels of reflectivity: technical rationality, practical action, and critical reflection, as depicted in Figure 11.1.

Reflectivity Continuum

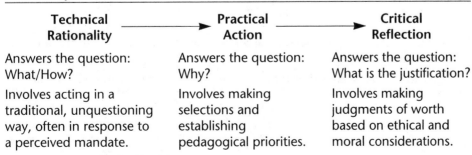

Technical Rationality	Practical Action	Critical Reflection
Answers the question: What/How?	Answers the question: Why?	Answers the question: What is the justification?
Involves acting in a traditional, unquestioning way, often in response to a perceived mandate.	Involves making selections and establishing pedagogical priorities.	Involves making judgments of worth based on ethical and moral considerations.

Figure 11.1 Levels of Reflectivity

Technical rationality refers to "delivering" the curriculum in much the way it is presented in the official documents of the school. Practical action involves teacher selection from among alternatives that are available in light of the projected practical outcomes of each. "At this level every action is seen as linked to particular value commitments, and the actor considers the worth of competing educational ends" (Zeichner and Liston, 1987, p. 24). Critical reflection transcends practical action by asking questions in the critical and moral dimension, involving "concerns for justice, equity, and concrete fulfillment, and whether current arrangements serve important human needs and satisfy important human purposes" (p. 25).

Teachers are encouraged to engage in reflectivity at the highest level that is pertinent in a given situation. Ongoing decisions are necessary at the level of technical rationality, of course, as teachers conduct the routines of teaching. A teacher's personal teaching style is largely defined by the nature and pattern of decisions at this level, for example, the methods the teacher prefers, the rules established for behavior, and the frequency and types of homework assignments.

Meanwhile, many opportunities will occur for making practical action decisions. The teacher needs to be alert to these occasions and consider pedagogical priorities and the particular characteristics and needs of the students. At this point, the teacher may decide not to have the class read *Romeo and Juliet* as the course of study stipulates but instead see a videotape of *West Side Story* with the intention of reading brief excerpts from the play that illustrate the relationship between them. Various forms of reflective teaching at the level of practical action can be found in schools around the country. For example, classroom teachers are:

- Participating in problem-solving groups and decision-making teams (Lieberman, 1995)
- Keeping reflective journals
- Writing and analyzing case studies of practice (Lieberman, 1995)
- Engaging in peer study groups
- Analyzing student work through self-assessment and student performance commentaries (Bambino, 2002; Danielson and McGreal, 2000)
- Keeping professional portfolios
- Participating in peer coaching teams

These various forms of reflective teaching can lead to informed decision making at the level of practical action.

Relatively few instances of critical reflection will occur, but these are ones that will profoundly affect educational experiences within the classroom. Should birth control information be made explicitly available to students? Should a student be failed who has passed the tests but attended irregularly? Should different standards be applied to students who are bused in? Should ethnic versions of English usage be accepted in the classroom? Should students who are found smoking be reported if the automatic three-day suspension will seriously affect their chance of passing?

Scenario Reprise

The scenario at the beginning of this chapter depicted Denton Coleman, a student teacher, and Kay Obrock, his cooperating teacher, involved in reflection on teaching. Denton, after reflecting on his teaching, speculated that the problem was students' motivation. Kay extended the reflection process and suggested an action research endeavor using data-collection and -analysis methods to further investigate the problem. This type of inquiry is an extended application of the principle of reflective teaching.

Consider on the other hand what might have occurred. Denton could have assumed that the Spanish III students were lazy or they were staging a conspiracy. He may immediately have resorted to using a verbal reprimand or threat or other punitive measure at the expense of any goodwill that had been accrued in the six weeks he had been their teacher. His approach, instead, represents the application of sound pedagogical principles, and he has a good chance of achieving his intended outcome of providing additionally for the students' motivation. Meanwhile, this learning about teaching experience is valuable for Denton.

The Teacher as Researcher

The professional development of a teacher is a career-long concern. Obtaining a teaching certificate, even an advanced certificate or degree, or tenure in one's position does not exempt one from the expectation of engaging in continuing development. Only the most arrogant of teachers would claim to have reached a level of optimum effectiveness beyond which further improvement is impossible, for teaching is a dynamic, evolving profession in which changes are ongoing. To remain static in one's skills and methods assures that one's practice will become outmoded. Consequently, there is the expectation that teachers will keep up with literature pertinent to their practice, attend courses and workshops as part of their in-service education, engage in professional dialogue with their colleagues, and be open to promising new ways of providing effective education for youth.

In recent years, a new emphasis has been placed on the role of the teacher as researcher, an aspect of reflective practice, as a means of improving teaching (Johnson, 1993). However, acceptance of this new role has been met with considerable reluctance by teachers. They have tended to view research with suspicion when they have viewed it at all (Bennett, 1993). They consider research to be closely associated with theory, and that theory is something that educational theorists are involved with that has little relevance to hands-on teaching. Research conjures up mountains of data in support of jargony-stated hypotheses. The purpose for doing research is often misunderstood by teachers, too. In their work on best practices in schools, Zemelman, Daniels, and Hyde (1998) contend that "because academic research is so often used in the educational world to prove one person's status higher than another's rather than to really improve schools, teachers often view 'theory' with well-justified suspicion" (p. 228). When teachers are asked how they use research in their classrooms, they typically reply, in effect, that they make no overt use of research in their teacher decision making. Teacher educators and researchers must accept some measure of blame for having failed to convince prospective teachers—who then become practicing teachers—of the potential of research to be a mainstay of their beliefs and practices.

All teachers conduct a kind of "soft research" in their classrooms, if research is broadly conceived as making thoughtful decisions about instruction based on information derived from their observation and experience. In this current context, however, research is defined as systematic problem solving based on data obtained for that purpose. Basically, we are construing research in a somewhat more formal way than that with which teachers routinely address concerns in their classrooms. We refer to it as *action research*, a term coined based on a concept introduced by John Dewey in the 1920s and further developed by Kurt Lewin in the 1940s. Check (1997) writes that this type of teacher research "can be a revolutionary form of professional development because it responds in a new way to a fundamental question: who can validly generate knowledge about teaching and learning?" (p. 7). Powerful professional development can result from action research, Check (1997) maintains, by "offering the possibility of major, long-term changes that are generated by teachers themselves, based on their own investigations of practice" (p. 7).

In the words of Glanz (1998), action research "is a form of research that is conducted by practitioners to improve practices in educational settings" (p. 20). Calhoun (2002) defines action research as "continual disciplined inquiry conducted to inform and improve our practice as educators" (p. 18). In a profession that is "anchored in activity" (Freeman, 1998), inquiring into one's practice can be a radical shift in orientation. Freeman believes that becoming a teacher-researcher can create tension. Teachers, he believes, are not "paid to ask questions about what they do; they are paid to *do*. The professional community that hosts their work is founded in the idea of action; it values doing, not asking questions" (p. 14).

Learning to balance teaching and inquiry is hard work but the benefits are invaluable, as reported by the International Reading Association (1989):

Helps solve classroom problems.

Encourages effective change.

Revitalizes teachers.

Empowers teachers to make decisions in their classrooms.

Identifies effective teaching and learning methods.

Promotes reflective teaching.

Verifies what methods work.

Promotes ownership of effective practice.

Widens the range of teachers' professional skills.

Provides a connection between instructional methods and results.

Helps teachers apply research findings to their classrooms.

Enables teachers to become change agents.

Avery (1990), reporting on her use of action research, made these comments:

Teaching was more exciting than it had ever been. I was no longer implementing someone else's instructional program. Instead, I was developing a responsive mode of teaching based on the needs of learners. As I listened to and observed children actively engaged in learning, I found myself becoming enthused and energized by the richness and multiplicity of ways in which they learned. I became involved in demonstrating strategies for writing and reading and in exposing my students to more literature as their appetite for literacy increased. Teaching had taken on new dimensions, and I was changing as a professional. (pp. 34–35)

I do not conduct investigations with findings that can be duplicated. I pursue questions that I find relevant within the context of my own teaching to better understand and respond to individual learning processes. (p. 35)

The connections between theory and practice became a reality for me because of my own classroom research. (p. 41)

Further testimony is provided by Bennett (1993) based on a study of 90 teachers who used action research in their classrooms:

Experienced teacher-researchers stated that their research brought them many personal and professional benefits, including increased collegiality, a sense of empowerment, and increased self-esteem. Teacher-researchers viewed themselves as being more open to change, more reflective, and better informed than they had been when they began their research. They now saw themselves as experts in their field who were better problem solvers and more effective teachers with fresher attitudes toward education. They also saw strong connections between theory and practice. (p. 69)

This sort of testimony on behalf of action research recommends it for use by any teacher or student teacher. What is more pertinent for student teachers especially than a process that helps them achieve their primary mission is to become increasingly effective teachers over the duration of student teaching.

Some practical examples of action research projects undertaken by student teachers include the following.

Curriculum-Based. Kasey, a student teacher in a general-level twelfth-grade English class, was concerned about teaching an upcoming unit on *Macbeth*. She had an uneasy feeling that the students would not be particularly interested in the play given that graduation was less than seven weeks away and that several had expressed disappointment in having to read Shakespeare. Kasey decided to turn this problematic situation into her action research project by posing the question, "What kind of unit plan can I develop that will engage the students with what the district has identified as a major objective in the English curriculum?" She began by surveying the students in the class to find out what kinds of activities they found to be most compelling in their past literature classes. Kasey also reviewed some literature on student engagement and on multiple intelligences. Finally, with the help of her cooperating teacher, Kasey identified specific learning activities that were most positively received by individual students. With this information before her, Kasey was able to develop a unit plan with a clear focus on ways to engage her students in the study of *Macbeth*. Kasey's reflections on this process revealed even more ways to engage students in her future literature classes and led to other questions such as "How can I vary learning activities and, at the same time, assess at the same level of cognition?" and "How can I involve my students in the design of learning activities and assessment activities?"

Discipline-Based.   In his seventh-grade geography class, Jack was concerned with what he called a discipline problem. After several discussions with his cooperating teacher, he came to realize that the "problem" existed in one class, third period. Jack decided to conduct an action research project around the behaviors of this class of rather active young adolescents. He began by collaborating on some initial data collection with his cooperating teacher, Sherry. Sherry observed during third period each day for one week. She used seating charts to record individual student behaviors and recorded notes that described Jack's behavior, movement, comments, and so on that occurred at the time of each off-task student behavior. Then Jack was able to form a question that would have noticeable impact on the remaining weeks left in his student teaching. He asked, "What can I do to increase the on-task behaviors of the students in my third-period class?" During the school day, Jack and Sherry would examine videotapes of the third-period class and Sherry's continued recorded observations. Jack also examined literature on teacher behaviors that have positive and negative effects on student task engagement. After two more weeks, Jack came up with three specific behaviors that seemed to be lacking in his classroom teaching—proximity to disengaged students, the design of multiple questions and activities that promoted involvement for all students, and specific techniques that raised the level of student concern. During the two weeks that Jack implemented these interventions, Sherry, again, recorded the relationships between Jack's behaviors and students' behaviors. Both Jack and Sherry were so impressed with the positive effect of his new approaches in increasing student on-task behaviors that they decided to continue the project in the other classes as well.

Instruction-Related.   The ninth-grade students in Tom's environmental science class did not appear to be overly concerned about completing homework assignments. Tom and his cooperating teacher, Dave, agreed to focus closely on this situation. Tom began by reviewing Dave's gradebook from the beginning of the year to see if he could determine a pattern in uncompleted homework. What he discovered was that the same students who were regularly not turning in homework in his class had missed a number of homework points in Dave's gradebook as well. Although Tom was concerned that the students had completed more homework for Dave than for him, he decided to address the homework problem in general by asking the question, "What can I do to increase the completed homework assignments in my classes?" After studying both his gradebook and Dave's even more closely, the two teachers discovered that the students who regularly completed homework assignments had parents who attended both the school's late autumn open house and the early winter parent–teacher conferences. Tom then decided to conduct a survey of his students to find out their experiences with parent input related to homework. Tom also read the literature on parental involvement with adolescent students and its effects on academic success. Tom's action research question became, "What can I do to increase the involvement of my students' parents with their academic work?" Tom worked closely with Dave to design a class newsletter that went home each week with the students. The newsletter explained weekly assignments and unit projects and offered specific suggestions for parental support and involvement. Tom also learned from his students and the literature that many parents feel out of touch with their children's teachers once their sons and daughters enter high school. Tom initiated a series of telephone calls home and even a "Portfolio Night" when students presented their work to parents. The intervention worked; more students completed more homework assignments. Tom's next action research project will focus on increasing parent involvement in specific unit projects.

The Process of Action Research

Action research may take place in at least three modes: individual-teacher research, collaborative-action research, and schoolwide-action research (Calhoun, 2002). For our purposes in this chapter, only the first is addressed, but we do acknowledge the others for their potential as approaches to team problem solving, faculty-development activities, and school reform.

The action research process is predicated on the general question, "What might I do to improve my teaching?" Embedded within this question is a tacit concern for apparent or suspected problems or deficiencies, as well as purely developmental interests. With the general intent of improvement in mind, more specific questions may be posed as a response to some particular problem or need that concerns the teacher. These can be framed as "if" questions; for example, will my teaching be more effective if I:

change my movement pattern?

ask more higher-level questions?

use cooperative-learning activities?

use classroom meetings to address group concerns?

This list could be extended to include many dozens of questions. A teacher planning to engage in action research might list several possible areas for attention and then prioritize on the basis of what is most pressing and what is readily doable.

Step 1 in the action research process is determining which question has the greatest potential to immediately affect one's teaching effectiveness. In student teaching, the student teacher and cooperating teacher as a team would do this. The question should be sufficiently limited in scope so that it is manageable.

Step 2 is devising a new approach/behavior that is an intended improvement over current teaching practice. This essentially becomes a hypothesis—that is, the teacher is taking the position that the new practice has the possibility of being more effective than the current practice—and eliminates or mitigates a perceived problem in current practice.

Step 3 involves determining the nature of the data that will be required to test the hypothesis and making provision to obtain them. Depending on the question asked, data may be collected by means of students' test performance, anecdotal records or journals, observation instruments or simple frequency counts, questionnaires, interviews, video recordings, or any available source. The observation instruments included at the end of many of the chapters in this book would serve to provide data regarding the practices they reflect. Step 3, it should be noted, would probably occur more or less concurrently with Step 2.

Two approaches are especially useful for collecting comparable data. The "pre-post" method involves obtaining baseline data prior to the new treatment and then obtaining data on the same sample (usually a group of students) following the treatment. The control-group method involves treating one group but withholding treatment from a second reasonably similar group. In either case, a difference in the data collected will be a measure of the change that has occurred.

Step 4 is implementing the new approach. The idea for the approach may be suggested in the educational literature, or it may be the teacher's creative response to a classroom situation.

Step 5 is tabulating and analyzing the data and reflecting on the outcome of the new practice, especially as it compares to the former practice.

An example of action research conducted by a student teacher was reported by Brooks (1994) based on her role as supervisor of that teacher. We note that the fact that the teacher involved is a student teacher is incidental; any teacher might have done this research.

Jackie was a nontraditional student teacher assigned to me for supervision. When I first conferenced with her, I was struck by her maturity, depth of preparation, and reflective skills. Her first formal observation gave credence to this initial impression. By the fourth week of the ten-week student teaching experience, Jackie approached me with an idea for her required action research project. Although her instructional work was outstanding, Jackie was not pleased with her students' scores on the first test she had administered. She began her analysis of the problem, low student grades, by looking at her reviewing techniques. As a result of much reading and brainstorming with her cooperating teacher, Jackie devised a series of daily reviews over previously learned material and supplemented this with a full day's review prior to the next test. The class period review utilized a spelling-bee format with teams using books and notes rather than individual players working from memory. When the tests were scored, the grades were just as disappointing as previously; in fact, several students scored lower on the second test than on the first. In discussions with students after the return of papers, it became clear to Jackie and me that because of the extensive in-class reviews, the students did not think they needed to study beyond that amount for the test. Obviously, emphasis on review was not the key to the correction of poor student performance on the tests.

At this point, I suggested that we begin to look at the evaluative instrument, the test itself. To determine if students missed more of one type of question than another, the cooperating teacher ran an item analysis of the test questions. No pattern emerged; students missed each and every question with similar frequency. Jackie then began to examine each test item, searching for ambiguities of language, trickiness of wording, complexity of concept. She found a few items of dubious nature, but not in sufficient quantity to explain the problem. That evening on the phone, I suggested another tactic: examine the questions for content, relate them to the lesson in which that material was covered, analyze the lesson plan, reflect on its enactment, and determine whether the information was covered appropriately for its subsequent importance. The following evening, an excited Jackie called. Through reflection, she discovered that the problem was far more subtle than even I had thought. Her lesson plan objectives for each day were not explicit enough to give her the guidance she needed. Therefore, even though the elements of a "good" workable plan were present, they were not adequate to help her to focus on the important material and to assist her students in making sense of all the information.

That weekend as Jackie reworked her plans for the coming week, she continually examined her objectives. Were they clearly worded? Was the focus sharp? Had she been explicit in stating what her students were to learn from each lesson? How could she help each student achieve understanding? How would she measure that understanding? The scores on the next tests were somewhat improved. Jackie continued to work on objectives, focusing, rewording, and analyzing. By the completion of her student teaching, every student's scores had risen, several more than doubling from the first test. Further, Jackie believed that even though her earlier test construction was not that much at fault, her later tests which built on the clearly stated objectives were better measures of her students' understanding of major social studies concepts than her earlier tests. (Brooks, p. 3)

Hints for the Beginning Teacher

How are you functioning as a "teacher-researcher"? What professional journals do you now read? A practical way to develop in this area of professional responsibility is to set aside at least two hours a week for professional reading.

■ EMPOWERING TEACHERS

This chapter has addressed the concern for empowering teachers. The conditions that attend teaching are well known, although unevenly reported, and a litany of them here is not necessary. The overwhelming task that has been given the school and its teachers in current society is unrealistic. In many instances teachers feel beleaguered and disempowered in the face of it. The context of classroom teaching that disempowers educators stems from traditions of American schools that have been around for over one hundred years. Lambert and colleagues (1996) describe these "limits or boundaries" that can make teaching "suffocating, frustrating, and even demeaning": lack of a clear purpose for schooling, educational hierarchies, patriarchy as leadership, isolationism and individualism, teaching as women's work, the status of schooling (pp. 2–7).

The hope for improving the profession lies in the expanding knowledge base of the profession and teachers subscribing to it as the defining trait of their practice.

These conditions are not going to go away. If teachers, and the education profession generally, are waiting for that to happen, they are naive. Of course, teachers need to be well organized politically to use whatever influence they can mount to affect legislation and funding, but this essentially only allows education to "stay even." If teachers are to make a breakthrough toward higher status and greater empowerment, it will occur more in pedagogical than political terms. Doing what they do better—teaching—and doing it so convincingly that it cannot be ignored by the community they serve, which ultimately is the nation, is the key to empowerment.

Shulman (1986) commented insightfully on the nature of a profession:

> *What distinguishes mere craft from profession is the indeterminacy of rules when applied to particular cases. The professional holds knowledge, not only of how—the capacity for skilled performance—but of what and why. The teacher is not only a master of performance but also of content and rationale, and capable of explaining why something is done. The teacher is capable of reflection leading to self-knowledge, the metacognitive awareness that distinguishes draftsman from architect, bookkeeper from auditor. A professional is capable not only of practicing and understanding his or her craft, but of communicating decisions and actions to others. (p. 13)*

Teachers need to frame their understanding of their role in these terms and to set about ordering their practice to conform to them. A suggested beginning is to attend to Francis Bacon's admonition long ago that knowledge is itself power. The profession will not be moved ahead very far by those gifted individual practitioners who practice their craft with insight and panache, but whose intuitive gifts retire with them. The hope lies in the expanding knowledge base of the profession and teachers subscribing to it as the defining trait of their practice. Teachers will think of themselves as more than technicians who implement pedagogy; they will be agents in the continual redefining of that pedagogy. Oberg and McCutcheon (1990) referred to this as they described the expansion of the role of the teacher into research:

> *The teacher-as-researcher is based on teachers liberating themselves from ideas solely imposed by others outside the classroom. In a sense it constitutes an acknowledgment that teaching belongs to teachers and as the experts about their own practice, teachers are the ones most able to understand and refine their work. (p. 142)*

APPLICATION for DIVERSE CLASSROOMS

The teacher as *role model* needs to be an empowering image for emphasizing the importance of teachers' work in helping to shape informed, contributing citizens, thus ensuring the continuation of our democratic way of life. Teachers need to understand their role as models of professional behaviors. The classroom is a community of learners in which teachers have a moral and ethical obligation to each student to uphold the fundamental values of our democracy—equality and social justice for all, along with the highest societal values of love and respect for human dignity.

And so this book completes a circle that began with a focus on teacher decision making. The professional educator is empowered by a systematic approach to decision making. The bases for this decision making evolve throughout the teacher's career as he or she adds to informed beliefs and practices. Through ongoing feedback, collaborative action research, reflection, and so on, the art of teaching and the science of teaching are refined.

Understanding one's discipline in terms of its organizing schemes and its structure, being able to use the concept of pedagogical content knowledge, having a repertoire of effective teaching strategies that are available to promote optimal learning, being committed to reflecting on one's teaching, using systematic approaches to analyze one's practice, and utilizing information from and methods of research in one's classroom are the bases for achieving empowerment. Through these, teaching will reach its potential to be a mature and fulfilling profession.

■ WEBSITE RESOURCE ■

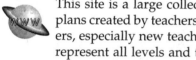 This site is a large collection of lesson plans created by teachers to help teachers, especially new teachers. The plans represent all levels and the major academic subject areas, including the arts and special education. There's even a section with lesson plans that are oriented to managing the classroom. Teachers are encouraged to communicate with other teachers from around the world and to submit plans:

http://www.pacificnet.net/~mandel/.

■ QUESTIONS FOR REFLECTION ■

1. What are the most common variables that affect the continuously emerging classroom scene, and what is the influence of each one you identify?

2. What aspects of clinical supervision qualify it to be considered an application of action research? How does action research, in turn, qualify as an aspect of reflective teaching?

3. How can you use the levels of reflectivity—technical rationality, practical action, and critical reflection—to help you translate the concept of reflective teaching into substantive teacher practice?

4. The notion of the teacher as researcher has emerged prominently in recent years. Why, in your view, has this happened, and what is the likely broad impact of it on teacher attitudes and teaching practices?

5. The nation broadly, and many states individually, have established higher standards and optimistic expectations for schools as we move into the twenty-first century. Given the commentary on teacher empowerment and teaching as a profession in this chapter, what can teachers do as individuals and as a profession to make gains toward those goals as well as to help define (redefine) pertinent and realistic goals?

■ REFERENCES ■

Acheson, K. A., and Gall, M. D. (1997). *Techniques in Clinical Supervision of Teachers Preservice and Inservice Applications* (4th ed.). New York: John Wiley.

Avery, C. (1990). "Learning to research, researching to learn." In M. Olson (Ed.), *Opening the Door to Classroom Research.* Newark, DE: International Reading Association.

Bambino, D. (2002). "Critical friends." *Education Leadership, 59*(6), 25–27.

Bennett, C. (1993). "Teacher researchers: All dressed up and no place to go?" *Educational Leadership, 51*(2), 69–70.

Brooks, E. (1994). *Action Research and Teacher Supervision.* Unpublished manuscript, Kent State University.

Calhoun, E. F. (2002). "Action research for school improvement." *Educational Leadership, 59*(6), 18–24.

Check, J. W. (1997, May/June). "Teacher research as powerful professional development." *The Harvard Education Letter.*

Cogan, M. (1972). *Clinical Supervision.* Boston: Houghton Mifflin.

Danielson, C., and McGreal, T. L. (2000). *Teacher Evaluation to Enhance Professional Practice.* Alexandria, VA: Association for Supervision and Curriculum Development.

Daresh, J., and Playco, M. (1995). *Supervision as a Proactive Process.* Prospect Heights, IL: Waveland Press.

Darling-Hammond, L., and McLaughlin, M. W. (1995). "Policies that support professional development in an era of reform." *Phi Delta Kappan, 76*(8), 597–604.

Dewey, J. (1933). *How We Think.* Boston: Heath.

Feiman-Nemser, S. (1990). "Teacher preparation: Structural and conceptual alternatives." In R. Huston (Ed.), *Handbook of Research on Teacher Education.* New York: Macmillan.

Freeman, D. (1998). *Doing Teacher-Research: From Inquiry to Understanding.* Pacific Grove, CA: Heinle & Heinle.

Ginsberg, M., and Clift, R. (1990). "The hidden curriculum of preservice teacher education." In R. Huston (Ed.), *Handbook of Research on Teacher Education.* New York: Macmillan.

Glanz, J. (1998). *Action Research: An Educational Leader's Guide to School Improvement.* Norwood, MA: Christopher-Gordon.

Glickman, C. D. (2002). *Leadership for Learning: How to Help Teachers Succeed.* Alexandria, VA: Association for Supervision and Curriculum Development.

Goldhammer, R, (1969). *Clinical Supervision: Special Methods for the Supervision of Teachers.* New York: Holt, Rinehart & Winston.

Guskey, T. R. (2000). *Evaluating Professional Development.* Thousand Oaks, CA: Corwin Press.

International Reading Association (1989). "Classroom Action Research: The Teacher as Researcher." *Journal of Reading, 33*(3), 216–218.

Johnson, B. (1993). *Teacher as Researcher.* Washington DC: Office of Educational Research and Improvement (ERIC Digest No. ED 355 205).

Kennedy, M. (1990). "Choosing a goal for professional education." In R. Huston (Ed.), *Handbook of Research on Teacher Education.* New York: Macmillan.

Lambert, L. (1998). *Building Capacity in Schools.* Alexandria, VA: Association for Supervision and Curriculum Development.

Lambert, L., Collay, M., Dietz, M. E., Kent, K., and Richert, A. E. (1996). *Who Will Save Our Schools? Teachers as Constructivist Leaders.* Thousand Oaks, CA: Corwin Press.

Lieberman, A. (1995). "Practices that support teacher development." *Phi Delta Kappan, 76*(8), 591–596.

Maeroff, G. (1988). "A blueprint for empowering teachers." *Phi Delta Kappan, 69*(7), 472–477.

Oberg, A., and McCutcheon, G. (1990). "Teacher as researcher." *Theory into Practice, 29*(3), 142–143.

Shulman, L. (1986). "Those who understand: Knowledge growth in teaching." *Educational Leadership, 15*(2), 4–14.

Zeichner, K., and Liston, D. (1987). "Teaching student teachers to reflect." *Harvard Educational Review, 57*(1), 23–48.

Zemelman, S., Daniels, H., and Hyde, A. (1998). *Best Practice: New Standards for Teaching and Learning in America's Schools* (2nd ed.). Portsmouth, NH: Heinemann.

Index